Macroeconomic Policy:
Inflation, Wealth and the
Exchange Rate

Macroeconomic Policy: Inflation, Wealth and the Exchange Rate

MARTIN WEALE, ANDREW BLAKE, NICOS CHRISTODOULAKIS,
JAMES MEADE AND DAVID VINES

London
UNWIN HYMAN
Boston　　Sydney　　Wellington

© M. R. Weale, A. P. Blake, N. Christodoulakis, J. E. Meade, D. A. Vines 1989

Published by the Academic Division of
Unwin Hyman Ltd
15/17 Broadwick Street, London W1V 1FP, UK

Unwin Hyman Inc.,
8 Winchester Place, Winchester, Mass. 01890, USA

Allen & Unwin (Australia) Ltd,
8 Napier Street, North Sydney, NSW 2060, Australia

Allen & Unwin (New Zealand) Ltd in association with the
Port Nicholson Press Ltd,
Compusales Building, 75 Ghuznee Street, Wellington 1, New Zealand

First published in 1989

British Library Cataloguing in Publication Data

Macroeconomic policy: inflation, wealth and the exchange
rate.
1. Open economics. Macroeconomics aspects
I. Weale, Martin
330.12′2

ISBN 0-04-445428-7

Library of Congress Cataloging-in-Publication Data

Macroeconomic policy: inflation, wealth, and the exchange rate/by
Martin Weale ... [et al.].
    p.   cm.
Bibliography: p.
Includes index.
ISBN 0-04-445428-7
1. Great Britain—Economic policy—1945— —Econometric models.
2. Economic policy—Mathematical models. 3. Keynesian economics.
I. Weale, Martin, 1955–
HC256.6.M28   1989   89-5819
338.941′001′51—dc20   CIP

Typeset in 10 on 12 point Times by Mathematical Composition Setters Ltd, Salisbury, Wilts
and printed in Great Britain by The University Press, Cambridge

Contents

Part II

Application

Part III

Method

Part IV

Conclusion

List of Tables

List of Figures

Notation

We use the following notation in Chapters 1 to 4 and again in Chapter 6. In Chapter 5, where we present equations taken directly from our computer model rather than algebraic analysis, we, of necessity, use an *ad hoc* notation which is explained in each case. Chapters 10 and 11, which are concerned with the properties of linear models in general, and not with specific economic relationships, also use their own notation.

A real exchange rate (measured in units of foreign product/unit of home product)

B budget deficit measured in units of domestic product

C private consumption measured in units of domestic product

D monetary base measured in money value

E nominal exchange rate (measured in units of foreign currency/unit of home currency)

F net capital outflow in units of domestic product

G government consumption measured in units of domestic product

H stock of net foreign assets measured in units of domestic product

I domestic investment in units of domestic product

J the sum of domestic and net foreign investment, measured in units of domestic product

K domestic capital stock

L labour

M imports measured in units of domestic product

N national wealth measured in units of domestic product

P price of net domestic product (GDP deflator)

R rate of interest on short-term bills

S rate of tax

T tax revenue measured in units of domestic product

U national debt measured in units of domestic product

V post-tax real wage measured in terms of consumption goods

W money wage
X exports measured in units of domestic product
Y real gross domestic product
Z money gross domestic product

We make use of the following superscripts

e   expected future value
F   foreign
-      indicates a constant value
^   indicates a percentage change
*   indicates a target value
~   used for *ad hoc* purposes as indicated in the text

Subscripts to these variables are used only to indicate time, with ∞ being used to indicate a steady-state value.

We use capital letters to describe the levels of the variables concerned. Small letters are used to define partial derivatives in Chapters 1 and 2 and logarithms in Chapter 3. This is indicated in the text and should not be a source of confusion.

Greek letters are generally used to represent model parameters. The following conventions are used in Chapters 2–4.

α, β wage equation parameters
ε trade price elasticity
η propensity to import
ζ interest semi-elasticity of the demand for money
θ, ϕ capital flow parameters
ι interest effect on investment
$\varkappa$ propensity to consume
λ adjustment parameter
μ multiplier
ν accelerator
π mark-up
σ, Σ slopes of lines
χ control parameters

δ and ψ are used for parameter combinations.

δ is used in Chapter 2 to represent small deviations. ω is not a parameter, but is used as an index of comparative advantage. Superscripts and subscripts are used to distinguish parameters within these broad groupings.

Δ is used to represent determinants. It is also used in Chapters 5–11 as a difference operator with $\Delta x_t = x_t - x_{t-1}$.

Preface

Macroeconomic policy in advanced Western countries is now in a difficult position. It is not just that policies have recently become more unsatisfactory, or that, at least in Europe, we are living through the worst period of unemployment since the 1930s. Both these things are true. But the problem lies deep. Policy-makers are adrift, without a framework to guide them, in a way that has not been true since the 1930s. Gone is the confidence which characterized policy-making in the Keynesian heyday of the 1950s and 1960s. Gone too is the promise, which monetarism offered in the 1970s, of providing a new framework for policy. It is not enough simply to muddle through, applying *ad hoc* common sense to each crisis as it arises. A new framework of ideas is needed.

This book is an attempt to present such a fresh coherent package of ideas, for application to macroeconomic decision-making in open economies. These ideas are explained in Chapters 1–4. Then in Chapters 5–9 we try out this package of ideas on an econometric model of one particular economy, the United Kingdom, with simulated reruns of history for the UK economy over the years 1975–89. As well as presenting new proposals, our suggestions are extensively compared with ideas for reform put forward by others. Technical aspects of our work are described in Chapters 10 and 11. Chapter 12 summarizes our conclusions.

The main features of our proposals are that

i)   Fiscal and monetary instruments should be used *together* in the pursuit of two policy targets: inflation and wealth accumulation.

ii) The anti-inflation objective should be implemented by means of control of the Money GDP leaving it to the institutional and other forces in the private sector to determine the outcome, or the 'trade-off', between high output and low prices on the one hand and low output and high prices on the other.

iii) There should be a real exchange-rate intermediate target as a guide to the setting of monetary policy.

We demonstrate that the design of fiscal and monetary policy must pay attention to the structure of the labour market (in particular to whether there is strong real wage resistance or not.) We also investigate fully the sensitivity of our packages to the way in which expectations are formed and conclude that, although the nature of expectations formation has a major impact on the precise working of our control rules, it is quite possible to find a set of illustrative policy rules which performs satisfactorily for both types of expectational mechanisms (model-consistent and adaptive) which we consider.

Our analysis is confined to a single open economy in the world economy (such as the United Kingdom) rather than considering problems of multilateral policy co-ordination. This has allowed us to study more closely certain basic issues which must be resolved as a prelude to work on the international co-ordination of national policies.

The research which we are reporting here began in 1984. Preliminary results have already been presented by Christodoulakis, Vines and Weale (1986), Christodoulakis and Weale (1987), Vines (1986), Blake and Weale (1988), Blake, Vines and Weale (1988) and Meade and Vines (1988). Our research has its roots in an earlier book *Stagflation Volume II: Demand Management* (Vines, Maciejowski and Meade, 1983) which itself developed ideas in Meade's Nobel Prize lecture (Meade, 1978).

What follows extends the existing literature on open economy macroeconomics in five important ways.

i)   There are four theoretical chapters (1-4) which explore systematically the interconnections between fiscal and monetary instruments, on the one hand, and the objectives of policy for an open economy, on the other. These chapters pay close attention to the technical questions currently concerning open economy macroeconomists – for example, the stability of prices in forward-looking asset markets, the stability of processes of wealth accumulation, and the stability of closed-loop feedback policies. Yet the models presented are simple and clear. Thus these chapters can serve as an expository guide, from one particular point of view, to the theory of macroeconomic policy-making in the late 1980s. They are addressed to the practitioner. Nevertheless, they can be read with no more than advanced undergraduate training, and could serve as a complement to a final year undergraduate, or graduate, course in the theory of macroeconomic policy.

ii) The relationships between the wage equation and the conduct of macroeconomic policy are carefully spelled out. This exposition shows, in ways not previously analysed, just how great are the consequences of real wage resistance (extensively documented in Europe by Layard and Nickell, 1985) for the conduct of fiscal policy, of monetary policy, and of exchange-rate management.

iii) We analyse in great detail the operation of an exchange-rate intermediate target. We are both sympathetic to, and critical of, the proposals of McKinnon (1984) and Williamson (1985).

iv) A detailed study of a single country has allowed us to build an empirical model for the thorough analysis of alternative policy scenarios. This model treats carefully the problems of wealth accumulation and also attempts to deal in a new way with the question of expectations formation. It does this because both of these features are shown to be important in the theoretical chapters. The model is presented in Chapter 5 and contains new uses of the rational expectations hypothesis in economic modelling. It is simulated in Chapters 6 to 8. Those chapters make a new contribution to the literature on the design of macroeconomic policy with rational expectations. We are able to present policies which are stable irrespective of whether expectations are model-consistent or adaptive.

v) We have developed techniques, described in Chapters 10 and 11, for the solution of economic models with endogenous policy rules when expectations are assumed to be model-consistent. We hope that these techniques will be of general use to model-builders, since they have a number of advantages over conventional model-solution techniques (Lipton *et al.*, 1982, Spencer, 1984).

The five authors have worked on various stages of the project. Andrew Blake joined in October 1986, and has worked mainly on computational problems. Nicos Christodoulakis was a member of the project from January 1985 to September 1986, and during the summer of 1987, and made a large contribution, both in putting our econometric model together and in pioneering our model-solution techniques. James Meade has worked on the project throughout its life, and has paid particular attention to Chapters 1 to 4 and to the structure of the model used in Chapter 5. David Vines has worked on both the economic-theoretical and control-design aspects, travelling regularly to Cambridge from Glasgow for this purpose. Martin Weale has worked full-time on the project throughout its life, and has been responsible for its day-to-day running.

The techniques which we have used have their origins in Jan Maciejowski's contribution to the earlier project on which some members of our team were engaged (Vines, Maciejowski and Meade, 1983).

We are very grateful for the insights he has offered, although he is, of course, in no way responsible for any of the material in this book.

The Centre for Economic Policy Research kindly supported a conference held at Clare College, Cambridge, in July 1987, at which some of our results were discussed. We are most grateful to everyone who took part in this conference and made it possible. We are also much indebted to the participants of seminars at which this work has been presented.

The Centre for Economic Policy Research also provided part of the funding for research work during the period June 1986–September 1987. The Economic and Social Research Council covered all the costs from January 1985 until June 1986 and a part of the cost until September 1987. The Houblon-Norman Fund awarded Martin Weale a fellowship at the Bank of England from October 1986 until July 1987 which gave him an invaluable opportunity to discuss the ideas in this book with colleagues at the Bank of England. The Department of Applied Economics at Cambridge University has met incidental expenses not covered by the other sources and supported Andrew Blake from October 1987 until the end of the project. The University of Glasgow has covered a large part of David Vines' travel expenses from Glasgow to Cambridge.

The econometric model which we have used for our study has been built from Version 7 of the National Institute of Economic and Social Research model of the UK economy. Without their kindness in making this model available, our research would not have been possible.

Thanks are due to the assistant staff in the Department of Applied Economics. In particular, we would like to acknowledge Shirley Seal's help in preparing the text.

Part I
Theory

Chapter One

A New Keynesian framework for macroeconomic policy

1.1 AN OVERVIEW OF THE IDEAS IN THIS BOOK

1.1.1 New Keynesian financial policy: objectives and instruments

We propose in this study what we call a New Keynesian assignment of fiscal and monetary policies. In the Old or Orthodox Keynesian prescription it was the function of financial policies to maintain a high and stable level of real demand for the United Kingdom's products and so for the level of employment; and in so far as this threatened to lead to an inflation of money costs and prices, it was the function of the reform of wage- and price-setting institutions (incomes policy) to prevent this. In our New Keynesian system this prescription is reversed. We propose that the function of fiscal and monetary policies should be to prevent monetary inflation by maintaining the level of total monetary expenditures on the country's products (the Money GDP) on a steady stable growth path; it would then become the function of structural reform of wage-setting and price-fixing institutions to ensure that, so long as there are unemployed resources available, increased money expenditures lead to an increase in real output and employment at uninflated levels of money costs and prices rather than to a rise in the money wages and prices of the existing levels of employment and output. This Money GDP target is the centrepiece of our proposals.

In addition, we argue that the Money GDP target should not be the sole objective of fiscal and monetary policy. Policy-makers face an understandable temptation to control inflation through policies which reduce inflationary pressures by raising current living standards at the expense of future living standards. We advocate the use of a target value for national wealth concurrently with a target value for Money GDP, as a means of preventing this.

In this book we propose financial policy rules – for both fiscal and monetary policy – which steer both Money GDP and national wealth to target values. We argue that both sets of policies should share in the pursuit of both objectives. The design of financial policy needs to consider all of the relevant linkages – from each target to each instrument. And policy-makers should, we argue, adopt what we call the right instrument-target emphasis in policy choice – a relative weight on each of the objectives of policy which reflects the structure of the economy – when they set each of the instruments of policy.

1.1.2   The labour market

We shall see that particularly if wages are strongly indexed to prices, and thus if real wages are sticky, the temptation for the authorities to buy out inflation at the expense of wealth will be strong. For example, if real wages are sticky a real exchange-rate appreciation will be attractive as a means of reducing inflationary pressures, despite the fact that it reduces both domestic and foreign investment. We seek to design policy rules which will take account of such dangers, and argue that the appropriate form for these rules is determined by the structure of the economy and in particular by the extent of wage-price indexation observed in the labour market.

More generally we seek to explore systematically the connections between financial policy and labour market behaviour and the implications of labour market behaviour for the design of financial policy. Our second major contribution thus concerns the crucial importance of the structure of the labour market for the design of both monetary policy and fiscal policy. We show that different types of policy rules must be designed, depending on whether wages are indexed or unindexed, at least on the basis of the plausible assumption which we make, namely, that fiscal policy has to be carried out by variations in tax rates.

1.1.3   An exchange-rate intermediate target

Our book has a third objective. Intermediate targets can provide a useful guide for short-term policy-making. Movements in the money stock have at times been used as a guide to indicate the appropriate setting of the short-term interest rate. However, more recently the use of the money stock as an intermediate target has become less popular. This is partly a consequence of the practical difficulties of monetary control. It is also partly because the use of the money stock as an intermediate target has led policy-makers to set interest rates at levels which have had undesirable and unintended effects on the exchange rates (cf. Poole, 1970, Dornbusch, 1976, Artis and Currie, 1981, Buiter and Miller, 1982).

Increasingly the exchange rate has been adopted as an intermediate target of policy. This need not necessarily imply that policy-makers aim to stabilize exchange rates at levels fixed either in nominal or in real terms. A more flexible use of the exchange rate as an intermediate target can be achieved if a rule is specified indicating how this target is to be set. Within such a context the operation of monetary policy requires another set of rules (i.e. for the interest rate and for foreign-exchange market intervention) in order to guide the actual exchange rate to its target value. The third aim of this book is to describe the use of the exchange rate as an intermediate target in this fashion.

Thus the financial policy rules to be studied in this book examine the pursuit of targets for Money GDP and national wealth when, in the conduct of monetary policy,

i)   monetary policy steers the exchange rate to its target,
ii) the exchange-rate target is not fixed but follows a 'closed-loop' feedback rule.

One important conclusion is that it is impossible to operate a system of fixed real exchange-rate targets; such a system is inherently unstable and therefore not sustainable.

1.1.4   Expectations formation

A fourth subsidiary theme of the book concerns the role of expectations formation. In common with other economists over the past ten years we have taken the Lucas critique (Lucas, 1976) seriously. We give explicit analysis of the role of expectations, allowing us to examine the workings of economic policy on the assumption that the effects of policy may be understood by the agents in the economy. However, we do not limit ourselves to this assumption. Thus in the analytical work of Chapters 3 and 4 we assume either adaptive or 'rational' – i.e. model-consistent – expectations in the foreign-exchange market. This allows us to investigate whether the process of expectations formation for exchange rates is or is not important in policy design. But our major response to the Lucas critique is to be found in our empirical work, reported in Chapters 5 to 9, where we allow for the possibility of forward-looking model-consistent expectations formation in the determination of the exchange rate (which influences trade flows and prices), of human capital (which influences consumption), of the rate of interest on consols (which also influences consumption), and of the stock market valuation ratio (which influences investment and consumption). In addition, a simple form of model-consistent expectations is allowed for in wage-fixing. We find, in both our theoretical and our analytical work, that policy rules can be found which perform satisfactorily independently of whether expectations are model-consistent or adaptive. This issue, we conclude, is not nearly as important as the issues of wage-fixing and of exchange-rate targeting in influencing the design of appropriate policy rules.

1.1.5   Small models, large models, and control theory

We also have a fifth, methodological, message. We suggest that much insight into policy design on large empirical macroeconomic models is provided by small analytic representations of them. We show that analysis, on small algebraic models, of

– steady-state instrument movements,
– stability,
– comparative advantage of instruments,

is helpful. It provides a useful guide when choosing the structure of simple control rules to regulate an actual large empirical economic model. However, since small algebraic models cannot possibly summarize all the important feedbacks in the economy, excessive reliance on them can be misleading. They do not form a substitute for a systematic study of a coherent macroeconomic model.

1.2   THREE POLICY FRAMEWORKS COMPARED

We write at a time of some confusion about the principles of macroeconomic policy-making. It is thus useful to explain briefly how our ideas relate to other policy-making frameworks.

1.2.1 The Keynes-Bretton Woods framework and its demise

The quarter of a century after the Second World War was a period of unprecedented, sustained economic growth in the world economy. It was based on a regime of policy-making with four essential elements.

i)   There was an explicit, or implicit, recognition of the Keynesian prescription that national governments in devising their financial policies should so control the demand for goods and services as to maintain a 'high and stable level of employment', or 'full employment' for short.

ii)   It was believed that, short of full employment, wages were 'sticky', meaning that the pursuit of high employment would not lead to a permanent runaway inflation. Temporary inflationary difficulties caused by undue wage pressure or 'supply-side shocks' (for example, a rise in the price of oil) were to be dealt with by incomes policy.

iii) Internationally governments pursued the Bretton Woods objective of freeing international payments in an exchange-rate regime of 'adjustable pegs' under which rates of exchange were fixed but subject to *ad hoc* large adjustments when a country found itself in a 'fundamental balance of payments disequilibrium' (Nurkse, 1945).

iv)   The importance of expectations was recognized. Indeed, Keynes' *General Theory* was addressed to the problem caused when investors' animal spirits sagged. And expectations were felt to be crucially important for the success of policy, too: the expectation that policy was promoting full employment would buoy up investors' animal spirits (Matthews, 1968).

This Keynesian-Bretton Woods package broke down for two basic reasons. First, when a country's internal level of money costs and prices moved out of line with that of other countries, as happened to the UK, there was an unhappy conflict between the internal and external requirements of the system. Either the promotion of a high and stable level of employment must be abandoned in order to maintain the pegged exchange rate, or else the peg must be devalued in order to get out of a fundamental disequilibrium. But if the system of pegged exchanges was to have any validity these changes of peg must be infrequent and must be postponed until they were inevitable. The build-up to such an exchange-rate cataclysm then invited speculation against the threatened currency. The experience of Stop-Go balance-of-payments crises in the UK and the final debâcle when the international currency, the dollar, was faced with this problem indicate the basic deficiencies of the Bretton Woods regime.

Secondly, a more basic cause for the breakdown of the system, at least in the UK, was the recurrent threat of a runaway inflation of money wages and prices. This was promoted by the undertaking implicit in Keynesian policies to expand money expenditures on goods and services whenever unemployment rose above a very moderate level. Difficulties in trying to control such inflationary movements by incomes policies of one kind or another were such that in the end it was a Labour Government in the UK which explicitly abandoned the idea of maintaining full employment by expansionist financial policies. The ultimate breakdown of the Keynesian-Bretton Woods system in the UK was due to the inability to ensure that an expansion of money expenditures on goods and services would lead to an increase in output and employment at existing prices and costs rather than to an inflation of money prices and costs at existing levels of output and employment.

1.2.2 The monetarist framework and its demise

The Keynesian-Bretton Woods era was succeeded by an era of monetarism in the 1970s and early 1980s. It is more difficult to pin down the basic ideas which lie behind 'monetarism', but this term can be used to describe different packages of the following four ingredients, arranged in an order similar to that used in section 1.2.1.

i)   Financial policies should be designed to maintain the level of the nation's money income on an uninflated path rather than, as in the Keynesian prescription, to maintain the level of real national output and employment; and this could best be achieved by a control of the money stock at an uninflated level.

ii) A second ingredient was associated with the idea of the virtues of free market mechanisms. Wages and prices should be left uncontrolled – a far cry from the Keynesian world of incomes policies – to find their own 'market levels'. It was believed that wages and prices would be sufficiently flexible to enable a high level of employment and output to be continually achieved within the constraint of a restrained rate of growth of money incomes and expenditure. (Friedman, 1968).

iii) The third ingredient was also associated with the idea of the virtues of free market mechanisms. Internationally, it was argued, foreign-exchange rates should be left uncontrolled to find their own levels in free foreign-exchange markets (Friedman, 1953, Meade, 1966a).

iv) A fourth and very important idea has become associated with 'monetarism', although it is more recent than the original doctrine of monetarism. This is the belief that in forming their expectations economic agents assess the probability of the future effects of present events (including the future effects of the present economic policies themselves) rationally and with a full understanding of how the economy works. In its most extreme form such a 'rational expectations' view can lead to the conclusion not merely that decisions are best left to unrestricted free markets but that a whole range of macroeconomic policies is in fact incapable of having any meaningful effect whatsoever on the development of the real economy (Sargent and Wallace, 1975).

We now briefly evaluate each of these four different ingredients in turn.

Financial policy

We accept whole-heartedly the basic ingredient of the monetarist view that financial policy should be used for the control of a country's Money GDP rather than for the control of real GDP (and thus for the control of employment). In this fundamental matter we side with the monetarists, and against the Orthodox Keynesians (see Meade, 1978, 1982, and Vines *et al.*, 1983).

But we have grave doubts about the validity of the other monetarist prescriptions for financial policy. We argue later that the control of the Money GDP should not be the sole macro objective of financial policy but that there are basic economic reasons for the introduction of a 'wealth target' which relates to the distribution of national income between present consumption and investment for the future. Moreover, as we demonstrate in Chapter 4, without a target of this type financial policy control rules are actually likely to be unstable. With two financial objectives, control of the level of money income and control of its distribution between consumption and investment, there must be two sets of financial instruments, fiscal as well as monetary, used together, to control Money GDP and wealth together. Experience of monetarist regimes has confirmed that, without the active use of both of these instruments, things tend to go awry.

Experience has also shown that one cannot regard the stock of money as a good intermediate target for the control of the flow of money expenditure. This is partly because revolutions in modern financial institutions have made it difficult or indeed meaningless to draw a hard and fast line between what one does and what one does not include in the stock of money. But also, even without these particular difficulties, the idea can be seen to be inappropriate. Occasions have arisen when holders of wealth, including large fund-holding institutions, decide that they want to go 'liquid'. It is absurd to use a criterion which regards as an inflationary threat an increase in the supply of money which is in fact needed to offset a serious deflationary threat due to a desire on the part of wealth-holders to hold their wealth in a more liquid form. Indeed, it is a recipe for financial destabilization. Put simply, targeting the money supply can be a useful policy only if the demand for money is a 'stable function of a few economic variables' (Friedman, 1956). But it is not; fluctuations, frequently wild, in the demand for money have thus given monetarism a very bad name in the past few years in both Britain and the United States. They have sent the policy authorities scurrying from one monetary target to another, in search of an asset, the demand for which was 'stable', which they could then use as their new monetary target.

Wage and price flexibility

The optimism engendered by Friedman (1968) that inflation could be controlled by stabilizing the growth of money incomes, without generating difficulties of high unemployment, has proved completely unfounded. Wage stickiness is an important fact of life. There are two types. In the first case money wages are sticky but, at least gradually over time, real wages are flexible. In the second case it is real wages which are sticky (the 'real wage resistance' case). Macroeconomic policy must be designed in the recognition of such stickiness.

Floating exchange rates

Experience has shattered, as it did in the 1930s, the application to the foreign-exchange market of an unconditional belief in the virtues of completely free markets. The volatility of free foreign exchange rates and the huge swings that have occurred have led to the widespread (but not universal) acceptance of the need for some degree of official concern with their determination; but how much influence, on what principles, and by what means remain undecided.

Rational expectations

The fourth ingredient in modern 'monetarism', namely, the rational expectations hypothesis, raises important issues. But it is impossible to accept the rational expectations hypothesis, that all economic agents make efficient use of all information available to them, in undiluted form (cf. Currie, 1985).

First of all, the Sargent and Wallace policy-ineffectiveness proposition is destroyed by either of the above-noted types of wage stickinesses (cf. Buiter, 1980). It is also destroyed by other lags in or costs to the adjustment of prices in the economy. Even with very rapid adjustment of wages to prices, in an empirical model we shall find a need for an effective stabilization policy, and a need to design it in a way sensitive to the actual wage formation process.

But the problems connected with the rational expectations hypothesis go further than the question of allowing for certain lags. In fact, the future is in many ways so uncertain that a statistical calculation of probabilities often becomes inappropriate. There are many once-for-all events which are not suitable for probability calculations; this applies not only to events such as wars but also to such events as the political formation of a monopoly like OPEC with its devastating effect on a major price. In a democracy with frequent elections between different parties with different and continually changing programmes, how long does one expect a given policy to last, and how does one weigh the probability of particular changes to the next batch of policies? In view of many important uncertainties about the way in which the regular 'inside' relationships work in the economy, does one use the Treasury model, the National Institute of Economic and Social Research model, or the London Business School model of the economy to decide what will be the outcome for one's own future in a complicated economy with a network of many dynamic interrelationships? What weight does one put upon the possibility, in an economy in which there are complex interrelated decisions to take, that many agents may accept satisficing rules of thumb and customary institutional procedures for expectation formation rather than the sophisticated processes of information-gathering required for the formation of 'rational expectations'?.

We conclude that there are fundamental flaws in monetarism, just as there were in the earlier Keynesian approach. These two sets of findings lead to our own new proposals.

1.2.3   The New Keynesian framework

We may summarize our own policy proposals under four similar headings.

   i)   On financial policy, we embrace the objective of attempting to control the rate of growth of total money incomes, or Money GDP; but we believe that this should not be done through an intermediate target set by the stock of money. Moreover, we add to this the objective of controlling wealth accumulation, and in the pursuit of these two objectives we recommend a combination of fiscal and monetary policy. The principles by which this combination should be determined are explained at length in our study.

   ii)   On wage-fixing, we assume that wage increases are fixed as a result of both demand-pull pressures and cost-push features, and that wages adjust sluggishly. This means that wage determination is not considered to be either under the direct control of the authorities (as in the Orthodox Keynesian system) or instantaneously flexible according to the needs of policy (as in the monetarist system); instead we argue that economic policy ought to be designed in the light of a detailed understanding of how wages and prices are actually set.

   iii)   As to exchange rates, we argue that the rate of foreign exchange ought to be incorporated as an intermediate target in the process of formulation of fiscal and monetary policy. We argue this for three reasons; first, to avoid undue volatility in foreign-exchange markets, secondly to prevent undue swings in the foreign balance and thus in the accumulation of foreign wealth, and thirdly to prevent undue interference with the process of international trade.

   iv)   Finally, we argue that economic policy should not rely on any single type of expectational behaviour, but should be robust across expectational mechanisms.

For the remainder of this chapter we introduce the reader to our proposals in more detail. It is convenient to do this in the same order as that in the above list.

1.3   FINANCIAL POLICY EXPLAINED

In this study we use the term financial policy to embrace both fiscal and monetary policy. In this section we explain our proposals for financial policy. We take the basic principles of 'Keynesian economic management' to be that financial policy should be actively pursued in response to developments in the spending and saving of the nation as a whole (rather than the spending and saving of some subsection such as public-sector spending or borrowing). This principle was first adopted in the UK in the 1941 budget and remained the overriding one until the late 1970s. We believe that such a principle ought to be re-established.

1.3.1 Money GDP as a financial target

Our fundamental postulate is that financial policies should be assigned to the control of inflation and wealth rather than to the control of output and employment. This means that we have deliberately eschewed the use of financial policies to maintain real output and employment. Rather we advocate their use to prevent inflation, by means of a policy designed to keep the nation's Money GDP on an uninflated path. The first question to ask is whether it would not be more appropriate to take the price level itself, rather than the level of Money GDP, as the objective for the control of inflation. There are two reasons for choosing the Money GDP. The first and fundamental reason is the fact that, as explained below, it may be helpful to have a target which stresses the demand-pull considerations in wage-setting (what is the total demand for labour going to be?) rather than the cost-push element (what is going to happen to the cost of living?). The adoption of Money GDP as a financial target may be hoped, on its own, to have an influence on the behaviour of the labour market (see section 1.4 below). It creates a direct trade-off between inflation and increased output. It is not possible, by means of any economic model, to predict how large this effect will be, although we can be reasonably confident that it will not lead to a worsening of the supply-side position. If a price index were taken as the objective of financial control it would presumably have to be one (such as the GDP deflator) which excluded the price of imports and the level of indirect taxes and similar charges, since it would be undesirable to demand an absolute reduction of money wage rates and costs in order to offset a rise in the price of imported goods or a rise in tax charges specifically imposed to raise revenue. If one must in any case desert the cost-of-living price level as the objective, it is better to go the whole way towards an index (the Money GDP) of the total money demand for the products of labour.

But there is a second reason for the choice of the Money GDP as the financial target. Suppose that for one reason or another there was a cost-push incident in wage-setting which pushed money costs and prices 5 per cent above the target level. The financial commitment would then be to deflate total money expenditure until a volume of unemployment had been created which would exercise a sufficient downward demand-pull influence on wage bargaining to reduce money rates of pay by the 5 per cent needed to cancel the undesired 5 per cent rise. This might well involve an increase in the unemployment percentage of much more than 5 per cent. The maintenance of the Money GDP at its unchanged level would require at the most no more than a 5 per cent reduction in output to offset an unwanted 5 per cent rise in money prices and costs. The implications of stabilization through a stable price level run the risk of much greater disturbances than does a background of a moderate steady growth in the total of money expenditures on the nation's products. This seems to us to be the most suitable general financial background against which labour market and other decisions can be taken. We are not sympathetic to the suggestion made by Edison, Miller and Williamson (1987) that the policy authorities should allow the Money GDP target to slip upwards whenever there is upward wage pressure. In our view this does not seem likely to create an economic environment of financial stability.

1.3.2 National wealth as a financial target

Next we must consider in a little detail our second proposed target for financial policy, namely, the wealth target. It is, we believe, essential to have such a target, so as to ensure that adequate attention is paid to the distribution of the country's product (the GDP) as between current consumption, on the one hand, and the maintenance and development of the country's capital resources, on the other. Otherwise it becomes all too easy, even with the most inflationary cost-push wage-setting institutions, to combine full employment with uninflated prices by means of lax fiscal policy. In this case excessive government borrowing is needed to raise funds to keep down money costs and prices by reducing tax rates and/or paying subsidies, while a tight monetary policy is adopted which seriously restricts all forms of expenditure on the maintenance and development of real capital resources. As a result prices are kept at uninflated levels even though money wage and other income costs are inflated, the difference being covered by the low level of taxes or high level of positive subsidies of one kind or another. The resources for an excessively high level of consumption are offset by the deficient expenditure on capital projects. Full employment with a control of price inflation is achieved by living on capital (eating up the seed corn or 'selling the family silver') with adverse longer-term results. Accordingly an essential feature of our package of policy prescriptions is the existence of two, instead of only one, major objectives of financial policies, namely, some form of wealth target as well as a Money GDP target, against which must be set the two separate sets of financial instruments of control (namely, monetary policy and fiscal policy).

A wealth target can take many different forms. There are at least four important features to be considered.

i)   Should the target be concerned solely with the public sector (i.e. the National Debt) or with the public plus private sector (i.e. the total of real national assets of the country)?
ii) Should it be concerned with the absolute amount of such wealth or with the rate of change of that amount (i.e. the budget deficit or the rate of national investment in real capital assets)?
iii) Should it measure these wealth variables in real terms or in money values?
iv) Should it be concerned with the level of these variables or with the ratio between them and, say, the national income?

On the assumption that the ratios in item (iv) would be the same in real terms as in money terms, this catalogue presents a choice between twelve possible combinations of these four features. Any one of these twelve possible definitions of a wealth target would serve to put some constraint on spendthrift financial policies; but the choice could have a number of other important implications.

For example, the choice between the level and the rate of change of the level of the wealth variable (item (ii) above) will have an obviously very important significance for control purposes. Suppose that, in the case of a national wealth target, it is the rate of current new investment that is taken as the target. Any failure to meet the target in any one period would reduce the national wealth below what it would otherwise have been. A requirement to reach a certain level for the stock of wealth would mean that this deficiency would later have to be restored, whereas a requirement to restore the rate of investment to its target level would, at least in a static economy, simply write off this once-for-all deficiency.

A similar issue could arise in the case of a Money GDP target. Instead of choosing a given path for the level of the Money GDP, one might choose a given rate of increase in the Money GDP as the target for the control of inflation. In the former case any excess rate of inflation in any one period would have to be made good in a later period, whereas in the latter case it would be ignored.

By choosing the level of the stock of national wealth and the level of the Money GDP we have in this book in both cases, wisely or unwisely, adopted the more rigorous criteria.

We believe that the precise choice of wealth target may make an important difference to the problems involved in designing effective and appropriate rules for the operation of monetary and fiscal controls. In Chapter 2 of this book we include a preliminary investigation, in terms of the comparative statics of an IS/LM type of model, of the important difference which may be made to the problems of financial macro-economic control as a result of selecting a particular form of wealth target. But from Chapter 3 onwards throughout the discussion of the dynamic problems of control and in our simulations of the rerunning of history we have confined our analysis to a single form of wealth target, namely, a suitably defined path for the growth of the total real stock of the country's wealth.[1] We are certain that there should be some wealth target; we are not certain whether this is the most appropriate form. There is in our view a great deal of further important work to be done on the whole subject of wealth targets. At this stage in this book we are not ready to do more than to insist on the need to include a wealth target of some kind in any worthwhile control package and to show in our reruns of history what an important role such an objective can play in complicating the problem of control.

The dynamic function of financial policy, then, comes to be to keep both the Money GDP and the wealth target simultaneously close to their target paths by a skilful combination of adjustments of monetary and of fiscal policies. This does not, of course, mean that in the process the wealth target variable will be kept exactly on its target path. It is much more important to prevent serious inflations or deflations of the Money GDP than to prevent short-term swings in a wealth target. Short-term fluctuations in the former can become unstable and lead to cumulative booms or slumps of activity; changes in a wealth target are of more long-term structural importance. It may be part of a good dynamic control design to allow or even to engender short-term fluctuations in wealth in order to achieve greater short-term stability in the GDP. What is important is that there should be no long-run continuing and uncorrected divergence from the wealth target. The design of appropriate combined rules for the uses of monetary and fiscal policies, as we show below, involves considerations of just this kind.

1.3.3   The rate of interest as the instrument of monetary control

As has been argued in section 1.2.2, modern developments in banking institutions and in methods of payment, combined with massive shifts of wealth-holders' preferences between liquid and illiquid assets, frustrate any attempt to select a precisely defined stock of money as the instrument to be used for purposes of monetary control. But while the monetary authorities cannot readily for any good purpose determine what stock of money should be supplied to the market, they can significantly affect the rate of interest at which assets of a particular kind (e.g. Treasury bills) should be bought and sold. Within reasonable limits they could indeed operate a buffer stock in Treasury bills with buying and selling prices announced from time to time. Accordingly, in our policy framework we treat the short-term rate of interest (R) as the instrument to be used for monetary purposes.

It is often believed that the definition of monetary policy in terms of the rate of interest rather than the stock of money makes the price level indeterminate. In Chapter 3 we demonstrate that an active monetary policy rule, defined in terms of the rate of interest, can be used to remove this indeterminacy. It is perfectly possible to adopt a counter-inflationary monetary policy without defining this in terms of the stock of money. Indeed, we demonstrate in both theoretical models and in simulations throughout the book that satisfactory control of the price level can be maintained without any reference to the money stock.

It is important to counter immediately a common objection to such a policy framework, due most influentially, to Friedman (1968). The objection runs as follows.

> If the monetary authorities fix the nominal rate of interest, then this may lead to an explosive indeterminacy of prices. Suppose that inflation threatens, then, if the nominal interest rate is fixed, real interest rates fall, stimulating more expenditure and so more inflation. This process can become explosive.[2]

This objection is irrelevant to our work because it contains a basic ambiguity in the use of the word 'fixed'. In our policy framework the authorities 'control' the short-term rate of interest, and on a day-to-day basis it is 'fixed'. But the level at which it is fixed is altered by the authorities over time − in conjunction with alterations in tax rates − precisely in such a way as to ensure that inflation is controlled.

Another common objection to our policy framework also needs to be dismissed. Sometimes we shall say something like the following. 'The nominal rate of interest has to be set in such a way as to ensure that, given the developments on the inflation front, the real rate of interest is low enough to ensure that there is sufficient new investment so as to ensure that national wealth grows as desired.' An objector then replies 'but surely that would prevent monetary policy from restricting demand as may be necessary for the control of inflation, and so leaves the economy vulnerable to inflation, or even hyperinflation'. It does not. In our policy framework, however high or low the real interest rate needs to become in order to ensure the required evolution of wealth, it is then the task of fiscal policy to ensure that consumption is at a level which would bring about the desired evolution of Money GDP. By such means the control of inflation is pursued, not abandoned.

1.3.4   The rate of tax as the instrument of fiscal control

Macroeconomic fiscal policy is devised to suck purchasing power out of the market, or to pour purchasing power into the market, through a surplus or deficit of government revenue over government expenditures. The control can thus be operated on either side of the budget accounts.

Operating the control through variations in the rate of government expenditures raises two kinds of problem. First, all government expenditures are designed for some specific purpose (defence, health, education, police, social benefits and so on), and this makes it inappropriate to turn these flows of expenditure on and off in the interests of general control over the level of the GDP or of its distribution between consumption and investment. Secondly, government expenditure programmes need for the most part careful planning in advance together with administrative arrangements which are not rapidly flexible. On the whole, expenditure programmes cannot be rapidly changed

The adjustment of rates of tax such as the general rate of income tax, or of VAT, or of compulsory national insurance contributions are of a much more generalized kind pervading the whole of the economy and are for this reason probably more appropriate for use as instruments of control over the general levels of activity in the economy. Moreover, arrangements could be made more easily in the case of taxes than in the case of expenditures for frequent and prompt changes in response to fluctuations in the economy (Vines, Maciejowski and Meade, Part III, 1983, Baas, 1987).

There is, however, one serious disadvantage in the use of rates of tax in place of rates of expenditure as the fiscal controller. Any general tax is bound to affect the real value of the worker's post-tax take-home pay. If there is a marked cost-push element in wage-setting arrangements, a rise in the rate of tax will accordingly lead to an increased upward inflationary pressure on wage costs. It may be customary, for more or less irrational considerations, to lay more stress on changes in the cost of living than on changes in the PAYE deductions from pay in pressing a wage claim. Certain taxes (indirect taxes such as VAT) may thus have a more marked cost-push effect than other taxes (direct taxes such as income tax). But the cost-push element is likely to exist to a greater or lesser degree in all taxation cases.

In the policy framework presented in this book we illustrate the operation of fiscal controls for the most part by changes in the rate of tax (S) on the grounds that we seek to use an instrument which has a general effect over the whole economy and which is capable of fairly prompt and frequent adjustment in spite of the cost-push problem to which this gives rise. Such a use of prompt feedback response through tax adjustment is in no way incompatible with less prompt and less frequent adjustments of expenditure programmes which take into account the desirability of relaxation or restriction in general fiscal policy. Indeed, there is much to be said for the old-fashioned idea that public works programmes on schemes whose precise timing is not essential for the project itself should be prepared well in advance, providing a range of schemes which can be taken off the shelf for implementation with as little delay as possible. A periodic review (e.g. an annual budget) of expenditure plans which takes account of the forward probabilities of the need for general fiscal expansion or restriction, combined with arrangements for frequent and prompt feedback adjustments of certain general tax rates, may well be the most satisfactory procedure. It is in no way incompatible with the fiscal feedback controls through tax rates which form a basic part of the policy framework presented in this book. Nevertheless, we regard it as remarkable that, in Chapters 8 and 9, we have been able to stabilize the economy during a period long enough for three five-year plans, solely by means of our simple policy rules which operate through changes in taxes alone.

1.3.5 'Instrument-target emphasis': the linkages of financial targets to financial instruments

We can see a great deal to recommend a situation in which responsibility for economic policy is clearly divided between the various authorities involved. It would be easier for policies to be understood by all concerned if it were known that the fiscal authority was responsible for the control of wealth, and the monetary authority responsible for the control of inflation or *vice versa*. Vines, Maciejowski and Meade (1983) presented policy rules of this type. But there are practical disadvantages. Policy rules with this division of responsibility tend to require complex lag structures and often result in sudden instrument movements. They may also be slower and less smooth in achieving the desired result.

Here we do not argue that each of the two policy instruments should be 'assigned' to only one of the two policy targets. Instead we investigate a range of possible linkages between the two targets and the two instruments. We deliberately investigate cross-linkages between instruments and targets, in which both instruments are moved in response to a deviation of either of the targets from its desired value.

But we do consider an 'assignment' problem in a modified form: what we call 'instrument-target emphasis' in policy-making. We examine the conditions which make it appropriate to rely primarily on monetary policy for inflation control and on fiscal policy for wealth control, or *vice versa*.

The question of instrument-target emphasis will recur throughout this book. It is worth pausing now to note two opposing extreme views. Williamson (1985) has argued that very strong emphasis ought to be placed on the use of monetary policy to control (via 'exchange-rate target zones') the foreign balance (a part of the accumulation of wealth). Thus, effectively, monetary policy would be strongly emphasized in the control of wealth. This means that strong emphasis would then need to be placed on fiscal policy for the control of inflation. Another commonly expressed view is that strong emphasis should be placed on monetary policy in the control of inflation (perhaps exploiting the cost-reducing effects of exchange-rate appreciation, cf. Dornbusch, 1976, Buiter and Miller, 1982). This then means that strong emphasis would need to be placed on fiscal policy for the control of wealth accumulation (or its components domestic investment and the trade balance) (cf. Boughton, 1988). These opposing extreme views about instrument-target emphasis in the conduct of financial policy can be evaluated; this will be one of our main tasks in this book. That comparison will emerge naturally from the main exercise which runs throughout the book: an investigation, in detail, of what kind, and what strength, of instrument-target emphasis is likely to give a macroeconomic policy which performs well.

1.4 WAGE FIXING AND ITS IMPLICATIONS FOR FINANCIAL POLICY

It is an important feature of the framework presented in this book not merely to stress the reversal of roles between financial policies and wage- and price-setting institutions which we proposed at the outset of this chapter, but also to emphasize the intimate relationship between the nature of wage-setting institutions and the choice of appropriate financial policies. We believe that this basic relationship can have far-reaching implications.

Wage-setting arrangements are very diverse in character, dependent upon a number of psychological attitudes and customary procedures, and in consequence notoriously difficult to model satisfactorily. Nevertheless there is a basic distinction to be made between two sets of conditions which may lead to wage and price inflation. The first set may be called 'demand-pull' elements. When the demand for the products of labour is high and rising, employers can afford to grant wage claims more easily; workers will have little fear of pricing themselves out of a job; and there will be little availability of unemployed alternative sources of labour. High and rising demand is likely to lead to a higher rate of wage rises. Essentially these factors lie behind the famous Phillips curve. The second set of inflationary elements in the setting of wages may be called the 'cost-push' elements. If the real take-home pay of workers is below some customary or aspiration level which those in employment consider fair or if their real take-home pay falls below its existing level because of increases in the cost of living or in taxation, there may be additional increased pressure for wage increases. In such cases there is an inflation of money wages due to a push on the side of costs rather than a pull on the side of demand. In the framework presented in this book great stress is put upon the effect of the relative importance of demand-pull and cost-push factors in the ruling wage-setting arrangements upon the appropriate design of financial policies for the control of inflation.

This book in no way attempts to analyse existing wage-setting arrangements or to discuss the positive forms of wage reform which might shift the balance between demand-pull and cost-push factors. Throughout the book our purpose is to stress the different implications for the design of macroeconomic policies of different balances between these two sets of elements in wage-setting institutions. The importance which we put on this balance is emphasized in our theoretical work. It is again stressed in our empirical work by the fact that the reruns of history which in Chapter 8 are performed on an assumption of unreformed wage-setting institutions (i.e. with a wage equation which purports to resemble the effects of existing wage institutions in the United Kingdom) are then repeated in Chapter 9 on the assumption of reformed wage-setting institutions (in which cost-push becomes less important relative to demand-pull). This is not meant to suggest how, if at all, wage institutions could be so reformed; it is an exercise to show how far-reaching an effect wage reform would have had on the problems of financial controls.[3]

We should again stress that we have designed our framework of policy on the New Keynesian prescription that financial policies should be designed to prevent unwanted inflations or deflations of money values, with the structural reform of wage-setting arrangements as the method of achieving and maintaining the full-employment levels of real output. It is hoped that this will prove a more effective arrangement for the control of inflation than was the Old Keynesian prescription. Attempts to cope with the problem by means of direct anti-inflation arrangements, restricting increases in money rates of pay, work against the grain of the market. When business is overbuoyant, employment is overfull, and prices and profits are rising, this is just the time when it is most difficult to prevent rises in money pay, but is precisely the time when, for the control of inflation, reductions rather than rises are needed. The opposite atmosphere in which wage increases are to be encouraged when and where the demand for labour is excessive and to be discouraged when demand is deficient, sets a more natural market background. Moreover, to announce that the total money demand for the products of labour and so for labour itself is going to rise at a steady rate of, say, 5 per cent per annum suggests that if one group gets more than 5 per cent some other group must get less than 5 per cent or else the level of employment must fall. This may help to set a recognized norm. It is not suggested that no further reform of wage-setting institutions would be needed in order to promote sufficiently the demand-pull elements in wage-setting; it is suggested only that this sort of arrangement is more likely to be helpful than is a set of direct anti-inflationary controls over the setting of rates of pay.

1.5   EXCHANGE RATE MANAGEMENT

1.5.1   The case for foreign exchange rate targeting

Strong arguments are often made that foreign exchange rates ought to be stabilized in some form. For example, McKinnon (1984, 1986) argues that if nominal exchange rates are stabilized in a general environment of world monetary control, then importers and exporters will be able to plan on the basis of reasonably certain knowledge of the prices of traded goods in home currency. Williamson and Miller (1987) argue that if real exchange rates are stabilized in some way, then firms will be able to form plans on the basis of reasonably secure knowledge of the real profit margins to be earned on traded goods. And Crockett and Goldstein (1987) argue that the adoption of internationally consistent exchange-rate targets will force national policy-makers to adopt internationally consistent policies.

These proposals are not all capable of being adopted. Exchange rates cannot be stabilized both in nominal terms and in real terms. We present in the next section, and then in Chapters 3 and 4, ways of stabilizing the exchange rate in a manner which offers both McKinnon's and Williamson and Miller's proposals as special cases (although we do not address the question of international consistency, see section 1.8). Common to all these proposals for exchange-rate stabilization is a belief that, left to itself, the foreign exchange rate may take on, and hold for quite a long period, a value which is damaging to the rest of the economy and hinders rather than helps to achieve policy objectives. In markets like the foreign-exchange market there are elements of two different kinds of 'irrationality'. First, changes of sentiment of bullishness or bearishness are likely to be infectious in closely linked market networks of this kind; uncertainties are so great that precisely formulated views about the future are impossible, but moods change from optimism to pessimism in an infectious manner. Secondly, there may be elements of speculative bubble, during which many operators may think that an upward (or downward) movement of price has gone too far off any sustainable trajectory but intend nonetheless to stay in the market some time longer with the expectation that others are going to continue to support the upward movement for some time. In such cases the time comes when some speculators do decide to get out, others follow suit, and the market collapses. It is difficult to interpret movements in exchange rates without assuming some such elements of 'irrationality'.

These are likely to be features of all asset markets and many raw materials markets. Theoretical models which help explain such phenomena are offered by Tirole (1983). But why is the case for stabilizing the foreign-exchange market of greater macroeconomic importance than that for stabilizing the many other markets which are prone to bubbles? The answer is that, in an economy with any degree of openness, the foreign exchange rate is a variable of macroeconomic importance with powerful effects on the demand for imports and exports and on the price of imports. These give the foreign exchange rate an importance absent from other asset prices and suggest *prima facie* a case for stabilizing it in a manner consistent with economic policy objectives.

The arguments for stabilization hinge, of course, on the assumption that the means used for it do relatively little damage to the economy. For example, if interest-rate setting is subordinated to exchange-rate stabilization (as it is in our policy proposals), then an inappropriate interest rate with an appropriate exchange rate is assumed to be more desirable than an appropriate interest rate with an inappropriate exchange rate. This assumption can, in turn, be justified if the main route by which the interest rate affects the economy is through its impact on the exchange rate. We believe this to be the case in an open economy such as the United Kingdom.

In the light of these arguments for stabilization of the exchange rate close to a level consistent with policy objectives, we now set out a framework which shows how this can be achieved. It involves treating the exchange rate as both a target and an instrument of policy.

1.5.2 The foreign exchange rate as an intermediate target

In section 1.3 above we sketched out a framework for policy which may be depicted in the following general manner:

$$\begin{bmatrix} \Delta S \\ \Delta R \end{bmatrix} = \begin{bmatrix} s_z & s_n \\ r_z & r_n \end{bmatrix} \begin{bmatrix} Z - Z^* \\ N - N^* \end{bmatrix} \tag{1.1}$$

where $Z - Z^*$ depicts the extent to which the actual Money GDP (Z) diverges from its target level (Z^*), and $N - N^*$ similarly depicts the divergence of the national wealth (N) from its target level (N^*); where ΔS and ΔR depict the adjustments which the fiscal and monetary policy rules require to be made in the rate of tax and the rate of interest; and where s_z, s_n, r_z, and r_n depict the quantitative details of the policy rules which require certain adjustments in each controller in response to the divergence from target of each objective. The design of the nature and force of such rules is, of course, the basic subject-matter of the rest of this book and it is not our purpose to discuss such matters in this chapter, which is confined to a description of the main structure of controls contained in our package of policy recommendations. But for this purpose it is necessary to consider in what way the simple structure depicted in (1.1) needs to be interpreted in order to take account of the international relationships of an open economy such as the UK.

The main structural arrangement of (1.1) can be applied equally well to a closed or to an open economy, but in an open economy the actual operation of the structure is greatly affected, indeed in some cases dominated, by the country's international economic and financial relations. Thus reductions of tax and of interest are both likely to lead to some increases in domestic expenditure, the former primarily on consumption and the latter primarily on investment. In an open economy both are thus likely to lead to increases in the demand for imports which in turn will cause a reduction in the country's balance of trade, which in turn would represent a reduction in foreign investment (i.e. in the accumulation of real wealth overseas). Thus the national wealth objective (N^*) in the open economy must include net assets held abroad (H) as well as assets held domestically (K).

A reduction in the rate of interest would have another extremely important set of repercussions in an open economy. It would encourage owners of capital funds to invest more of their funds abroad if foreign rates of interest had not also been reduced. This factor is a very important one in modern conditions in which national capital markets are so closely interconnected. Such an outflow of funds in a regime of free exchange rates would lead to some depreciation of the currency with a consequential positive effect on the balance of trade (and so on foreign investment) and on the price of imports (and so on the cost of living and any cost-push elements in the formation of domestic wage costs). It is not the purpose of this introductory chapter to pursue these topics, which are analysed at length in the rest of this book. All that is relevant here is to point out that the general structure of controls and of objectives of policy shown in (1.1), with the two weapons (S and R) being used to control the two target variables (Z and N), is valid for an open economy provided that N includes assets abroad as well as assets at home; but the open-economy control parameters s_z, s_n, r_z, and r_n need much elaboration to take into account the direct and indirect effects of changes in S and R not only on domestic expenditure and costs but also on imports and exports and so on foreign investment and on the rate of foreign exchange and so on the import content of the cost of living and thus on cost-push inflation.

There remains, however, one complication which will arise if, in addition, it is desired to take steps to moderate fluctuations in rates of foreign exchange. We noted above a widespread view that ill-informed and volatile expectations, speculative bubbles, and political and other scares may cause excessive and unhelpful movements in foreign-exchange markets. We seek some foreign-exchange regime which would moderate this.

A scheme of policy like that mentioned up to now would be prey to a serious problem in this regard for the following reason. All of the control parameters s_z, s_n, r_z and r_n would, as already noted, depend upon how the exchange rate responded to changes in the instruments S and R. But in the presence of speculative bubbles this would become particularly unreliable. Even without actual bubbles the 'excessive and unhelpful' movements in the exchange rate would impose unwanted shocks to the targets, Money GDP and wealth. But in the policy framework just described, with freely floating exchange rates, that would not cause any corrective action on the instruments S and R unless and until these unwelcome disturbances to the targets had occurred.

What we therefore seek is an exchange-rate regime which would avoid these problems. What is required is a 'halfway house' between the over rigid adjustable pegs of the Bretton Woods system, on the one hand, and complete benign neglect, on the other. Proposals are under discussion for a system of target exchange rates or target zones for exchange rates with monetary and official intervention policies designed to keep actual exchange rates with a greater or lesser degree of strictness near to their target rates or within their target zones. We are in full agreement with the need to devise an intermediate system of this kind.[4]

The management of the foreign exchange rate so as to keep it near a given target level would depend upon the use of monetary policy for this purpose, raising interest rates when it was desired to attract funds in the foreign exchange market and so to raise the exchange rate, and lowering interest rates if it was desired to reduce an appreciation of the currency. In other words, the rate of interest would be assigned as the instrument to be used to move the actual exchange rate towards its target level.[5] But in (1.1) we need the rate of interest as one of the two instruments to control the two target variables Z and N. Can that be reconciled with the use of the rate of interest to control the rate of foreign exchange?

There is, in fact, no conflict between these two suggestions provided that the target exchange rate (the attainment of which is a policy objective) is itself also treated as an instrument of control for the attainment of one of the two basic policy objectives, namely, the control either of inflation or of the national wealth.

The general idea is depicted in the revised (1.2):

$$
\begin{bmatrix} \Delta S \\ \Delta E^* \\ \Delta R \end{bmatrix} = \begin{bmatrix} s_z & s_n & . \\ e_z & e_n & . \\ . & . & r_e \end{bmatrix} \begin{bmatrix} Z - Z^* \\ N - N^* \\ E - E^* \end{bmatrix} \tag{1.2}
$$

where E represents the foreign exchange rate (foreign currency per unit of home currency) and E^* represents a target level for the exchange rate. If the actual exchange rate is appreciated above the target level ($E > E^*$), the rate of interest will be lowered ($r_e < 0$) in order to encourage a downward movement in the exchange rate. But the target rate itself E^* in (1.2) now takes over the control role which the rate of interest played in (1.1).

A depreciation of the exchange rate by encouraging exports and discouraging imports would tend (i) to increase foreign investment and so to raise N and (ii) to increase the total demand for the country's product and so to raise Z. In (1.2) it is the target exchange rate E^* which undertakes these tasks.

An example may serve to show how the system would work. Suppose the actual rate of exchange to be on target ($E = E^*$) and the GDP to be on target ($Z = Z^*$) but the national wealth to be below target ($N < N^*$); and suppose that according to the structure in (1.1) it would have been the function of a reduction in the rate of interest (through the parameter r_n) to raise N to N^*. In the structure in (1.2) the target exchange rate (E^*) is depreciated (through the parameter e_n) in order to stimulate more foreign investment through an improvement in the balance of trade. But the actual exchange rate is now off target ($E > E^*$). According to the third row of (1.2) R is now reduced (through the parameter r_e) in order to bring E down towards E^*. This reduction in the rate of interest will also have its effect in raising N through the stimulation of domestic as well as foreign investment. The net result is a reduction of R which stimulates both domestic investment (directly) and foreign investment (indirectly through the exchange rate effect on the balance of trade).

A similar compatibility of functions would demonstrate itself if in (1.1) it had been the function of a fall in the rate of interest (through the parameter r_z) to stimulate an increase in Z. In (1.2) it is now the function of a depreciation of the target exchange rate (through the parameter e_z) to stimulate the external demand for the country's products and thus to raise Z. But the rate of interest must now be reduced in order to bring the actual exchange rate (E) down in line with the new target exchange rate (E^*). Once again a reduction in R has been used to stimulate Z, directly in (1.1) and indirectly in (1.2).

The interposition of the target exchange rate (E^*) in between the use of the rate of interest (R) and its effect on the two basic objectives (Z and N) is suggested as a means of modifying the use of R for these purposes of control in such a way as to moderate the large swings and great volatility of rates of foreign exchange that such use of R might otherwise entail. Throughout the dynamic analysis of this book we rely on the use of the exchange rate as an intermediate target of this kind for the purpose of combining an effective use of the market rate of interest for its basic control purposes with the avoidance of excessive perturbations in the foreign exchange market. This constitutes a basic element in our proposed policy framework.

1.6 EXPECTATIONS

We now discuss the way in which we have treated the formation of expectations in our work.

There is, in fact, an important element of truth which results from the rational-expectations school of thought. There is no doubt that, when monetary and fiscal policies are changed, economic agents take into account some of the probable future effects of these policies, that this affects the behaviour of the system, and that accordingly in designing economic policies one must take into account the effect of these policies on the behaviour of the economic system which is the subject of control. How to do this remains one of the most important unsolved problems of macroeconomic control, awaiting much more advanced empirical investigation about the ways in which economic agents do in fact form their expectations. In the meantime one must do one's best without any certain knowledge of the precise ways in which expectations are formed.

In the markets for financial assets the assumption of rational expectations may be especially useful in this respect, but it should still be employed with care. It is often used, as noted above, to assert that, following any shock, asset prices jump onto a convergent saddlepath to their new equilibrium, along which expected yields are always realized. Such an assumption makes asset prices very volatile in model simulations in response to changes in policy instruments, a stylized fact which an adaptive-expectations assumption cannot 'explain'. Herein lies the attractiveness of the assumption of rational expectations as applied to asset markets. But in reality we do not have much idea at all of how expectations in financial markets are formed. This makes it vital that policies are not designed which rely on the assumption of rational expectations: since it is unlikely to be in fact true, such policies may themselves fail!

We are unable to examine, in all its complexity, the assumption of rational expectations as applied to financial markets. We study, instead, the closely related and much simpler assumption of model-consistent expectations. In this book we argue that policies should work on the assumption of model-consistent expectations in financial markets (since to rely on their consequences being inaccurately understood also seems a recipe for failure). But they should also be robust to the possibility of expectations not being model-consistent.

The assumption of model-consistent expectations may also be useful in other applications, if employed with care. If, for example, consumption depends on expected future income, or investment on expected future profits, and if policy is likely to change these, then the implications of particular policy designs should, at least, be investigated with the assumption of model-consistent expectations. But, again, for policy to rely on future income or future profits being correctly anticipated seems dangerous; robustness to other types of expectations should also be tested.

What we have done in this book is to admit the uncertainty as to the way in which expectations are formed and to search for policy rules which are robust in the sense that they would operate reasonably effectively on different assumptions about the formation of expectations. Thus in conducting the rerunning of history in the UK between 1975 and 1989 in Chapters 8 and 9 below, we have rerun history twice; first, on the assumption of simple adaptive expectations and, second, on the assumption of model-consistent expectations; and we have devised a single set of control rules which work reasonably well in both cases. If one knew precisely how expectations were formed, we could no doubt on that basis design a still more satisfactory set of rules. But the design of policy rules which are robust across different assumptions about the formation of expectations is an important element in the framework of policy presented in this volume.

1.7   THE FORM OF CONTROL

For our policy framework we have chosen to operate through simple and robust feedback rules designed to stabilize movements of the Money GDP and the national wealth around paths which are themselves determined independently in advance on simple welfare criteria. We have chosen to adopt this method rather than a more sophisticated optimal-control procedure for a number of reasons.

The welfare functions which have to be used in optimal control exercises in order to give sensible results are usually nothing like any plausible utility function. Optimal policies can only be designed with reference to specific shocks. It is true that stochastic weighting is possible to produce a rule which is optimal in the face of a probabilistic combination of shocks, but there are some events such as wars and OPEC behaviour to which no sensible probability can be attached. In the presence of uncertainty as well as risk optimal design is not possible.

Further problems arise with the design of optimal rules. Conventional techniques, used on non-linear models, do not test the working of the rules beyond some terminal date. It is quite possible for conventional optimization to produce rules which are unstable and therefore unsustainable.

In any case, the whole procedure is unfamiliar and not easily understood by the layman or, indeed, by most of the ministers and officials who would be required to operate it. Optimal policy rules are invariably very complex, and do not show any obvious links between their specification and the structure of the economy which they are intended to control.

On the other hand, the framework of policy which we propose is in many ways a familiar one, the good sense of which is easily understood. If one substituted the Money GDP for the stock of money ($M_0,...M_3,...$ etc) and the national wealth for the Public Sector Borrowing Requirement one would be operating something very similar to the present Medium-Term Financial Strategy.[6] There would be target paths set for the GDP and the national wealth. To implement this there would be simple proportional and integral control rules to keep the economy on the chosen path (such as to raise tax rates and/or interest rates in so far as the GDP was above target and was rising rapidly).[7] Our search is for simple rules of this kind which are easy to understand and which would be as robust as possible in the face of various uncertainties about how the economy worked, how people formed expectations, and so on. At the present stage of the game it is not possible to expect perfection; but in our view it should be possible to make important improvements in the present arrangements.

Our approach to policy design allows us to sidestep the whole issue of policy credibility. We test our rules with model-consistent expectations on the assumption that the public understand and believe the rules and assume that the government will adhere to these rules and to its published targets to the bitter end. As Kydland and Prescott (1977) and Barro and Gordon (1983) have clearly demonstrated, in a forward-looking model, the government gains extra room for manoeuvre if it treats expectations of future policies as an instrument to be varied independently of actual policies. If the public are assumed to be aware of this they may try to take account of the temptation for the government to cheat. In this case, the behaviour of an economy with forward-looking variables will differ from that of one in which a government was expected to, and did, keep its word.

There is no practical way of modelling the extent to which policy announcements will in fact be believed. On the other hand, as noted above, we would not want to prescribe policies which worked only if they were to be believed. We note that our simple rules have the advantage over optimal rules that it is reasonably clear when they are being broken. They do not offer much of a smoke-screen for a government which intends to break its promises. However, by choosing two quite different forms of expectations formation, and checking that our rules work even when expectations are backward-looking, so that the government cannot exploit them independently of its actions, we can be reasonably confident that our rules will not fail because they are not believed.

There is one other important aspect of our control rules. There are some policy adjustments (e.g. changes in tax rates for the control of the GDP) which can be made only after a certain lag either because the data on which their change must be based become available only at discrete intervals or because of administrative and other institutional factors; but there are other adjustments (e.g. changes in short-term interest rates to control the rate of foreign exchange) which can be made at any time and for which the necessary statistical data are currently available. An important feature of the design of our framework of rules is to distinguish on this principle between what may be called lagged and simultaneous rules. We thus have a structure of rules some of which are applied with a lag of one or more quarters and others of which are applied without any significant lag. Nor are our proposals in any way incompatible with the continuation of a general annual review of the economy (as at the time of an annual budget) at which the forward planning of the economy is considered in the light of what are thought to be the most probable future developments. Our framework of simple, robust feedback rules can supplement an annual review with more rapid and automatic reaction to divergences from the planned future path as they occur.

1.8 INTERNATIONAL ASPECTS OF POLICY RULES

In this book we consider the problem of policy design from the perspective of a small country in the world economy. This is probably not very different from the situation which the United Kingdom has faced, at least since exchange rates started floating in 1972.

It is true that during this period there have been summit meetings between the major economic powers, and that attempts have been made to co-ordinate economic policy. This book does not address the problem of policy co-ordination. That is the subject of a separate and lengthy study upon which some members of our group are now embarking. While we cannot, of course, anticipate the results of that study we would note that the major issue which will interest us is whether the policy rules which we identify in Chapter 6 can be extended to form the basis for international 'rules of the game' within which each participant can pursue a decentralized approach to economic management. In such an environment there may well be exchange-rate targets. One very important point to note about exchange-rate targets, in an international context, is that, as intermediate targets, they may serve as an important focus for international co-operation, even if those target values are not always internationally consistent.[8]

Our examination of the possibilities of control of the UK economy in the virtual absence of organized international co-operation over the years 1975–89 is of more than historic interest. It is directly relevant to the present search for a new formal framework for the setting of international policy. The major relationships examined in our study (for example, in the labour market, in the setting of target exchange rates, in the treatment of the GDP and wealth targets, in the treatment of expectations) are of basic importance for the construction of an effective system of international co-operation. Without a correct appreciation of these national relationships it is impossible to construct an efficient and acceptable system of international co-operation.

1.9   OUTLINE OF SUBSEQUENT CHAPTERS

Chapters 2 to 4 continue the theoretical explanation of our proposals. The chapters present a portfolio of simple illustrative algebraic models, differing in detail from each other as required, in order to highlight key questions.

   The purpose of these chapters is to begin the discussion of policy–target emphasis, that is the question of the relative weights which should be placed upon fiscal and monetary policy in the pursuit of the two financial targets. In these chapters we simplify by replacing the Money GDP target with a price target, solely for reasons of algebraic tractability. (We have explained in Section 1.3.1 above the important practical advantages of choosing Money GDP rather than the price level as a policy target.)

   Chapter 2 examines three issues. How do the relative weights (what we shall call the emphases) which should be put upon the use of fiscal policy and of monetary policy for the attainment of the price target and of the wealth target depend upon:

i)   the balance between demand-pull and cost-push in wage determination,
ii)   the nature of the wealth target, and
iii)   the effects of international trade and capital movements?

This model is a simple static model and all variables are in levels.

   Chapters 3 and 4 turn to dynamics. This is tricky, since we want to analyse at most third-order equation systems so as to be able to interpret the results clearly. We thus split up our problem, and consider in these chapters perhaps the two most important pieces of it.

   Chapter 3 explores dynamic aspects of (i) the wage price spiral and (ii) the operation of an exchange-rate intermediate target. The focus is on the interactions between inflation control, interest-rate setting, exchange-rate targeting and the instabilities which can stem from a wage-price spiral. A preliminary discussion of these issues was provided by Blake and Weale (1988) and Blake, Vines and Weale (1988). The model is in logarithms which in this case produce a very simple set of linear differential equations.

In Chapter 4 we present simple models to elaborate the implications for policy of dynamic aspects of wealth accumulation. We believe that this has more important implications for the design of dynamic financial control policies than has been generally recognized. In particular, the possibility of instability in an open economy due to the accumulation of interest on overseas assets or liabilities has proved more troublesome to us than we had expected. The model is in levels again because of the need to deal carefully with interest payments on debt.

Part II contains a detailed attempt to evaluate how our proposals might be applied. In Chapter 5 we present key aspects of the macro-economic model of the UK which we have built from version 7 of the National Institute of Economic and Social Research model. It contains a number of interesting new features, important for our problem. In Chapter 6 we present our policy rules and demonstrate their ability to achieve target 'step-changes' in the target variables in this new model.

Chaper 7 discusses our approach to the problem of counterfactual simulation with model-consistent expectations. In Chapters 8 and 9 we have applied our simple lagged and simultaneous feedback rules to reruns of history over the period 1975–89 in an attempt to keep the economy on a combination of GDP-national wealth target trajectories so as to reduce the rate of inflation with a minimum of other adverse effects. In the search for a set of rules which combine simplicity, effectiveness and robustness over different institutional and behavioural assumptions, we have four possible combinations of (i) reformed or unreformed wage-fixing institutions with (ii) assumptions of adaptive or of rational behaviour in the formation of expectations. We have produced two sets of control rules to cover these four possible cases. We find that an economy in which cost-push dominates in the wage-setting institutions probably requires a different set of rules from those needed in an economy in which demand-pull dominates. But for each of these two cases we can find a single set of rules which is surprisingly robust whether expectations are formed adaptively or on the basis of rational expectations.

In Part III we turn to questions of method. Chapter 10 describes how we construct a linear representation of our model, as an essential tool for our empirical study. Technical details of the way in which we design our control rules are described in the Chapter 11

Part IV presents a summary of our conclusions.

The linkages between financial weapons and financial targets: a comparative static analysis

2.1 LINKAGES AND EMPHASIS

This chapter begins the detailed theoretical analysis of our New Keynesian policy proposals. We start to examine our proposals for financial policy introduced in section 1.3: the joint use of fiscal policy (taxes) and monetary policy (the interest rate) in the pursuit of the two objectives of policy. We noted at the end of Chapter 1 that we use here a price target as one of our objectives, in place of a Money GDP target; this simplifies our algebraic analysis. The other objective is a national wealth target. Our concern is with the emphasis which should be put on the two targets in the setting of each of the two instruments.

We do not assume that each of the two policy instruments should be linked exclusively to one and only one of the financial targets. We allow for cross-linkages between the two weapons and the two targets, and examine the conditions which make it appropriate to set monetary policy mainly with regard to the desired outcome for the inflation target and fiscal policy mainly with regard to the control of wealth, or *vice versa*. That is what we call 'emphasis' in the setting of policy.

The model presented in this chapter is entirely static. Clearly a full evaluation of these issues requires a dynamic model. But a very simple static model provides an important vehicle for an exploration of the following three key questions. How does the emphasis which should be placed upon the two targets in the setting of monetary policy and fiscal policy, respectively, depend upon

i) the balance between demand-pull and cost-push elements in the wage equation,
ii) the form chosen for a national wealth target, and
iii) international trade and capital movements in an open economy?

These three questions recur throughout the book. We shall use a more complex dynamic model to analyse them in the next chapter, and we undertake an exhaustive dynamic analysis with our empirical econometric model later in the book. But we can say much with the simple static model of this chapter.

In order to simplify the algebra we assume in this chapter that the price-control objective is to maintain the rate of inflation of the domestic factor-cost price level (rather than of the Money GDP) at a moderate predetermined level. The choice of wealth targets which we consider is as between given levels for (i) the total national expenditure on real capital development, (ii) the current account surplus or deficit on the government's budget. Since the analysis is short-period, these wealth targets defined in flow terms are exactly analogous to wealth targets defined as either the stock of real capital assets or the stock of the net national debt; the flow during the short period determines uniquely the stock at the end of the period.

We assume that the monetary and fiscal policies take the form of the setting at specified levels by the authorities of the short-term rate of interest and of the rate of universal income tax.

2.2   THE MODEL OF A CLOSED ECONOMY

2.2.1   Assumptions

We deliberately start in this chapter with a highly simplified model. The economy is initially closed but subsequently opened. The model is designed on lines which are suitable for a 'static' IS/LM type of analysis. For this purpose we make use of what may be called Marshallian-Keynesian short-period analysis, with the following characteristics:

i)   The period is short enough for it to be reasonable to assume no significant change in any capital stocks.

ii) Certain factors, however, such as labour can be varied and indeed are varied in amounts immediately at the beginning of each period.

iii) There are no appreciable time-lags in the adjustment of consumption, investment, exports, imports, production etc. to the conditions ruling at the beginning of the period.

iv) Expectations are given exogenously and are not influenced by the choice of policy variables at the beginning of each period.

v)   The money-wage rate is fixed at the beginning of each period, but the rate at which it will be set at the beginning of the next period depends upon what happens during this period, this difference measuring what we will call this period's rate of inflation ($\hat{W}_0 = (W_1 - W_0)/W_0$).

The questions which we set to our simple model are of the following kind. What difference would be made to the rate of inflation ($\hat{P}$), the level of investment (I), the budget balance (B), the level of total output (Y), and the level of consumption (C) during this period if the control variables (the rate of tax (S) and/or the rate of interest (R)) were set at the beginning of the period at different levels? We are thus comparing different equilibria which might rule during this short period according to the choice at the beginning of the period about the level of the control variables to operate during the period.

The *LM* side of the *IS–LM* is in this model represented by an assumption that the monetary authorities set the rate of interest which rules during the period under analysis by providing automatically whatever money or liquidity is necessary for that purpose. This means that the monetary policy instrument is the rate of interest, rather than the stock of any monetary aggregate. The *IS* side of the model is represented by the fact that, with the rate of interest together with the rate of tax being thus set by the authorities, the multiplicand of the Kahn-Keynes multiplier (e.g. government expenditure and investment expenditure) and the consumption multiplier itself will be determined. The reader can then interpret the following analysis in either of two ways:

i)   If the Keynesian 'short' period is sufficiently 'long' for all the relevant relationships (e.g. the level of consumption dependent upon a given level of post-tax income) to have settled down to equilibrium, but sufficiently short that the assumptions (i) to (v) hold good, then the following model can be used to represent a full Keynesian type of analysis.

ii) But alternatively – and this is the form in which the following model is precisely formulated – the 'short' period can be regarded as very 'short', indeed no longer than, say, the quarter which is often used as the relevant short period for a fully dynamic difference-equation type of analysis. The insights which are then gained from the model refer only to what may be called the 'impact' effects of changes in the policy variables, dealing with questions such as what would be the immediate effects of a given change in S or R on I, C, Y etc. regardless of their implications for any longer-period new steady-state of the economy or of its subsequent path to, or away from, or around, such a steady-state.

The actual level of money prices and costs ruling during the period under analysis is determined by assuming that a fixed money wage is set at the beginning of the period and that prices are determined by a fixed mark-up of prices on these money costs. But it is an essential feature of the model to consider the factors at work during the period under analysis which will influence, indeed will determine, the rate at which the money wage will be set at the beginning of the next period. In this respect the model does stray away from the strictly static nature of an *IS/LM* model. (Turnovsky, 1977, Chapter 4, presents a model in the spirit.)

2.2.2   Basic equations

Consider then the following nine equations of a greatly simplified short-period model of a closed economy:[1]

$$Y = L \tag{2.1}$$

Output (Y) per worker (L) is assumed constant.

$$P = (1 + \pi) W \tag{2.2}$$

The factor-cost of price of output is equal to a marked-up $(1 + \pi)$ value of the money wage costs (W).

$$C = \varkappa_1 (1 - S) Y + (\tilde{\varkappa}_1 - \varkappa_1)(1 - S_{-1}) Y_{-1}$$
$$= \varkappa_1 (1 - S) Y + \overline{C} \tag{2.3}$$

The amount of product consumed in any given short period (C) depends upon a proportion ($\tilde{\varkappa}_1$) of the post-tax income from which it is financed. There may by a distributed lag so that this period's consumption (C) is partly financed out of this period's post-tax $(1 - S)$ income (Y) and partly ($\tilde{\varkappa}_1 - \varkappa_1$) out of last period's post-tax $(1 - S_{-1})$ income (Y_{-1}). But for this period everything due to last period's events becomes a given constant effect ($\overline{C}$) on this period's consumption (C), so that the parameter $\varkappa_1$ shows the impact effect of any change in this period's post-tax income on this period's consumption.

$$I = \bar{I} - \iota R - (\tilde{\iota} - \iota) R_{-1} + \nu (Y - Y_{-1}) + (\tilde{\nu} - \nu)(Y_{-1} - Y_{-2})$$
$$= - \iota R + \nu Y + \bar{I} \tag{2.4}$$

The amount of product invested in new capital by the private sector is equal to a constant ($\bar{I}$) minus a constant ($\bar{\iota}$) times the rate of interest (R) and an accelerator ($\bar{\nu}$) times the rate of increase in the total demand for the products of the economy ($Y - Y_{-1}$). But these two effects may be partially lagged. The parameters ι and ν show the impact effects on investment during the period of a reduction in R or a rise in Y during this period.

$$Y = \bar{G} + I + C \tag{2.5}$$

The amount of product produced in this period is equal to the sum of consumption by the government sector which is assumed to be constant ($\bar{G}$) plus private investment (I) and consumption (C).

$$B = YS - \bar{G} \tag{2.6}$$

This period's budget balance (B) is defined as this period's income (Y) multiplied by this period's rate of tax (S) minus this period's government spending ($\bar{G}$). A major simplification of the model is to ignore the effects of the national debt and the payment of interest on the debt. Thus equation (2.3) neglects any effect on consumption of expenditures financed by the private sector's receipt of interest on the national debt and equation (2.6) neglects interest income both on the expenditure side of the budget and as an element of the tax base. A true dynamic analysis would necessitate the abandonment of these assumptions since the growth of national debt resulting from a growing interest charge upon the budget can be an important destabilizing influence (Blinder and Solow, 1973).

$$V = \frac{W(1 - S)}{P}$$

$$= \frac{1 - S}{1 + \pi}, \text{ using (2.2)} \tag{2.7a}$$

The real value of a worker's take-home pay (V) is his money wage (W) less tax (S) divided by the cost of living (P).[2]

$$\tilde{V} = \bar{V} + \frac{L}{\beta'} \tag{2.7b}$$

The term $\tilde{V}$ represents what may be called the worker's 'aspiration' level of real post-tax take-home pay, which is assumed to be an increasing function of the level of employment (L) and so a decreasing function of the level of unemployment.

$$L_s = \beta'(V - \bar{V}) \tag{2.7c}$$

The phenomenon of an aspiration rate of pay which may differ from the actual rate of pay can, if preferred, be translated into terms of an upward-sloping labour supply curve as given in (2.7c) by writing $V = \tilde{V}$ in (2.7b) and then solving for L. The resulting expression shown in (2.7c) then shows what the level of employment would have to be to make the workers content with their actual pay. Actual employment is demand determined so that L represents the demand for labour. If $L > L_s$, the demand for labour exceeds the supply. This can in alternative language be stated as a situation in which workers aspire to, or demand, a wage which is higher than the actual wage.

$$\hat{W} \equiv \frac{W_{+1} - W}{W} = \beta_3(\tilde{V} - V) + \beta_5(V_{-1} - V) \tag{2.8a}$$

Alternatively

$$\hat{W} = \beta_4(L - L_s) + \beta_5(V_{-1} - V) \tag{2.8b}$$

Equations (2.8a) and (2.8b) are alternative ways of expressing the pressures which build up during this period to cause the money wage rate set at the beginning of the next period (W_{+1}) to exceed the money wage rate which was set at the beginning of this period. In (2.8a) the rate of wage inflation is made to depend upon the excess of the aspired over the actual wage ruling in this period and in (2.8b) on the excess of labour demand over labour supply ruling during this period; and in both cases it is also made to depend upon a 'catching-up' term, i.e. upon any reduction of the rate of real post-tax pay ruling during this period below its level in the previous period. If one uses (2.1) to write $Y = L$ and also writes $\beta_4\beta' = \beta_3$, both formulations of $\hat{W}$ can be written as

$$\hat{W} = \beta_6 Y + \beta_7 S + \hat{\bar{W}} \tag{2.8c}$$

where $\beta_6 = \beta_3/\beta'$, $\beta_7 = (\beta_3 + \beta_5)/(1 + \pi)$, and $\hat{\bar{W}} = \beta_3\bar{V} + \beta_5 V_{-1} - (\beta_3 + \beta_5)/(1 + \pi)$.

Thus if $\beta_3 = \beta'\beta_4$, the two formulations are merely different ways of expressing the same real factors. In either case the rate of wage inflation ($\hat{W}$) can be seen to depend upon two factors, Y and S.

The first is measured by $\beta_6 Y$ and may be called the 'demand-pull' factor. The higher is the demand for output and so for labour, the greater will be the aspiration wage and thus the upward pressure on money wage rates. This corresponds to the familiar Phillips-curve effect. The second factor is measured by $\beta_7 S$ and may be called the 'cost-push' factor. It can be divided into two parts corresponding to the terms $\beta_3/(1 + \pi)$ and $\beta_5/(1 + \pi)$ which make up the term β_7. (i) The higher is S, the lower will be the actual post-tax real take-home pay and the greater, therefore, will be the gap between the aspired and the actual rate of pay. (ii) The higher is S, the lower will be this period's real post-tax pay relative to that of the previous period and the greater, therefore, will be the catching-up pressure on wage claims.[3]

If we eliminate L and W from equations (2.1) to (2.7) and use (2.8c) we obtain the model in summary form.

Table 2.1   The short-term model of a closed economy

$$Y = \mu\{\bar{G} + \bar{C} + \bar{I} - \iota R\} \tag{2.9a}$$
$$C = \varkappa_1(1 - S)Y + \bar{C} \tag{2.9b}$$
$$I = -\iota R + \nu Y + \bar{I} \tag{2.9c}$$
$$B = SY - \bar{G} \tag{2.9d}$$
$$\hat{P} = \beta_6 Y + \beta_7 S + \hat{w} \tag{2.9e}$$

where $\mu = 1/(1 - \varkappa_1[1 - S] - \nu)$, the Kahn-Keynes multiplier, with $G + \bar{C} + \bar{I} - \iota R$ as the multiplicand. $[\varkappa_1(1 - S) + \nu]$ is assumed to be less than unity so that μ is positive.

2.2.3   Comparative statics

By substitution of the value for Y from the first of these equations into the remaining five equations one can obtain expressions for the inflation target ($\hat{P}$) and the two possible wealth targets (I, B) and also for total income (Y) and consumption (C) in terms of the two control variables (S and R).

Then by differentiation of (2.9) with respect to S and R one obtains:

$$\begin{bmatrix} \delta\hat{P} \\ \delta I \\ \delta B \\ \delta C \\ \delta Y \end{bmatrix} = \begin{bmatrix} p_s & p_r \\ i_s & i_r \\ b_s & b_r \\ c_s & c_r \\ y_s & y_r \end{bmatrix} \begin{bmatrix} \delta S \\ \delta R \end{bmatrix} \tag{2.10}$$

with the parameters in the matrix taking the following values:

$$p_s = -\beta_6\mu x_1 Y + \beta_7 \qquad p_r = -\beta_6\mu\iota$$
$$i_s = -\nu\mu x_1 Y \qquad i_r = -(1 + \nu\mu)\iota$$
$$b_s = (1 - x_1 - \nu)\mu Y \qquad b_r = -S\mu\iota$$
$$c_s = -(1 - \nu)\mu x_1 Y \qquad c_r = -\{(1 - \nu)\mu - 1\}\iota$$
$$y_s = i_s + c_s \qquad y_r = i_r + c_r$$
$$= -\mu x_1 Y \qquad = -\mu\iota$$

It should be emphasized that the small changes in the variables (δS, δR, $\delta\hat{P}$, δB etc.) in (2.10) do not represent the change in the variable over time. (Changes in the variables listed in the left-hand vector in (2.10) may take place between one period and the next even if S and R remain unchanged; for example, in the consumption equation (2.3) C may be higher or lower in this period because Y was high or low in the last period, an influence which is captured by the element $\bar{C}$, even though S and R remained unchanged from one period to the next.) All that the first equation in (2.10), namely $\delta\hat{P} = p_s\delta S + p_r\delta R$, expresses is the extent to which $\hat{P}$ would be higher or lower than it would otherwise have been in the short period under examination if S and/or R were raised or lowered above or below what they would otherwise have been.

Thus the matrix (2.10) expresses the way in which a change in the levels of instrument variables S and R at the beginning of any one period would cause the values of the other variables in the system during the coming short period to differ from what they would otherwise have been. The five equations in (2.10) represent five independent relationships between the seven variables ($\hat{P}$, I, B, C, Y, S, and R). It is, of course, possible to rearrange these equations by selecting a pair of variables other than S and R to play the role of the 'knowns' in the right-hand vector in (2.10) while S and R join the unknowns in the left-hand vector.

It is first helpful to define five parameters

$$\sigma_p = -\frac{p_s}{p_r} = \frac{-\beta_6\mu x_1 Y + \beta_7}{\beta_6\mu\iota}$$

$$= -\frac{\beta_6\mu x_1 Y - \beta_7}{\beta_6\mu x_1 Y} \cdot \frac{x_1 Y}{\iota}$$

$$\sigma_i = -\frac{i_s}{i_r} = -\frac{\nu\mu}{1 + \nu\mu} \cdot \frac{x_1 Y}{\iota}$$

$$= -\frac{\nu}{1 - x_1(1 - S)} \cdot \frac{x_1 Y}{\iota} \qquad\qquad (2.11)$$

$$\sigma_b = -\frac{b_s}{b_r} = \frac{1 - \varkappa_1 - \nu}{S\varkappa_1} \cdot \frac{\varkappa_1 Y}{\iota}$$

$$\sigma_c = -\frac{c_s}{c_r} = -\frac{(1 - \nu)\mu}{\{(1 - \nu)\mu - 1\}} \cdot \frac{\varkappa_1 Y}{\iota}$$

$$= -\frac{1 - \nu}{\varkappa_1(1 - S)} \cdot \frac{\varkappa_1 Y}{\iota}$$

$$\sigma_y = -\frac{y_s}{y_r} = -\frac{\varkappa_1 Y}{i}$$

Each σ measures, respectively, the extent to which R must change, given a unit change in S, in order to keep the variables ($\hat{P}$, I, B, C, or Y) at an unchanged level. We shall call the value of σ_p 'the slope of the $\hat{P}$-contour' since it measures the change in R per unit change in S which is needed to keep $\delta\hat{P} = 0$. It will be an upward or downward slope according as σ_p is positive or negative. We shall call the absolute value of σ_p regardless of sign 'the steepness of the $\hat{P}$-contour'. Thus the steepness will be a gentle upward slope if a small increase in R is associated with a unit increase in S and a steep downward slope if a large decrease in R is associated with a unit increase in S; and *vice versa*. And similarly, for σ_b, σ_i, σ_c, and σ_y.

Suppose one chooses to take $\delta\hat{P}$ and δI as two predetermined changes in the inflation and the investment targets which one wishes to achieve. One can then transform the five equations of (2.10) into the following five equations:

$$
\begin{bmatrix} \delta S \\ \delta R \\ \delta B \\ \delta C \\ \delta Y \end{bmatrix} = \frac{1}{\Delta_I}
\begin{bmatrix}
i_r & -p_r \\
-i_s & p_s \\
b_s i_r - b_r i_s & b_r p_s - b_s p_r \\
c_s i_r - c_r i_s & c_r p_s - c_s p_r \\
y_s i_r - y_r i_s & y_r p_s - y_s p_r
\end{bmatrix}
\begin{bmatrix} \delta\hat{P} \\ \delta I \end{bmatrix} \tag{2.12}
$$

with $\Delta_I = p_s i_r - p_r i_s = \iota\{\beta_6 \mu \varkappa_1 Y - \beta_7(1 + \nu\mu)\}$

In this case $\delta\hat{P}$ and ΔI represent the 'known' changes which are to be effected in the two target variables; δS and δR then measure the 'unknown' change in the two control variables which are needed to effect the predetermined changes in the target variables; and δB, δC, and δY indicate the changes which will result in the other variables.

If one took B instead of I as the wealth target, one would need in matrix (2.12) to substitute δB for δI, b_r for i_r, b_s for i_s, and Δ_B for Δ_I where

$$\Delta_B = p_s b_r - p_r b_s = \iota\mu\{\beta_6 Y - \beta_7 S\}$$

In the following section of this chapter we shall illustrate the economic implications of the results of the formal analysis contained in equations (2.8) to (2.12) by examining in some detail the economic aspects of two particular short-period policy decisions. For this purpose it will be useful first to note in advance certain features of these equations.

2.2.4 Comparative advantage and emphasis

(1) The signs of the parameters in (2.10) are unambiguous except in the case of p_s. In the case of p_s we have

$$p_s \gtreqless 0 \qquad \text{as} \qquad \beta_7 \gtreqless \beta_6 \mu \varkappa_1 Y \qquad (2.13)$$

which expresses the fact that the effect of an increase in the rate of tax will lead to a net increase (or decrease) in the rate of inflation according as the cost-push element (β_7) exceeds (or is less than) the demand-pull element ($\beta_6 \mu \varkappa_1 Y$) in the wage equation.

(2) As already explained, the expressions in equation (2.11) measure the slopes of the contour lines for the relevant variables. The signs of these contour slopes are all unambiguous except for σ_p. The sign of this slope is ambiguous because of the ambiguity of the sign of p_s.

(3) In the economic analysis of the following section it will become clear that an important role is played by the comparative steepness of the various contour-slopes, a comparison which is particularly important where any two slopes have the same sign (either upward or downward). In (2.11) we express all these slopes as multiples of $\varkappa_1 Y / \iota$, i.e. of the downward steepness of the Y-contour. (i) As can be seen from the first row of (2.11) the downward steepness of the $\hat{P}$-contour would be the same as that of the Y-contour if $\beta_7 = 0$, but that if $\beta_7 > 0$ any downward slope of the $\hat{P}$-contour must be less steep than that of the Y-contour. (ii) We must, however, have $\varkappa_1(1 - S) + \nu < 1$, as has already been assumed. It follows that any negative slope for the I-contour must be less steep than for the Y-contour. (iii) In the case of the C-contour for the same reason we must have $1 - \nu > \varkappa_1(1 - S)$ so that the C-contour is more steeply sloped than the Y-contour.

(4) In the matrix (2.12) the expressions i_r / Δ_I and i_s / Δ_I in the first two rows represent the extent to which the control instruments S and R will need to be adjusted in order to lead to a change in the inflation target variables by $\delta \hat{P}$ without any change in the wealth target variable I; and similarly for the corresponding expressions in the other rows of the first column of the matrix for the resulting changes in the other variables. The

signs of these expressions (such as i_r/Δ_I) thus depend not only upon the sign of the numerator (such as i_r) but also upon the sign of the denominator (such as the determinant Δ_I). The signs of the determinants Δ_I and Δ_B, will accordingly play an important role in the following economic analysis since they will determine in which direction, upward or downwards, the instruments of control must be adjusted in order to achieve a given adjustment of the levels of the target variables.

(5) In Section 2.1 it was shown that a proper 'linkage' of different instruments as means of control over particular target variables does not imply that each instrument should be exclusively tied to one particular target. Indeed, the example given in the previous paragraph illustrates the fact that if it is desired in (2.12) to change $\hat{P}$ by $\delta\hat{P}$ without changing I one should change S by i_r/Δ_I and R by $-i_s/\Delta_I$, which means that $|i_s/i_r|$ represents the relative weight which should be put on R as compared with S in the control of $\hat{P}$. Similarly if it is desired in (2.12) to change I by δI without changing $\hat{P}$, one would need to change S by $-p_r/\Delta_I$, and R by p_s/Δ_I, which means that $|p_s/p_r|$ represents the relative weight to be put on R as compared with S in the control of I.

Thus if

$$\left|\frac{p_s}{p_r}\right| > \left|\frac{i_s}{i_r}\right|, \text{ i.e. if } \left|\frac{p_s/i_s}{p_r/i_r}\right| \equiv \left|\frac{\sigma_p}{\sigma_i}\right| > 1$$

more weight should be put upon S relative to R in the control of $\hat{P}$ as compared with the weight to be put upon S relative to R in the control of I (cf. Mundell, 1962). Accordingly we can define σ_p/σ_i as a comparative weighting index measuring the comparative emphasis which should be put upon S relative to R in the control of $\hat{P}$. At the same time we can see from the matrix (2.10) that $|p_s/p_r|$ measures the effectiveness of S relative to the effectiveness of R in the control of $\hat{P}$, while $|i_s/i_r|$ measures the effectiveness of S relative to that of R in the control of I. Thus we could equally well describe $|\sigma_p/\sigma_i|$ as a comparative advantage index measuring the comparative efficiency of S relative to that of R in the control of $\hat{P}$.

If B instead of I were the wealth target, $|\sigma_p/\sigma_i|$ would be replaced by $|\sigma_p/\sigma_b|$. Thus we can define

$$\omega \equiv \frac{\sigma_p}{\sigma_i} \text{ if } I \text{ is the wealth target}$$

$$\text{or } \omega \equiv \frac{\sigma_p}{\sigma_b} \text{ if } B \text{ is the wealth target}$$

$$(2.14)$$

as a comparative weighting index or a comparative advantage index.[4] If $|\omega| > 1$, we can say either that in the control of $\hat{P}$ one should emphasise the use of S and in the control of I one should emphasise the use of R or that S has a comparative advantage in the control of P and R in the control of I.

From (2.11) it can be seen that $|\sigma_p|$ measures the steepness of the slope of the $\hat{P}$-contour and that $|\sigma_i|$ or $|\sigma_b|$, as the case may be, measures the steepness of the slope of the wealth-target contour. One can thus describe the above conclusions about the relative emphasis to be put upon the two instruments of control in the following words:

> When two target variables are under consideration the emphasis should be put upon R for the control of that target variable whose contour line has the smaller absolute magnitude of slope and on S for the control of that target variable whose contour line has the larger absolute magnitude of slope. This reflects the fact that emphasis should exactly reflect the comparative advantage of the instruments in influencing the targets.

This rule has a straightforward implication for the design of policies in the case of the static analysis of this chapter. But its application in a dynamic analysis of an economy changing through time is less straightforward for a number of reasons discussed in the concluding section of this chapter.

2.3 THE CONTROL OF INFLATION AND WEALTH IN A CLOSED ECONOMY

In this section we consider some of the economic policy implications of the formal analysis of section 2.2 by applying the analysis to the control of our two policy objectives. We suppose that it is desired so to change the setting of the control instruments (i.e. so to set δS and δR) as to cause a unit decrease in the rate of inflation below what it would otherwise have been (i.e. so as to cause $\delta \hat{P} = -1$) without having any effect upon the level of a wealth target expressed as the level of investment (i.e. while keeping $\delta I = 0$). Then, separately, we suppose that it is desired to change the setting of the control instruments so as to cause a unit increase in this wealth target variable ($\delta I = +1$) without having any effect on inflation. In the analysis special attention will be paid to the question whether the demand-pull or the cost-push element is predominant in the wage equation (i.e. whether $p_s \gtrless 0$). We shall then consider the substitution of the budget balance (B) for investment (I) as the wealth target and ask whether the use of B (with an upward contour slope) instead of I (with a downward contour slope) would greatly affect the problem of control over inflation.

In Figure 2.1 the relevant contour maps are illustrated, the slopes of the contour-lines in this figure being as given in (2.11). We start in each case at an origin O where S and R are set at their existing levels. In Figure 2.1(a) we draw the line marked $\delta\hat{P} = 0$ which shows the combination of changes in S and R which would be needed to keep $\delta\hat{P} = 0$. The continuous line shows the combination if the demand-pull element exceeds the cost-push element $(p_s < 0)$, while the broken line shows the case in which the cost-push element is dominant $(p_s > 0)$. If it were desired to reduce $\hat{P}$ by a certain amount (e.g. $\delta\hat{P} = -1$) it would be necessary with $p_s < 0$ to raise either the rate of tax or the rate of interest or some combination of both. The contour line for $\delta\hat{P} = -1$ would lie above that for $\delta\hat{P} = 0$ as shown by the contour for $\delta\hat{P} < 0$. If, however, $p_s > 0$, then to reduce $\hat{P}$ would require either a fall in the rate of tax or a rise in the rate of interest; and once again the contour line for $\delta\hat{P} < 0$ would lie above the contour line for $\delta\hat{P} = 0$.

In Figure 2.1(b) we show similar contour lines for the two alternative wealth target variables I and B, as defined from the second and third lines of (2.11). The I-contours have a downward slope since a fall in R will directly raise I, while a rise in S through its restrictive effect on C and so on Y will lower the accelerator influence on I. Since a decrease in R, with S constant, will raise I, the I-contour for $\delta I > 0$ will pass below the I-contour for $\delta I = 0$. The B-contours have an upward slope because a rise in R by reducing I and so Y will reduce the tax base which must be offset by a rise in S if the budget balance is to stay unchanged $(\delta B = 0)$. If it is desired to raise B $(\delta B > 0)$ then either the tax base must be raised by a reduction of R or the yield raised by a rise in S, so that the contour $\delta B > 0$ passes to the right of the contour $\delta B = 0$.

Finally, Figure 2.1c shows the contour lines for Y and C, as derived from the fourth and fifth rows of (2.11). In both cases the slopes are downwards since any stimulating effect of a cut in the rate of interest must be offset by a rise in the rate of tax. The slope is steeper for the C- than for the Y contours because a change in S operates directly only on the C-component of Y, whereas a change in R operates directly only on the I-component of Y. In both cases the contour lines for an increase in Y or C (i.e. δY or $\delta C > 0$) pass below the original contour line (i.e. δY or $\delta C = 0$) because a reduction in S or R or any combination of such changes will expand both Y and C.

We have already noted in the previous section in commenting on (2.11) that the downward slopes of the $\hat{P}$- and I-contours are necessarily less

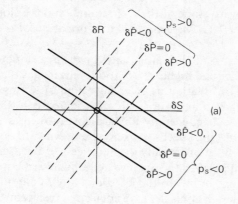

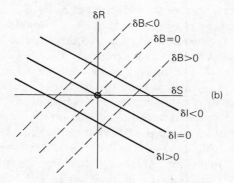

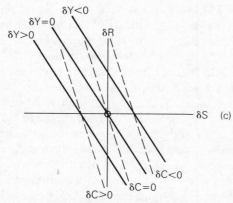

Figure 2.1   Contour maps for the closed economy

steep than the downward slope of the Y-contours and *a fortiori* less steep
than the downward slope of the C-contours; and the slopes have been so
drawn in Figure 2.1. The economic interpretation of these relationships
is as follows.

As one moves to the left along any downward sloping $\hat{P}$-contour one
will cross a higher and higher Y-contour. This means that as one controls
any given level of inflation by reducing S and offsetting any inflationary
effect by raising R, there will result a net increase in the level of Y. The
reduction in S will reduce any upward cost-push pressure on inflation.
The offsetting rise in R needs to exercise a downward demand-pull effect
which is sufficient to offset only the net excess of the S-generated upward
demand-pull effect over the S-generated downward cost-push effect.

Similarly as one moves to the left along any I-contour one will cross a
higher and higher Y-contour. Consider any given reduction in S. For Y
to be constant there must be a rise in R which causes a decrease in I equal
to the impact effect on C of the reduction of S. For I to be constant there
need not be so great a rise in R and thus there would be some increase in
Y. There must be some rise in R because if there were not there would be
an accelerator boost to I due to the rise in Y. The rise in R must exercise a
sufficient restraint on I to offset the accelerator boost to I due to the rise
in Y; but with I thus constant there will be some increase in Y as a result
of the reduction in S combined with a moderate rise in R. Since the
B-contours slope upwards and Y- and C-contours slope downwards, it
follows that as one moves to the left along any B-contour, so one moves
on to higher and higher Y- and C-contours. Thus we may reach the
following most important conclusion that any movement to the left
along a wealth target contour will imply a rise in Y and C.

We now use the contours of Figure 2.1 to examine the effects of
various degrees of cost-push in the wage equation on policies designed
either (i) to reduce the rate of inflation by one unit while keeping the level
of investment unchanged or (ii) to raise the level of investment by one
unit while keeping the level of inflation unchanged. In Figure 2.2 we
display four cases in each of which the targets are either (i) $\delta\hat{P} = -1$ with
$\delta I = 0$ or (ii) $\delta I = +1$ with $\delta\hat{P} = 0$. In all four cases the slopes of the
I-contour are the same. The only difference is the slope of the
$\hat{P}$-contours. As we move from diagram (a) to (b) to (c) to (d), so the
cost-push parameter β_7 in the wage equation increases and the slope of
the $\hat{P}$-contour swings round in an anti-clockwise direction, passing
between diagrams (b) and (c) from a position in which demand-pull
exceeds cost-push to one in which cost-push is dominant.

R exerts its influence on $\hat{P}$ only through the demand-pull element. As
we are assuming no change in β_6, the force of the demand-pull element,
the same increase in R would be needed in all four cases to produce a

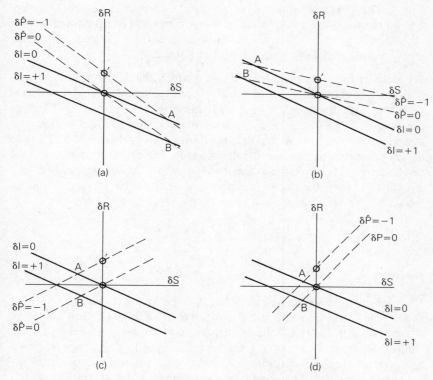

Figure 2.2   Changing prices and changing investment

reduction in $\hat{P}$ of one unit, so that the distance $O\,O'$ is the same in all four diagrams. Only the slope of the $\delta\hat{P} = -1$ contour swings round on the point O'.

We shall briefly comment on the outcomes in the four cases from the point of view of four features:

i)   *The signs of movements in the instruments of control*. In which direction, up or down, must S and R move to obtain a given reduction in $\hat{P}$ or a given rise in I?

ii) Which target (inflation or wealth) must have the *major weight* in the setting of S and R?

iii) *Controllability*. By this we measure the extent to which large or small changes in the controls (S and R) are needed to obtain a given effect on $\hat{P}$ or on I. If large changes in S and/or R are needed to obtain a small change in $\hat{P}$ or on I, controllability will be defined as bad.

iv) *The 'welfare' effects.* What effects in each case will a given reduction of inflation on its own or increase in investment on its own have on C and Y? Increases in C, I, Y and B will be considered as in themselves desirable.

We start by examining the conditions in which the demand-pull element is dominant (i.e. diagrams (a) and (b) in Figure 2.2). We know from (2.11) that the lower is the cost-push factor β_7, the steeper will be the downward slope of the $\hat{P}$-contour. However, we also know that the steepness of this slope will have a maximum value when $\beta_7 = 0$ and that at this point the steepness of the downward slope of the $\hat{P}$ contour would be equal to $\varkappa_1 Y/\iota$ (the same as the steepness of the downward slope of the Y-contour). Thus the maximum steepness of the slope of the $\hat{P}$-contour would be greater than the steepness of the slope of the I-contour if

$$\frac{\varkappa_1 Y}{\iota} > \frac{\nu}{1 - \varkappa_1(1 - S)} \cdot \frac{\varkappa_1 Y}{\iota}$$

i.e. if $\nu < 1 - \varkappa_1(1 - S)$

But this must be so, if the multiplier is to be kept below infinity.

There is therefore some initial low range of values of β_7 for which the downward slope of the $\hat{P}$-contour is steeper than the downward slope of the I-contour; and over this range $|\omega| = |\sigma_p/\sigma_i| > 1$. This range is shown in diagram 2.2(a). In diagram 2.2(b) a somewhat larger value of β_7 has caused the steepness of the downward slope of the $\hat{P}$-contour to fall below that of the downward slope of the I-contour and in 2.2(c) a still higher value of β_7 has caused the slope of the $\hat{P}$-contour to become positive but with a steepness which remains less than the steepness of the downward slope of the I-contour. In both these cases $|\omega| = |\sigma_p/\sigma_i| < 1$. Finally in 2.2(d) when the cost-push influence on inflation of tax reductions becomes sufficiently strong, the upward slope of the $\hat{P}$-contour becomes steeper than the downward slope of the I-contour and $|\omega| = |\sigma_p/\sigma_i| > 1$ again.

We now discuss the control of our two targets, beginning with diagram (a) of Figure 2.2. The contour line showing $\delta P = -1$ lies above that for $\delta P = 0$, as discussed above. Since both of these lines are steeper than the $\delta I = 0$ line, the $\delta P = -1$ line intersects with the $\delta I = 0$ line to the south east of O, at point A. This shows that taxes must be raised, and interest rates reduced, if inflation is to be brought down without investment being reduced.

The contour line $\delta I = +1$ lies below that for $\delta I = 0$, as discussed above. Since both of these lines are flatter than the $\delta \hat{P} = 0$ line, the $\delta I = +1$ line interesects with the $\delta \hat{P} = 0$ line to the south east of O, at point B. This shows that interest rates must be reduced, and tax rates raised, if investment is to be stimulated without any change in inflation.

But we can say more than this. In diagram (a) the ratio of the change in S to the change in R is greater in the reduction of inflation (the move from the origin to the point A) than in the raising of investment (the move from the origin to the point B). This illustrates geometrically the proposition which we have earlier expressed algebraically (see the discussion preceding (2.14)), namely that with the slope of the $\hat{P}$-contour steeper than the slope of the I-contour (i.e. with $|\omega| = |\sigma_p/\sigma_i| > 1$) S should be emphasised in the control of $\hat{P}$ and R in the control of I. But it is important to consider the correct instrument-target emphases to be put on S and R not only when one is comparing one policy with another (e.g. the policy to reduce $\hat{P}$ without affecting I with the policy to raise I without affecting $\hat{P}$), but also when one is considering only one policy (e.g. the policy to reduce $\hat{P}$ without affecting I). In this case in diagram (a) with $|\omega| = |\sigma_p/\sigma_i| > 1$, it is clear that the emphases should be put on S for bringing about the reduction of $\hat{P}$ and on R for the control of I at its unchanged target level. From the values for p_s and p_r in (2.10) it can be seen that if it were merely a question of reducing $\hat{P}$ it would be helpful to raise R as well as S. But in fact in diagram (a) R is reduced, this movement being needed in order to stimulate investment so as to offset the depressing accelerator effect on I of the rise in S. Thus in diagram (a) the mere fact that it is necessary to raise S and to reduce R shows that the emphasis should be on S to reduce $\hat{P}$ and on R to prevent I from falling below its existing target level.

In diagram (b) of Figure 2.2 the slope of the $\hat{P}$-contours remains negative but is now more or less steeper than the downward slope of the I-contours. As a result $|\omega| = |\sigma_p/\sigma_i|$ is now < 1, and the instrument-target emphasis is reversed. R must now rise to fulfil its primary task of reducing $\hat{P}$ and S must now be reduced in order to exert an upward accelerator effect on I so as to prevent I from being depressed below its existing target level by the rise in R. (Between diagrams (c) and (b) the determinant Δ_I in (2.12) has changed sign and the movements in (b) have become a mirror image of those in (a)).

In diagrams (c) and (d) the $\hat{P}$-contours are upward-sloping which means that the negative demand-pull effects of tax increases on inflation are swamped by the positive cost-push effects. In these cases it can be seen from Figure 2.2 that whatever may be the correct instrument-target emphasis (i.e. whether $|\omega| = |\sigma_p/\sigma_i| \gtrless 1$), a reduction of S with a rise in R will be needed to reduce $\hat{P}$ on its own and a reduction in both S and R will be needed to raise I on its own. These results can be explained in the following way.

Consider first a policy of reducing inflation without changing investment. Both a fall in S and a rise in R will be helpful in reducing inflation. The fall in S would alone exert an upward accelerator effect on I, but this would be offset by the rise in R; and the rise in R would alone exert a downward demand-pull effect on $\hat{P}$, which would simply mean that the fall in S needed to reduce inflation would be smaller than would otherwise be the case. Similarly for a policy of raising investment on its own, both a fall in S and a fall in R would be helpful in raising I. And the deflationary cost-push effect on $\hat{P}$ of the fall in S can be offset by the inflationary demand-pull effect of the fall in R; and any upward accelerator effect on I of the fall in R will simply mean that the reduction of S would be less than would otherwise be necessary.

The instrument-target emphases of S and R on $\hat{P}$ and I will, however, differ as between diagrams (c) and (d) according as the upward slope of the $\hat{P}$-contour is less (as in diagram (c)) or greater (as in diagram (d)) than the downward slope of the I-contour, i.e. according as $|\omega| = |\sigma_p/\sigma_i| \gtrless 1$.[5]

We turn next to a consideration of the effects of replacing the downward sloping investment wealth target (I) with an upward-sloping budget-balance wealth target (B). In Figure 2.3 we reproduce the lines and slopes for the $\delta I = 0$ and $\delta \hat{P} = -1$ contours just as they are in Figure 2.2, so that the points A in Figures 2.2 and 2.3 represent the same adjustments of the instruments S and R that are needed to reduce $\hat{P}$ without affecting I. But we now add in all four cases of Figure 2.3 the $\delta B = 0$ contour line which, unlike the $\delta I = 0$ contour line, is upward-sloping. Figure 2.3 thus shows the changes in control policies which are needed to obtain $\delta \hat{P} = 1$ if B instead of I is chosen for the unchanged wealth target.

In diagrams (a) and (b) of Figure 2.3 if $|\sigma_p/\sigma_b| > 1$, i.e. if the downward slope of the $\hat{P}$-contour is steeper than the upward slope of the B-contour, the emphasis will be on S for the control of $\hat{P}$ and on R for the control of B. In this case S is raised to deflate $\hat{P}$; and R is raised to reduce Y and so to deflate the tax base to offset the effect of the rise in the rate of tax on B. There is a combined rise in R and S to the new equilibrium point C. Much the same point is reached if the $\hat{P}$-contour is less steeply sloped than the B-contour. In this case R is raised to exert a downward demand-pull effect on $\hat{P}$. S is raised to offset the deflationary effect on the tax base Y due to the rise in R. Thus in both diagrams (a) and (b) with B as the wealth target both S and R would be raised.

In diagram (c) as in diagram (b) of Figure 2.3 the emphasis will be on S for the control of B and on R for the control of $\hat{P}$. R is raised to deflate $\hat{P}$. S is raised in order to offset the effect on B of the reduction in the tax base Y caused by the rise in R. The process meets at the point C in diagram (c). In diagram (d) the instrument-target emphasis is reversed. S is reduced in order to exert its cost-push effect so as to reduce $\hat{P}$; R is

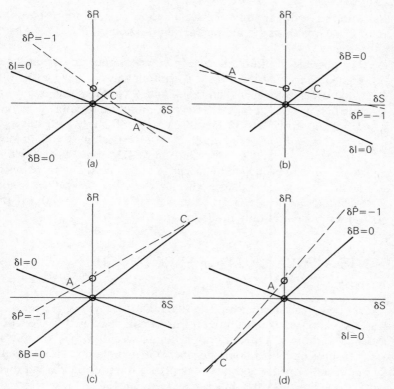

Figure 2.3   Budgetary targets and investment targets

reduced in order to inflate the tax base Y to offset the budgetary effect of the fall in S. The process meets at point C in diagram (d).

An examination of Figures 2.2 and 2.3 reveals the following differences between the various policy outcomes:

i)   It is clear that the signs of the necessary movements of the controls do not depend solely upon the value of $|\omega|$. Whether or not a control instrument should be raised or lowered depends, as is illustrated in the Figures, not only on the value of $|\omega|$ but also upon the signs of σ_p and of σ_i or σ_b.

ii)   The appropriate instrument-target emphases do depend upon the value of $|\omega|$. In Figure 2.3 the emphasis for the control of inflation should be on S in diagrams (a) and (d) but on R in diagrams (b) and (c), regardless of whether I or B is chosen for the wealth target.

iii) Controllability is, however, much affected by the choice of wealth target; it can be very bad if the inflation contour is nearly parallel

with the wealth contour. This can happen in diagrams (a) or (b) if
I is the wealth target and in diagrams (c) and (d) if B is the wealth
target.

iv)   The possible 'welfare' effects can be very important. It has been
argued above that the Y- and C-contours always have a negative
slope which is steeper than the I- and $\hat{P}$-contours.[6] If one bears
this fact in mind it is clear that any equilibrium points in Figure
2.2 or 2.3 to the left of the vertical axis will imply increases in Y
and C and any to the right of the vertical axis will involve
decreases in Y and C. Thus in Figure 2.2 with I as the wealth
target decreases in Y and C occur in diagram (a) and increases in
diagrams (b), (c) and (d), whereas in Figure 2.3 with B as the
wealth target decreases in Y and C occur in diagrams (a), (b) and
(c) and increases only in diagram (d).

2.4   THE AVAILABILITY OF FREE LUNCHES

We have seen that in some of the diagrams of Figures 2.2 and 2.3
increases in output and consumption can be combined with a reduction
of inflation without any deterioration of the wealth target or with an
increase in investment without any increase in inflation. Such results
make one's mouth water and one may perhaps appropriately call them
cases of a free lunch. A free lunch may seem startling.

First, the result depends upon the assumption that the economy is
below its full-employment level; it possesses unused resources which
make an increase in output possible if the demand is forthcoming.
Secondly, it can be seen from Figures 2.2 and 2.3 that free lunches are
available if, and only if, the slope of the inflation contour is greater (i.e.
has either a smaller negative value or a larger positive value) than the
slope of the wealth-target contour, i.e. if and only if $\sigma_p > \sigma_i$ or $\sigma_p > \sigma_b$ as
the case may be. Thirdly, this fact, as shown below, imposes a further
strict limit to the availability of free lunches even if unemployed
resources remain available.

Figures 2.2 and 2.3 show that the attainment of free lunch always
involves a reduction in S. But the slopes of σ_p and σ_i (as can be seen from
(2.11)) are not independent of the level of S. In particular as S falls, so
the multiplier μ increases; and this raises the demand-pull element
relatively to the cost-push element in the wage equation, because any
initial increase in consumption or investment due to a reduction in S or R
is swollen by the multiplier into a bigger increase in total output and thus
into a greater ultimate demand-pull effect. Indeed, it can be seen from

the definition of μ in (2.9) that as S approaches the critical low value of $S = 1 - (1 - \nu)/\varkappa_1$ the multiplier and so the demand-pull effect in the wage equation will approach ∞.

It can be shown that as a result there is a strict limit to the process by which successive cumulative reductions in S can continue to provide free lunches. When S has been reduced to some critical level the slope of the $\hat{P}$-contours will cease to be such as to allow still further free lunches to be enjoyed.

From (2.11) we see that the condition for a further free lunch with I as the wealth target, namely $\sigma_p > \sigma_i$, implies

$$-\frac{\beta_6 \mu \varkappa_1 Y - \beta_7}{\beta_6 \mu \varkappa_1 Y} > -\frac{\nu}{1 - \varkappa_1(1 - S)}$$

which can be expressed as

$$\beta_6 \varkappa_1 Y < \beta_7\{1 - \varkappa_1(1 - S)\} \tag{2.15a}$$

But in all the cases examined in Figure 2.2 we shall have

$$Y = \bar{G} + I^* + \bar{C} + \varkappa_1(1 - S)Y$$
$$= \frac{\bar{G} + I^* + \bar{C}}{1 - \varkappa(1 - S)} \tag{2.16a}$$

since I will be kept at a target level I^* regardless of the value of Y, whether this target level is the original level I (with $\delta \hat{P} = -1$) or the new target level $I + 1$ (with $\delta P = 0$).

Substituting this value of Y in (2.15a) and solving for S we obtain

$$S > \sqrt{\frac{\beta_6}{\varkappa_1 \beta_7}(\bar{G} + I^* + \bar{C})} - \frac{1 - \varkappa_1}{\varkappa_1} \tag{2.17a}$$

as the necessary and sufficient condition for a further free lunch

If the critical value of S on the right-hand side of (2.17a) is greater than 1 there is no possible value of $S < 1$ which provides an opportunity for a cheap lunch. It is possible that the expression on the right-hand side of (2.17a) is less than zero, in which case one would have to replace the tax S with a subsidy before cheap lunches became unavailable. But if the expression on the right-hand side of (2.17a) were a positive fraction, there would be a range of higher positive values of S which would make a cheap lunch possible.

A similar result can be shown for the case of a free lunch which is possible with B as the wealth target as is shown at point C in diagram (d)

of Figure 2.3. Instead of (2.15a) we use the condition $\sigma_p > \sigma_b$ which can be expressed as

$$S\beta_7 > \beta_6 Y \qquad (2.15b)$$

From (2.6) we have

$$Y = \frac{\bar{G} + B^*}{S} \qquad (2.16b)$$

Substituting for Y in (2.15b) we obtain

$$S > \sqrt{\frac{\beta_6}{\beta_7}} \, (\bar{G} + B^*) \qquad (2.17b)$$

If the expression on the right-hand side of (2.17b) is < 1, there can be a range of higher values of S for which a free lunch is still available.

We know from (2.9e) that $\hat{P} = \beta_6 Y + \beta_7 S + \hat{\bar{W}}$. In those cases in which there is a range of feasible values of S which offer the opportunity of a free lunch, we can find the minimum possible value of the rate of inflation which is compatible with the maintenance of the wealth target by taking the relevant value for Y in (2.16a or b) and the critical value for S in (2.17a or b) and substituting these values in (2.9e).

The minimum possible value of $\hat{P}$ is then found to be

$$\hat{P} = 2\sqrt{\frac{\beta_6 \beta_7}{\varkappa_1}} \, (\bar{G} + \bar{C} + I^*) - \beta_7 \frac{1 - \varkappa_1}{\varkappa_1} + \hat{\bar{W}} \qquad (2.18)$$

if I is the wealth target and

$$\hat{P} = 2\sqrt{\beta_6 \beta_7 (\bar{G} + B^*)} + \hat{\bar{W}} \qquad (2.19)$$

if B is the wealth target.

If these minimal values for the rate of inflation are unacceptable, either the inflationary pressures in the wage-setting institutions must be modified, or the country must be prepared to make less provision for the future by relaxing the wealth target, or the government must reduce its demand for goods and services. We shall find that this observation provides great insight into our simulations in Chapter 8 where the cost-push element in wage inflation is strong and where, consequently, the temptation of a free lunch is great. Nevertheless, if these minimal values are unacceptable inflation control without reform of wage-fixing institutions inevitably forces us into one of the two remaining unsatisfactory alternatives mentioned above: relaxing the wealth target, or reducing the purchase of goods and services by government.

2.5 THE OPEN ECONOMY

We next consider a small open economy in which trading and financial transactions take place within a world economy, the single economy not being large enough to affect trading conditions in the rest of the world. The equations of the previous model (2.1) to (2.9) are now modified in the following way:

$$Y = L \tag{2.20}$$

$$P = (1 + \pi)W \tag{2.21}$$

$$C = \varkappa_1(1 - S)Y + \bar{C} \tag{2.22}$$

$$I = -\iota R + \nu Y + \bar{I} \tag{2.23}$$

The equations for Y, P, C and I remain unchanged.

$$J = \bar{I} - \iota R + \nu Y + X - M \tag{2.24}$$

We are now dealing with total investment (J), i.e. with domestic plus foreign investment instead of only domestic investment.

$$Y = \bar{G} + J + C \tag{2.25}$$

The national product now contains foreign investment as well as domestic investment.

$$M = \eta'(Y - X + M) = \eta(Y - X) \tag{2.26}$$

$$\text{where } \eta = \frac{\eta'}{1 - \eta'}$$

We assume that all imports take the form of finished goods and not of raw materials. This justifies the assumption in (2.21) above that the price of home products is set by a mark-up only on domestic labour costs. We assume that the expenditure and price elasticities of demand for imports are both unity so that the amount spent on imports in terms of home products (M) is a constant proportion (η') of total expenditures on finished goods bought for domestic use.

$$X = \bar{X}A^{-\varepsilon} \tag{2.27}$$

where

$$A = \frac{EP}{\bar{P}^F} \tag{2.28}$$

A measures the real terms of trade where P is the price of home products, E is the rate of exchange (units of foreign money per unit of home money) and $\bar{P}^F$ is the price of foreign products in terms of foreign money. ε then measures the price elasticity of the foreign demand for the country's exports (X).

$$F = \lambda\{\phi(\bar{R}^F - R) - \bar{H}\} \tag{2.29}$$
$$= -\theta R + \bar{F}$$

It is assumed that foreign capital movements (F = net outflows of capital funds measured in terms of domestic products) take the form solely of transactions initiated by residents of the home country. Such residents are assumed to wish to hold an amount of foreign assets which have a value in terms of domestic products ($\phi[\bar{R}^F - R]$) which depends upon the difference between the yield abroad ($\bar{R}^F$) and the yield at home (R) and to move funds abroad (F) at a rate (λ) which depends upon the extent to which this desired portfolio holding ($\phi[\bar{R}^F - R]$) falls below the portfolio holding actually held at the beginning of this period ($H_{-1} = \bar{H}$). With $\theta = \lambda\phi$ equation (2.29) then determines the value of this period's net outward flow of capital funds

This analysis assumes that there is imperfect mobility of capital. In the simpler case of perfect mobility of capital (which we adopt in Chapters 3 and 4), the current balance does not enter into the determination of the exchange rate. With expectations of the future exchange rate fixed (as they are in this chapter), a 1-point increase in the per-period interest rate would cause an increase in the nominal exchange rate of 1 per cent. This would cause an expected capital loss of 1 per cent and would eliminate completely the expected excess yield on home assets.

$$X = F + M \tag{2.30}$$

Equilibrium implies that the value of exports equals the value of imports plus value of foreign lending, if one neglects interest earned on foreign assets. This neglect of interest payments in the balance of payments could represent a very serious distortion for dynamic analysis since accumulation of foreign interest can be a serious cause of instability as is shown later in Chapter 4. But for a comparative static analysis it is an acceptable simplification. Equation (2.30), using (2.27) and (2.29), could be written as $(1 + \eta)\bar{X}A^{-\varepsilon} = \eta Y - \theta R + \bar{F}$ and this is in fact the equation which serves to determine the real terms of trade which will clear the market. If X were less than $F + M$, then the currency would depreciate, the terms of trade would deteriorate and the foreign demand for the country's exports would rise, and *vice versa*. A settles at the level required to satisfy this equation.

$$P_c = P^{1-\eta'}(\bar{P}^F/E)^{\eta'} \tag{2.31}$$

$$= PA^{-\eta'}, \text{ using (2.28)}$$

The cost of living is a weighted average of the cost of domestic finished goods (P) and of imported finished goods ($\bar{P}^F/E$), the weights being dependent on the proportion of domestic expenditures spent on imports (η'). If one uses (2.28) one can write (2.29) in the form of $P_c = PA^{-\eta'}$.

$$B = SY - \bar{G} \tag{2.32}$$

This expression for the budget deficit is the same as for the closed economy in equation (2.6).

$$V = \frac{W(1-S)}{P_c}$$

$$= \frac{(1-S)A^{\eta'}}{1+\pi}, \text{ using (2.21) and (2.31)} \tag{2.33a}$$

The real value of a worker's take-home pay (V) is his money wage (W) less tax (S) divided by the cost of living (P_c).

We have as in (2.7b) and (2.7c) for the closed economy:

$$\tilde{V} = \bar{V} + \frac{L}{\beta'} \tag{2.33b}$$

and
$$L_s = \beta'(V - \bar{V}) \tag{2.33c}$$

We can also express the two alternative ways of expressing the factors leading to wage inflation, as in (2.8a) and (2.8b) for the closed economy:

$$\hat{W} = \beta_3(\tilde{V} - V) + \beta_5(V_{-1} - V) \tag{2.34a}$$

and

$$\hat{W} = \beta_4(L - L_s) + \beta_5(V_{-1} - V) \tag{2.34b}$$

which can now both be expressed as:

$$\hat{W} = \beta_6 Y - \beta_7(1 - S)A^{\eta'} + \hat{\bar{\bar{W}}} \tag{2.34c}$$

where, as before, $\beta_6 = \beta_3/\beta'$ and $\beta_7 = (\beta_3 + \beta_5)/(1 + \pi)$ but $\hat{\bar{\bar{W}}} = \beta_3\bar{V} + \beta_5 V_{-1}$.

As before the terms in β_6 and β_7 express the demand-pull and the cost-push forces affecting the rate of wage inflation. But, while the price level of domestic products is determined by a mark-up on money wage cost in the same way as before, the cost of living now depends upon the price of imports as well as upon this marked-up price of home products; and this involves a modification of the formulation of the wage equations. The import-price modification of the cost of living ($A^{\eta'}$) must now be applied to the post-tax $(1 - S)$ value of the money wage to obtain the real value of take-home pay.

If we now eliminate L, W, I, M, X, E, F, P_c and V from equations (2.20) to (2.34) and rearrange terms we obtain:

Table 2.2   The short-term model of an open economy

$$Y = \bar{G} + \bar{C} + \varkappa_1(1 - S)Y + \bar{I} - \iota R + \nu Y + \bar{F} - \theta R = \mu\{ - (\iota + \theta)R + \bar{Y}\} \tag{2.35a}$$

where

$$\bar{Y} = \bar{G} + \bar{C} + \bar{I} + \bar{F}$$

and

$$\mu = \frac{1}{1 - \varkappa_1(1 - S) - \nu}$$

$$C = \varkappa_1(1 - S)Y + \bar{C} \tag{2.35b}$$

$$J = -(\iota + \theta)R + \nu Y + \bar{I} + \bar{F} \tag{2.35c}$$

$$B = SY - \bar{G} \tag{2.35d}$$

$$\hat{P} = \beta_6 Y - \beta_7(1 - S)A^{\eta'} + \hat{\bar{\bar{W}}} \tag{2.35e}$$

$$A^{-\varepsilon} = \frac{1}{(1 + \eta)\bar{X}} \{\bar{F} - \theta R + \eta Y\} \tag{2.35f}$$

The assumptions that the international flow of capital funds measured in terms of the home product depends solely on the relative rates of interest and that the exchange rate and terms of trade adjust so as to maintain the balance of trade (i.e. the level of real foreign investment) equal to the flow of funds have two important effects upon these equations. First, total investment (J) continues to depend solely on the rate of interest and income as it did in the closed economy, because foreign investment adjusts (through variations in the terms of trade) so as to be equal to the flow of funds which in turn depends solely on the rate of interest and the level of income. Secondly, variations in S and so in Y have no effect upon foreign investment. It is true that a change in Y causes a change in M; but if F is constant, the terms of trade adjust so as to cause a change in X which exactly offsets the change in M. For this reason the multiplier (μ) in the open economy remains the same as it was in the closed economy. The multiplicand is changed by the addition of any positive foreign invest-ment; but a change in Y does not affect this item, so the multiplier is unchanged.

This would cease to be true if the flow of funds depends upon expectations of changes in the exchange rate which in turn depend on movements of the exchange rate itself (whether lagged, contemporan-eous or expected in the future). For these movements in the exchange rate will, as equation (2.35f) makes clear, depend upon a whole mixture of other parameters, including export price elasticities. Thus (i) investment will no longer depend only upon the interest rate and the level of income, and (ii) variations in S and Y will cause changes in foreign investment.

By substituting the value of Y from (2.35a) into equations (2.35b) to (2.35f) we can obtain expressions for Y, C, J, B, $\hat{P}$, and A in terms of certain constant parameters and the two control variables S and R.

Differentiation of (2.35f) and normalizing by writing $A = 1$ (i.e. defining units of home and foreign products so that the real terms of trade are unity in the period under examination), we obtain

$$\delta A = \frac{\theta \delta R - \eta \delta Y}{\varepsilon(1 + \eta)\overline{X}} \tag{2.36}$$

Differentiation of (2.35a) to (2.35e) using (2.36) to eliminate δA, gives matrix (2.37) which has for the open economy the same form as matrix (2.10) for the closed economy:

$$\begin{bmatrix} \delta \hat{P} \\ \delta J \\ \delta B \\ \delta C \\ \delta Y \end{bmatrix} = \begin{bmatrix} p_s & p_r \\ j_s & j_r \\ b_s & b_r \\ c_s & c_r \\ y_s & y_r \end{bmatrix} \begin{bmatrix} \delta S \\ \delta R \end{bmatrix} \tag{2.37}$$

where

$$p_s = \{ - \beta_6 \mu \varkappa_1 Y + \beta_7(1 - \psi\eta\mu) \} \quad \text{with} \quad \psi = \frac{\eta(1 - S)\varkappa_1 Y}{(1 + \eta)^2 \varepsilon X}$$

$$p_r = - \{ \beta_6 \mu(\iota + \theta) + \frac{\beta_7 \psi}{\varkappa_1 Y}(\eta\mu[\iota + \theta] + \theta) \}$$

$$j_s = - \nu\mu\varkappa_1 Y \qquad\qquad j_r = -(1 + \nu\mu)(\iota + \theta)$$

$$b_s = (1 - \varkappa_1 - \nu)\mu Y \qquad b_r = - S\mu(\iota + \theta)$$

$$c_s = -(1 - \nu)\mu\varkappa_1 Y \qquad c_r = - \{(1 - \nu)\mu - 1\}(\iota + \theta)$$

$$y_s = j_s + c_s \qquad\qquad y_r = j_r + c_r$$

$$\quad = - \mu\varkappa_1 Y \qquad\qquad\quad = - \mu(\iota + \theta)$$

From these values of the various parameters one can derive the following slopes of the relevant contours:

$$\sigma_p = \frac{- \beta_6 \mu \varkappa_1 Y + \beta_7(1 - \psi\eta\mu)}{\beta_6 \mu \varkappa_1 Y + \beta\psi(\eta\mu + \theta/[\iota + \theta])} \cdot \frac{\varkappa_1 Y}{\iota + \theta}$$

$$\sigma_j = - \frac{\nu\mu}{1 + \nu\mu} \cdot \frac{\varkappa_1 Y}{\iota + \theta} \tag{2.38}$$

$$\sigma_b = \frac{1 - \varkappa_1 - \nu}{S\varkappa_1} \cdot \frac{\varkappa_1 Y}{\iota + \theta}$$

$$\sigma_c = - \frac{(1 - \nu)\mu}{\{(1 - \nu)\mu - 1\}} \cdot \frac{\varkappa_1 Y}{(\iota + \theta)}$$

$$\sigma_y = - \frac{\varkappa_1 Y}{\iota + \theta}$$

The forms of (2.37) and (2.38) are similar to the forms of (2.10) and (2.11) for the closed economy. There are, however, certain changes in the values of the various parameters

(1) The expression for the parameters j_s (in place of i_s), b_s, c_s and y_s are all unchanged. These similarities all result from the fact noted above that changes in Y (resulting from a change in S) have no effect on $(X - M)$ and so no effect upon the multiplicand whether it includes or excludes $(X - M)$. (Recall that we ignore the effects of endogenous exchange-rate expectations on capital flows, and also ignore the Laursen-Metzler, 1951, effect.)

(2) On the other hand, the expressions for the parameters j_r (in place

of i_r), b_r, c_r, and y_r are all multiplied by $(\iota + \theta)/\iota$. The reason for this is that the rise in R now causes total investment to fall by $\theta\delta R$ (the effect on foreign investment) as well as by $\iota\delta R$ (the effect on home investment). The response to a change in R is thus multiplied up by the same factor in all these cases.

(3) The really notable changes are in the parameters p_s and p_r. As far as p_s is concerned there is a reduction in the cost-push element equal to $\beta_7\psi\eta\mu$. This is due to the fact that a rise in S by reducing Y will cause a reduction in M which will lead to an appreciation of the exchange rate and so to a fall in the import-goods element in the cost of living. The aspiration wage will thereby be more fully met.

(4) But the changes in the parameter p_r will be even more striking. In this case the deflationary response to a rise in the rate of interest will be increased by three factors: (i) $\beta_6\mu\theta$ (ii) $(\beta_7\psi/\varkappa_1 Y)\eta\mu(\iota + \theta)$ and (iii) $(\beta_7\psi/\varkappa_1 Y)\theta$. Factor (i) occurs because the rise in the rate of interest will reduce the outflow of funds which will cause an appreciation of the currency which will cause a fall in exports which after enlargement by the multiplier will result in a decreased inflationary demand-pull effect. Factor (ii) represents the fact that the decreased income due to the multiplier effect of the decreases in domestic and foreign investment brought about by the higher rate of interest will cause a reduction in the demand for imports and so an appreciation of the currency which in turn will lower the cost of living and so reduce the cost-push effect. Factor (iii) shows the favourable cost-push effect due to the appreciation of the currency which was noted in factor (i) to result from the reduction in the outflow of capital funds.

These changes in the parameters affect the contour-slopes shown in (2.11) and (2.38) respectively for the closed and the open economies.

It will be seen that all the contour slopes with the exception of the $\hat{P}$-contour slope are simply multiplied by the same factor $\iota/\iota + \theta$. This means that the steepnesses of all the slopes (except the σ_p slope) as shown in Figures 2.1, 2.2 and 2.3 for the closed economy are reduced by a factor $\iota/\iota + \theta$, regardless of sign, simply because a smaller change in R is now needed to offset any change in S because R operates on foreign as well as domestic investment. We can, therefore, continue to use Figures 2.1, 2.2 and 2.3 for all the contour slopes (except those for $\hat{P}$) since they all preserve an unchanged sign and an unchanged relationship to each other. For example, it is still true that as one moves to the left along any one wealth-target contour, so one moves on to higher and higher Y- and C-contour lines.

In (2.11) and (2.38) the slopes of the contour lines for $\hat{P}$, J, B and C are all expressed as multiples of $\varkappa_1 Y/\iota$ or of $\varkappa_1 Y/(\iota + \theta)$, respectively, i.e. of the absolute value of the slope of the Y-contour line. In the case of J, B

and C these multiples are the same in the open economy as in the closed economy. But this is not so in the case of the $\hat{P}$-contour lines where the multiple of the downward steepness of the Y-contour changes from Σ_c to Σ_o as between the closed and open economies, where

$$\Sigma_c = \frac{-\beta_6\mu\varkappa_1 Y + \beta_7}{\beta_6\mu\varkappa_1 Y}$$

$$\Sigma_o = \frac{-\beta_6\mu\varkappa_1 Y + \beta_7(1 - \psi\eta\mu)}{\beta_6\mu\varkappa_1 Y + \beta_7(\psi\eta\mu + \psi\theta/[\iota + \theta])}$$

(2.39)

Since all the other relationships remain unchanged it is the change in this relationship from Σ_c to Σ_o which expresses the basic change due to the opening of the economy. What changes must be made to the features of the $\hat{P}$-contour slopes in Figures 2.1, 2.2 and 2.3 as a result of the changes in the relative slopes of the $\hat{P}$-contours shown in (2.39)?

(1) From (2.39) we have

$$\frac{\delta\Sigma_c}{\delta\beta_7} = \frac{\beta_7}{\beta_6\mu c V} > 0 \text{ and } \frac{\delta\Sigma_o}{\delta\beta_7} = \frac{\beta_6\mu\varkappa_1 Y(1 + \psi\theta/[\iota + \theta])}{\{\cdot\}^2} > 0$$

so that it remains true that the relative slope of the open-economy $\hat{P}$-contour swings round anti-clockwise as one moves from diagram (a) to (b) to (c) to (d) in Figures 2.2 and 2.3.[7] If $\beta_7 = 0$, then from (2.39) it can be seen that $\Sigma_c = \Sigma_o = -1$. In other words, it also remains true that the $\hat{P}$-contour can never have a negative slope which is steeper than the negative slope of the Y-contour. However, as $\beta_7 \to \infty$ so $\Sigma_c \to \infty$, but $\Sigma_o \to (1 - \psi\eta\mu)/(\psi\eta\mu + \psi\theta/[\iota + \theta])$. Thus in the open economy there is a strict upper limit to Σ_o, a limit which will actually be < 0 if $\psi\eta\mu > 1$.[8] This is a most important effect of opening the economy. It may, with decreasing probabilities, rule out the existence of diagrams (d), (c) and (b) of Figures 2.2 and 2.3.

(2) The effect of changes in income on the demand for imports and so on the real terms of trade and the cost of living is shown by the introduction of the term $\beta_7\psi\eta\mu$ in the expression Σ_o in (2.39). Its appearance as a negative element in the numerator shifts the slope of the $\hat{P}$-contour in a clockwise direction and makes probable a movement of the actual situation in the direction from diagram (d) to (c) to (b). Its appearance as a positive element in the denominator leads to a decrease in the steepness of the slope of the $\hat{P}$-contour relative to the steepness of the slopes of all the other contours.

(3) The introduction of the term $\psi\theta/(\iota + \theta)$ into the denominator of Σ_o has the unequivocal effect of decreasing the relative steepness of the slope of the $\hat{P}$-contour regardless of sign.

(4) The opening of the economy has one other effect on the contour for $\delta\hat{P} = -1$ in Figures 2.2 and 2.3. It can be seen from the expressions for p_r in (2.10) and (2.37) that a rise in β_7 has no effect on p_r in the closed economy, whereas a rise in β_7 will lower the value of p_r in the open economy; in the closed economy a rise in R has only its deflationary demand-pull effect, whereas in the open economy it has in addition a deflationary cost-push effect. This means that if one is to use Figures 2.2 and 2.3 for the analysis of the open economy, the distance OO' (i.e. the rise in R needed to cause $\delta\hat{P} = -1$) falls as one moves from diagram (a) to (b) to (c) to (d).

With these interpretations of the signs, the relative slopes, and the distances OO' from origin on the vertical axis, Figures 2.2 and 2.3 with their subsequent analysis can be used for the open economy as they were used for the closed economy. All combinations are still conceivable and it is not possible to reach definite conclusions about the effect of opening the economy. There are, however, some very important probabilities.

(1) A positive slope for σ_p becomes more unlikely. This is because of the reduction in the cost-push effect of tax increases, noted in point (3) beneath equations (2.38), because in an open economy higher taxes means lower income and imports, and an appreciation of the exchange rate. That lowers cost-push inflationary pressure and so makes p_s more likely to be negative, thereby making σ_p more likely to be negative. As a result diagrams (c) and (d) become less probable as compared with diagrams (a) and (b).

(2) The steepness of the $\hat{P}$-contour relative to the steepness of the other contours is more likely to fall than to rise. This is because of the higher size of p_r likely in an open economy, for reasons explained in point (4) beneath equations (2.38). This implies an increased probability that it would be appropriate to put the emphasis on R as the means of controlling $\hat{P}$.

2.6 CONCLUSION

Five key insights may be gained from the greatly simplified comparative-static analysis of this chapter.

(1) Given (i) the initial position in the economy, (ii) the model of the economy and (iii) the values of the target variables which are to be achieved, the use of the control variables (S and R) is determined. That is to say, the signs and the absolute values of the necessary δS and δR are in no sense arbitrary. This obvious conclusion is not without its importance.

These matters are sometimes discussed as if it were an open matter of choice whether, for example, one should use fiscal policy or monetary policy as the primary instrument for the control of inflation. In a comparative-static model of the kind discussed in this chapter and with two instruments of control to achieve two objectives of policy, no open choice exists. The emphasis to be put on each instrument for the control of each target variable is not an arbitrary matter.[9]

(2) The analysis in the preceding sections has indicated the basic importance which must be ascribed to the balance between demand-pull and cost-push factors in the determination of rates of pay. Different balances between these factors can cause quite basic changes in sign of the required movements in, and changes in the required emphasis on, financial instruments of control. For example, as we have seen, it may determine whether fiscal policy or monetary policy should be emphasized for the control of inflation; and it may even determine whether the rate of tax should be raised or lowered in order to reduce inflation.

(3) If the cost-push factor in wage setting is extremely powerful and if tax rates are high, it is possible that a reduction of tax will provide a free lunch in the sense of leading to a simultaneous reduction of inflation, increase of investment, increase of consumption, increase of output, and increase of employment. But in the model examined in this chapter it is clear that this possibility will reach a limit when the rate of tax has been reduced to a certain critical level; and at this point the rate of price inflation will have reached a minimum level which in turn may well still be unacceptably high.

(4) The controllability of the economy depends upon the interaction between the degree of the cost-push element in the wage-setting institutions and the choice of wealth target. In the rest of this book we have chosen to treat the level of the country's total investment in, or stock of, capital assets as the wealth target. From diagrams (a) and (b) of Figure 2.2 it can be seen that controllability could in this case become a serious problem if there was a moderate degree of cost-push in the wage equation which matched the accelerator element in the investment equation so that the $\hat{P}$-contour became nearly parallel with the I-contours.

(5) The outstanding effect of opening a small economy to international influences shows itself through the sensitivity of capital movements to changes in the country's rate of interest relative to the rates of interest in the rest of the world. The resulting changes in the rate of foreign exchange, in the real terms of trade, and in the import content of the cost of living, together with the effects of monetary policy upon the balance of trade and so on foreign investment, make it a much more potent instrument of control. Foreign as well as domestic investment is now

sensitive to monetary control. Moreover, the price of imports and so the cost of living is now affected by changes in the rate of interest, so that monetary policy now exercises an important influence over the cost-push factor in wage determination. The probability of needing to emphasize monetary policy in the control of inflation is thus markedly enhanced.

This chapter has contained a static analysis. Our conclusions cannot be carried over to our subsequent dynamic analysis of macroeconomic policy without some modification. In particular the first conclusion needs to be changed as follows. One would need to say that given (i) the initial position, (ii) the model of the economy, (iii) the values of the target variables to be achieved, and (iv) the path to be taken by the economy as it moves towards the desired values for the target variables, the use of the control variables over time would be fully determined. A simple example may serve to show the need for the final extra condition. Suppose the final wealth target to be a given level of investment expenditure. The path to the position at which investment was as desired might be one along which investment expenditures were at a high, or alternatively at a low, level. In the former case the new equilibrium would enjoy the advantage of a higher stock of real capital equipment than in the latter case. Thus the economy might in the new equilibrium enjoy the same final financial targets (rate of price inflation and level of investment expenditures) but might find itself in a different real situation because of the difference in the dynamic path with which it had chosen to attain the new target objectives. This important, but subtle, dynamic question is taken up in our empirical reruns of history in Chapters 8 and 9.

Moreover, as will become clear in subsequent chapters of this book, in a dynamic analysis the choice of an appropriate instrument-target emphasis and its derivation from the comparative advantage index ω become more complicated matters than may have been suggested by the static analysis in the present chapter. This is so for three reasons.

(1) The lags in the economy might be such that there is a very big but a much delayed response of, say, inflation to the rate of interest. In this case fiscal policy might have a comparative advantage over monetary policy in the control of inflation in the immediate future, while monetary policy might have the comparative advantage if one was concerned with the later effects of today's policy changes. The instrument-target emphasis would depend upon the extent to which one put weight on immediate or delayed effects.

(2) In a non-linear structure of economic relationships the comparative advantage of a particular control variable may well depend upon whether the economy is near to or far removed from its ultimate steady-state target values. Thus if investment far exceeded the wealth target, inflation far exceeded the inflation target, and the demand for labour far exceeded

the available supply, the cost-push element in the wage equation might be much greater relative to the demand-pull factor than it would become in the ultimate steady state with both investment and inflation at their target levels. Thus the comparative advantage of fiscal policy in controlling inflation might be much greater in an initial disequilibrium position of the economy than it would be in the ultimate well-controlled steady state.

(3) In order to avoid otherwise unacceptably large and frequent changes in certain variables it might from time to time be desirable to disregard the emphasis which comparative-advantage considerations would otherwise put upon them.

Meanwhile, two absolutely fundamental dynamic problems which need theoretical clarification relate to the wage—price spiral and wealth accumulation. We analyse these issues in the next two chapters. In these chapters, we also analyse the issue of exchange-rate targeting, and begin to tackle the question of expectations formation.

Chapter Three

The dynamics of price stabilization

3.1 INTRODUCTION

So far we have studied the problem of economic policy in a static context. Taking a particular structure of the economy we have investigated the necessary adjustments to monetary and to fiscal policy which are needed to achieve particular short-term variations in prices and in national wealth. In this chapter we extend the previous analysis to a dynamic context so as to focus on two particular dynamic problems: (i) the wage–price spiral and (ii) the role of a target exchange rate. We neglect other important dynamic issues and, in particular, the dynamics of wealth accumulation, which we leave to Chapter 4.

We set out a model, which is intrinsically dynamic. Throughout this chapter, as in the previous one, we work with a price target rather than a Money GDP target. The motive for doing this is once again to maintain algebraic simplicity.

We first explore the steady-state properties of the model, showing the adjustments to policy instruments which are needed to achieve particular long-run variations in target values or supply-side conditions. These steady-state changes are a consequence solely of the character of the model, and cannot reflect any preference to use policy rules in any particular way.

We then consider various ways in which one could specify an active policy designed to achieve price stability, indicating that either monetary policy (which we demonstrate can be expressed using the interest rate as an instrument, and working through the medium of a target exchange rate) or fiscal policy should be emphasized for this purpose. We test for the asymptotic stability of the economy using either monetary or fiscal stabilization rules and show that, if the fiscal instrument is a tax rate, and if wages are strongly indexed to prices, a fiscal rule is likely to be unstable. This result meets the Lucas critique, since it is found when expectations are model-consistent. It is robust to the way in which expectations are formed, since it also holds when expectations are assumed to be adaptive.

It is not possible in a simple analytic model to investigate jointly the dynamics of the monetary and the fiscal rules which would stabilize simultaneously both prices and national wealth. In this chapter we are concerned with the problems arising in the stabilization of prices; and for this purpose we have proceeded as follows. To study the dynamic problems which arise if monetary policy is used to stabilize prices, we assume that the fiscal control is held constant at the level at which it would be operative in the steady state (in which both prices and national wealth would be at their target levels) and then study the dynamic problems of adjusting the monetary control so as to keep prices on a target path. Conversely, to study the dynamic problems of control of inflation by means of fiscal policy, we assume the monetary control to be kept constant at its steady-state value and then examine the problem of varying the fiscal control in such a way as to keep prices on their target trajectory.

Our model does not allow us to study the simultaneous dynamic operation of both controls to achieve both targets, but it does allow us to investigate the comparative advantage of fiscal measures relative to monetary measures in controlling inflation and national investment. In our static model of Chapter 2 there was a direct link between the pattern of comparative advantage and the appropriate target-instrument emphasis of policy rules. In a dynamic model in which the pattern of comparative advantage changes over time the link cannot be as clear. Nevertheless it has been our experience that the short- to medium-term pattern of comparative advantage is reflected in the structure of well-designed policy rules. In this chapter, therefore, we investigate how the pattern of comparative advantage depends on the structure of the wage equation as a preliminary to our empirical investigation of Chapter 6.

3.2   THE ANALYTIC MODEL

We use an expanded version of Dornbusch's (1976) model. The model is one in which stock effects are neglected despite their undoubted importance; investment behaviour is modelled in a very simple way; no role exists for foreign-exchange intervention and the model does not incorporate any proper production function. Nevertheless the model does allow us to explore the effects of attempting to stabilize prices by means of either monetary or fiscal policy and in the context of an exchange-rate target. The model is derived from that presented by Blake and Weale (1988) and is very similar to Miller and Williamson's (1988) model. However, our analysis differs from that of Miller and Williamson mainly in that we have a more developed model of wage formation (see Fischer, 1988). We attach very considerable importance to the fact that the model allows us to consider issues such as steady-state outcomes and the stability of different policies, as well as some short-term responses.

3.2.1 Policy objectives

There is a target path, p^*, for the level of the domestic (factor cost) output prices, p. It is sometimes convenient to express this as equal to the original price level, p_0, augmented over time by the target inflation rate, $\dot{p}^*$. Prices are measured in logarithms, thus we may write $p^* = p_0 + \dot{p}^* t$.

There is also a target, j^*, for the level of national investment, j.[1] We measure j as the logarithm of investment expenditures, in units of gross domestic product; j includes both domestic and foreign investment (the latter is equal to the surplus on the current account of the balance of payments).

These objectives are consistent with our New Keynesian approach to economic policy, although, for reasons of analytical simplicity we adopt a target for the price level rather than for the level of Money GDP. In particular, we avoid setting a target for the level of real output, on the grounds that this is determined by the structure of the labour market.

3.2.2 The labour market

Wage rates, w, are assumed to respond to excess demand in the labour market, to price inflation and to changes in the rate of tax. Prices and quantities are measured in logarithms with the base value of log prices set at zero. Thus we write

$$\dot{w} = \bar{\alpha} + \alpha_1(l^d - l^s) + \alpha_2(\dot{p} - \eta'\dot{a}) + \alpha_3\dot{S} + \alpha_4\dot{p} \qquad (3.1)$$

where $\bar{\alpha}$ is a constant and l^d and l^s represent logarithms of labour demand and labour supply respectively; a is the logarithm of the real exchange rate, measured in units of foreign currency per unit of domestic currency adjusted for inflation in domestic output prices, so that a fall in

a represents a real depreciation. The (pre-tax) price of consumption goods is $p - \eta' a$ (and its rate of change is $\dot{p} - \eta' \dot{a}$) since it is assumed, as in Chapter 2, that a fraction η' of spending is directed towards imports. It is widely argued that the inflationary consequences of indirect tax changes are much stronger than are those of direct tax changes. This is a phenomenon which we would not wish to rely on for purposes of economic management, because we suspect that any systematic attempt to exploit it would result in labour market behaviour changing so that it was no longer true. In this equation we therefore do not distinguish the effects of direct taxes from those of indirect taxes; we use a single index of the rate of tax (S). Inflationary pressures are augmented if this increases.

$\dot{p}$ is the 'core' rate of inflation, and is exogenous. We assume that it is equal to the target rate of inflation adopted by the authorities. We do not consider mechanisms by which the core rate might be brought into equality with the target rate if there is initially some discrepancy between the two. Thus we write

$$\dot{p} = \dot{p}^* \qquad (3.2)$$

Homogeneity of degree 1 of wage inflation with respect to price inflation requires $\alpha_2 + \alpha_4 = 1$ and we also assume this from now on.

A simple labour supply curve is specified

$$l^s = \bar{l}^s + \alpha_5(w - [p - \eta' a]) - \alpha_6 S \qquad (3.3)$$

where $\bar{l}^s$ is a constant. This labour supply curve is of the same form as that in Chapter 2 (equation 2.7c). We abstract from shifts in the supply curve over time, due, for example, to the growth in workers' aspirations. We do not embody any intertemporal substitution effects in this supply curve.

In addition to the labour supply and labour demand curves, an embryonic short-run production function may be embodied in the assumption that labour demand is proportional to output, y. We abstract from productivity growth and choose our units so that the constant of proportionality is unity. This gives

$$l^d = y \qquad (3.4)$$

Productivity is assumed to be constant. This means that w measures the logarithm of unit labour costs, as well as the logarithm of the real wage.

3.2.3 Output

Output is demand-determined and is represented by a simple *IS* curve

$$y = \bar{y} - \mu(\iota' [R - \dot{p}] + \varepsilon' a + \varkappa_1' S - \bar{g}) \tag{3.5}$$

where $\bar{y}$ is a constant. y is measured as the logarithm of output. ι', ε' and $\varkappa_1'$ represent the 'impact effects' on demand, as a proportion of the level of output, of changes in the real interest rate $(R - \dot{p})$, a and S respectively; $\bar{g}$ is real government spending, measured in deviations from its initial proportion of the initial level of output. μ is the Kahn–Keynes multiplier which augments all these impact effects on demand in the usual way. (Care is needed here in the choice of units and proportions because the model is log-linear.) We abstract from any trends in the constant $\bar{y}$, or in government spending.

3.2.4 Prices and the real exchange rate

The price of domestic output is, as in Chapter 2, set by a mark-up, π, on unit labour costs, w; it is assumed that there are no imported raw materials. In logarithms we write

$$p = \pi + w \tag{3.6}$$

The real exchange rate is simply the sum of the nominal exchange rate and the price level, since all these variables are measured in logarithms, and foreign prices are assumed to be constant.

$$a = p + e \tag{3.7}$$

3.2.5 National investment

National investment, j, is the logarithm of the sum of home and foreign investment. It plays no role in the dynamics of the model but, since the economy is assumed to have a target for the level of investment, it is essential to consider its determinants. A real interest-rate term ι' represents the effects of that variable on domestic investment, while a term in the real exchange rate is included as a consequence of its effect on the net foreign balance. An increase in output has two effects on national investment in opposite directions. There is a positive accelerator effect on domestic investment. In Chapter 2 this was represented by the parameter, ν. But there is a negative effect on net foreign investment, since imports are assumed to rise. This is represented by the parameter η' defined in Chapter 2. We assume that the foreign investment dominates $(\delta = \eta' - \nu > 0)$, so that an increase in output depresses investment overall. The coefficient $\bar{j}$ is a constant; we abstract from any trend in this. [2]

$$j = \bar{j} - \iota'(R - \dot{p}) - \varepsilon'a - \delta y \tag{3.8}$$

where $\delta = \eta' - \nu > 0$.

This equation differs from the analogous equation of Chapter 2 (equation 2.35c) because the real exchange rate is entered explicitly, whereas there it was solved out. The main consequence of this is that, with the exchange rate as explicit, the sign of the output term is negative. In Chapter 2, the floating exchange rate offset the effect of imports on overall investment, and only the positive accelerator effect remained.

3.2.6 The financial markets

It is assumed that there is perfect substitutability between home and foreign assets, so that the expected rate of change of the exchange rate depends only on the gap between the foreign $(\bar{R}^{\text{F}})$ and home (R) rates of interest

$$\dot{e}^e = \bar{R}^{\text{F}} - R \tag{3.9}$$

There is a simple *LM* curve which could be used in the model, showing the relation between nominal income $(y + p)$, the nominal interest rate and the money stock, d. Nominal income and the money stock are measured in logarithms.

$$d = \bar{d} + y + p - \zeta R \tag{3.10}$$

If a monetary target were to be adopted then this equation would play a crucial role as the determinant of interest rates in the short term and the price level in the long term. However, in the examples which we consider in detail an interest-rate rule is used. In such circumstances the *LM* curve is an appendage required solely for the sake of completeness. It is true that the *LM* curve is important because the proportion of outstanding government debt in the form of money affects the amount of interest the government has to pay and therefore the budget deficit. This is an issue which we take up empirically in Chapter 5. The present model does not show the effects of that deficit on interest payments, and therefore the extent to which the national debt is financed by non-interest-bearing rather than interest-bearing debt has no effect on the behaviour of other variables.

3.2.7 Expectations

We consider two naive assumptions about the formation of expectations in the foreign exchange markets. The easiest approach is that of model-consistent expectations. This assumption is very simply

$$\dot{e}^e = \dot{e} \tag{3.11a}$$

The assumption of model-consistent expectations is often regarded as a convenient working hypothesis, even though it is at best an approximation to the more realistic assumption of rational expectations.

The other expectational assumption which we consider is that of adaptive expectations. Depreciation of the real exchange rate in one period is expected to be followed by appreciation in the next period. An adjustment must be made for steady-state inflation, in order to ensure that expectations are consistent in the long run. In the limiting case of continuous time, this reduces to

$$\dot{e}^e = -\phi(\dot{e} + \dot{p}^*) - \dot{p}^* \tag{3.11b}$$

Expectations are not fulfilled except in the steady state, when $\dot{e} = -\dot{p}^*$, and the exchange rate responds only gradually when the model is shocked.

This regressive form of adaptive expectations is not completely satisfactory. It means that, at any time when the rate of depreciation is faster than the core rate of inflation, it is expected to be below the core rate of inflation. This feature could only be avoided if we were to introduce more complicated dynamics, or use a common alternative regressive form of adaptive expectation, which depicts the real exchange rate as expected to return gradually to some long-run steady-state level, rather than (as here) being expected to reverse the direction of its present change. The second form is not suitable for simulating in our empirical model later since it requires the identification of a long-run steady-state exchange rate. (We were in any case reluctant to make the assumption, in our adaptive expectations model, that the long-run steady-state real exchange rate was easily identifiable.)

3.2.8   The complete model

The equations above may be brought together in the following summary table

Table 3.1   The dynamic model

$$\dot{w} = \bar{\alpha} + \alpha_1(l^d - l^s) + \alpha_2(\dot{p} - \eta'\dot{a}) + \alpha_3\dot{S} + \alpha_4\dot{p} \qquad (3.12a)$$

$$\dot{p} = \dot{p}^* \qquad (3.12b)$$

$$l^s = \bar{l}^s + \alpha_5(w - [p - \eta'a]) - \alpha_6S \qquad (3.12c)$$

$$l^d = y \qquad (3.12d)$$

$$y = \bar{y} - \mu(\iota'[R - \dot{p}] + \varepsilon'a + \varkappa_1'S - \bar{g}) \qquad (3.12e)$$

$$p = \pi + w \qquad (3.12f)$$

$$j = \bar{j} - \iota'(R - \dot{p}) - \varepsilon'a - \delta y \qquad (3.12g)$$

$$\dot{e}^e = \bar{R}^F - R \qquad (3.12h)$$

$$d = \bar{d} + y + p - \zeta R \qquad (3.12i)$$

$$\dot{e}^e = \dot{e} \qquad (3.12ja)$$

$$\dot{e}^e = -\phi(\dot{e} + \dot{p}^*) - \dot{p}^* \qquad (3.12jb)$$

$$a = e + p \qquad (3.12k)$$

3.2.9   Three basic equations

By elimination of the eight variables, $w, \dot{p}, l_s, l_d, y, e, e^e$ and d, from the eleven equations of Table 3.1, we obtain three equations expressing the relationships between five basic variables, namely, the two target variables, p and j, the intermediate target variable, a, and the two control variables, R and S, in terms of the exogenous constants.

The first of these equations shows the level of price inflation. From equations (3.12a,b,c,d and e), after elimination of $\dot{p}, l_s, l_d$ and y we obtain[3]

$$\dot{w} = \bar{\alpha}' + \alpha_1\{\bar{y} - \mu(\iota'[R - \dot{p}] + \varepsilon'a + \varkappa_1'S - \bar{g})\} + \alpha_2(\dot{p} - \eta'\dot{a}) + \alpha_3\dot{S}$$
$$+ \alpha_4\dot{p}^* - \alpha_1\alpha_5(w - [p - \eta'a]) + \alpha_1\alpha_6 S$$

where $\bar{\alpha}' = \bar{\alpha} - \alpha_1\bar{l}^s$.

Noting that $\dot{w} = \dot{p}$ and $w - p = -\pi$ (from equation (3.12f)) we may re-express this, after elimination of w and regrouping terms, as

$$\dot{p} = \bar{\beta} - \beta_1\mu\iota'R - (\beta_1\mu\varepsilon' + \beta_5\eta')a - (\beta_1\mu\varkappa_1' - \beta_6)S - \beta_2\eta'\dot{a} + \beta_3\dot{S} + \beta_4\dot{p}^*$$

$$(3.13)$$

where

$$\bar{\beta} = (\bar{\alpha}' + \alpha_1[\bar{y} + \mu\bar{g}] + \alpha_1\alpha_5\pi)/(1 - \alpha_2 - \alpha_1\mu\iota')$$
$$\beta_i = \alpha_i/(1 - \alpha_2 - \alpha_1\mu\iota'), \ i = 1, 2, 3$$
$$\beta_i = \alpha_1\alpha i/(1 - \alpha_2 - \alpha_1\mu\iota'), \ i = 5, 6$$
$$\beta_4 = \alpha_4/(1 - \alpha_2 - \alpha_1\mu\iota') = (1 - \alpha_2)/(1 - \alpha_2 - \alpha_1\mu\iota')$$

The sign of the expression $(1 - \alpha_2 - \alpha_1\mu\iota')$ is of crucial importance since the signs of all the β-parameters in (3.13) depend upon it. There are two important ways in which an inflationary price rise may feed back upon itself in such a way as to cause an explosive inflationary effect. First (as measured by the parameters $\alpha_1\mu\iota'$), a rise in prices reduces the real rate of interest and will thus encourage an increase in investment expenditures which in turn will exert a demand-pull inflationary effect. Secondly (as measured by α_2), a rise in prices will raise the cost of living which will exert a cost-push inflationary effect on wages and so on prices. We first assume $\alpha_2 + \alpha_1\mu\iota' < 1$ so that all the β-parameters are positive in sign.

In this case we can interpret equation (3.13) in the following way. A depreciating real exchange rate causes upward cost-push pressure on prices, as does a low level of the real exchange rate. The latter also causes demand-pull pressure through its effects on the trade balance. A rising tax rate causes upward cost-push pressure on inflation, as does a high level of the tax rate. But the latter also causes downward demand-pull pressure and thus the direction of the effect of the level of the tax rate on inflation is ambiguous. A high real interest rate obviously dampens inflation — for a given level and rate of change of the real exchange rate — by means of demand-pull influences.

If, however, $\alpha_2 + \alpha_1\mu\iota' > 1$, then the β-parameters become negative and the effects of the right-hand side variables appear to be reversed. However, the effect is in fact more dramatic. Unless some of the right-hand side variables are suitable functions of $\dot{p}$, a rise in prices would lead to a larger 'second-round' rise in prices. The process would continue, and the wage–price loop would be instantaneously unstable. The rate of inflation implied by (3.13) would never be established. An important part of our subsequent analysis is to investigate whether any of the right-hand side variables are, or can be made, functions of $\dot{p}$ so as to ensure that the price equation is stable even if $\alpha_2 + \alpha_1\mu\iota' > 1$.

The second of the three basic equations shows the rate of appreciation of the real exchange rate. In the case of model-consistent expectations we use (3.12h), (3.12ja) and (3.12k) to eliminate e and e^e, and obtain

$$\dot{a} = \bar{R}^F - (R - \dot{p}) \tag{3.14a}$$

whilst, for the case of adaptive expectations, use of (3.12jb) instead of (3.12ja) gives

$$\dot{a} = -\frac{(\bar{R}^F - R + \dot{p}^*)}{\phi} + \dot{p} - \dot{p}^* \tag{3.14b}$$

Finally the equation for the level of national investment may be written – after substituting the *IS* equation into (3.12g) – as

$$j = \bar{j}' - \iota'(1 - \delta\mu)(R - \dot{p}) - \varepsilon'(1 - \delta\mu)a + \delta\mu\varkappa_1'S \tag{3.15}$$

where $\bar{j}' = \bar{j} - \delta[\bar{y} + \mu\bar{g}]$. We make the standard assumption that, taking the real exchange rate as given, $\delta\mu < 1$. This implies that import leakages cannot be large enough to reverse the direction of influence on national investment of the negative impact effect of the real interest rate on domestic investment. It also ensures that provided $\varepsilon' > 0$ (which is the Marshall-Lerner condition) a real depreciation has a positive effect on the national investment. Higher taxation increases national investment because it reduces imports more than it depresses domestic investment.

The policy problem addressed in the analytic part of the chapter may now be stated formally. It concerns the use of the two policy instruments S and R so as to obtain from equations (3.13) to (3.15) the desired outcomes p^* and j^* for the two policy objectives of the price level and national investment. We examine both long-run comparative static and then dynamic effects.

3.3 THE STEADY STATE OF THE REAL ECONOMY

Before considering the way in which the price level might be stabilized, it is helpful to investigate the consequences of such stabilization. The logic of adopting this particular order is to reinforce the vital point made in Chapter 2 that the steady state of the real economy is independent of the control rules which are adopted. We also show that this steady state is independent of the inflation target.

A steady state is defined as

$$p = p^* = p_0 + \dot{p}^* t \tag{3.16a}$$

$$j = j^* \tag{3.16b}$$

$$\dot{a} = 0 \tag{3.16c}$$

Equation (3.16a) implies that $\dot{p}_\infty = \dot{p}^*$. Using this together with equations (3.12h, ja, jb and k) we find that $R_\infty = \bar{R}^F + \dot{p}^*$; this in fact follows from our assumption of perfect capital mobility. Substitution of $\bar{R}^F + \dot{p}^*$ for R in (3.13) and noting that $\beta_4 - \beta_1 \mu \iota' = 1$ leads to (3.17a), equation (3.16b) enables (3.15) to be written as (3.17b):

$$\dot{p} - \dot{p}^* = 0 = \bar{\beta} - \beta_1 \mu \iota' \bar{R}^F - (\beta_1 \mu \varepsilon' + \beta_5 \eta')a - (\beta_1 \mu \varkappa_1' - \beta_6)S \tag{3.17a}$$

$$j^* = \bar{j}' - \iota'(1 - \delta\mu)\bar{R}^F - \varepsilon'(1 - \delta\mu)a + \delta\mu\varkappa_1'S \tag{3.17b}$$

These steady-state conditions indicate the relationship between the policy instruments and the policy targets. Notice that, in the steady state the real exchange rate is treated as though it is an instrument. This reflects its status as an intermediate target; i.e. as a target variable in guiding short-term policy, but also as an instrument which can be adjusted in order to achieve the overall aims of economic policy, namely, inflation at its target rate and investment at its desired level. It is also worthy of note that the condition for inflation to be at its target rate (3.17a) does not depend on the value taken by that target rate. The model is homogeneous of degree zero in inflation in the long run; that is, its steady state does not depend on the rate of inflation. Despite this, the analytical techniques of Chapter 2 remain highly relevant. Equations (3.17) can be used to find the steady-state values of S_∞ and a_∞. They are

$$S_\infty = \{\bar{\beta}\varepsilon'(1 - \delta\mu) + (\beta_1 \mu \varepsilon' + \beta_5 \eta')(j^* - \bar{j}') + \iota'(1 - \delta\mu)\beta_5 \eta' \bar{R}^F\}/\Delta \tag{3.18a}$$

$$a_\infty = \{\bar{\beta}\delta\mu\varkappa_1' - (\beta_1\mu\varkappa_1' - \beta_6)(j^* - \bar{j}') - (\iota'\beta_1\mu\varkappa_1' - \beta_6\iota'\,[1 - \delta\mu])\bar{R}^F\}/\Delta$$

(3.18b)

where

$$\Delta = \beta_1\mu\varepsilon'\varkappa_1' + \beta_5\eta'\delta\mu\varkappa_1' - \beta_6\varepsilon'(1 - \delta\mu)$$

It is important to note that the steady-state values are uniquely defined by the target rate of investment and the condition that inflation should proceed at its core rate. In normal circumstances this rules out the permanent tax cut proposed by Buiter and Miller (1982) as a way of 'costlessly reducing inflation'. Their proposal in fact finances a reduction in inflation by a subsidy to current consumption.

The expression Δ will be positive unless the upwards long-run cost-push effect of an increase in the tax rate, β_6, is so large as to outweigh the downward demand-pull effect $\beta_1\varkappa_1'$ by enough to offset the other term. We describe an economy with these abnormal properties as 'very long-run cost-push'. We note that if β_5 is large, i.e. if the real exchange rate has powerful cost-push effects, then the chance of the economy being very long-run cost-push is reduced.

We illustrate the comparative static properties of this solution in Figures 3.1 and 3.2. In Figure 3.1 we show the effect of a change in supply-side conditions, while in Figure 3.2 we show the effect of a shift in the investment target.

The line in Figures 3.1 and 3.2 marked $\bar{\beta}$ is derived from equation (3.17a) and shows the combinations of a and S which deliver inflation at its target rate given the value of $\bar{\beta}$. It is replaced by the line marked $\bar{\beta}'$ if $\bar{\beta}$ is replaced by $\bar{\beta}'$ in (3.17a), with $\bar{\beta}' > \bar{\beta}$. From the expression for $\bar{\beta}$ in (3.13) it can be seen that a rise in $\bar{\beta}$ to $\bar{\beta}'$ could occur from any exogenous change which would put an inflationary pressure on prices, such as an increased demand-pull pressure from an exogenous decrease in the labour supply or increase in the demand for labour, or an increased cost-push effect from an exogenous rise in the mark-up of prices over costs. A higher rate of interest could offset or a lower rate of interest could intensify in (3.17a) the inflationary effects of these pressures on $\bar{\beta}$ in the conventional Keynesian manner. The slope of the $\bar{\beta}$ contour can be derived from (3.17a) as $\partial a/\partial S = -(\beta_1\mu\varkappa_1' - \beta_6)/(\beta_1\mu\varepsilon' + \beta_5\eta')$. This is negative so long as $\beta_6 < \beta_1\varkappa_1'$, but swings round in the anti-clockwise direction as the cost-push factor, β_6, increases, changing from a negative to a positive slope when β_6 exceeds $\beta_1\mu\varkappa_1'$.

Similarly the line marked j^* in Figures 3.1 and 3.2 is derived from (3.17b), and shows the combinations of a and S which are needed to keep j at its target value, j^*. It may be noted that, while the j^* contour slopes

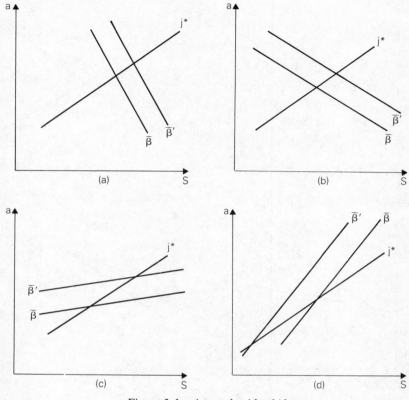

Figure 3.1   A supply-side shift

upwards in Figure 3.1 in the $S{-}a$ plane, the J-contour slopes downwards in Chapter 2 in the $S{-}R$ plane, as can be seen from the negative value of σ_y. These two results are in no way in conflict. In fact in Chapter 2 the J-contour would also slope upwards if it had been drawn in the $S{-}a$ plane instead of in the $S{-}R$ plane.[4]

In Figure 3.1 we consider four cases, showing the long-term policy response which is necessary to achieve both the price target and the investment target in the face of a worsening of the supply side, or an increase in exogenous demand pressure (an increase in $\bar\beta$).[5] In Figures 3.1(a) and 3.1(b), the demand-pull effect of taxes in the wage equation exceeds the cost-push effect. In Figure 3.1(a) the downward slope of the $\bar\beta$-contour exceeds the upward slope of the j^*-contour, and so the comparative advantage lies with fiscal policy in responding to the increased inflationary pressure represented by the shift in $\bar\beta$. In Figure 3.1(b) the cost-push term is stronger, and so the comparative advantage

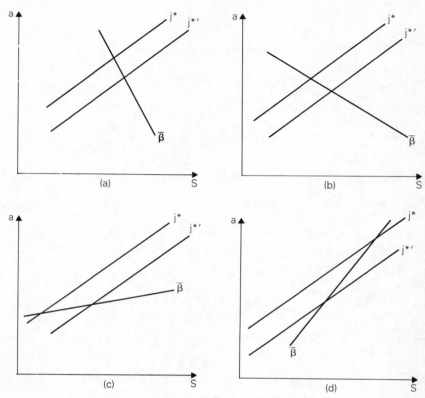

Figure 3.2   An investment target shift

now lies with the real exchange rate. But in both cases the policy response is to appreciate the real exchange rate and to raise taxes. Controllability would be described as good.

In Figure 3.1(c) we move on to the case in which the cost-push term in the wage equation exceeds the demand-pull term. The upward slope of the $\bar{\beta}$ line is less than that of the j^* line, and so once again we find an increase in taxes and an appreciation of the real exchange rate. Comparative advantage still lies with the real exchange rate in suppressing the inflationary disturbance, but controllability must be described as poor. Large movements in a and S are required.

In Figure 3.1(d) the whole pattern is changed. The cost-push term is now so powerful that the slope of the j^*-contour is less than that of the $\bar{\beta}$ line. The response to a worsened supply condition, or to an increase in exogenous public or private demand, is to reduce taxes (so as to generate extra output) and depreciate the real exchange rate (so as to offset the effect of the expansion on the import bill). In this very cost-push case the controllability is poor and the pattern of control is reversed as compared with the other three cases.

An increase in the target rate of investment is shown in Figure 3.2. It is represented by a rightward shift in the j^*-contour. It can be seen that in cases (a) and (b) this will be associated with a higher tax rate and a lower real exchange rate. In cases (c) and (d) the real exchange rate will still be reduced, but the tax rate will also be lower.

Finally we note that a reduction in the foreign interest rate will affect both the $\bar{\beta}$- and j^*-contours. The $\bar{\beta}$-contour will be moved in the direction of β' and the j^*-contour will also move to the right. In cases (a), (b) and (c) the new equilibrium will have a higher real exchange rate, although whether the tax rate is increased or reduced depends on the magnitudes of the various parameters. In case (d) the tax rate will undoubtedly fall, and the issue of whether the exchange rate is increased or reduced depends on the magnitude of the model parameters.

3.4   REGIME 1 :THE UNCONTROLLED ECONOMY

We now present standard results (see, for example, Adams and Gros, 1986) about the dynamic behaviour of an economy in which no active policy rule is used. We define this to be one in which the nominal interest rate is held constant, at a value $\bar{R}$, and the tax rate is held at $\bar{S}$.

We then find from (3.13) and (3.14a), with model-consistent expectations,

$$\dot{p} = \bar{\beta} - \beta_1 \mu\iota'\bar{R} - (\beta_1\mu\varepsilon' + \beta_5\eta')a - (\beta_1\mu\varkappa_1 - \beta_6)\bar{S} - \beta_2\eta'\dot{a} + \beta_4\dot{p}^* \quad (3.19a)$$

$$\dot{a} = \bar{R}^F - \bar{R} + \dot{p} \quad (3.19b)$$

From these we may solve for $\dot{p}$ and $\dot{a}$ as

$$\dot{p} = \frac{\{\bar{\beta} - \beta_1\mu\iota'\bar{R} - (\beta_1\mu\varepsilon' + \beta_5\eta')a - (\beta_1\mu\varkappa_1 - \beta_6)\bar{S} - \beta_2\eta'(\bar{R}^F - \bar{R}) + \beta_4\dot{p}^*\}}{1 + \beta_2\eta'}$$

$$(3.20a)$$

$$\dot{a} = \bar{R}^F - \bar{R} + \frac{(\bar{\beta} - \beta_1\mu\iota'\bar{R} - (\beta_1\mu\varepsilon' + \beta_5\eta')a - (\beta_1\mu\varkappa_1 - \beta_6)\bar{S} - \beta_2\eta'(\bar{R}^F - \bar{R}) + \beta_4\dot{p}^*)}{1 + \beta_2\eta'}$$

$$(3.20b)$$

This system has one zero root, since p does not feature in either equation. This zero root means that the price level is indeterminate. The dynamic behaviour of the system does not depend on the price level. The second root is given by the coefficient of a in (3.20b). Using the values of β_1, β_2 and β_5 from (3.13), this can be expanded as

$$\frac{-(\beta_1\mu\varepsilon' + \beta_5\eta')}{(1 + \beta_2\eta')} = \frac{-(\alpha_1\mu\varepsilon' + \alpha_5\alpha_1\eta')}{(1 - \alpha_2 - \alpha_1\mu\iota' + \alpha_2\eta')}$$

This root is negative if $\alpha_2(1 - \eta') + \alpha_1\mu\iota' < 1$, a condition which must be fulfilled if instantaneous price instability of the type mentioned in section 3.2 is to be avoided. This stability condition is weaker than that in section 3.2 ($\alpha_2 + \alpha_1\mu\iota' < 1$) because we see in (3.19b) that the real exchange rate is now endogenous. Rising prices lead to a rising real exchange rate. This exerts a downward pressure on prices; it can stabilize the instantaneous wage–price loop even if the condition of section 3.2 does not hold. However, a negative root means that the model has no unstable root associated with the real exchange rate. The uncontrolled economy is overstable when expectations are model-consistent.

When expectations are adaptive, $\dot{p}$ is once again given by (3.19a), while $\dot{a}$ is now given by (3.14b). We now find, after substituting, that

$$\dot{p} =$$

$$\frac{\{\bar{\beta} - \beta_1\mu\iota'\bar{R} - (\beta_1\mu\varepsilon' + \beta_5\eta')a - (\beta_1\mu\varkappa_1 - \beta_6)\bar{S} + \beta_2\eta'(\bar{R}^F - \bar{R})/\phi + (\beta_4 + \beta_2\eta'[1 + 1/\phi])\dot{p}^*}{1 + \beta_2\eta'}$$

$$(3.21a)$$

$$\dot{a} = -(\bar{R}^F - \bar{R})/\phi +$$

$$\frac{\{\bar{\beta} - \beta_1\mu\iota'\bar{R} - (\beta_1\mu\varepsilon' + \beta_5\eta')a - (\beta_1\mu\varkappa_1 - \beta_6)\bar{S} + \beta_2\eta'(\bar{R}^F - \bar{R})/\phi + (\beta_4 - [1 + 1/\phi])\dot{p}^*\}}{1 + \beta_2\eta'}$$

$$(3.21b)$$

The model now has roots of 0 and

$$\frac{-(\beta_1\mu\varepsilon' + \beta_5\eta')}{1 + \beta_2\eta'} = \frac{-(\alpha_1\mu\varepsilon' + \alpha_5\alpha_1\eta')}{1 - \alpha_2(1 - \eta') - \alpha_1\mu\iota'}$$

The condition for instantaneous price stability is the same as it was when expectations were model-consistent and, when prices are instantaneously stable, the root is negative. This negative root means that the real exchange rate is stable.

The root has the same sign independently of the way in which expectations are formed, because a high real exchange rate has both cost-push and demand-pull effects which lead to falling prices. Other things being equal, these falling prices have the effect of reducing the real exchange rate. This is a stabilizing influence. This effect, which is overstabilizing with model-consistent expectations, arises from the use of the nominal interest rate as the exogenous instrument of monetary policy.

This model allows at best a partial analysis. It is possible to argue that it neglects possible stabilizing features such as the Pigou effect whereby a rise in the price level would damp demand because of the fall in the value of cash balances. Nevertheless the results are very clear. The price level is indeterminate. With model-consistent expectations the real exchange rate is overstable. These facts create a clear need for some sort of active policy rule.

3.5   THE POLICY FRAMEWORK

3.5.1   Four types of inflation control

Having considered the comparative statics of the steady state and looked at the behaviour of the uncontrolled economy, we now investigate policy rules which could be used to control inflation. In each exercise we assume that only one policy instrument is used to control inflation at any one time. This means that our results can be used to illustrate the proposals of McKinnon (1986) who advocates the use of monetary policy to fight inflation, and Williamson and Miller (1987) who advocate the use of fiscal policy to fight inflation. Our results also indicate the sort of pitfalls which might be encountered in setting up cross-linked rules of the type which we use in Chapter 6.

We assume that if fiscal policy is used to control inflation, then the monetary control 'instrument', the target real exchange rate, is held constant at its steady-state value, while if monetary policy is used to control inflation, the fiscal policy instrument (the tax rate) is held at its steady-state value. This means that we do not consider the dynamic problems in attaining the investment target. That will be investigated in Chapter 4. But our assumption does imply that in any steady state which is achieved by our control of inflation, the wealth target will also be achieved.

The model allows us to consider four possible types of counter-inflationary policy. The first policy is that of monetary targets. The nominal money stock is allowed to grow at the target rate of inflation and the interest rate is determined by inverting (3.12i). The second approach also uses monetary policy as the route to keeping prices on their target path. However, as discussed in the introduction, an intermediate target is established for the exchange rate, with reference to the level of prices. The home interest rate is then set with reference to the gap between the actual and target exchange rates. The remaining approaches to maintaining price stability rely on fiscal policy; either government spending or the tax rate is varied so as to stabilize inflation. In this section we discuss some of these alternative methods of disinflation.

A monetary target

The use of monetary targets in an open economy results in a system very similar to that described by Dornbusch (1976). It is now well documented that disturbances to international capital markets or shifts in the velocity of circulation will, in a regime with a fixed money stock, lead to fluctuations in the real exchange rate and disturbances to output even though there may be no inflationary pressure (Artis and Currie, 1981). We can see no advantages in such a system compared with one in which the interest rate is used explicitly for counter-inflationary purposes. It has been much discussed elsewhere and we do not consider it further.

An exchange-rate target

The main route by which monetary policy achieves inflation control in an open economy is through the exchange rate. We may therefore set out an anti-inflationary policy in which (i) a target exchange rate is set at a level which depends on the deviation of actual prices from their target value and (ii) an interest-rate policy (specified below) shows how the interest rate is used to steer the exchange rate to that target. This is monetary control of inflation, although by rather different means from those presented by Dornbusch (1976) and Buiter and Miller (1982). In our analytic model we write

$$a^* = a_\infty + \chi_1(p - p^*) \qquad \chi_1 > 0 \qquad (3.22)$$

This implies that the real exchange-rate target is appreciated above its steady-state level if prices are above their target level. (Note that the special case of $\chi_1 = 1$ corresponds to a fixed nominal exchange rate target.) Interest-rate policy now becomes subordinated to the attainment of this target exchange rate in a manner discussed below. This formulation assumes that the authorities know a_∞ and can use this information in the setting of a^*. We do not assume this in our empirical work, but to do so here greatly simplifies our analytic investigation.[6]

There are a number of reasons why it might be desirable to adopt a target real exchange rate as a focus for counter-inflationary monetary policy, rather than relying on the money stock as an intermediate target or letting the interest rate respond directly to the price level. It is often argued that exchange-rate stabilization, such as would be expected to follow from exchange-rate targeting, is desirable *per se*. Or it may be that, without any exchange-rate target, there will be bubbles in the exchange rate which may have a disruptive effect on the other variables in the economy. We discussed some of these in more detail in Chapter 1. We do not now add to this normative case for the use of the exchange rate as an intermediate target. To do so would inevitably extend our material to an unreasonable degree. What we do offer is a positive demonstration of the way in which such a target works, and a solid demonstration that it can replace the money stock as an intermediate target on which a counter-inflationary policy can be based.

A tax-rate rule

A third approach is to set the tax rate with reference to the deviation of prices from their desired level. In our analytic model we write

$$S = S_\infty + \chi_2(p - p^*) \tag{3.23}$$

This implies that taxes are set above their steady-state level whenever prices are above target.

This formulation assumes for simplicity that the authorities know S_∞; we do not assume this in our empirical work.[7]

A public expenditure rule

Public expenditure could be used as an alternative fiscal instrument, giving the fourth means of price stabilization. We use it in this way in Chapter 4, so as to simplify our exposition. For the purposes of this chapter it can be treated in the same way as the tax rate. The only major difference is that we assume that the cost-push effects of both the level and rate of change of public expenditure (β_3 and β_6) are zero.

3.5.2   The fiscal-monetary mix

None of the options outlined above is sufficient to close the system. If monetary policy is used for counter-inflationary purposes, some principle is needed for the setting of fiscal policy. If, on the other hand, fiscal policy is used to suppress inflation, some guidance is needed to indicate an appropriate monetary stance.

We assume in our analytical model that the 'spare' policy instrument is set in a manner which ensures that the investment target is achieved in the steady state. In fact it may be desirable to use this missing policy instrument actively in order to damp down disturbances; indeed in our empirical work discussed below this is done. However, the dynamic model presented here would become intractable if any attempt were made to extend it in this way, and we do not make any such attempt.

Thus, if the real exchange rate intermediate target is used for disinflation, and if it is assumed that the level of real government spending is exogenous, then the tax rate is set to ensure that the investment target is met. The appropriate tax rate is given by equation (3.24)

$$S = S_\infty \tag{3.24}$$

If fiscal policy is used for disinflation, then we assume that a target real exchange rate, consistent with the desired investment target, is adopted. The required target value is given by equation (3.25)

$$a^* = a_\infty \tag{3.25}$$

3.5.3   Specification of interest-rate policy

Target values for the real exchange rate have been specified in three of the four 'policy rules': it is now necessary to indicate how monetary policy should respond when the actual real exchange rate is away from its target. There might in reality be two arms to monetary policy, foreign-exchange intervention and interest-rate setting. However, by making the simplifying assumption that there is perfect substitutability between home and foreign assets, any role for intervention is lost. And so it remains to consider only the setting of the interest rate. An obvious suggestion in the context of our model is to adopt a high real interest rate when the real exchange rate is below its target, and a low real rate when the real exchange rate is above its target. If the domestic interest rate is also set with reference to world interest rates then an appropriate simple rule is, with no inflation abroad,

$$R = \bar{R}^{F} + \chi_3(a^* - a) + \dot{p} \qquad \chi_3 > 0 \qquad (3.26)$$

We use just such a rule in our analytical model. In our empirical work, the use of integral control means that it is possible to specify a control rule without explicit reference to the foreign rate of interest or the domestic rate of inflation and so the structure is slightly different.

3.5.4 Why investigate decoupled control rules?

In order to investigate stability with our simple analytic model it is necessary to restrict the system to be second-order. As a consequence we make the following assumptions which have already been noted. When the active exchange-rate target rule is used to stabilize prices, the tax rate is assumed to be set permanently to S_∞. On the other hand, if an active fiscal rule is used to stabilize prices, the target real exchange rate is assumed to be set to a_∞. In both cases interest-rate policy is used as in (3.26). In neither case is there any dynamic feedback from the level of investment to the policy instruments.

We are now equipped to compare the dynamics of two more regimes:

(a) Regime 2: monetary disinflation using a target exchange rate (with S constant at S_∞),
(b) Regime 3: fiscal disinflation (during which a^* is constant at a_∞).

The reader may doubt the relevance of such 'decoupled' regimes in which one instrument is exclusively assigned to the control of one target. We perform these investigations for two reasons.

(1) Other people propose assignments. It is apparently a UK Treasury view (see also Boughton, 1988) that inflation control should take place as in Regime 2, with the fiscal instrument only being adjusted for 'longer-term structural reasons' (i.e. in pursuit of a wealth target?). By contrast Edison *et al.* (1987) have advocated Regime 3, with the real exchange rate being kept at or near a_∞. Our approach means that we can compare the dynamics of their proposed assignments.
(2) This investigation also gives preliminary indications concerning the appropriate instrument-target emphasis for our more complex empirical investigations (where we do not confine ourselves to decoupled designs).

3.6   REGIME 2: MONETARY CONTROL OF INFLATION BY AN EXCHANGE RATE TARGET

In Chapter 2 we looked at the way in which policy instruments could be used to change the short-term rate of inflation, which raised the same problems as those which arise in coping with the inflationary pressures resulting from an adverse change in supply-side conditions. The exercises were equivalent. However, in this chapter the real economy is homogeneous of degree zero in prices in the long run, which makes them different. In section 3.3 we were able to look at the effect of a permanent supply-side shift, and we noted that a permanent change in the core-target rate of inflation does not require any permanent instrument movement.

Now we study the dynamic convergence properties of the system, showing how, if we start off with the price level displaced from its target value for any reason, active policy rules can be used to bring it towards its target value. We assume that the core-target inflation rate, $\dot{p}^*$, and the values of a_∞ and S_∞ consistent with the model parameters are known.

The dynamic system into which we insert our control rules for the purpose of this dynamic analysis is a subset of the full system described in equations (3.13) to (3.15). We need only consider the evolution of prices (3.13) and of the real exchange rate (3.14a or 3.14b). The investment equation (3.15) can be ignored.[8] Our aim is to investigate whether this system will converge to the steady-state trajectory. Substituting R from (3.26) into (3.13) we obtain

$$\dot{p} = \bar{\beta} - \beta_1\mu\iota'(\bar{R}^F + \chi_3[a^* - a] + \dot{p}) - (\beta_1\mu\varepsilon' + \beta_5\eta')a$$
$$- (\beta_1\mu\varkappa_1' - \beta_6)S - \beta_2\eta'\dot{a} + \beta_3\dot{S} + \beta_4\dot{p}^* \quad (3.27)$$

Model-consistent expectations

Taking first the case of model-consistent expectations and substituting for R from (3.26) into (3.14a), we obtain

$$\dot{a} = -\chi_3(a^* - a) \quad (3.28)$$

It remains to substitute for the exchange-rate target, a^*, and the tax rate, S, in equations (3.27) and (3.28). We substitute for a^* from (3.22) and for S from (3.24) and so obtain in matrix form

$$
\begin{bmatrix} \dot{p} \\ \dot{a} \end{bmatrix} = \begin{bmatrix} \dfrac{-\beta_1\mu\iota'\chi_3\chi_1 + \beta_2\eta'\chi_3\chi_1}{1 + \beta_1\mu\iota'} & \dfrac{\beta_1\mu\iota'\chi_3 - (\beta_1\mu\varepsilon' + \beta_5\eta') - \beta_2\eta'\chi_3}{1 + \beta_1\mu\iota'} \\ -\chi_3\chi_1 & \chi_3 \end{bmatrix} \begin{bmatrix} p \\ a \end{bmatrix}
$$

$$+ \text{constants} \tag{3.29}$$

Using the values of the βs from (3.13), the determinant can be expressed as

$$-\chi_3\chi_1(\beta_1\mu\varepsilon' + \beta_5\eta')/(1 + \beta_1\mu\iota') = -\chi_1\chi_3(\alpha_1\mu\varepsilon' + \alpha_5\alpha_1\eta')/(1 - \alpha_2)$$

In order to avoid instantaneous price instability, we require $\alpha_2 < 1$. This says simply that wages must not be fully and instantaneously indexed to prices. We assume that this condition is met. The determinant is then negative provided that χ_1 is chosen to be positive, and the system then has the one unstable root [9] which we require for saddlepath stability. We assume that this unstable root is removed by a 'jump' in the nominal exchange rate which sets the system on a saddlepath to the steady state. The condition $\chi_1 > 0$ implies that, although the nominal exchange-rate target need not rise in order to rein in prices, the real exchange rate must be allowed to rise. The case of a fixed nominal exchange rate ($\chi_1 = 1$) is obviously consistent with stable adjustment.

Figure 3.3 illustrates this. From (3.29) the $\dot{a} = 0$ line, along which

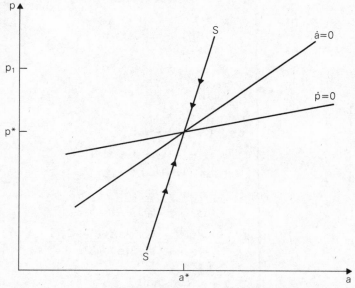

Figure 3.3   The price/real exchange rate phase diagram

$a = a^*$, has a positive slope. The $\dot{p} = \dot{p}^*$ line is flatter, and may have a negative slope (although for sufficiently high χ_3 the slope is certainly positive). *SS* is the saddlepath. When p is higher than p^*, at p_1 then the following happens: a^* is raised, so R is raised, a is then assumed to jump upwards (but not by as much as the change in a^*) and we can converge back to p^* along *SS*.

Adaptive expectations

With adaptive expectations we substitute for R from (3.26) into (3.14b) and obtain

$$\dot{a} = \{\chi_3(a^* - a)\}/\phi + (\dot{p} - \dot{p}^*)(1 + 1/\phi) \tag{3.30}$$

We also substitute in (3.27) and (3.30) for a^* and S from (3.22) and (3.24) and the system becomes in matrix form

$$
\begin{bmatrix} \dot{p} \\ \dot{a} - (1 + 1/\phi)\dot{p} \end{bmatrix} =
$$

$$
\begin{bmatrix} \dfrac{-\chi_3\mu\beta_1\iota'\chi_1 - \beta_2\eta'\chi_3\chi_1/\phi}{1 + \beta_2\eta'(1 + 1/\phi) + \beta_1\mu\iota'} & \dfrac{\beta_1\mu\iota'\chi_3 - \beta_1\mu\varepsilon' - \beta_5\eta' + \beta_2\eta'\chi_3/\phi}{1 + \beta_2\eta'(1 + 1/\phi) + \beta_1\mu\iota'} \\[3mm] \chi_3\chi_1/\phi & -\chi_3/\phi \end{bmatrix}
\begin{bmatrix} p \\ a \end{bmatrix}
$$

$$+ \text{ constants} \tag{3.31a}$$

or

$$
\begin{bmatrix} \dot{p} \\ \dot{a} \end{bmatrix} =
\begin{bmatrix} \dfrac{-\chi_3\mu\beta_1\iota'\chi_1 - \beta_2\eta'\chi_3\chi_1/\phi}{1 + \beta_2\eta'(1 + 1/\phi) + \beta_1\mu\iota'} & \dfrac{\beta_1\mu\iota'\chi_3 - \beta_1\mu\varepsilon' - \beta_5\eta' + \beta_2\eta'\chi_3/\phi}{1 + \beta_2\eta'(1 + 1/\phi) + \beta_1\mu\iota'} \\[5mm] \chi_3\chi_1/\phi - \dfrac{(1 + 1/\phi)(\chi_3\mu\beta_1\iota'\chi_1 + \beta_2\eta'\chi_3\chi_1/\phi)}{1 + \beta_2\eta'(1 + 1/\phi) + \beta_1\mu\iota'} & -\chi_3/\phi + \dfrac{(\beta_1\mu\iota'\chi_3 - \beta_1\mu\varepsilon' - \beta_5\eta' + \beta_2\eta'\chi_3/\phi)(1 + 1/\phi)}{1 + \beta_2\eta'(1 + 1/\phi) + \beta_1\mu\iota'} \end{bmatrix}
\begin{bmatrix} p \\ a \end{bmatrix}
$$

$$+ \text{ constants} \tag{3.31b}$$

With model-consistent expectations we required there to be one unstable root which would be cleared by a jump in the exchange rate. With adaptive expectations it is assumed that variables do not jump and so there should be no unstable roots. This is assured if the trace is negative and the determinant is positive.

The determinant is $\chi_3\chi_1(\beta_1\mu\varepsilon' + \beta_5\eta')/\{1 + \beta_2\eta'(1 + 1/\phi) + \beta_1\mu\iota'\}\phi = \chi_3\chi_1(\alpha_1\mu\varepsilon' + \alpha_5\alpha_1\eta')/\{1 - \alpha_2 + \alpha_2\eta'(1 + 1/\phi)\}\phi$. With $\phi > 0$, the condition for instantaneous stability is now $\alpha_2(1 - \eta'[1 + 1/\phi]) < 1$. This is weaker than the condition, $\alpha_2 < 1$, which we met with model-consistent expectations. The reason for this is that we have assumed expectations about the nominal exchange rate to be adaptive. This means that rising prices raise the real exchange rate, thereby damping the wage–price spiral. Provided that this condition holds, positive values of χ_1 and χ_3 will ensure that the determinant is positive. The trace is

$$\frac{\chi_3\mu\beta_1\iota'(1 + 1/\phi - \chi_1) + \chi_3\beta_2\eta'(1/\phi - \chi_1 + 1)/\phi - (\beta_1\mu\varepsilon' + \beta_5\eta')(1 + 1/\phi)}{1 + \beta_2\eta'(1 + 1/\phi) + \beta_1\mu\iota'} - \chi_3/\phi$$

It is increasingly negative in χ_1 and so, by choosing a value of χ_1 (the coefficient of the target real exchange rate on the price level) large enough, it is always possible to ensure stable control. This condition is tighter than when expectations were model-consistent. A policy rule which is stable when expectations are adaptive will be saddlepath stable when expectations are model-consistent, but the converse is not necessarily true.

Thus our analytical investigation has shown in a stylized way how such a policy regime would work, and has not revealed any difficulties concerning potential instabilities.

3.7 REGIME 3: FISCAL CONTROL OF INFLATION BY A TAX RULE

Model-consistent expectations

With fiscal control of inflation, and a fixed real exchange-rate target, we substitute for S from (3.23) and for a^* from (3.25) into (3.27); (3.28) completes the system to give

$$\begin{bmatrix} \dot{p} \\ \dot{a} \end{bmatrix} = \begin{bmatrix} \dfrac{-(\beta_1\mu\chi_1' - \beta_6)\chi_2}{1 - \beta_3\chi_2 + \beta_1\mu\iota'} & \dfrac{\beta_1\mu\iota'\chi_3 - \beta_1\mu\varepsilon' - \beta_5\eta' - \beta_2\eta'\chi_3}{1 - \beta_3\chi_2 + \beta_1\mu\iota'} \\ 0 & \chi_3 \end{bmatrix} \begin{bmatrix} p \\ a \end{bmatrix}$$

$$+ \text{constants} \qquad\qquad (3.32a)$$

This has determinant

$$\frac{-\chi_3\chi_2(\beta_1\mu\varkappa_1' - \beta_6)}{1 - \beta_3\chi_2 + \beta_1\mu\iota'} = \frac{-\chi_3\chi_2(\alpha_1\mu\varkappa_1' - \alpha_1\alpha_6)}{1 - \alpha_2 - \alpha_3\chi_2}$$

We first note that the condition for instantaneous price stability has been modified. It is now $\alpha_2 + \alpha_3\chi_2 < 1$. This condition sets an immediate upper limit to the value of χ_2. The reason for this is very simple. If $\alpha_3 > 0$, so that an increase in taxes has an immediate cost-push effect on wages, then any policy of raising taxes in response to inflation will aggravate the instantaneous wage-price spiral. A sufficiently powerful positive response will lead to instantaneous instability. χ_2 must be small enough to ensure that this does not happen.

We now consider the (unlikely) case in which the positive long-run cost-push effects of a higher level of taxes dominate the negative demand-pull effects (i.e. $\beta_6 > \beta_1\mu\varkappa_1'$). Then inspection of equation (3.32) shows that stable control is possible with a 'perverse' signed fiscal controller (i.e. with $\chi_2 < 0$).[10] In this case if p begins above p^*, then taxes are cut and we converge stably to the lower price level p^*. But our empirical work suggests that this case is not a relevant one. The relevant case is $\beta_1\mu\varkappa_1' > \beta_6$: i.e. positive long-run cost-push effects of a high level of taxes are less strong than the negative demand-pull effects. In this case the requirement of instantaneous price stability discussed above sets an upper limit to the value of χ_2. This important result means that, with cost-push pressures in the wage equation, there are limits to the use of fiscal policy in controlling price evolution.

We now check to see if our results survive the translation to adaptive expectations.

Adaptive expectations

With fiscal stabilization the system is

$$
\begin{bmatrix} \dot{p} \\[2ex] \dot{a} - (1 + 1/\phi)\dot{p} \end{bmatrix} =
$$

$$
\begin{bmatrix} \dfrac{-\chi_2(\beta_1\mu\varkappa_1' - \beta_6)}{1 + \beta_1\mu\iota' + \beta_2\eta'(1 + 1/\phi) - \beta_3\chi_2} & \dfrac{\beta_1\mu\iota'\chi_3 - \beta_1\mu\varepsilon' - \beta_5\eta' + \beta_2\eta'\chi_3/\phi}{1 + \beta_1\mu\iota' + \beta_2\eta'(1 + 1/\phi) - \beta_3\chi_2} \\[3ex] 0 & -\chi_3/\phi \end{bmatrix}
\begin{bmatrix} p \\[2ex] a \end{bmatrix}
$$

$$+ \text{constants} \hspace{4cm} (3.33a)$$

or

$$
\begin{bmatrix} \dot{p} \\ \dot{a} \end{bmatrix} = \begin{bmatrix} \dfrac{-\chi_2(\beta_1\mu\varkappa_1' - \beta_6)}{1 + \beta_1\mu\iota' + \beta_2\eta'(1 + 1/\phi) - \beta_3\chi_2} & \dfrac{\beta_1\mu\iota'\chi_3 - \beta_1\mu\varepsilon' - \beta_5\eta' + \beta_2\eta'\chi_3/\phi}{1 + \beta_1\mu\iota' + \beta_2\eta'(1 + 1/\phi) - \beta_3\chi_2} \\[2.5em] \dfrac{-\chi_2(\beta_1\mu\varkappa_1' - \beta_6)(1 + 1/\phi)}{1 + \beta_1\mu\iota' + \beta_2\eta'(1 + 1/\phi) - \beta_3\chi_2} & -\chi_3/\phi + \dfrac{(\beta_1\mu\iota'\chi_3 - \beta_1\mu\varepsilon' - \beta_5\eta' + \beta_2\eta'\chi_3/\phi)(1 + 1/\phi)}{1 + \beta_1\mu\iota' + \beta_2\eta'(1 + 1/\phi) - \beta_3\chi_2} \end{bmatrix} \begin{bmatrix} p \\ a \end{bmatrix}
$$

$$+ \text{ constants} \tag{3.33b}$$

We require no unstable roots (i.e. negative trace and positive determinant).

The problems previously found with fiscal management recur. The determinant is now

$$
\chi_3\chi_2(\beta_1\mu\varkappa_1' - \beta_6)/\{1 + \beta_1\mu\iota' + \beta_2\eta'(1 + 1/\phi) - \beta_3\chi_2\}\phi =
$$
$$
\chi_3\chi_2(\alpha_1\mu\varkappa_1' - \alpha_6\alpha_1)/\{1 - \alpha_2 + \alpha_2\eta'(1 + 1/\phi) - \alpha_3\chi_2\}\phi.
$$

The determinant condition for instantaneous price stability is now, with $\phi > 0$, $1 - \alpha_2 + \alpha_2\eta'(1 + 1/\phi) - \alpha_3\chi_2 > 0$. Once again it sets an upper limit to χ_2. If this condition does hold, then we require $\chi_2 > 0$ if the economy is long-run demand-pull ($\beta_6 < \beta_1\mu\varkappa_1'$) and $\chi_2 < 0$ in the empirically less relevant case where the economy is long-run cost-push ($\beta_6 > \beta_1\mu\varkappa_1'$).

The trace is

$$
\frac{-\chi_2(\beta_1\mu\varkappa_1' - \beta_6) + (\beta_1\mu\iota'\chi_3 - \beta_1\mu\varepsilon' - \beta_5\eta' + \beta_2\eta'\chi_3/\phi)(1 + 1/\phi)}{1 + \beta_1\mu\iota' + \beta_2\eta'(1 + 1/\phi) - \beta_3\chi_2} - \chi_3/\phi
$$

Provided that prices are instantaneously stable, a sufficiently large value of χ_2 will, with $\beta_6 < \beta_1\mu\varkappa_1'$, ensure that the trace is negative. However, if the degree of wage indexation (α_2) is close to 1, and if the economy is long-run demand-pull, so that we need $\chi_2 > 0$, then it may not be possible to find a value of χ_2 large enough to deliver a negative numerator without, at the same time, leading to instantaneous price instability.

We may summarize these results by concluding that the use of fiscal policy to stabilize prices may face problems if the fiscal controller has a cost-push effect on wages. If the long-run demand-pull effects of fiscal policy dominate the cost-push effects, and this is believed to be the empirically relevant case, then there is an upper limit to the value which the control parameter, χ_2, can take. With adaptive expectations there is also a lower limit to χ_2, and so there may be no value of χ_2 which yields a stable solution. More generally, as with monetary control of prices, it seems that a value of the control parameter which yields a stable solution with adaptive expectations will yield a saddlepath solution with model-consistent expectations, but that the converse is not the case.

3.8 THE COMPARATIVE ADVANTAGE OF FISCAL AND MONETARY POLICY

3.8.1 The relevance of comparative advantage for policy design

We now turn away from simple policy regimes in which particular instruments are assigned to the control of particular targets. Instead we ask the following more complex question: in cross-coupled regimes[11] which instrument should be mainly relied upon to control which target?

In order to consider the question of whether reliance should be placed mainly on fiscal or mainly on monetary policy in order to damp inflation, it is helpful to use the concept of the comparative advantage or comparative weighting index, ω, which we introduced in Chapter 2. This was defined as follows. If we consider the problem of controlling two variables, y_1 and y_2, by means of the instruments x_1 and x_2 in the system

$$y_1 = \chi_{11}x_1 + \chi_{12}x_2 + \text{other terms}$$
$$y_2 = \chi_{21}x_1 + \chi_{22}x_2 + \text{other terms} \tag{3.34}$$

we may define a comparative advantage index as

$$\omega = (\chi_{11}/\chi_{12})/(\chi_{21}/\chi_{22}) \tag{3.35}$$

Then as in Chapter 2 we may say that x_1 has a comparative advantage in controlling y_1 if $|\omega| > 1$.

In a dynamic framework this index will probably change over time. By short-term comparative advantage we summarize the relative impact effects of the two policy instruments on our target variables. By long-term comparative advantage we summarize the steady-state effects of step changes in the instrument variables. The medium term relates to effects between these two extremes.

The pattern of long-term comparative advantage indicates the relative magnitude of changes in the policy instruments which will have to be made in order to achieve particular target values in the steady state. It is an indication, but not always a very good indication, of the structure of the integral components needed for well-behaved policy rules. We have found that short- to medium-term comparative advantage provides a good indication of the structure of the proportional component of control rules. [12] If x_1 has a comparative advantage in controlling y_1, then the proportional component of a control rule designed to damp a disturbance in y_1 should rely mainly on x_1. Indeed relative instrument movements can differ from what is indicated by the parameter ω only to the extent that one or both of the targets are allowed to slip. We express these ideas in more detail in section 3.8.5.

3.8.2 Long-term comparative advantage

We consider first the question of long-term comparative advantage. This is simple, in that it is independent of the way in which expectations are formed (because with both our expectational rules, expectations are fulfilled in the long run).

However a complication arises in the long run. The tax rate is one policy instrument, but the long-term real rate of interest is, at least in this model, constrained to equal that of the rest of the world. In studying long-term comparative advantage it is necessary to regard the real exchange-rate target as the instrument of monetary policy. This in fact follows naturally from our analysis in section 3.3.

With this in mind we can use equations (3.17) to write

$$\omega = \frac{\partial(\dot{p} - \dot{p}^*)/\partial S}{\partial(\dot{p} - \dot{p}^*)/\partial a}\bigg|\frac{\partial j/\partial S}{\partial j/\partial a} = \frac{(\beta_1\mu x_1' - \beta_6)\delta\mu x_1'}{(\beta_1\mu\varepsilon' + \beta_5\eta')\,\varepsilon'(1 - \delta\mu)} \qquad (3.36)$$

This represents the long-run (i.e. steady-state) comparative advantage of fiscal policy relative to exchange-rate policy in influencing the inflation target as compared with the investment target. Notice that, since always in the long run $\dot{p} - \dot{p}^* = 0$, the effects of policy instruments on the inflation target need to be thought of as relating to ability to remove an inflationary disturbance caused by, say, a change in $\bar{\beta}$.

With the cost-push parameter, β_6 equal to 0, ω will be negative; depending on the parameters of the model, we may find $\omega < -1$, giving a comparative advantage to a demand-pull fiscal policy in fighting inflation.

It can be seen that as β_6 increases from zero the value of ω rises towards zero. It becomes more likely that the monetary policy will have a long-run advantage in fighting inflation. As β_6 increases further ω will exceed 0 and eventually the pattern of comparative advantage will lie with a cost-push fiscal policy in fighting inflation; the long-term target-instrument emphasis of the policy rules may need to reflect this.

3.8.3 Short-term comparative advantage

The evaluation of short-term comparative advantage is more complicated. We take as our starting point equations (3.13) and (3.15). In order to consider short-term comparative advantage, we work in discrete time and consider the one-period effect of a change in the real exchange rate and the tax rate. It is necessary to specify how the real exchange rate is affected by change in the interest rate in the short term. The real exchange rate may be assumed to respond to a change in the real interest rate; but this response depends on the way in which expectations are formed and, if expectations are forward-looking, on the expected future level of the real interest rate. However, we shall see that it is possible to come to reasonably firm qualitative conclusions about the pattern of short-term comparative advantage merely by assuming that an increase in the real interest rate causes some increase in the real exchange rate in the short term. The magnitude of this increase turns out to be relatively unimportant. Thus we put

$$\Delta a = \sigma \Delta \tilde{R} \tag{3.37}$$

where the real interest rate is represented by

$$\tilde{R} = R - \dot{p} \tag{3.38}$$

Substituting $\tilde{R}$ for $R - \dot{p}$ in (3.13) and (3.15) and taking discrete differences in the variables we obtain

$$\Delta\dot{p}(1 + \beta_1\mu\iota') = -\beta_1\mu\iota'\Delta\tilde{R} - (\beta_1\mu\varepsilon' + \beta_5\eta')\Delta a$$
$$- (\beta_1\mu\varkappa_1' - \beta_6)\Delta S - \beta_2\eta'\Delta a + \beta_3\Delta S \tag{3.39}$$

and

$$\Delta j = -\iota'(1 - \delta\mu)\Delta\tilde{R} - \varepsilon'(1 - \delta\mu)\Delta a + \delta\mu\varkappa_1'\Delta S \tag{3.40}$$

Then, using (3.37) to replace $\Delta\tilde{R}$ by $\Delta a/\sigma$ we obtain

$$\omega = \frac{\delta\Delta p/\delta\Delta S}{\delta\Delta p/\delta\Delta a} \bigg| \frac{\delta\Delta j/\delta\Delta S}{\delta\Delta j/\delta\Delta a}$$

$$= \frac{\beta_3 + \beta_6 - \beta_1\mu x_1'}{\delta\mu x_1'} \cdot \frac{(1 - \delta\mu)(\iota'/\sigma + \varepsilon')}{\beta_1\mu(\iota'/\sigma + \varepsilon') + (\beta_5 + \beta_2)\eta'} \quad (3.41)$$

$$= -\frac{1 - \delta\mu}{\delta\mu} \cdot \frac{\beta_1\mu x_1' - (\beta_3 + \beta_6)}{\beta_1\mu x_1' + \dfrac{(\beta_5 + \beta_2)\eta' x_1'}{\iota'/\sigma + \varepsilon'}}$$

We may analyse this expression in stages.

First ignore all cost-push effects of taxes, i.e. set $\beta_3 = \beta_6 = 0$ and ignore the effects of the interest rate on the exchange rate. Then the interest rate affects investment directly, but there is an offsetting effect arising from the fact that an interest rate increase reduces demand. This second-round effect offsets the initial fall in investment, because the reduction in imports (net foreign investment) is larger than the accelerator effect ($\delta = \eta' - \nu > 0$). The combined effect on investment is therefore $-(1 - \delta\mu)$, while the effect on inflation, which is not shown in the expression, is simply $-\beta_1\mu$. A tax increase, which reduces inflation by an amount $-\beta_1\mu$, will raise investment by an amount $\delta\mu$ because, once again, the effect of the fall in imports dominates the accelerator effect. The ratio of these two effects is therefore the value of the comparative advantage index. High values of both δ and μ reduce the comparative advantage of monetary policy in affecting investment because they enhance the effect of demand on investment.

With $\sigma > 0$ the effects of monetary policy on both investment and on inflation are augmented since an increase in interest rates reduces net exports ($\varepsilon' > 0$). But the relative influence on inflation is strengthened because costs and prices fall directly ($\beta_2 + \beta_5 > 0$). This lowers ω.

Thus the effects of high import leakages (high δ) and strong effects of interest rates on the exchange rate point in the same direction; the one reduces the ability of high interest rates to restrict investment and the other raises the ability of high interests rates to damp inflation. Both lower ω. Thus there is some presumption that, in an open economy, monetary policy will have a comparative advantage in fighting inflation.[13]

The presumption is strengthened given non-zero but moderate sizes of the cost-push effects, $\beta_3 + \beta_6$ of taxes on inflation. Their effect is to counteract the demand-pull effects of tax increases in damping inflation and so to strengthen the comparative advantage of monetary policy in dealing with inflation. These moderate effects raise ω towards zero. As they increase further they make ω positive and possibly even greater than one, giving cost-push fiscal policy the comparative advantage in fighting inflation.

3.8.4 A graphical representation of comparative advantage

We may plot ω against $\beta_3 + \beta_6$ in Figure 3.4. This shows that the pattern of comparative advantages is indeed sensitive to the parameters of the wage equation. It is an empirical question of how much ω increases as β_3 and β_6 rise to values consistent with our unreformed wage equation of Chapter 6 (equation 6.2). Our results of Chapter 6 suggest that, at least in the short term, with full wage indexation and the estimated value of β_6, ω may be greater than 1. The implication of this is that we should not expect to be able to find policy rules which work successfully in economies both with unindexed and with fully indexed wages.

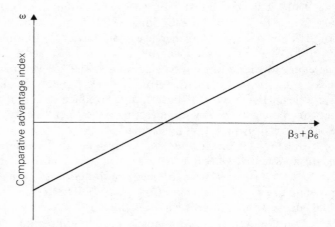

Figure 3.4   Comparative advantage index in our analytical model

3.8.5   Comparative advantage and the structure of policy rules

The structure of comparative advantage may be used as a guide in the design of economic policy rules. We do this in Chapter 6.

Long-term comparative advantage and integral components of policy rules

Long-term comparative advantage was discussed in section 3.8.2. As already noted we would expect this to be a guide to the choice of the integral components of policy rules. The former shows the relative emphasis which should be put on each of the policy instruments in removing completely disturbances to each of the policy targets. The latter show that direction and size of movements in the policy instruments which continue whenever the targets of policy are not attained: it is these components of the rules which ensure that the disturbances are in fact completely removed.

The first and obvious implication is that the relative sizes of the movements of each policy instrument dictated by the relative sizes of the integral components of the control rules should reflect the (absolute) magnitude, $|\omega|$, of the comparative advantage index. The signs, as well as the sizes of the instrument movements are problematic, because the size and sign of the effects of taxes on inflation cannot be specified *a priori*; it all depends on the size of the cost-push effects of tax increases.

In Figures 3.1 and 3.2 we identified four cases. Case (a) corresponded to $\omega < -1$. Case (b) represented $-1 < \omega < 0$. In case (c) $0 < \omega < 1$ and in case (d) $\omega > 1$. In Figures 3.1 and 3.2 we were discussing the long-term adjustments to S and a which were needed in response to a change in supply-side conditions or a change in the investment target. We may read off from the two sets of graphs the signs of changes in S and a which are needed in response to these disturbances. For example with $\omega < -1$, we see from Figure 3.1(a), that taxes rise and the exchange rate is reduced in response to a worsening of supply conditions leading to inflationary pressure. We read off, in the shift from $\bar{\beta}$ to $\bar{\beta}'$ the policy response to an adverse supply shift. In Figure 3.2 the response to investment being above target is represented by the shift from $j^{*\prime}$ to j^*. In order to bring down investment Figure 3.2(a) shows us that taxes are reduced and the real exchange rate must be raised. On the other hand, with $\omega > 1$, we see, in Figure 3.1(d) that both taxes and the real exchange rate are reduced in response to inflationary pressure. A reduction in the investment target (Figure 3.2(d)) requires higher taxes; the inflationary effects of these must be offset by a higher real exchange rate. These two cases, and the two intervening ones, with $-1 < \omega < 0$ and $0 < \omega < 1$, can be summarized in Table 3.2, which shows the signs of the adjustments in each case.

We have represented the inflationary shock in Table 3.2 by $\delta\bar{\beta}$. Changes to investment are shown as δj^*. A positive value of δj^* represents an excess of investment over its target value. In cases (a) and (b) Table 3.2 shows us that this is brought back to zero by means of tax

Table 3.2   Comparative advantage and instrument adjustment

$$\begin{bmatrix} \delta S \\ \delta a \end{bmatrix} = \begin{bmatrix} + & - \\ + & + \end{bmatrix} \begin{bmatrix} \delta \bar{\beta} \\ \delta j^* \end{bmatrix} \qquad\qquad \begin{bmatrix} \delta S \\ \delta a \end{bmatrix} = \begin{bmatrix} + & - \\ + & + \end{bmatrix} \begin{bmatrix} \delta \bar{\beta} \\ \delta j^* \end{bmatrix}$$

(a) $\omega < -1$ $\qquad\qquad\qquad\qquad$ (b) $-1 < \omega < 0$

$$\begin{bmatrix} \delta S \\ \delta a \end{bmatrix} = \begin{bmatrix} + & - \\ + & - \end{bmatrix} \begin{bmatrix} \delta \bar{\beta} \\ \delta j^* \end{bmatrix} \qquad\qquad \begin{bmatrix} \delta S \\ \delta a \end{bmatrix} = \begin{bmatrix} - & + \\ - & + \end{bmatrix} \begin{bmatrix} \delta \bar{\beta} \\ \delta j^* \end{bmatrix}$$

(c) $0 < \omega < 1$ $\qquad\qquad\qquad\quad$ (d) $1 < \omega$

cuts and an exchange-rate appreciation; in the other cases, however, the required adjustments change sign. A positive value of $\delta \bar{\beta}$, however, indicates the signs of the adjustments which would be needed to offset the consequences of an inflationary supply-side shift. The required adjustments change sign between cases (c) and (d).

Short-term comparative advantage and the proportional components of policy rules

Short-term comparative advantage was discussed in section 3.8.3. As already noted, we would expect this short-term comparative advantage to be a good guide to the choice of proportional components of policy rules. The former shows the relative emphasis which should be put on each of the policy instruments if it were desired to remove disturbances in a short period of time. The latter show the immediate movements in the policy instruments which the policy rules will cause as a result of such disturbances to the policy targets. It is these components of the rules which ensure that disturbances can be removed reasonably promptly, and we have found that the structure of short- to medium-term comparative advantage does help us to choose the structure of the proportional components of our policy rules.

As with our integral rules, the relative sizes of the proportional components of our policy rules should reflect the absolute magnitude of the comparative advantage index in the short to medium term. But we also need to determine the appropriate signs of the proportional components of the policy rules. An argument, analogous to that applied to Table 3.2, can be constructed. (Now the table is re-interpreted as showing the desired short- to medium-term adjustments in the policy targets, and the signs in the matrices show the required signs of the proportional components of the policy rules.) Depending on the size and sign of ω we can find exactly the same implications for the signs of the proportional components of the policy rules.

We return to this issue in Chapter 6, where we show empirically the connection between the pattern of comparative advantage and the structure of effective policy rules.

3.9 CONCLUSION

This chapter has allowed us to consider some aspects of economic policy in a dynamic context. The model which we have used has allowed us to emphasize the link between labour-market behaviour and the structure of economic policy rules which are dynamically stable. We have demonstrated that the long-run adjustments to taxes and the real exchange rate, which are needed after a permanent supply-side shock or a change in the investment target, depend crucially on the strength of cost-push relative to demand-pull terms in the wage equation. Looking at dynamic stability we conclude further that, once cost-push elements are present in the wage equation, there is an upper limit to the extent to which fiscal policy can be used to regulate inflation.

Our dynamic analysis indicated limits to the feasibility of fiscal control of inflation. We then looked at the pattern of comparative advantage and showed how, in both the short and the long term, this too depended on the magnitude of the cost-push terms. We studied the comparative advantage index, and found we were able to identify a link between this and the structure of policy rules. This is particularly helpful in assessing the proportional component of our policy rules and proves to be of empirical relevance in Chapter 6.

This chapter has not addressed the question of whether the wealth target poses problems of its own. Our *IS–LM* model was not capable of capturing any stock effects, but their absence from that model does not mean that they are unimportant. In the next two chapters we study the role of stock effects in the economy and the impact that they have on the stability of policy rules and on the effect of policy instruments on the economy.

Chapter Four

Wealth targets, stock instability and macroeconomic policy

4.1 INTRODUCTION

The previous chapter carried forward discussion of the linkages between the targets (inflation and national wealth) and the instruments (fiscal and monetary) of financial policy. In the context of a dynamic model we showed how the use of policy instruments was constrained by the balance between cost-push and demand-pull effects in wage determination. We also described the working of an exchange-rate intermediate target and investigated whether the way in which expectations were formed had an important bearing on our results.

This chapter continues our discussion of the working of policy rules in a dynamic context and introduces a new theme. We show that, if the accumulation of wealth is correctly modelled (which it was not in Chapter 3), a source of potential instability is introduced. Unless the policy rules take explicit account of the wealth target, the cumulation of property income is likely to make the economy completely unstable. We demonstrate that the pursuit of a target real exchange rate, as advocated by Williamson and Miller (1987), suffers from this fault, unless that target exchange rate is sufficiently flexible. We also demonstrate that control of inflation by monetary means will be unstable unless a suitable fiscal policy rule is adopted.

This so-called stock instability arises in the following way. Suppose that initially a country's budget is balanced at a rate of tax which covers all expenditure including the interest on the national debt; there is some exogenous rise in, say, government consumption of goods and services, but the tax rate is not changed. The resulting deficit adds to the national debt; the interest on the additional debt causes a further rise in expenditure which adds further to the national debt. In the absence of some offsetting stabilizing change a vicious spiral of debt accumulation may be triggered off. Another example is provided by the accumulation of foreign assets as a consequence of some exogenous rise in the demand for a country's exports. The resulting surplus on the current account leads to an increase in the country's foreign assets and so to receipts of interest. The interest receipts add to the surplus on the current account and so the holding of foreign assets builds up further. The process can continue *ad infinitum*. The possible resulting instability, and associated stabilizing factors, have been extensively investigated in closed economies (Blinder and Solow, 1973, Tobin and Buiter, 1976). For the open economy, Whittaker *et al.* (1986) present some computer simulations of an open-economy model which explores these effects; Obstfeld (1980) has also looked at some aspects of the problem, although in a model which neglects some crucial property income flows and valuation effects. Our model is most closely related to that presented by Sachs and Wyplosz (1984).

The purpose of this chapter is to illustrate stock instability by means of a simple analytical model. The construction of a model which is sufficiently simplified to investigate these issues analytically necessitates, as with the model used in the previous chapter, an heroic degree of simplification of a vast range of many other important dynamic relationships. The extent to which the results of this chapter are general rather than model-specific can be inferred only from a numerical analysis of an empirical model. Such an investigation is an essential part of our later work on policy design.

Accordingly, for this chapter, we make the following basic assumptions. First, we assume that there are no cost-push elements in the wage equation; the wage equation then simplifies to an expression showing that there is simply a 'full employment' level of real output and employment at which the rate of inflation of money wages is equal to the core rate of inflation.

Secondly, we assume, as in Chapters 2 and 3, in the control exercises discussed in this chapter, that the inflation control objective is to keep the rate of price inflation, rather than the level or rate of growth of Money GDP, stable. Thirdly, we assume that this objective is achieved continuously and instantaneously without any time lag.

The implication of these three assumptions about the workings of the wage-fixing mechanism and the control-of-inflation mechanism is that, by fiscal policy or by monetary policy, output and inflation are maintained at the 'full employment' level. This ensures that, in our controlled economy, money wages, money labour costs and so money prices all rise at the core rate of inflation.

The result is that in the control exercises in this chapter the spare limb of financial policy (i.e. monetary policy if fiscal policy is used to control inflation, and *vice versa*) can be freely used to achieve a wealth target.

We assume that this target is to keep the stock of real national wealth (or in our last exercise in this chapter, the real national debt) at some prescribed target level. As a result of the above assumptions a much simplified analysis of the control of national wealth can be carried out against a background of a constant level of real output and a fixed rate of inflation.

4.2   A STOCK-FLOW MODEL

Our basic model differs from that of the previous chapter in that it is additive rather than logarithmic. We make such a jump because we require additive properties in order properly to account for the cumulation of debt interest. The basic model is as follows:

4.2.1   Output, imports and exports

$$Y = C + G + X - M + \dot{K} \tag{4.1}$$

Net domestic product (Y) is the sum of private consumption, government consumption, exports and domestic investment, less the real value in terms of home products of expenditures on imports. It is assumed that there are no imported raw materials but that a constant proportion (η') of total domestic expenditure on finished products $(C + G + \dot{K})$ is spent on the import of such goods (M). Thus

$$M = \eta'(C + G + \dot{K}) = \eta'(Y - X + M) = \eta(Y - X)$$

where $\eta = \eta'/(1 - \eta')$ so that

$$X - M = (1 + \eta)X - \eta Y \tag{4.2}$$

The assumption that η' is constant implies that both the income and the price elasticities of demand for imports are unity. This assumption greatly simplifies that analysis since it implies that the proportion η', and thus the parameter η, is independent of the real terms of trade between the country's imports and exports

$$X = \bar{X} - \varepsilon_1 A \tag{4.3}$$

The real rate of exchange is measured as $A = EP/\overline{P}^F$, where E is the nominal exchange rate, P is the price of domestic output and $\overline{P}^F$ is the price of foreign output, which is assumed to be constant. It determines the volume of exports (X), a rise in E representing an appreciation of the domestic currency. There is no lag between a change in E and its effect on X, i.e. there is no J-curve effect.

4.2.2 Tax revenue

$$T = S(Y + [R - \dot{P}/P]U + \overline{R}^F H) \tag{4.4}$$

Total tax revenue (T) depends upon a rate of tax (S) levied on private incomes, which are the sum of income earned on home production, plus the interest yield on national debt and foreign assets held by the private sector. Since we are assuming perfect substitutability between home and foreign assets, there is no purpose to be served by intervention in the foreign exchange markets. Accordingly we assume that all foreign assets (H) are held by the private sector of the economy. We assume also that there are no foreign holdings of domestic assets, so that the whole of the national debt (U) is held in the private sector of the economy. H is a net figure of foreign assets less foreign liabilities. Both H and U are valued in real terms in units of home products, but it is assumed that H is denominated in foreign currency. At any given real terms of trade, the real return on H is the foreign rate of interest (since we assume that foreign prices measured in foreign currency are constant over time). The real rate of return on the national debt is, however, the domestic money rate of interest (R) less the rate of domestic price inflation $(\dot{P}/P)$. We assume that the tax authorities allow an inflation offset, so that they only tax the real yield on the national debt, and thereby treat it in the same way as foreign assets.

4.2.3 Consumption

$$C = \varkappa_1'(1 - S)\lambda Y + \varkappa_2(H + U + K) \tag{4.5}$$

We use a consumption function which distinguishes between consumption financed from wage-earned income and that financed from the enjoyment of capital assets. If a constant proportion (λ) of income from domestic production accrues to wages which are taxed at a rate (S) and if a constant proportion $(1 - \varkappa_1')$ of this net earned income is saved, then $\varkappa_1'(1 - S)\lambda Y$ measures consumption out of earnings. If an appropriate assumption is made about the spenders' utility function,[1] consumption out of unearned income can be treated as a constant proportion $(\varkappa_2)$ of the current value of the private sector's holding of assets $(H + U + K)$ regardless of the level of the rate of yield on the assets. This consumption function has the property that the national debt is regarded as net wealth. The model would be more complex if a rational expectations consumption function were used. However, unless agents were also assumed to have infinite horizons, the national debt would continue to influence net wealth (Blanchard, 1985), and we do not expect that the results would be much affected.

4.2.4   Investment

$$\dot{K} = \gamma_2(\nu Y - K) \tag{4.6}$$

Fixed investment depends positively on output but negatively on the existing stock of capital. This equation can be regarded as a continuous time expression of an accelerator relationship. It does not prove possible, in the simple model which we use in this chapter, to take account of forward-looking investment behaviour. We defer a discussion of the effects of this to the next chapter.

4.2.5   The output equation

From equations (4.1), (4.2), (4.3), (4.5) and (4.6) we can eliminate C, M, X, and $\dot{K}$ to obtain

$$Y = \mu_1\{\varkappa_2(H + U + K) - \varepsilon_2 A + G + (1 + \eta)\bar{X} - \gamma_2 K\} \tag{4.7}$$

where

$$\varepsilon_2 = (1 + \eta)\varepsilon_1 \text{ and } \mu_1 = 1/(1 - \lambda\varkappa_1'[1 - S] + \eta - \gamma_2\nu)$$

Thus μ_1 measures the open-economy Kahn–Keynes multiplier which, with our assumptions about the demand for imports, is independent of the rate of exchange and of the real terms of trade. For the multiplier to be positive we require that $1 + \eta - \gamma_2\nu - \lambda\varkappa_1'(1 - S) > 0$. Provided that the propensity to save is positive, this condition can only fail to hold if the accelerator coefficient is too large. In such circumstances the multiplier process would fail to converge and the economy would be unstable.

We add to equations (4.6) and (4.7) the following nine equations (4.8 – 4.16) to represent the other behavioural relationships and identities of the economy.

4.2.6 Net external wealth

$$\dot{H} = \bar{R}^F H + X - M - H\dot{A}/A$$
$$= (\bar{R}^F - \dot{A}/A)H - \varepsilon_2 A - \eta Y + (1 + \eta)\bar{X} \qquad (4.8)$$

An increase in the real value of the country's assets arises either from a revaluation of existing assets due to a change in the rate of exchange $(-H\dot{A}/A)$ or from any surplus on the country's balance of payments $(\bar{R}^F H - \varepsilon_2 A - \eta Y + [1 + \eta]\bar{X})$.

4.2.7 Financial markets

$$\dot{E}^e/E = \bar{R}^F - R \qquad (4.9)$$

We assume that there is perfect substitutability between domestic and foreign assets. As a consequence the expected change in the nominal exchange rate, $\dot{E}^e/E$, is equal to the difference between the domestic and foreign interest rates.

We assume that all the national debt is interest-bearing, and as a consequence our model, unlike that of Chapter 3, does not have an *LM* curve.

4.2.8 The national debt

$$\dot{U} = (R - \dot{P}/P)U + G - S(Y + [R - \dot{P}/P]U + \bar{R}^F H) \qquad (4.10)$$

The increase in national debt is the excess of real expenditure $([R - \dot{P}/P]U + G)$ over the sum of tax revenue. We assume that, since home and foreign assets are perfect substitutes, the government does not hold any foreign-exchange reserves; as a consequence the government receives no interest income.

4.2.9 The production function

$$L = Y \tag{4.11}$$

The amount of labour employed is proportional to the level of output, and we measure units of labour so that the constant of proportionality is unity. The supply of labour is taken as independent of the consumption wages, and so there is a recognizable level of output, $\bar{Y}$, at which the labour requirement, $\bar{L}$, is equal to full employment.

4.2.10 The labour market

The working of the labour market is assumed to be represented by a wage equation simpler than that used in Chapter 3. The equation is expressed with all variables in terms of levels rather than logarithms.

$$\dot{W}/W = \beta_2''(L - \bar{L})/\bar{L} + (\dot{P}/P)^* \tag{4.12}$$

Wages are shown as responding to excess demand, $(L - \bar{L})/\bar{L}$, and the core-target rate of increase in the cost of living, $(\dot{P}/P)^*$.

4.2.11 Domestic prices

$$P = (1 + \pi)W \tag{4.13}$$

Prices are set by a constant mark-up on costs. Since we have assumed that there are no intermediate imports, wages are the only component of domestic costs.

$$\dot{P}/P = \beta_9(Y - \bar{Y}) + (\dot{P}/P)^* \tag{4.14}$$

where $\beta_9 = \beta_2'' / \bar{Y}$

An equation linking changes in the price level to the deviation of output (Y) from its full employment level ($\bar{Y}$) can be found by using (4.11) to eliminate L and (4.13) to eliminate W from (4.12).

4.2.12   The terms of trade

$$\dot{A}/A = \dot{E}/E + \dot{P}/P \qquad (4.15)$$

With the real exchange rate given as $A = EP/\bar{P}^F$ and foreign prices constant, the proportional change in the real terms of trade is the sum of the proportional changes in the exchange rate and in domestic prices.

4.2.13   Policy instruments

$$R = ? \qquad (4.16)$$
$$G = ? \qquad (4.17)$$

Out of equilibrium, the home rate of interest and the rate of government spending depend upon the nature of the ruling policy regime. In this chapter we treat the level of government expenditure (G), rather than the rate of tax, as the fiscal control variable. This choice of fiscal variable has no basic economic significance in our present model in which the wage equation does not contain any cost-push factors.[2] But it eases the exposition and in particular avoids one problem of linearization in the use of the models.

4.2.14   Expectations

In this chapter we continue to consider two types of expectational mechanism for the nominal exchange rate. The first is that of model-consistent expectations:

$$\dot{E}^e = \dot{E} \qquad (4.18a)$$

The second type is the regressive mechanism which we have considered in Chapter 3:

$$\dot{E}^e/E = -\phi(\dot{E}/E + [\dot{P}/P]^*) - (\dot{P}/P)^* \qquad (4.18b)$$

Equation (4.18a) implies that real exchange rate expectations are also model-consistent. On the other hand, (4.18b) implies that the foreign exchange market has adaptive expectations of a regressive type about the nominal exchange rate. The adjustment for the core-target rate of inflation ensures that, when this inflation rate is achieved, the nominal exchange rate is expected to depreciate at this rate. If the core-target inflation rate is achieved in a steady state, expectations will be model-consistent.

4.2.15   The model as a whole

Using (4.11) and (4.13) to eliminate L and W from equations (4.6)–(4.10), (4.12) and (4.15)–(4.18), we are left with ten equations which describe our basic model as summarized in Table 4.1:

Table 4.1   A simple stock-flow model

$$Y = \mu_1\{x_2(H + U + K) - \varepsilon_2 A + G + (1 + \eta)\bar{X} - \gamma_2 K\} \tag{4.19a}$$

where $\mu_1 = 1/(1 - \lambda x_1[1 - S] + \eta - \gamma_2 \nu)$

$$\dot{K} = \gamma_2(\nu Y - K) \tag{4.19b}$$

$$\dot{H} = (\bar{R}^F - \dot{A}/A)H - \varepsilon_2 A - \eta Y + (1 + \eta)\bar{X} \tag{4.19c}$$

$$\dot{E}^e/E = \bar{R}^F - R \tag{4.19d}$$

$$\dot{U} = (R - \dot{P}/P)(1 - S)U + G - SY - S\bar{R}^F H \tag{4.19e}$$

$$\dot{P}/P = \beta_9(Y - \bar{Y}) + (\dot{P}/P)^* \tag{4.19f}$$

$$\dot{E}^e/E = \dot{E}/E \tag{4.19ga}$$

$$\dot{E}^e/E = -\phi(\dot{E}/E + [\dot{P}/P]^*) - (\dot{P}/P)^* \tag{4.19gb}$$

$$\dot{A}/A = \dot{E}/E + \dot{P}/P \tag{4.19h}$$

$$R = ? \tag{4.19i}$$

$$G = ? \tag{4.19j}$$

Where necessary, we linearize $\dot{A}/A$ by $\dot{A}/A_\infty$, $\dot{A}H/A$ by $\dot{A}H_\infty/A_\infty$, RU by $RU_\infty + R_\infty(U - U_\infty)$, and $U\dot{P}/P$ by $U_\infty(\dot{P}/P - [\dot{P}/P]_\infty)$ $+ (U - U_\infty)(\dot{P}/P)_\infty$, where A_∞, H_∞, U_∞, R_∞ and $(\dot{P}/P)_\infty$ are steady-state values of these variables.

These ten equations in the ten variables, Y, A, E, E^e, U, H, K, $\dot{P}/P$, G and R constitute the framework within which everything that follows is constructed.

4.3 POLICY REGIMES

In Chapter 3 we looked at three policy regimes. The first was a *laissez-faire* policy or an uncontrolled economy. We then looked at the role of either fiscal or monetary policy as a means of ensuring that a particular price target was achieved. We looked at a one-target-one-instrument problem, contenting ourselves with setting the spare policy instrument so as to achieve the investment target in the steady state.

In this chapter we conduct similar exercises. We first look at an uncontrolled economy. In our second and third regimes we distinguish between two cases where fiscal policy is used to control inflation. In our second regime the real exchange-rate target is held constant. We demonstrate that this is unstable, even if the level chosen for the fixed real exchange rate could deliver the desired wealth target in the steady state. In our third regime a target real exchange rate is so set as to achieve the desired wealth target in a manner which is stable.

We find in our fourth regime that the use of monetary policy to control inflation, while fiscal policy is inactive, is unstable. We describe a fifth regime in which fiscal policy is used to achieve the wealth target while monetary policy controls inflation. Our final regime has no real parallel with those of the previous chapter. We present a simple-minded regime in which monetary policy is used to control inflation, while fiscal policy is used to balance the budget. We do not study this sixth regime in our later investigation; it is included as a representation of a popular view of economic policy.

As in Chapter 3, we limit ourselves to simple proportional policy rules, and we assign each instrument to only one target. This framework is much simpler than the policy regimes which we adopt in practice, but it has two advantages. First, as we noted in Chapter 3, policy issues are often popularly debated on the assumption that only one instrument is assigned to a particular target. And secondly it does allow us to identify potential instability and to suggest certain minimum conditions which are necessary to remove that instability.

In summary, our six regimes are:

1. First we consider an uncontrolled economy, in which the nominal rate of interest and the level of government spending are fixed ($R = \bar{R}$, $G = \bar{G}$).
2. We now assume that fiscal policy is used to stabilize the rate of growth of Money GDP, and thus to hold the rate of inflation at the core rate ($\dot{P}/P = (\dot{P}/P)^*$). Monetary policy is used to hold the real exchange rate constant ($A = A^*$).

3. We retain the assumptions that fiscal policy is used to keep inflation at the core rate. However, we now assume that monetary policy (through the medium of a target real exchange rate) is used to bring national wealth ($N = H + K$) to a target value N^*.

4. Here we consider the use of monetary policy, again expressed through a target exchange rate, to keep inflation at its core rate ($\dot{P}/P = [\dot{P}/P]^*$). We take the level of government spending to be exogenous ($G = \bar{G}$).

5. The previous regime is extended. Monetary policy is once again used to control inflation ($\dot{P}/P = [\dot{P}/P]^*$). Fiscal policy is now used to bring national wealth to a target value ($H + K = N = N^*$).

6. Finally we assume that the budget is balanced, so that the national debt is always held to its initial value ($U = U_0$), by suitable use of fiscal policy. Monetary policy is used to keep inflation at its core rate ($\dot{P}/P = [\dot{P}/P]^*$).

In the next section we compare the steady states generated by these six policy regimes. We then continue to explore the stability properties of each successive regime.

4.4   THE STEADY STATES

A steady state is defined as one in which the rate of change of each real variable is zero, so that $\dot{K} = \dot{H} = \dot{U} = \dot{A} = 0$. We shall also assume that in any steady state the rate of inflation $(\dot{P}/P)_\infty$ must be equal to the core-target rate of inflation $(\dot{P}/P)^*$. If this were not the case, the economy would be in a situation in which the actual rate of inflation remained constant at a rate different from the expected core-target rate of inflation. Such a steady state would not be expected to persist, since in the end agents would alter their expectations to reflect reality.

With $\dot{A} = 0$ and $(\dot{P}/P)_\infty = (\dot{P}/P)^*$, we obtain from (4.19g) and (4.19h) $(\dot{E}^e/E)_\infty = -(\dot{P}/P)^*$. Substituting this value of $(\dot{E}^e/E)$ in (4.19d) and writing $\dot{K} = \dot{H} = \dot{U} = \dot{A} = 0$ we obtain from (4.19a) to (4.19f)

$$Y_\infty = \mu_1\{\varkappa_2(H_\infty + U_\infty) + (\varkappa_2 - \gamma_2)K_\infty - \varepsilon_2 A_\infty + G_\infty + (1 + \eta)\bar{X}\}$$

$$K_\infty = \nu Y_\infty$$

$$\varepsilon_2 A_\infty = \bar{R}^F H_\infty - \eta Y_\infty + (1 + \eta)\bar{X} \tag{4.20'}$$

$$R_\infty = \bar{R}^F + (\dot{P}/P)^*$$

$$SY_\infty = (R_\infty - [\dot{P}/P]^*)(1 - S)U_\infty - S\bar{R}^F H_\infty + G_\infty$$

$$Y_\infty = \bar{Y}$$

These equations can be rearranged as

$$Y_\infty = \bar{Y} \tag{4.20a}$$

$$K_\infty = \nu\,\bar{Y} \tag{4.20b}$$

$$R_\infty = \bar{R}^F + (\dot{P}/P)^* \tag{4.20c}$$

$$\varepsilon_2 A_\infty = \bar{R}^F H_\infty - \eta\,\bar{Y} + (1 + \eta)\,\bar{X} \tag{4.20d}$$

$$\bar{Y}(1/\mu_1 - [\varkappa_2 - \gamma_2]\nu - \eta) = (\varkappa_2 - \bar{R}^F)H_\infty + \varkappa_2 U_\infty + G_\infty \tag{4.20e}$$

$$S\,\bar{Y} = \bar{R}^F(1 - S)U_\infty + G_\infty - S\bar{R}^F H_\infty \tag{4.20f}$$

The six equations (4.20a–f) must all be satisfied in the steady state of our model, whether or not it is being controlled and irrespective of the regime with which it is being controlled. They describe the relationships between seven unknowns, namely Y_∞, K_∞, R_∞, A_∞, H_∞, U_∞ and G_∞. There is one missing equation which will, in each case, be provided by the specification of each particular regime as we come to discuss it.

But before any discussion of individual regimes, it is interesting to consider the general steady-state properties which, as described in (4.20a–f), are common to all the regimes of control or lack of control. There are three variables, namely Y_∞, K_∞ and R_∞, which will have the same value in all regimes. Somehow or other Y_∞ must be kept to $\bar{Y}$ (i.e. the level which brings the demand for labour into equality with its supply) if the rate of inflation of money costs and prices is to be kept equal to its expected rate, $(\dot{P}/P)^*$. Equation (4.19b), in which investment is determined solely by an accelerator effect, shows that the capital stock, K_∞, will remain unchanged only if it is equal to a fixed value, ν, of the level of output, $\bar{Y}$. This is expressed in (4.20b). With perfect substitutability between home and foreign assets, and with a constant unchanging expectation of change in the money exchange rate of $-(\dot{P}/P)^*$, the home rate of interest, R_∞, must be equal to $\bar{R}^F + (\dot{P}/P)^*$, giving (4.20c).

Equation (4.20d) expresses the relation between A_∞ and H_∞ which is necessary to keep the balance of payments in equilibrium in the steady state. If $\dot{H}$ is to be zero, the current account must balance. With Y constant at $\bar{Y}$, the volume of imports is determined. There remains only the balance between exports (determined by the real rate of exchange, $\varepsilon_2 A_\infty$) and the interest earned on foreign assets ($\bar{R}^F H_\infty$).

Equation (4.20e) is obtained by substituting for $\varepsilon_2 A_\infty$ and $\bar{Y}$ in the first equation of (4.20)'. It expresses the combination between the three variables, H_∞, U_∞ and G_∞, which somehow or another must be brought about in order to keep the demand for home-produced goods equal to the supply, $\bar{Y}$.

Equation (4.20f), which is obtained by substitution of the value of R_∞ into the last equation of (4.20)', expresses the combination between the three variables, H_∞, U_∞ and G_∞, which is necessary in order to keep government revenue equal to government expenditure, since a balanced budget in current account is needed if $\dot{U} = 0$.

It is interesting to examine the relationship between equations (4.20e) and (4.20f). Equation (4.20e) shows the combinations of G_∞, H_∞ and U_∞ which ensure that demand is equal to supply in the goods market. Higher values of H_∞ and U_∞ require a lower value of G_∞ because they raise the private demand for consumption goods. The effect of U_∞ is larger than that of H_∞, because a holding of foreign assets raises the steady-state exchange rate (4.20d) and so exerts a depressing effect on demand which goes some way to offsetting any stimulus from G_∞. However, provided that $\varkappa_2 > \bar{R}^F$ the stimulus is positive.

This condition states that the propensity to consume out of wealth should be larger than the steady-state (foreign) rate of interest. Since, in our model, consumers spend out of their wealth, but not out of the income earned on their wealth, it is, from the point of view of the nation as a whole, likely to be an important stability condition. If the propensity to consume out of wealth is larger than the rate of interest, then the wealth-consumption interaction, taken on its own, will be stable. If on the other hand the propensity to spend is below the rate of interest, then wealth will be accumulated faster than it is spent, and the wealth-consumption interaction, taken on its own, will be unstable. The precise nature of the condition (i.e. whether, as here, it is the interest rate gross, $\varkappa_2 > \bar{R}^F$, or, as later in the chapter, net of tax, $\varkappa_2 > \bar{R}^F(1 - S)$, which is relevant) depends on the configuration of the model, but the general importance of conditions of this type was first identified by Blinder and Solow (1973). Furthermore the condition identified here relates to a static economy. In a growing economy (Chapter 5) the condition relates to the interest rate net of the growth rate, and we then find that, empirically, the condition is met. Throughout this chapter we make the assumption that this condition holds, noting that, if $\varkappa_2 > \bar{R}^F$, then it follows that $\varkappa_2 > \bar{R}^F(1 - S)$. We refer to the condition as the Blinder–Solow condition. With $\varkappa_2 > \bar{R}^F$ and for given values of G_∞ we may plot the line of this equation in H_∞, U_∞ space. It is shown as AA' in Figure 4.1.

Secondly we may consider the condition for budget balance as expressed in (4.20f). This suggests that, for a given value of G_∞, a high value of U_∞ will require a high value of H_∞. The reason for this is that a high national debt requires service payments. If output and government consumption are fixed, then the only other source of revenue is tax on property income from abroad. A high level of foreign investment is

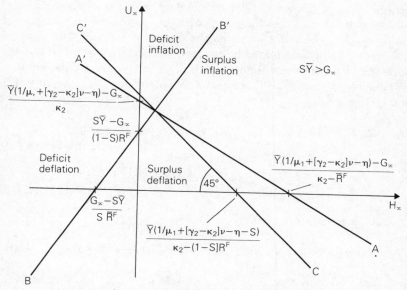

Figure 4.1   The steady state of our model

required to produce the tax revenue needed to service the national debt. For a given value of G_∞ we may plot the line BB' on Figure 4.1.

The intersection of these two lines determines the steady-state values of H_∞ and U_∞. While we defer the question of dynamic analysis until later, it is worth noting that, to the right of the AA' line, demand for goods exceeds supply and so there will be inflation, while to the left supply exceeds demand and so there is deflation. Above the BB' line there is a budget deficit, while below the line there is a budget surplus. However, these observations only hold for a given value of G_∞ and they do not form the basis of any policy prescriptions.

We may also calculate the combinations of H_∞ and U_∞ which ensure equilibrium for different values of G_∞. We are allowing G_∞ to vary, and calculating the set or locus of points $(U_\infty(G_\infty), H_\infty(G_\infty))$ to which this gives rise. We simply eliminate G_∞ between (4.20e) and (4.20f) to find that

$$H_\infty(G_\infty) + U_\infty(G_\infty) = Y_\infty(1/\mu_1 + [\gamma_2 - \varkappa_2]\nu - \eta - S)/(\varkappa_2 - [1 - S]\bar{R}^F)$$

$$(4.20g)$$

This locus of steady states, represented as CC' on the diagram, illustrates that, for a given value of Y_∞, there is one-for-one crowding out between foreign assets and the national debt. Since $N_\infty = H_\infty + K_\infty$ there is also one-for-one crowding out between national wealth and the national debt. The point at which the economy actually settles on the CC' locus can be determined by choice of (i) G_∞, (ii) H_∞ or (iii) U_∞, but once one of these three variables is fixed, the other two are determined.

Using (4.20e) and (4.20f) we may solve for H_∞ and U_∞ in terms of $\bar{Y}$ and G_∞:

$$H_\infty = G_\infty/\bar{R}^F + \bar{Y}\{(1/\mu_1 + [\gamma_2 - \varkappa_2]\nu - \eta)(1 - S)\bar{R}^F - \varkappa_2 S\}/$$
$$\bar{R}^F(\varkappa_2 - [1 - S]\bar{R}^F) \quad \text{(4.21a)}$$

$$U_\infty = - G_\infty/\bar{R}^F + \bar{Y}\{S\bar{R}^F(1/\mu_1 + [\gamma_2 - \varkappa_2]\nu - \eta - 1) + \varkappa_2 S\}/$$
$$\bar{R}^F(\varkappa_2 - [1 - S]\bar{R}^F) \quad \text{(4.21b)}$$

so that, as noted in (4.20g),

$$H_\infty + U_\infty = \bar{Y}(1/\mu + [\gamma_2 - \varkappa_2]\nu - \eta - S)/(\varkappa_2 - [1 - S]\bar{R}^F) \quad \text{(4.21c)}$$

and finally we note that $N_\infty = H_\infty + K_\infty$ and use (4.20b) to find national wealth:

$$N_\infty = G_\infty/\bar{R}^F + \bar{Y}\{(1/\mu_1 + [\gamma_2 - \varkappa_2]\nu - \eta)(1 - S)\bar{R}^F - \varkappa_2 S +$$
$$\nu(\varkappa_2 - [1 - S]\bar{R}^F)\bar{R}^F\}/\bar{R}^F(\varkappa_2 - [1 - S]\bar{R}^F) \quad \text{(4.21d)}$$

These expressions give H_∞, U_∞ and N_∞ in terms of G_∞, but they may of course be easily reversed so as to find the value of G_∞ which is permitted by a given value of H_∞, U_∞ or N_∞. It is also interesting to note that in all steady states, $U_\infty + H_\infty$ has the same value, given in (4.20g) regardless of the value of G_∞.

It should be stressed once again that these equations show steady-state relationships only. For example, from (4.21b) we see that a high level of government spending is associated with a low national debt. This is a necessary equilibrium condition because, other things being equal, a high debt-service burden competes with government spending for tax revenues. It does not mean that high government spending will necessarily cause a low national debt. An attempt to set out policy in that way might well be unstable.

The six policy regimes imply different ways of providing the missing equations discussed above. In all these regimes, as noted above, we assume that $Y_\infty = \bar{Y}$ and $(\dot{P}/P)_\infty = (\dot{P}/P)^*$. Otherwise there would have to be permanent money illusion in the labour market. This assumption has already provided one basic restriction. The other restriction depends very much on the regime in force. Table 4.2 shows the additional equation

Table 4.2   The policy regimes

Regime 1	$G_\infty = \bar{G}$
2	$A_\infty = A^*$
3	$H_\infty + K_\infty = N^*$
4	$G_\infty = \bar{G}$
5	$H + K_\infty = N^*$
6	$U_\infty = U_0$

needed together with the six equations of (4.20)' to determine the steady state for each regime.

4.4.1   Regimes 1 and 4: exogenous government spending

Regimes 1 and 4 will deliver the same steady state, though the dynamics of the regimes will be very different. In Regime 1 the rate of interest is set at the constant rate of $R_\infty = \bar{R}^F + (\dot{P}/P)^*$, since, as we have seen, this is the only rate consistent with an ultimate steady state. There is no assumption in Regime 1 that $\dot{P}/P$ remains constant at its steady-state value, during the process of dynamic adjustment. In Regime 4, on the other hand, it is assumed that, by means of a flexible monetary policy, $\dot{P}/P$ is kept constant and equal to $(\dot{P}/P)^*$. In both cases, however, G is set at an arbitrary value, $\bar{G}$, so that the steady-state values of H_∞, U_∞ and N_∞ are found very simply by replacing G_∞ by $\bar{G}$ in (4.21a, b and d). The steady-state real exchange rate is found by substituting for H_∞ in (4.20d). In these two regimes the equilibrium position on the CC' line of Figure 4.1 is determined by the choice of $\bar{G}$. Everything else follows from this.

4.4.2   Regime 2: a target real exchange rate

For Regime 2, with A set at an arbitrary value of A^*, it follows from (4.20d) that $H_\infty = \{\eta \bar{Y} - (1 + \eta)\bar{X} + \varepsilon_2 A^*\}/\bar{R}^F$. We put this value for H_∞ into (4.21c) so as to find

$$U_\infty = \bar{Y}(1/\mu_1 + [\gamma_2 - \varkappa_2]\nu - \eta - S)/(\varkappa_2 - [1 - S]\bar{R}^F)$$
$$- (\eta \bar{Y} - [1 + \eta]\bar{X} + \varepsilon_2 A^*)/\bar{R}^F \quad (4.22a)$$

and use this value of U_∞ in (4.21b) to solve for G_∞

$$G_\infty = \varepsilon_2 A^* - (1 + \eta)\bar{X} + \eta \bar{Y} -$$
$$\bar{Y}\{(1/\mu_1 + [\gamma_2 - \varkappa_2]\nu - \eta)(1 - S)\bar{R}^F - \varkappa_2 S\}/(\varkappa_2 - \bar{R}^F[1 - S]) \quad (4.22b)$$

This result indicates that a high target real exchange rate will be associated with a high level of foreign assets, a low national debt and high government spending. Once again we stress that this comparative static result does not mean that the fixing of a high target real exchange rate will automatically lead to these desirable outcomes. The regime may not be stable.

4.4.3   Regimes 3 and 5: a wealth target and controlled inflation

In both Regimes 3 and 5 the target for national wealth ($N^* = H_\infty + K_\infty$) is assumed to be met, and we can derive the steady-state holding of foreign assets as $H_\infty = N^* - K_\infty = N^* - \nu\bar{Y}$.

The steady-state exchange rate is then given by substituting for H_∞ into (4.20d) as

$$A_\infty = \{\bar{R}^F(N^* - \nu\bar{Y}) - \eta\bar{Y} + (1 + \eta)\bar{X}\}/\varepsilon_2 \qquad (4.23a)$$

We now have to find the values of G_∞ and U_∞. We may take (4.22a and b) and replace A^* by the value given in (4.23a) so as to find the steady-state values of G and U which are produced by cases 3 and 5.

This gives

$$U_\infty = \frac{\bar{Y}(1/\mu_1 - S + \nu\gamma_2 - \eta - \bar{R}^F\nu[1 - S])}{\varkappa_2 - \bar{R}^F[1 - S]} - N^* \qquad (4.23b)$$

$$G_\infty = \frac{\bar{Y}\{\nu\bar{R}^F(\bar{R}^F[1 - S] - \varkappa_2 S) + \varkappa_2 S - (1 - S)\bar{R}^F(1/\mu_1 + \nu\gamma_2 - \eta)\}}{\varkappa_2 - \bar{R}^F(1 - S)} + N^*\bar{R}$$

$$(4.23c)$$

The main difference between these and Regime 2 is that there the steady-state real exchange rate determined the level of national wealth, whereas now the level of national wealth determines the steady-state real exchange rate.

These results also illustrate points which can be seen in (4.21a–d). In particular we observe once again crowding out between the steady-state national debt and steady-state national wealth (4.23b). We also see that the property income earned on incremental national wealth (4.23c) is entirely used for public sector consumption. The reason for this is quite straightforward. The private sector is indifferent between national debt and national wealth. Private consumption will not be affected if one unit of national wealth displaces one unit of national debt. The government will save a service charge net of tax of $(1 - S)\bar{R}^F$. But in addition it earns incremental tax revenue of $S\bar{R}^F$ on the incremental national wealth. So net government income rises by an amount $\bar{R}^F$ per unit of incremental national wealth. For the budget to be balanced at a constant tax rate, this must all be spent on consumption goods.

4.4.4   Regime 6: a balanced budget and controlled inflation

Finally we may investigate the steady state which is generated by a policy of balancing the budget. We define a balanced budget to be a situation in which the national debt is always equal to its initial value, $U = U_0$. In the steady state this implies that $U_\infty = U_0$. We may insert the exogenous value of U, U_0, into (4.21b, c) to find the resulting values of G_∞ and H_∞:

$$G_\infty = \{ \bar{Y}S(\varkappa_2 + \bar{R}^F[1/\mu_1 + (\gamma_2 - \varkappa_2)\nu - \eta - 1])/(\varkappa_2 - \bar{R}^F[1 - S])\} - \bar{R}^F U_0 \tag{4.24a}$$

$$H_\infty = \{ \bar{Y}(1/\mu_1 + [\gamma_2 - \varkappa_2]\nu - \eta - S)/(\varkappa_2 - \bar{R}^F[1 - S])\} - U_0 \tag{4.24b}$$

with

$$N_\infty = H_\infty + \nu\bar{Y} \tag{4.24c}$$

This result shows, once more, one-for-one crowding out between the national debt and net foreign assets (and therefore between the national debt and national wealth). It also illustrates that, once the crowding out effects are taken into account, the burden of the national debt (as a constraint on the level of government spending) depends on the interest rate gross rather than net of tax. The reason for this is very simple. It is exactly analogous to the result of the previous section. One-for-one crowding out means that the tax earned on interest payments on the national debt is exactly offset by tax receipts lost on the foreign wealth which has been crowded out. When this is taken into account, the overall tax burden is measured by the interest burden gross of tax.

4.4.5   A summary of the steady states

These results illustrate, yet again, that, in an economy with two instruments, monetary and fiscal policy, and two targets, inflation and a wealth target, the steady states do not depend on the routes adopted so as to reach those targets, and therefore do not depend on the policy rules.

In cases 1 and 4 we had an exogenous level of government spending rather than a wealth target. These two regimes gave the same steady state with the same rate of interest. The regime with an exogenous real exchange rate again had to take the level of national wealth as endogenous. The other three regimes all used wealth targets. In 3 and 5 these were targets for national wealth, while in 6 there was a target value for the national debt. However, since there is one-for-one crowding out between the national debt and national wealth, a target could be adopted expressed in terms of either variable.

We turn next to an examination of the dynamic properties of these various regimes.

4.5   REGIME 1: THE UNCONTROLLED ECONOMY

We note from (4.20c) that a steady state with $Y = \bar{Y}$ and $\dot{P}/P = (\dot{P}/P)^*$ can be reached only if $\bar{R}$ has been set at $\bar{R} = \bar{R}^F + (\dot{P}/P)^*$. We now assume that $\bar{R}$ has been set at this level and that G has been set at an arbitrary constant level, $\bar{G}$. We then test whether the system will converge to the steady state. This gives the following dynamic equations for the uncontrolled economy. From (4.19d) with $\bar{R} = \bar{R}^F + (\dot{P}/P)^*$ we obtain $\dot{E}^e/E = -(\dot{P}/P)^*$, so from (4.19ga) or (4.19gb) we obtain $\dot{E}^e/E = -(\dot{P}/P)^*$. Using this value of $(\dot{E}/E)$ in (4.19h), we obtain

$$\dot{A}/A = \dot{P}/P - (\dot{P}/P)^* \tag{4.25a}$$

From (4.19a) we obtain

$$Y = \mu_1 \varkappa_2 (H + U) + \mu_1 (\varkappa_2 - \gamma_2)K - \mu_1 \varepsilon_2 A + \text{constants} \tag{4.25b}$$

From (4.19b), using (4.25b) to eliminate Y, we obtain

$$\dot{K} = -\gamma_2(1 - \mu_1 \nu [\varkappa_2 - \gamma_2])K + \gamma_2 \nu \mu_1 \varkappa_2 (H + U) - \gamma_2 \nu \mu_1 \varepsilon_2 A + \text{constants} \tag{4.25c}$$

From (4.19f) using linearized (4.25a) and (4.25b) to eliminate $(\dot{P}/P)$ and Y, we obtain

$$\dot{A} = \beta_9 \{\mu_1 \varkappa_2 (H + U) + \mu_1 (\varkappa_2 - \gamma_2)K - \mu_1 \varepsilon_2 A\}A_\infty + \text{constants} \tag{4.25d}$$

From linearized (4.19c), using (4.25b) and (4.25d) to eliminate Y and $\dot{A}/A$, we obtain

$$\dot{H} = -\mu_1(\varkappa_2 - \gamma_2)(\eta + \beta_9 H_\infty)K + (\bar{R}^F - \mu_1\varkappa_2[\eta + \beta_9 H_\infty])H$$
$$-\mu_1\varkappa_2(\eta + \beta_9 H_\infty)U - \varepsilon_2(1 - \mu_1[\eta + \beta_9 H_\infty])A + \text{constants} \qquad (4.25e)$$

From linearized (4.19e), using (4.25b) and (4.19f) to eliminate Y and $\dot{P}/P$, we obtain

$$\dot{U} = \{(1 - S)\bar{R}^F - \mu_1\varkappa_2(S + [1 - S]\beta_9 U_\infty)\}U$$
$$- \{S\bar{R}^F + \mu_1\varkappa_2(S + [1 - S]\beta_9 U_\infty)\}H$$
$$-\mu_1(\varkappa_2 - \gamma_2)(S + [1 - S]\beta_9 U_\infty)K + \mu_1\varepsilon_2(S + [1 - S]\beta_9 U_\infty)A + \text{constants}$$
$$(4.25f)$$

These equations (4.25c–f) can be set out in matrix form, in order to allow us to investigate the stability of the system.

$$
\begin{bmatrix} \dot{K} \\ \dot{H} \\ \dot{U} \\ \dot{A} \end{bmatrix} =
\begin{bmatrix}
-\gamma_2(1 - \mu_1\nu[\varkappa_2 - \gamma_2]) & \gamma_2\nu\mu_1\varkappa_2 \\
-\mu_1(\varkappa_2 - \gamma_2)(\eta + \beta_9 H_\infty) & (\bar{R}^F - \mu_1\varkappa_2[\eta + \beta_9 H_\infty]) \\
-\mu_1(\varkappa_2 - \gamma_2)\tilde{S}_\infty & -(S\bar{R}^F + \mu_1\varkappa_2\tilde{S}_\infty) \\
\beta_9 A_\infty\mu_1(\varkappa_2 - \gamma_2) & \beta_9 A_\infty\mu_1\varkappa_2
\end{bmatrix}
$$

$$
\begin{bmatrix}
\gamma_2\nu\mu_1\varkappa_2 & -\gamma_2\nu\mu_1\varepsilon_2 \\
-\mu_1\varkappa_2(\eta + \beta_9 H_\infty) & -\varepsilon_2(1 - \mu_1[\eta + \beta_9 H_\infty]) \\
\{(1 - S)\bar{R}^F - \mu_1\varkappa_2\tilde{S}_\infty\} & \mu_1\varepsilon_2\tilde{S}_\infty \\
\beta_9 A_\infty\mu_1\varkappa_2 & -\beta_9 A_\infty\mu_1\varepsilon_2
\end{bmatrix}
\begin{bmatrix} \dot{K} \\ \dot{H} \\ \dot{U} \\ \dot{A} \end{bmatrix} \qquad (4.26)
$$

$$+ \text{constants}$$

where $\tilde{S}_\infty = S + [1 - S]\beta_9 U_\infty$. It is to be noted that since (4.25a) is valid whether expectations are model-consistent or adaptive, these equations remain unchanged however expectations are formed.

If expectations were model-consistent, we would expect there to be one unstable root in the above matrix. We would then be able to make the conventional assumption that the real exchange rate 'jumps' so as to clear that unstable root, with the implication that the model then converges along a saddlepath to the equilibrium values found above.

It is not easy to find analytically the roots of the matrix. However, the product of the roots is equal to the determinant. A negative determinant indicates that there are either one or three unstable roots, and so a necessary condition for there to be the one unstable root is that the determinant of the matrix is negative.

The determinant of the matrix turns out to be

$$\gamma_2 \beta_9 A_\infty \mu_1 \{\varepsilon_2 \bar{R}^F([1-S]\bar{R}^F - \varkappa_2)\}$$

This is unambiguously negative, provided that the post-tax home real rate of interest, $\bar{R}^F(1-S)$, is smaller than the propensity to consume out of wealth, $\varkappa_2$. We have already noted the importance of this 'Blinder–Solow' condition, and note that we expect it to be fulfilled in practice.

Even if our model is saddlepath stable with model-consistent expectations (and we have just demonstrated that a necessary condition for this is accepted), it remains the case that the price level is, as in section 3.4, indeterminate. This indeterminacy raises one objection to an attempt at *laissez-faire* economic policy.

As already noted, the model will also be described by equations (4.25a–f) when expectations are adaptive. The dynamic properties do not depend on the way in which expectations are formed. The determinant is still negative, indicating that there are either one or three unstable roots. With model-consistent expectations this did not exclude the possibility that the economy could be saddlepath stable, but with adaptive expectations we must reject saddlepath stability as a satisfactory solution. The economy is then unstable.

We may draw useful comparisons between these results and our study of the behaviour of the uncontrolled economy in section 3.4, where we neglected stock effects. In both cases we found that the number of unstable roots in the system did not depend on the way in which expectations were assumed to be formed. In Chapter 3 there were no unstable roots; the economy was overstable with model-consistent expectations and stable with adaptive expectations. Our model in this chapter serves to demonstrate that stock effects can introduce instability, giving us either one or three extra unstable roots. With model-consistent expectations the economy could now be saddlepath stable, and with adaptive expectations it will not be stable. In any case an attempt to analyse policy on a model which neglected stock effects could be very misleading.

In the remainder of this chapter we look at the question of stability on the assumption that the authorities pursue active control of Money GDP. Having investigated the uncontrolled economy, we move on to investigate the remaining regimes of section 4.3, beginning with the fiscal control of inflation and a target real exchange rate.

4.6   REGIME 2: FISCAL CONTROL OF INFLATION AND A FIXED REAL EXCHANGE RATE

In this section we investigate a form of control similar to the Williamson–Miller (1987) proposal, in which fiscal policy is used to control inflation and monetary policy to maintain the real exchange rate at a predetermined target level.

From (4.19f) it can be seen that stabilization of price inflation at the target-core rate, $(\dot{P}/P)^*$, involves keeping $Y = \bar{Y}$, and from (4.19a) it can be seen that this implies adjusting government expenditure (G) so as to maintain

$$G = \bar{Y}/\mu_1 - \varkappa_2(H + U) - (\varkappa_2 - \gamma_2)K + \varepsilon_2 A^* - (1 + \eta)\bar{X} \quad (4.27)$$

where A^* is the chosen level of the fixed real exchange rate.

The real exchange rate is assumed to be maintained at this given target level in the following way. The money rate of interest is raised or lowered by means of the rule (4.28) according to whether the real exchange rate is below or above its target value.

$$\dot{R} = \chi_4(A^* - A) \quad (4.28)$$

If we let the control parameter, χ_4, tend to infinity, we then find that $A = A^*$, so that $\dot{A} = 0$. With $\dot{A} = 0$ and $\dot{P}/P = (\dot{P}/P)^*$ we obtain from (4.19h) $\dot{E}/E = -(\dot{P}/P)^*$, so that from (4.19g) $\dot{E}^e/E = -(\dot{P}/P)^*$. Thus from (4.19d) the rate of interest which delivers $A = A^*$ is in fact $R = \bar{R}^F + (\dot{P}/P)^*$.

With Y maintained at $\bar{Y}$ through fiscal policy and A at A^* through monetary policy, and with the value of G as given in (4.27), we can use (4.19b), (4.19c) and (4.19d) to derive the following equations for $\dot{K}$, $\dot{H}$ and $\dot{U}$ in this partially controlled economy.

$$\dot{K} = \gamma_2(\nu \bar{Y} - K) \quad (4.29a)$$

$$\dot{H} = \bar{R}^F H - \varepsilon_2 A^* - \eta \bar{Y} + (1 + \eta)\bar{X} \quad (4.29b)$$

$$\dot{U} = -(\varkappa_2 - [1 - S]\bar{R}^F)U - (\varkappa_2 + S\bar{R}^F)H \\ - (\varkappa_2 - \gamma_2)K + \bar{Y}(1/\mu_1 - S) + \varepsilon_2 A^* - (1 + \eta)\bar{X} \quad (4.29c)$$

The roots of these three equations can be observed directly. (4.29a) implies that there is a root of $-\gamma_2$ since no endogenous variable except K

enters the equation. For the same reason we can observe, from (4.29b) a root of $\bar{R}^F$. The third root of the model is then given as the coefficient of the term in U in equation (4.29c); this third root is therefore $-(\varkappa_2 - [1 - S]\bar{R}^F)$. This system is much simpler than that describing the uncontrolled economy because output is held constant. This means both that the rate of inflation is constant, so that price dynamics can be neglected, and that the rate of change of the capital stock depends only on its existing level. It greatly simplifies the structure of the dynamic system. A great deal of complexity would be introduced if either $\dot{H}$ or $\dot{K}$ depended on the domestic real interest rate.

We can immediately deduce that the first root is unambiguously stable, while the second root is unambiguously unstable. The third root is stable provided that the propensity to consume out of wealth, $\varkappa_2$, is larger than the real post-tax rate of interest on the national debt, $(1 - S)\bar{R}^F$. We have already, in section 4.4, assumed this to be the case.

It also follows from (4.29b) that the unstable root, $\bar{R}^F$, can be removed if A^* is equal to $(\bar{R}^F H_0 - \eta \bar{Y} + [1 + \eta]\bar{X})\varepsilon_2$. Unless the exchange rate is initially at a level at which the current account deficit is zero, foreign assets, and so national wealth, will either decline or grow without limit and the current account will also be cumulatively unstable.

It is worth noting that if we combine (4.29b) and (4.29c) to give an equation in $H + U$ we can find a stable solution for $H + U$. For

$$\dot{H} + \dot{U} = -(\varkappa_2 - [1 - S]\bar{R}^F)(H + U) - (\varkappa_2 - \gamma_2)K + \bar{Y}(1/\mu_1 - \eta - S)$$

$$(4.30a)$$

The term in K can be neglected, since neither H nor U enter into (4.29a), and so the root can be identified as $-(\varkappa_2 - [1 - S]\bar{R}^F)$, which we take to be negative. The steady-state value for K_∞ is $K_\infty = \nu\bar{Y}$ and so

$$H_\infty + U_\infty = \bar{Y}(1/\mu_1 - \eta - S - \nu[\varkappa_2 - \gamma_2])/(\varkappa_2 - [1 - S]\bar{R}^F) \quad (4.30b)$$

as already noted in (4.21c). We infer from this that the private sector can happily settle at an equilibrium in which its wealth, $K_\infty + H_\infty + U_\infty$, is stable, although the wealth of the nation, $K_\infty + H_\infty$ is unstable.

This paradoxical result can be understood in the following way. Suppose we start in a steady state with the real exchange rate set at a level at which the country's international payments are in balance on current account. Suppose that the real exchange rate is then fixed at a somewhat higher level so that the country's trade balance is worsened, leading to a deficit in the international current account, which starts to grow at a cumulative rate because of the loss of foreign assets. A demand-pull deflation will threaten. Government spending will be raised to the rate needed to offset the fall in private expenditure. Rising government spending will lead to a rising budget deficit, and thus to a rising rate of increase in the national debt. A point will come at which government expenditure is at a sufficiently high level for the budget deficit, and thus the rate of rise in the national debt, to be as high as the rate of fall in the private sector's holding of foreign assets. At this point the private sector's holding of all assets, and thus its expenditure out of capital wealth, will be constant. The government will have a budget deficit leading to the issue of additional national debt which is just as great as the private sector's loss of foreign assets. U will be rising as rapidly as H is falling, with G at a constant level. With home and foreign assets perfect substitutes for each other, the government is now producing more assets (national debt) and the foreigners are providing fewer assets for the private sector to hold.

A depreciation of the real exchange rate would reduce the deficit in the country's balance of payments on current account, by improving the trade balance. The government would then need to reduce its real consumption of goods (G) (or to restrict the private sector's real consumption by a rise in taxation) in order to offset the demand-pull inflationary effect of the improvement in the trade balance. To this extent the country would be stopping the loss of its foreign capital wealth by a restriction of either private or government consumption.

But unless the real rate of exchange is set at the level which will reduce the current account surplus to zero, there will be an unstable cumulative effect on the government's holding of assets, and on the composition of the private sector's holding of assets. Even if the real exchange rate has originally been set at this equilibrium level, any accidental change in H or in the trade balance will set in motion this cumulative instability. We conclude from this that a partial control of the Williamson–Miller type, with fiscal policy devoted to the control of inflation and monetary policy to the maintenance of a given real exchange rate, is likely to be unstable. This is true for any target real exchange rate, including what Williamson calls the 'Fundamental Equilibrium Exchange Rate'.

There are a number of ways in which the instability could be removed. One would be to abandon all hope of using fiscal policy in the manner suggested by Williamson and Miller, using it instead to ensure that the stock instability is suppressed. We consider this in section 4.9 of this chapter. An alternative, closer to the spirit of exchange-rate stabiliz-ation, is to investigate whether there may be some stabilizing rule by which the real exchange rate could be set. This would still be in keeping with the spirit of real exchange-rate stabilization but would also succeed in removing the instability to national wealth arising from interest payments on foreign assets. We investigate this in the next section.

4.7 REGIME 3: FISCAL CONTROL OF INFLATION AND MONETARY CONTROL OF NATIONAL WEALTH

In the previous section we have shown that a policy of stabilizing the real exchange rate at a constant level is not stable and therefore not sustainable. In this section we investigate the active use of a policy rule for the real exchange rate as a means of removing stock instability. This rule is run in tandem with the same fiscal policy as that considered in the previous section, namely, one designed to hold the rate of price inflation to its core-target value, as described in the previous section.

First, as in the previous section,

$$G = \overline{Y}/\mu_1 - \varkappa_2(H + U) - (\varkappa_2 - \gamma_2)K + \varepsilon_2 A - (1 + \eta)\overline{X} \qquad (4.31)$$

provides a rule for government spending which keeps $Y = \overline{Y}$ and so $\dot{P}/P = (\dot{P}/P)^*$.

Now we set a target exchange rate with reference to the deviation of national wealth $(H + K = N)$ from its target value (N^*)[3]

$$A^* = \chi_5(H + K - N^*) + A_\infty \qquad (4.32)$$

and we assume, for simplicity, that the interest rate rule, (4.28), is used with infinite gain, so as to keep $A = A^*$. We then find, by differentiating the equation for A^*, that

$$\dot{A} = \chi_5(\dot{H} + \dot{K}) \qquad (4.33)$$

Substituting for $A = A^*$ from (4.32) and for $\dot{A}$ from (4.33) into linearized (4.19c) we obtain

$$\dot{H} = \overline{R}^{\mathrm{F}}H - \chi_5 H_\infty(\dot{H} + \dot{K})/A_\infty - \eta\overline{Y} + (1 + \eta)\overline{X}$$
$$- \varepsilon_2\chi_5(H + K - N^*) - \varepsilon_2 A_\infty$$

or

$$\dot{H} = \frac{(\overline{R}^{\mathrm{F}} - \varepsilon_2\chi_5)H - \eta\overline{Y} + (1 + \eta)\overline{X} - \varepsilon_2\chi_5(K - N^*) - \chi_5 H_\infty\dot{K}/A_\infty - \varepsilon_2 A_\infty}{1 + \chi_5 H_\infty/A_\infty}$$

$$(4.34)$$

We also have equation (4.19b) for $\dot{K}$, which is unchanged:

$$\dot{K} = \gamma_2(\nu\overline{Y} - K) \qquad (4.35)$$

Two of the roots of the system may be determined from the two equations (4.34) and (4.35). The root, $-\gamma_2$, is unchanged from the previous section, since H and U do not enter into the equation for $\dot{K}$. It is also true that U does not enter into the equation for $\dot{H}$, because the policy of stabilizing Y at $\bar{Y}$ offsets the accelerator and wealth effects which were present in the uncontrolled economy. It then follows that a second root of the system is identified as the coefficient of the term in H in the equation for $\dot{H}$. This root is

$$(\bar{R}^F - \varepsilon_2\chi_5)/(1 + \chi_5 H_\infty/A_\infty)$$

and for the controlled economy to be stable it must be negative. A_∞ is undoubtedly positive. With $H_\infty > 0$, the root is negative provided that $\chi_5 > \bar{R}^F/\varepsilon_2$. If the target real exchange rate is held constant, then the effect of property income means that, if $\dot{H} > 0$, then $\dot{H}$ is rising because H is increasing. With our proportional control rule, the exchange rate is rising if $\dot{H} > 0$. This rising exchange rate has the effect of reducing $\dot{H}$. Our condition for a negative root says that the rule must be sufficiently powerful for the effect of the rising exchange rate to dominate that of the property income. If it is large enough for $\dot{H}$ to be negative when H is above H_∞, then the stock instability will be removed. This will be true provided that the rate of adjustment of the exchange-rate target is correcting the balance of payments at a rate faster than interest payments are worsening it. As a corollary, if $\chi_5 = 0$, which was the case considered in the previous section, the economy is unstable.

These conclusions appear to be reversed if $H_\infty < 0$ and χ_5 is sufficiently large to result in $1 + \chi_5 H_\infty/A_\infty$ being negative. This reversal happens because the valuation effect of a change in the exchange rate on interest payments is sufficiently large to result in a depreciation worsening the current balance of payments, despite the fact that it improves the balance of trade. The issue is discussed in more detail by Christodoulakis, Meade and Weale (1987), and we merely note here that we regard it as unlikely that a sufficiently negative value of H_∞ would be found in practice.

We have shown that the stock instability of the previous section can be cured if a flexible rather than a rigid target exchange rate is adopted, and have identified a sufficient condition for that flexibility. These results hold independently of the way in which expectations are formed. The reason for this is that the exchange rate target rule defines the actual movement of the real exchange rate and, in our simple model, the home interest rate needed to ensure this movement enters into neither the equation for $\dot{K}$ nor that for $\dot{H}$. However, the home interest rate inevitably enters into the equation for $\dot{U}$, since interest payments on the national debt depend on this home rate of interest. The equation for $\dot{U}$ will therefore depend on the way in which expectations are formed.

When expectations are model-consistent, we have from (4.19ga, h) and (4.19d)

$$(R - \dot{P}/P) = \bar{R}^F - \dot{A}/A \qquad (4.36)$$

If we substitute for $(R - \dot{P}/P)$ from (4.36), and for G from (4.31) into linearized equation (4.19e), and then substitute for $A = A^*$ and for $\dot{A}$ from (4.32) and (4.33), we obtain

$$\dot{U} = -(\varkappa_2 - [1 - S]\bar{R}^F)U - (\varkappa_2 + S\bar{R}^F - \varepsilon_2\chi_5)H - (\varkappa_2 - \gamma_2 - \varepsilon_2\chi_5)K$$
$$- \chi_5(1 - S)U_\infty(\dot{H} + \dot{K})/A_\infty + (\bar{Y}(1/\mu_1 - S) - \varepsilon_2\chi_5N^* - (1 + \eta)\bar{X} + \varepsilon_2 A_\infty \qquad (4.37)$$

If expectations are adaptive (4.36) is replaced by $(R - \dot{P}/P) = \bar{R}^F + \phi\dot{A}/A$ (since $\dot{P}/P = [\dot{P}/P]^*$). The only change to (4.37) is that the term

$$- \chi_5(1 - S)U_\infty(\dot{H} + \dot{K})/A_\infty$$

is replaced by the term

$$\phi\chi_5(1 - S)U_\infty(\dot{H} + \dot{K})/A_\infty.$$

In both these cases the fact that U does not enter into the equations for $\dot{K}$ and $\dot{H}$ means that the third root can be identified from the coefficient of U alone. This root can therefore be read off as

$$-(\varkappa_2 - [1 - S]\bar{R}^F)$$

and is also independent of the way in which expectations are formed. We have already noted that we expect the propensity to consume out of wealth to be larger than the real post-tax rate of interest in the steady state, and that this root, which is minus the difference between the two, will therefore normally be negative.

We therefore conclude that the problem of stock instability, encountered in an economy with a fixed real rate of exchange and a fiscal policy used to control Money GDP, can be avoided if the fixed real rate of exchange is replaced by a real exchange rate which is adjusted rapidly enough in response to a deviation in wealth from its target value. This demonstrates one of the main issues considered in this chapter. A regime with fiscal control of Money GDP and a real exchange-rate target will be unstable unless that target is flexible enough.

4.8   REGIME 4: MONETARY CONTROL OF INFLATION

So far we have assumed that fiscal policy is used to control price inflation. We now assume that monetary policy rather than fiscal policy is used to control inflation. We do not, at this stage, attempt to use fiscal policy for any defined control purpose. Instead government expenditure is held at a constant value $\bar{G}$. No attempt is made to regulate national wealth.

The absence of any restriction on fiscal policy places this exercise in the tradition of the analysis of monetary policy in an open economy (Dornbusch, 1976, Buiter and Miller, 1982). The fact that here monetary policy works through the exchange rate and the exchange rate is used to manipulate inflation is in one sense a detail. Like our study in section 3.6, this is part of the family of analyses in which monetary policy controls inflation and fiscal policy is not used.

Monetary policy takes the following form. The rate of interest is adjusted in the manner described by (4.27) so as to keep the real exchange rate, A, at a given target level, A^*. This target level is adjusted so as to control the rate of price inflation, being raised or lowered according to whether the rate of price inflation exceeds or falls short of its target-core level. With $A = A^*$ we can express this monetary control rule as follows:

$$\dot{A} = \chi_4'(\dot{P}/P - [\dot{P}/P]^*)$$

From (4.19f) it can be seen that this implies

$$\dot{A} = \chi_4'\beta_9(Y - \bar{Y}) \tag{4.38}$$

since the only reason price inflation is different from its core rate is as a result of the demand-pull factor in the wage equation. We assume that $\chi_4' \to \infty$ so that the monetary control in fact keeps $Y = \bar{Y}$ and thus $\dot{P}/P = (\dot{P}/P)^*$.

The *modus operandi* of this monetary rule can be explained as follows. From (4.19a) we can see that to keep $Y = \bar{Y}$ implies keeping

$$A = \{ - \bar{Y}/\mu_1 + \varkappa_2(H + U) + (\varkappa_2 - \gamma_2)K + \bar{G} + (1 + \eta)\bar{X}\}/\varepsilon_2 \tag{4.39}$$

In fact, the real exchange rate is so adjusted as to cause the balance of trade to be at such a level as to exert the degree of demand-pull required to keep $Y = \bar{Y}$ and thus $\dot{P}/P = (\dot{P}/P)^*$. This amounts to using the rate of interest as the means of control of inflation. It is simply that, in our model in which domestic expenditure is interest-insensitive, the interest rate affects demand through its impact on the exchange rate. Notice that, because we are controlling inflation of the output price index, not the consumer price index, and because there are no imported inputs into production, the interest rate must here work through the effects of the exchange rate on demand, rather than through the effects of the exchange rate on costs. These more immediate effects will be important in our empirical work.

We obtain the dynamic properties of the system in the following way. From (4.39) we obtain

$$\dot{A} = \{\varkappa_2\dot{H} + \varkappa_2\dot{U} + (\varkappa_2 - \gamma_2)\dot{K}\}/\varepsilon_2 \tag{4.40}$$

Substituting in linearized (4.19c) the values of A and $\dot{A}$ given in (4.39) and (4.40), we obtain

$$\dot{H} = \bar{R}^F H - H_\infty\{\varkappa_2(\dot{H} + \dot{U}) + (\varkappa_2 - \gamma_2)\dot{K}\}/A_\infty\varepsilon_2$$
$$+ \bar{Y}(1/\mu_1 - \eta) - \varkappa_2(H + U) - (\varkappa_2 - \gamma_2)K - \bar{G} \tag{4.41}$$

The determination of $\dot{H}$ in this equation depends upon the foreign rate of interest $(\bar{R}^F)$ and is not affected by the domestic rate (R). However, the determination of $\dot{U}$ depends upon the real domestic rate of interest $(R - \dot{P}/P)$, as can be seen from (4.19c).

From (4.19g, h) and (4.19d) we see that $R - \dot{P}/P = \bar{R}^F - \dot{A}/A$ in the case of model-consistent expectations, and that $R - (\dot{P}/P) = \bar{R}^F + \phi\dot{A}/A + \phi([\dot{P}/P]^* - [\dot{P}/P])$ in the case of adaptive expectations. However, $\dot{P}/P$ is controlled to equal $(\dot{P}/P)^*$ and so using (4.40) to substitute for $\dot{A}$, these expressions become

$$R - \dot{P}/P = \bar{R}^F - \{\varkappa_2(\dot{H} + \dot{U}) + (\varkappa_2 - \gamma_2)\dot{K}\}/\varepsilon_2A_\infty \tag{4.42a}$$

or

$$R - \dot{P}/P = \bar{R}^F + \phi\{\varkappa_2(\dot{H} + \dot{U}) + (\varkappa_2 - \gamma_2)\dot{K}\}/\varepsilon_2A_\infty \tag{4.42b}$$

in the cases of model-consistent or adaptive expectations respectively. With $\dot{P}/P$ kept equal to $(\dot{P}/P)^*$ these two equations show the way in which R must be adjusted so as to keep $A = A^*$.

In the case of model-consistent expectations, substituting for $(R - \dot{P}/P)$ from (4.42a) into linearized (4.19e) gives

$$\dot{U} = (1 - S)\bar{R}^F U - (1 - S)U_\infty\{\varkappa_2(\dot{H} + \dot{U}) + (\varkappa_2 - \gamma_2)\dot{K}\}/\varepsilon_2A_\infty$$
$$+ \bar{G} - S\bar{Y} - S\bar{R}^F H \tag{4.43}$$

From (4.19b) we have

$$\dot{K} = \gamma_2(\nu\bar{Y} - K) \tag{4.44}$$

The three equations (4.41), (4.43) and (4.44) then describe the dynamic evolution of the system.

The assumption that investment is insensitive to the domestic interest rate means that one root, $-\gamma_2$, can be identified immediately from (4.44). This root, arising from the adjustment of the domestic capital stock, is negative. We can now consider (4.41) and (4.43) so as to determine whether these remaining equations induce any instability. For the purpose of identifying stability it is only necessary to consider terms in H, U, $\dot{H}$ and $\dot{U}$. Since terms in H and U do not affect domestic capital accumulation, there is no risk that terms in K and $\dot{K}$ could induce instability, given the negative root of (4.44) which we have already noted. We may therefore summarize the equations as

$$\begin{bmatrix} 1 + \tilde{H}_\infty & \tilde{H}_\infty \\ \tilde{U}_\infty & 1 + \tilde{U}_\infty \end{bmatrix} \begin{bmatrix} \dot{H} \\ \dot{U} \end{bmatrix} = \begin{bmatrix} \bar{R}^F - \varkappa_2 & -\varkappa_2 \\ -S\bar{R}^F & \bar{R}^F(1 - S) \end{bmatrix} \begin{bmatrix} H \\ U \end{bmatrix} \quad (4.45)$$

$$+ \text{ terms in } K \text{ and constants}$$

where $\tilde{H}_\infty = \varkappa_2 H_\infty / \varepsilon_2 A_\infty$ and $\tilde{U}_\infty = \varkappa_2 U_\infty (1 - S) / \varepsilon_2 A_\infty$.

This may be rearranged as

$$\begin{bmatrix} \dot{H} \\ \dot{U} \end{bmatrix} = 1/\Delta$$

$$\begin{bmatrix} (1 + \tilde{U}_\infty)(\bar{R}^F - \varkappa_2) + \tilde{H}_\infty S\bar{R}^F & -\{(1 + \tilde{U}_\infty)\varkappa_2 + \tilde{H}_\infty \bar{R}^F(1 - S)\} \\ (\varkappa_2 - \bar{R}^F)\tilde{U}_\infty - S\bar{R}^F(1 + \tilde{H}_\infty) & \bar{R}^F(1 - S)(1 + \tilde{H}_\infty) + \varkappa_2 \tilde{U}_\infty \end{bmatrix} \begin{bmatrix} H \\ U \end{bmatrix}$$

$$+ \text{ constants and terms in } K \quad (4.46)$$

where $\Delta = 1 + \tilde{H}_\infty + \tilde{U}_\infty$. A study of the determinant and trace of the matrix in this equation allows us to determine whether the system is stable. The determinant of this matrix turns out to be

$$\bar{R}^F(\bar{R}^F[1 - S] - \varkappa_2)/\Delta.$$

This is negative, implying one unstable root unless either

$$\bar{R}^F(1 - S) > \varkappa_2 \text{ or } \Delta = 1 + \tilde{U}_\infty + \tilde{H}_\infty < 0.$$

The trace of the matrix is $\bar{R}^F + (\bar{R}^F(1 - S) - \varkappa_2\Delta)$. If Δ is positive and $\bar{R}^F(1 - S) > \varkappa_2$, both trace and determinant are positive and so there are two unstable roots.

A high propensity to consume out of wealth ($\varkappa_2 > \bar{R}^F[1 - S]$) will remove the source of stock instability identified by Blinder and Solow. But if Δ is still positive the determinant is now negative; there remains another source of instability arising from the cumulation of interest receipts on external assets. If, however, $\varkappa_2 > \bar{R}^F(1 - S)$ so that the system is Blinder–Solow stable, and also $\Delta < 0$, then there are two stable roots. For $\Delta < 0$ we require that there is a large external debt combined with a large negative national debt (national surplus). The combination of these two is highly unlikely to be observed (Figure 4.1) and we shall normally find that the monetary stabilization of price inflation results in a system with one extra unstable root. This unstable root cannot be removed by a jump in the exchange rate since that is stabilized by means of the policy rule.

The model is not changed very greatly when expectations are assumed to be adaptive. The movement of the real exchange rate is determined as before. For it has to be used to ensure price stability, whatever expectations may be. The equations for $\dot{K}$ and $\dot{H}$ are unchanged and shown below as (4.48a,b). However, the value for R, the rate of interest, is now given by (4.42b). This means that the equation for $\dot{U}$ is modified. U_∞ is replaced by $-\phi U_\infty$, giving (4.48c) to replace (4.43).

$$\dot{K} = \gamma_2 \nu \bar{Y} - \gamma_2 K \tag{4.48a}$$

$$\dot{H} = \bar{R}^F H - \bar{G} - \varkappa_2(H + U + K) + \gamma_2 K + (1/\mu - \eta)\bar{Y}$$
$$- H_\infty\{\varkappa_2(\dot{H} + \dot{U} + \dot{K}) - \gamma_2 \dot{K}\}/\varepsilon_2 A_\infty \tag{4.48b}$$

$$\dot{U} = [\bar{R}^F + \phi\{\varkappa_2(\dot{H} + \dot{U} + \dot{K}) - \gamma_2 \dot{K}\}/\varepsilon_2 A_\infty](1 - S)U_\infty$$
$$+ \bar{R}^F(1 - S)(U - U_\infty) + \bar{G} - S\bar{R}^F H - S\bar{Y} \tag{4.48c}$$

The stability of the root, $-\gamma_2$, is not affected. (4.48b) and (4.48c) may be set out as

$$\begin{bmatrix} 1 + \tilde{H}_\infty & \tilde{H}_\infty \\ -\phi \tilde{U}_\infty & 1 - \phi \tilde{U}_\infty \end{bmatrix} \begin{bmatrix} \dot{H} \\ \dot{U} \end{bmatrix} = \begin{bmatrix} \bar{R}^F - \varkappa_2 & -\varkappa_2 \\ -S\bar{R}^F & \bar{R}^F(1 - S) \end{bmatrix} \begin{bmatrix} H \\ U \end{bmatrix} \tag{4.49}$$
$$+ \text{ constants and terms in } K$$

with $\tilde{U}_\infty$ and $\tilde{H}_\infty$ defined as before.

This gives

$$\begin{bmatrix} \dot{H} \\ \dot{U} \end{bmatrix} = 1/\Delta'$$

$$\begin{bmatrix} (1 - \phi \tilde{U}_\infty)(\bar{R}^F - \varkappa_2) + \tilde{H}_\infty S\bar{R}^F & -\{(1 - \phi \tilde{U}_\infty)\varkappa_2 + \tilde{H}_\infty \bar{R}^F(1 - S)\} \\ -\phi(\varkappa_2 - \bar{R}^F)\tilde{U}_\infty - S\bar{R}^F(1 + \tilde{H}_\infty) & \bar{R}^F(1 - S)(1 + \tilde{H}_\infty) - \phi\varkappa_2 \tilde{U}_\infty \end{bmatrix} \begin{bmatrix} H \\ U \end{bmatrix}$$

$$+ \text{ constants and terms in } K \tag{4.50}$$

where $\Delta' = 1 + \tilde{H}_\infty - \phi \tilde{U}_\infty$.

The determinant of this matrix is found to be

$$\bar{R}^F\{\bar{R}^F(1 - S) - \varkappa_2\}/\Delta'$$

and the trace is $\bar{R}^F + (\bar{R}^F(1 - S) - \varkappa_2\Delta')$. For the system to be stable we require that the determinant is positive and that the trace is negative. Since now a negative value for Δ' will arise if a negative value of $\tilde{H}_\infty$ is combined with a positive value of $\tilde{U}_\infty$, there is a greater chance of this happening. But the values of H_∞ and U_∞ required for this are still fairly large (particularly if expectations are not very regressive and so ϕ is small). Outside this perverse case we note that for the determinant to be positive we need $\bar{R}^F(1 - S) - \varkappa_2 > 0$. In this circumstance, however, the trace is certainly positive, and there will be two unstable roots. The most that we can hope for is that the Blinder–Solow condition, $\bar{R}^F(1 - S) - \varkappa_2 < 0$, holds. In this case the determinant is negative and there remains one unstable root.

We find that, when monetary policy is used to stabilize the level of Money GDP, the accumulation of interest on debt normally makes the system unstable. This result is independent of whether expectations are model-consistent or adaptive, although it does not necessarily hold when H_∞ and U_∞ take very extreme values. The reason for this instability may be explained as follows. Suppose that the demand for goods tends to be higher than their supply. Then there would be inflationary pressure. Our monetary rule suppresses this by appreciating the exchange rate. But as a consequence a current account deficit is generated. There is no self-correcting process, since the exchange rate has to remain appreciated so as to suppress the inflation. The deficit leads to an increase in debt, on which interest payments cumulate in an unstable manner. In the next section we demonstrate that fiscal policy can be used to control this instability.

4.9   REGIME 5: MONETARY CONTROL OF INFLATION AND FISCAL CONTROL OF NATIONAL WEALTH

If monetary policy is used as above in conjunction with the workings of the labour market to stabilize in prices, it cannot also be used to stabilize national wealth. However, it is possible to use fiscal policy for this purpose. Thus we now assume that G is set to control national wealth. Ideally an integral rule would be adopted. This would be guaranteed to bring national wealth to any desired value. But the stabilizing role of the fiscal instrument can be demonstrated by means of a simpler proportional rule.

$$G = \chi_6(H + K - N^*) + G_\infty \tag{4.51}$$

where N^* is the target value for national wealth and G_∞ is the value of government spending consistent with N^* (section 4.4).

The value at which the real exchange rate must be set in order to keep $Y = \bar{Y}$ is given in the previous section by (4.39), since monetary policy is being used in the same way as in the previous section. If we substitute the value of G from (4.51) into (4.39) we obtain

$$A = \{ - \bar{Y}/\mu_1 + (\varkappa_2 + \chi_6)H + \varkappa_2 U + (\varkappa_2 + \chi_6 - \gamma_2)K - \chi_6 N^*$$
$$+ G_\infty + (1 + \eta)\,\bar{X}\}/\varepsilon_2 \quad (4.52)$$

so that

$$\dot{A} = \{(\varkappa_2 + \chi_6)\dot{H} + \varkappa_2\dot{U} + (\varkappa_2 + \chi_6 - \gamma_2)\dot{K}\}/\varepsilon_2 \quad\quad (4.53)$$

We can now examine the dynamic properties of the system. Substituting in linearized (4.19e) the values of A and $\dot{A}$ given in (4.52) and (4.53) we obtain

$$\dot{H} = \bar{R}^{\mathrm{F}}H - H_\infty\{(\varkappa_2 + \chi_6)\dot{H} + \varkappa_2\dot{U} + (\varkappa_2 + \chi_6 - \gamma_2)\dot{K}\}/A_\infty\varepsilon_2$$
$$+ \bar{Y}(1/\mu_1 - \eta) - (\varkappa_2 + \chi_6)H - \varkappa_2 U - (\varkappa_2 + \chi_6 - \gamma_2)K + \chi_6 N^* - \chi_6 G_\infty$$
$$(4.54)$$

Using the expression for $\dot{A}$ in (4.53), the equations (4.42) of the previous section, which ensure that A is kept at the level needed to keep prices on target, are replaced by

$$(R - \dot{P}/P) = \bar{R}^{\mathrm{F}} - \{(\varkappa_2 + \chi_6)\dot{H} + \varkappa_2\dot{U} + (\varkappa_2 + \chi_6 - \gamma_2)\dot{K}\}/\varepsilon_2 A_\infty \quad (4.55\mathrm{a})$$

with model-consistent expectations and

$$(R - \dot{P}/P) = \bar{R}^{\mathrm{F}} + \phi\{(\varkappa_2 + \chi_6)\dot{H} + \varkappa_2\dot{U} + (\varkappa_2 + \chi_6 - \gamma_2)\dot{K}\}/\varepsilon_2 A_\infty \quad (4.55\mathrm{b})$$

with adaptive expectations. These show the rate of interest which must be set so as to maintain $A = A^*$.

In the case of model-consistent expectations, substituting for $(R - \dot{P}/P)$ from (4.55b) and for G from (4.51) into linearized (4.19c) now gives

$$\dot{U} = \bar{R}^{\mathrm{F}}(1 - S)U - (1 - S)U_\infty\{(\varkappa_2 + \chi_6)\dot{H} + \varkappa_2\dot{U} + (\varkappa_2 + \chi_6 - \gamma_2)\dot{K}\}/\varepsilon_2 A_\infty$$
$$+ \chi_6(H + K - N^*) + G_\infty - S\bar{Y} - S\bar{R}^{\mathrm{F}}H \quad (4.56)$$

From (4.19b) we have as before

$$\dot{K} = \gamma_2(\nu\bar{Y} - K) \tag{4.57}$$

Equations (4.54), (4.56) and (4.57) now describe the dynamic evolution of the system.

Once again equation (4.57) gives a stable root of $-\gamma_2$, and in deriving the two remaining roots from (4.54) and (4.56) we can therefore neglect not only the constants but also all the terms in K and $\dot{K}$. These two equations can then be expressed in the form

$$\begin{bmatrix} 1 + \tilde{H}_\infty(1 + \chi_6/\varkappa_2) & \tilde{H}_\infty \\ \tilde{U}_\infty(1 + \chi_6/\varkappa_2) & 1 + \tilde{U}_\infty \end{bmatrix} \begin{bmatrix} \dot{H} \\ \dot{U} \end{bmatrix} = \begin{bmatrix} \bar{R}^F - \varkappa_2 - \chi_6 & -\varkappa_2 \\ \chi_6 - S\bar{R}^F & \bar{R}^F(1 - S) \end{bmatrix} \begin{bmatrix} H \\ U \end{bmatrix}$$

$$+ \text{ terms in } K \text{ and constants} \tag{4.58}$$

where $\tilde{H}_\infty$ and $\tilde{U}_\infty$ have the same values as those given in (4.45) in the previous section. This can be rearranged to give

$$\begin{bmatrix} \dot{H} \\ \dot{U} \end{bmatrix} = 1/\Delta \begin{bmatrix} -\tilde{H}_\infty(\chi_6 - S\bar{R}^F) + (1 + \tilde{U}_\infty)(\bar{R}^F - \varkappa_2 - \chi_6) \\ \{1 + \tilde{H}_\infty(1 + \chi_6/\varkappa_2)\}(\chi_6 - S\bar{R}^F) + \tilde{U}_\infty(1 + \chi_6/\varkappa_2)(\varkappa_2 + \chi_6 - \bar{R}^F) \end{bmatrix}$$

$$\begin{matrix} -\tilde{H}_\infty\bar{R}^F(1 - S) - \varkappa_2(1 + \tilde{U}_\infty) \\ \{1 + \tilde{H}_\infty(1 + \chi_6/\varkappa_2)\}\bar{R}^F(1 - S) + \tilde{U}_\infty(\varkappa_2 + \chi_6) \end{matrix} \Bigg] \begin{bmatrix} H \\ U \end{bmatrix}$$

$$+ \text{ constants and terms in } K \tag{4.59}$$

with $\Delta = 1 + \tilde{H}_\infty(1 + \chi_6/\varkappa_2) + \tilde{U}_\infty$. The trace of the transition matrix can be rearranged as

$$\bar{R}^F(1 - S) - \varkappa_2 - \chi_6 + \bar{R}^F\Delta + \tilde{H}_\infty\chi_6(\bar{R}^F(1 - S)/\varkappa_2 - 1)$$

and the determinant is

$$(\bar{R}^F - \chi_6)(\bar{R}^F[1 - S] - \varkappa_2)/\Delta$$

For the system to be stable we require that the trace should be negative and that the determinant should be positive. If $\tilde{H}_\infty(\bar{R}^F[1 - S]/\varkappa_2 - 1) < 1$, a sufficiently positive value of χ_6 will ensure that the trace is negative. The determinant is made increasingly positive by an increase in χ_6, provided that $(\bar{R}^F[1 - S] - \varkappa_2)/\Delta$ remains negative. Since our Blinder–Solow condition is assumed to hold, giving $\bar{R}^F(1 - S)/\varkappa_2 - 1 < 0$, these conditions will only break down if $\tilde{H}_\infty(1 + \chi_6/\varkappa_2) + \tilde{U}_\infty$ is sufficiently negative. We regard this as unlikely.

Outside this case fiscal policy can be used to remove the unstable root in national wealth.

The role of the parameter χ_6 can be easily understood. We note that, except when very negative values for H_∞ and U_∞ (and therefore $\tilde{H}_\infty$ and $\tilde{U}_\infty$) lead to perverse results, the determinant will be positive and the trace negative when the Blinder–Solow condition holds and when $\chi_6 > \bar{R}^F$. This condition simply states that the rate of adjustment of government spending must be sufficiently rapid to offset the effects of interest payments cumulating on the foreign debt. Otherwise the determinant will be negative and the system will be unstable. A direct comparison may be made with the results of section 4.6.

It is again the case that, when expectations are adaptive, the only terms directly affected are those in $\tilde{U}_\infty$. We use (4.55b) instead of (4.55a) as the equation for the domestic interest rate. Equations (4.54) and (4.57) are unchanged, while $\tilde{U}_\infty$ is replaced by $-\phi\,\tilde{U}_\infty$ in (4.56).

$$\dot{U} = \bar{R}^F(1 - S)U + \phi(1 - S)U_\infty\{(\varkappa_2 + \chi_6)\dot{H} + \varkappa_2\dot{U} + (\varkappa_2 + \chi_6 - \gamma_2)\dot{K}\}/\varepsilon_2 A_\infty$$
$$+ \chi_6(H + K - N^*) + G_\infty - S\bar{Y} - S\bar{R}^F H \quad (4.60)$$

In matrix form (4.54) and (4.60) may be rearranged as

$$\begin{bmatrix} \dot{H} \\ \dot{U} \end{bmatrix} = 1/\Delta' \left[\begin{array}{c} -\tilde{H}_\infty(\chi_6 - S\bar{R}^F) + (1 - \phi\,\tilde{U}_\infty)(\bar{R}^F - \varkappa_2 - \chi_6) \\ \{1 + \tilde{H}_\infty(1 - \chi_6/\varkappa_2)\}(\chi_6 - S\bar{R}^F) - \phi\,\tilde{U}_\infty(1 + \chi_6/\varkappa_2)(\varkappa_2 + \chi_6 - \bar{R}^F \end{array} \right.$$

$$\left. \begin{array}{c} -\tilde{H}_\infty\bar{R}^F(1 - S) - \varkappa_2(1 - \phi\,\tilde{U}_\infty) \\ \{1 + \tilde{H}_\infty(1 + \chi_6/\varkappa_2)\}\bar{R}^F(1 - S) - \phi\,\tilde{U}_\infty(\varkappa_2 + \chi_6) \end{array} \right] \begin{bmatrix} H \\ U \end{bmatrix}$$

$$+ \text{ constants and terms in } K \quad (4.61)$$

where $\Delta' = 1 + \tilde{H}_\infty(1 + \chi_6/\varkappa_2) - \phi\,\tilde{U}_\infty$. The trace and determinant of this differ from the previous case only in that Δ is replaced by Δ'. With $\Delta' > 0$, the stability condition is found to be $\chi_6 > \bar{R}^F$ as in the previous case. The only distinction lies in that a negative value of Δ' is more likely than a negative value of Δ. This has already been discussed in section 4.5. Outside these extreme cases we may conclude that, for both types of expectations, a sufficiently powerful fiscal rule will remove stock instability.

4.10   REGIME 6: A BALANCED BUDGET

We have seen in section 4.4 that it makes no real difference, at least as far as the steady state is concerned, whether the wealth target is set out in terms of national wealth or the national debt. It would be possible to investigate the stability of rules similar to those of Regimes 3 and 5 depending on whether fiscal or monetary policy was used to deliver the target value for U_∞.

However, we think it of greater interest to investigate the stability properties of a more simple-minded approach to maintaining a particular value for the national debt. In this section we look at the stability of an economy in which monetary policy is used to control inflation, and fiscal policy is adjusted so as to ensure that the budget is always balanced. This could be interpreted as a simple representation of a popular view of economic policy.

As in the previous section, we set monetary policy so as to keep $Y = \bar{Y}$, giving

$$A = \{ - \bar{Y}/\mu_1 + \varkappa_2(H + U_0) + (\varkappa_2 - \gamma_2)K + G + (1 + \eta)\bar{X}\}/\varepsilon_2 \quad (4.62)$$

The value of G which maintains budget balance is found from (4.19) as

$$G = S\bar{Y} + S\bar{R}^F H - (R - [\dot{P}/P]^*)(1 - S)U_0 \quad (4.63)$$

since, with $Y = \bar{Y}$, the rate of inflation is always $(\dot{P}/P)^*$.

We now substitute for G in (4.62) finding

$$A = \{ - \bar{Y}/\mu_1 + \varkappa_2(H + U_0) + (\varkappa_2 - \gamma_2)K + (1 + \eta)\bar{X} + S\bar{Y}$$
$$+ S\bar{R}^F H - (R - [\dot{P}/P]^*)(1 - S)U_0\}/\varepsilon_2 \quad (4.64)$$

This shows that, in order to maintain $Y = \bar{Y}$ with $U_0 > 0$ a low interest rate must be associated with a high real exchange rate. The reason for this is that, with budget balance, a low interest rate will be associated with high government spending. The inflationary effects of this have to be offset by the deflationary effects of a high real exchange rate.

We now differentiate (4.64)

$$\dot{A} = \{(\varkappa_2 + S\bar{R}^F)\dot{H} + (\varkappa_2 - \gamma_2)\dot{K} - \dot{R}(1 - S)U_0\}/\varepsilon_2 \quad (4.65)$$

From (4.19ga,h) and (4.19d) we obtain with model-consistent expectations

$$R = \bar{R}^F + (\dot{P}/P)^* - \dot{A}/A_\infty \quad (4.66a)$$

and with adaptive expectations

$$R = \bar{R}^F + (\dot{P}/P)^* + \phi\dot{A}/A_\infty \quad (4.66b)$$

Taking first the model-consistent case, after substituting for $\dot{A}/A_\infty$ from (4.64)

$$R = \bar{R}^F + (\dot{P}/P)^* - \{(\varkappa_2 + S\bar{R}^F)\dot{H} + (\varkappa_2 - \gamma_2)\dot{K} - \dot{R}(1-S)U_0\}/\varepsilon_2 A_\infty$$

$$(4.67)$$

We note that there is a positive feedback between $\dot{R}$ and R (provided that $U_0 > 0$). We have already seen that a low value of R is associated with a high value of G and a high value of A (4.63 and 4.64). But, from (4.66a), a low value of R also implies an appreciating value of A. This appreciating value of A means that government spending must be rising, in order to avoid a domestic deflation. Budget balance can then only be maintained by a falling value of R. This positive feedback is a possible source of instability.

We also have, from (4.19c),

$$\dot{H} = \bar{R}^F H - \dot{A}H_\infty/A_\infty - \varepsilon_2 A - \eta\bar{Y} + (1+\eta)\bar{X} \qquad (4.68)$$

After substituting for $\dot{A}$ and A from (4.64) and (4.65) this becomes

$$\dot{H} = \bar{R}^F H - \{\varkappa_2\dot{H} + (\varkappa_2 - \gamma_2)\dot{K} + S\bar{R}^F\dot{H} - \dot{R}(1-S)U_0\}H_\infty/\varepsilon_2 A_\infty$$
$$+ \bar{Y}/\mu_1 - \varkappa_2(H + U_0) - (\varkappa_2 - \gamma_2)K - S\bar{Y} - S\bar{R}^F H$$
$$+ (R - (\dot{P}/P)^*)(1-S)U_0 - \eta\bar{Y} \qquad (4.69)$$

The equations (4.67) and (4.69) can be set out as

$$\begin{bmatrix} 1 + H_\infty(\varkappa_2 + S\bar{R}^F)/\varepsilon_2 A_\infty & -H_\infty(1-S)U_0/\varepsilon_2 A_\infty \\ (\varkappa_2 + S\bar{R}^F)/\varepsilon_2 A_\infty & -(1-S)U_0/\varepsilon_2 A_\infty \end{bmatrix}\begin{bmatrix} \dot{H} \\ \dot{R} \end{bmatrix}$$

$$= \begin{bmatrix} \bar{R}^F - \varkappa_2 - S\bar{R}^F & (1-S)U_0 \\ 0 & -1 \end{bmatrix}\begin{bmatrix} H \\ R \end{bmatrix} \qquad (4.70)$$

$$+ \text{ terms in } \dot{K} \text{ and constants}$$

or, with $U_0 \neq 0$,

$$\begin{bmatrix} \dot{H} \\ \dot{R} \end{bmatrix} = \begin{bmatrix} -(\varkappa_2 - [1-S]\bar{R}^F) & (1-S)U_0 + H_\infty \\ \dfrac{-(\varkappa_2 - [1-S]\bar{R}^F)(\varkappa_2 + S\bar{R}^F)}{(1-S)U_0} & \varkappa_2 + S\bar{R}^F + \dfrac{(\varepsilon_2 A_\infty + H_\infty[\varkappa_2 + S\bar{R}^F])}{(1-S)U_0} \end{bmatrix}\begin{bmatrix} H \\ R \end{bmatrix} \qquad (4.71)$$

$$+ \text{ terms in } \dot{K} \text{ and constants}$$

For the purpose of stability analysis, the terms in $\dot{K}$ may be neglected, because, with $Y = \bar{Y}$, H and R do not feature in the equation for $\dot{K}$ (4.19b). We then require that the subsystem for H and R should be stable. This means that the trace of the above matrix must be negative, and its determinant positive.

The trace turns out to be

$$\bar{R}^F + (\varepsilon_2 A_\infty + H_\infty [\varkappa_2 + S\bar{R}^F])/(1-S)U_0$$

One can substitute for H_∞ and A_∞ in terms of (4.24b) and (4.20d). With $U_0 > 0$, the trace will be positive unless H_∞ is sufficiently negative. The determinant is

$$-(\varkappa_2 - [1-S]\bar{R}^F)\varepsilon_2 A_\infty/(1-S)U_0$$

We continue to assume that the Blinder–Solow condition holds $(\varkappa_2 > \bar{R}^F)$, and therefore this determinant is only positive if U_0, the national debt, is negative. We note that a negative U_0 turns the positive feedback of $\dot{R}$ on R into a negative feedback and conclude that the economy cannot be stable unless this source of instability is removed.[4] Even then stability requires a very negative value of H_∞.

With adaptive expectations we use (4.66b) as our equation for R, giving after substituting for $\dot{A}$,

$$R = \bar{R}^F + (\dot{P}/P)^* + \phi\{(\varkappa_2 + S\bar{R}^F)\dot{H} + (\varkappa_2 - \gamma_2)\dot{K} - \dot{R}(1-S)U_0\}/\varepsilon_2 A_\infty \tag{4.72}$$

We have to solve this equation jointly with the equation for $\dot{H}$ (4.69). Taken together we have

$$\begin{bmatrix} 1 + H_\infty(\varkappa_2 + S\bar{R}^F)/\varepsilon_2 A_\infty & -H_\infty(1-S)U_0/\varepsilon_2 A_\infty \\ -\phi(\varkappa_2 + S\bar{R}^F)/\varepsilon_2 A_\infty & \phi(1-S)U_0/\varepsilon_2 A_\infty \end{bmatrix} \begin{bmatrix} \dot{H} \\ \dot{R} \end{bmatrix} =$$

$$\begin{bmatrix} \bar{R}^F - \varkappa_2 - S\bar{R}^F & (1-S)U_0 \\ 0 & -1 \end{bmatrix} \begin{bmatrix} H \\ R \end{bmatrix} \tag{4.73}$$

$$+ \text{ terms in } \dot{K} \text{ and constants}$$

or

$$\begin{bmatrix} \dot{H} \\ \dot{R} \end{bmatrix} = \begin{bmatrix} \dfrac{-(x_2 - [1 - S]\bar{R}^F) \\ -(x_2 - [1 - S]\bar{R}^F)(x_2 + S\bar{R}^F)}{(1 - S)U_0} \\[4mm] \dfrac{(1 - S)U_0 - H_\infty/\phi}{x_2 + S\bar{R}^F - \dfrac{(\varepsilon_2 A_\infty + H_\infty[x_2 + S\bar{R}^F])}{(1 - S)U_0\phi}} \end{bmatrix} \begin{bmatrix} H \\ R \end{bmatrix} \quad (4.74)$$

+ terms in $\dot{K}$ and constants

The trace becomes

$$\bar{R}^F - (-\phi\varepsilon_2 A_\infty + H_\infty[x_2 + S\bar{R}^F]/\varepsilon_2 A_\infty)/(1 - S)U_0\phi$$

and the determinant is

$$(x_2 - [1 - S]\bar{R}^F)\varepsilon_2 A_\infty/(1 - S)U_0\phi$$

We observe that, since $A_\infty > 0$, the trace is more likely to be negative, and so this stability condition is more likely to be met. But the change in expectations formation changes the sign of the determinant. The reason for this is that the sign of the feedback of $\dot{R}$ on R is reversed by the change in expectational behaviour. With adaptive expectations the determinant is positive if $U_0 > 0$ and not if $U_0 < 0$.

These results illustrate two fatal flaws with a policy of using monetary policy to fight inflation, and using fiscal policy to pursue a simple-minded policy of budget balance. First, the stability of the system is sensitive to steady states. This was also true in Regimes 3 and 5, but in those cases we were able to find a minimum value for a control parameter which could offset the model instability. Here, since the policy is to balance the budget, there is no control parameter which can be used to offset natural instability. There is a second fundamental fault. The stability of the regime depends crucially on the initial conditions, as indicated by the sign of U_0, and the regime is not stable with both types of expectations formation.

4.11 CONCLUSION

In the previous chapter we demonstrated that an *IS–LM* model can be used to analyse the effects of monetary and fiscal approaches to the maintenance of price stability. In this chapter we have demonstrated that such an approach cannot be regarded as fully comprehensive. From the examples we have presented here we may infer that an economy is likely to be subject to stock instability, and that some sort of policy must be adopted to cure the stock instability. If monetary policy is used to stabilize prices, then fiscal policy can be used to cure stock instability and ensure that national wealth reaches a target value. Alternatively, if fiscal policy is used to stabilize prices, monetary policy can be used to stabilize national wealth.

In this chapter we have identified conditions which have to be be met for stock instability to be removed by active financial policy. This adds to our analysis of wage–price instability in Chapter 3. It indicates a second set of difficulties with which financial policy rules must cope, and marks the end of Part I of our book. In Part II we turn our attention to the problems raised by the empirical application of our New Keynesian policy framework. Chapter 5 begins this by a description of the stock effects found in a comprehensive economic model and gives an account of the interplay between these and expectational effects.

Part II
Application

Chapter Five

A stock-flow model with model-consistent or adaptive expectations

5.1 INTRODUCTION

In Chapter 1 of this book we presented our New Keynesian policy proposals. In Chapter 2 we used a static model to analyse the appropriate instrument-target emphasis of fiscal and monetary policies in the pursuit of policy objectives, and we showed how this was influenced by cost-push pressures in the wage equation and by the openness of the economy. This static model was clearly inadequate to study dynamic aspects of policy rules; we developed models to look at these in the next two chapters. In Chapter 3 we used a dynamic model to examine the wage-price spiral and to show how economic policy could be used to control inflation at the same time as wealth accumulation was being regulated. We also investigated, for the first time, the issue of exchange-rate targeting within our policy framework. In Chapter 4 we presented a more complex dynamic model which allowed us to look at the control of national wealth. We showed how this was complicated by the cumulation of debt on foreign assets.

These two sudies give important indications of the sort of problems that economic policy rules have to face. But they are incomplete as a guide to the practical operation of economic policy for three main reasons. First of all, they illustrate two distinct points, the stabilization of the wage-price spiral and the stabilization and control of national wealth. In Chapter 3 we used a detailed model of the wage-price spiral, and gave only rudimentary considerations to questions of control of national wealth. In Chapter 4 we looked at the control of national wealth in more detail, but the cost of this was a simplification of the wage-price spiral. However, the two issues of price stabilization and wealth control have to be considered jointly for an overall assessment of economic policy. Secondly, the models which we have used so far do not take account of possible lags in the major economic relationships. Yet these lags cannot be ignored, since they can easily make rules unstable, which would be stable in their absence. The third defect of the previous two chapters is that, while they have taken account of expectational effects in the foreign-exchange markets and implicitly, through the various specifications of the wage equation, in the labour market, expectational effects have otherwise been ignored. In particular we have neglected the facts that consumption is likely to depend on expected future income as well as current income, and investment is likely to depend on expected future profit. Also the market value of wealth, which was an influence on consumption in Chapter 4, will depend on the market value of long-term government debt and on the market value of the private capital stock; these asset values are likely to depend on expectations of future short-term interest rates and of future profits. Now the Lucas critique suggests that, particularly when studying economic policy, it is important to model the expectations process explicitly. This is because the way in which an economy evolves over time depends on the policy regime in force; and that is likely to make expectations of future events also sensitive to the policy regime. In order to take account of these points and of course of many other economic effects which we have left out of our analytical models, we share the view that it is necessary to use an econometric model to simulate the behaviour of the economy. Otherwise it is not possible to evaluate and test economic policy proposals properly.[1]

The basic quarterly models of the United Kingdom economy are the Bank of England model, the London Business School model, the National Institute of Economic and Social Research (NIESR) model and HM Treasury model. These are of course being continuously revised and updated but, as we engaged in our work, they were all basically income-expenditure models of a form similar to the theoretical models of Chapter 3. This had two consequences:

i) The effects of asset stock accumulation on the key behavioural variables were incorporated only in an *ad hoc* and rudimentary manner rather than in any sort of optimizing framework;
ii) The forward-looking variables were given at best limited roles.

Recent changes to the models have given greater emphasis to forward-looking variables, but they are generally introduced in a fashion which has no obvious link to intertemporal optimization, and therefore does not really meet the Lucas critique. Rather they are introduced on the basis of freely specified econometric equations. The resulting coefficients of the models reflect the economic policy regime in force during the estimation period and cannot therefore be used to investigate the effects of differing economic policy regimes on the assumption that these policies are properly understood.

It would have been possible for us to build a full computer model of the economy from scratch, so as to ensure that it reflected the basic issues with which we are concerned. But this would have been a time-consuming and unnecessary labour, given the macroeconomic models of the UK economy which already exist. We have therefore taken as our starting point version 7 of the NIESR model, and have modified the consumption and investment functions and the model of the foreign-exchange markets so as to embody expectational effects (and, in the case of the foreign-exchange markets, imperfect substitution between home and foreign assets) in the manner which we thought to be appropriate. As we demonstrate in this chapter, the consumption and investment functions which we adopt give an important role to stock variables. In order to keep track of these stock variables, we find it necessary to impose a consistent stock-flow accounting framework on our model; we have also developed this as required.

In this chapter we therefore present the modifications necessary to introduce consumption, investment and foreign-exchange market models which are robust to the Lucas critique, and we set these changes in the context of a consistent stock-flow accounting framework. There are of course many other areas of the model, such as stockbuilding, in which we have done nothing to represent the behaviour of forward-looking optimizing agents. But we claim that the major changes to the important parts of the model which we have made provide a basis for the thorough examination in Chapters 6 to 9 of the issues raised in the earlier chapters of this book.

Our model of stock-flow interactions is, in effect, a pathbreaking but simple application to the UK economy of the ideas expressed in Tobin's Nobel Prize Lecture (1982). (See also Tobin, 1969 and 1980.) The structure which we have adopted is less detailed than that described by Davis (1987a,b). But this simple structure has enabled us to avoid many of the pitfalls in this area of applied economics (Courakis, 1988) and allowed us to introduce model-consistent expectations in a much more satisfactory manner than has been done before. This goes far beyond Tobin's work. It has been made possible by the technical advances of the so-called 'rational expectations revolution'. The techniques which we have developed for the solution and simulation of this model can, indeed, be seen as a further contribution to this revolution.

We set out the rest of this chapter as follows. First, we give a very brief sketch of the NIESR Model 7, which we have used as our starting point. Next we present the balance-sheet structure which is needed to underpin our macroeconomic model. We then identify the roles of stock variables and asset prices as determinants of property income flows and of capital gains. The next section looks at the determination of asset prices, showing the role of stocks in this. The final section discusses the components of aggregate demand, consumption, investment and net foreign investment, which are affected by the changes we have made. There is one appendix to this chapter. It presents the numerical parameters which we have used.

5.2   THE NIESR MODEL: VERSION 7

This section gives a very brief summary of the version 7 of the National Institute model as made available to us by the National Institute of Economic and Social Research. For a fuller account of the underlying methodology the reader is referred to Britton (1983): he in fact describes an earlier version of the model (version 5); the equations in version 7 were re-estimated but there was no fundamental change in the underlying philosophy during that updating process. A full listing of the original model is available in the technical manual which the National Institute produced at the time (NIESR, 1984). The reader should note that the National Institute model has changed very substantially since 1984.

5.2.1   Components of demand

The model is essentially Keynesian in character. Consumer demand, split between non-durable and durable consumption, depends on current and lagged values of real disposable income and on the stock of financial assets held by the personal sector. The equations are essentially descendants of the consumption function produced by Davidson *et al.* (1978). Public sector consumption is exogenous. Fixed investment (excluding most public sector investment) is modelled in four distinct categories using accelerator equations. Only investment in dwellings is found to be interest-sensitive. Public sector investment is, apart from some nationalized industry investment, exogenous. Stockbuilding is represented, this time in three categories, again by accelerator equations. Exports depend on the level of world trade and on competitiveness, while imports depend on the level of demand and level of output of the home economy as well as on relative prices. Both exports and imports are disaggregated into a small number of broad categories.

5.2.2 Output and employment

Output is assumed to meet the difference between demand and imports. It is broken down into a number of component parts, but no use is made of an input–output table, and the economic interpretation of the decomposition is obscure. Employment is then determined from output, generally with a lag and with the assumption that there are economies of scale in some industries.

5.2.3 Factor incomes, wage rates and prices

Nominal factor incomes arise from three main sources. Labour income depends on employment and on the ruling wage rate. This in turn is determined by a wage equation which relates the change in the wage rate to expected inflation, the state of the labour market, the deviation of real wages from their target value and to terms indicating overtime activity. We discuss the wage equation at greater length in Chapter 6. Domestic prices are set by a mark-up on labour and import costs. Import and export prices depend on both world and domestic prices. Again lags are present in all price equations. For a given level of output, wage rate and employment, this means that profits can be calculated. These accrue to companies and to the self-employed, but do not feed through into personal sector property income.

5.2.4 Transfer income and taxes

Real grant income depends on the number of unemployed, and is paid by the government to the personal sector. Net property income flows are calculated for the personal, company and public sectors, on the basis of cumulated financial balances and interest rates. The net property income flow paid overseas is then calculated as a residual. Direct tax payments are calculated from tax functions applied to the incomes of the sectors concerned. Indirect taxes are calculated by rules of thumb. Personal disposable income is, of course, calculated from personal sector factor and grant income receipts less personal sector direct taxes. This then feeds back into the consumption function.

5.2.5   The real exchange rate

The real exchange rate is calculated from real interest-rate differentials, the trade balance and the value of oil reserves. The underlying model is one of relative capital immobility without forward-looking expectations. (This is one area which has been changed substantially since 1984.)

5.2.6   The financial sector

The financial sector is essentially an appendage to the model. Sectoral net stocks of financial asset holdings are calculated as the cumulated residual of income over consumption, investment and transfer expenditure. Changes in specific financial aggregates are determined by econometric equations including interest rates and a number of macroeconomic variables as well as net asset stocks. Short-term interest rates are treated as moving one for one with the Treasury bill rate, which is exogenous. The consol rate adapts gradually to changes in the Treasury bill rate. No other security prices are modelled.

5.2.7   Summary

The model is thus driven by the real demand for goods and services. Supply constraints are implicitly present in the specification of the employment and wage equations, but there is no clear production function, and no obvious role given to the capital stock in the productive process. There is no obvious role for asset stocks in expenditure decisions. Expectational effects are, throughout the model, implicit and backward-looking. We seek to remedy the last two points, but we have not had the resources available to investigate ways of introducing an explicit production function.

5.3 ASSET STOCKS IN A MACROECONOMETRIC MODEL

5.3.1   Balance sheet structure

To allow comprehensive modelling of stock and asset price effects it is, in fact, found to be necessary to maintain an inventory of seven assets in total. There are four key financial assets: foreign assets, private sector capital as valued by the stock market, long-term government bonds (consols) and short-term paper (Treasury bills). The stock of durable goods is an important component of domestic wealth which cannot be ignored. A sixth asset, the monetary base, has to be introduced to take account of the fact that base money does not bear interest while the other types of government debt do. This has implications for the amount of debt interest the public sector has to pay, but is otherwise of no other importance to our policy framework. Finally a seventh 'asset', human capital, must be explicitly identified so as to model satisfactorily the effects of current and expected future fiscal policy on consumption.

The simplest possible model would assume that the first five assets were perfect substitutes, in the sense that their current prices adjusted so that the expected short-period return on each of them was equalized.

Table 5.1 Balance sheet structure

Asset		Private	Sector	Public		Foreign
Home Assets	*HAP*	Home assets of the private sector	*HAG*	Home assets of the government (= – sterling national debt)	*HAF*	Home assets of foreigners
of which Interest-bearing	*HAP – D*	Land Capital Stock interest-bearing sterling national debt durable goods stocks, work in progress	*HAG + D*	Interest-bearing assets (= – sterling interest-bearing national debt)	*HAF*	
Non-interest-bearing	*D*	Monetary Base	*– D*	Monetary Base		
PLUS Foreign Assets	*FAP*	Foreign assets of the private sector	*FAG*	Foreign reserves	*FAF*	Foreign wealth
Total Wealth	*NWPR*	Net wealth of private sector	*NWG*	Net wealth of government	*WW*	World wealth

Note: *HAG* is normally negative and thus *HAG + D* is smaller than *HAG* in absolute magnitude.

However, given that we are particularly interested in the behaviour of the exchange rate, it seemed sensible to allow for a high, but finite, degree of substitution between home and foreign assets.[2] We have therefore constructed a model in which all home assets except currency are perfect substitutes[3] but in which home and foreign assets are not: portfolio allocation between home and foreign assets depends on existing holdings as well as on the expected yields of the home and foreign assets adjusted for expected exchange-rate changes.

This aggregation of assets is accompanied by an aggregation of institutional sectors into the private sector, the government and the rest of the world. The resulting asset classification, omitting human capital, is as set out in Table 5.1. This table shows the net asset position of each sector, and it neglects capital assets (such as roads and hospitals) which are owned by the public sector.[4,5]

5.3.2 Asset accumulation

There are two fundamental dynamic identities which link asset stocks in one period to those in the next. These, therefore, drive the components of the balance sheet, Table 5.1, through time.

i) The supply of home assets, adjusted for capital gains and purchases of durable goods, increases by the sum of private investment (at market prices) and the increase in the sterling national debt. This identity is shown in equation (5.1).
ii) Private sector saving equals private sector investment plus the budget deficit plus any current account balance-of-payments surplus. This identity is shown in equation (5.2).

These two key identities are used to maintain inventories of the stock of home assets. They allow the construction of a model in which the stock effects on expenditures can be considered.

The two identities are algebraically:

$$
\begin{aligned}
HAP_t + HAF_t = {} & (HAP_{t-1} + HAF_{t-1} - SDUR_{t-1}) \times DP_t \\
& + (INV_t - DEP \times K_{t-1} + SB_t) \times PDK_t \times Q_t \\
& + SDUR_t + BD_t - ZOF_t
\end{aligned}
\tag{5.1}
$$

and

$$
\begin{aligned}
HAP_t + FAP_t = {} & (HAP_{t-1} - SDUR_{t-1}) \times DP_t + FAP_{t-1} \\
& \times DF_t \times EX_{t-1}/EX_t + SDUR_t + (INV_t - DEP \times K_{t-1} \\
& + SB_t) \times Q_t \times PDK_t + BD_t + BPS_t
\end{aligned}
\tag{5.2}
$$

Here *HAP*   – home assets of private sector (£ million)
     FAP   – foreign assets of private sector (£ million)
     HAF   – net home assets of foreigners (£ million)
     DEP   – depreciation rate of fixed capital (1.2% per quarter derived from the National Accounts)
     DP   – 1 + fractional capital gain on home assets (excluding consumer durables)
     DF   – 1 + fractional capital gain on foreign assets in foreign currency (exogenous)
     INV   – gross fixed investment (1980 prices)
     K   – capital stock (1980 prices)
     SB   – private sector stock-building (1980 prices)
     PDK   – price of capital goods (1980 prices)
     ZOF   – official intervention (£ million)
     BD   – budget deficit (£ million)
     BPS   – balance of payments surplus (£ million)
     SDUR   – stock of consumer durable goods (£ million)
     Q   – ratio of stock exchange valuation of capital goods to replacement cost
     EX   – exchange rate index (foreign currency/£)

with all stocks indexed at end of period.

Three further identities, necessary for describing the evolution of components of the balance sheet, show the accumulation of stocks of fixed capital (K), consumer durables ($SDUR$) and foreign-exchange reserves (FAG). These are

$$K_t = (1 - DEP)K_{t-1} + INV_t \tag{5.3}$$

$$SDUR_t = (1 - DEPC) \times SDUR_{t-1} \times CPI_t / CPI_{t-1} + CPDUR_t \tag{5.4}$$

$$FAG_t = FAG_{t-1} \times EX_{t-1} / EX_t - ZOF_t \tag{5.5}$$

where

CPDUR   – purchases of consumer durables (£ million)
CPI   – consumer price index
DEPC   – rate of depreciation of consumer durables (4% per quarter)
FAG   – foreign exchange reserves (£ million)

It can be seen that the current price value of the stock of durable goods is adjusted with changes in the consumer price index, and the value of the foreign-exchange reserves reflects changes in the nominal exchange rate as well as official intervention.

We note one additional simple identity which shows the cumulation of stocks and work in progress (S) by the private sector.

$$S_t = S_{t-1} + SB_t \qquad\qquad (5.6)$$

where

S – private sector stocks and work in progress (1980 prices).

The quantity of stocks and work in progress proves important in sections 5.3.5 and 5.4.2. A similar stock-flow identity could be constructed for world wealth, but we choose to treat this as exogenous.

This balance-sheet structure provides the simplest possible means we have been able to devise of keeping track of stock variables in an economic model so as to allow an analysis of the effects of capital gains and interest payments together with other aspects of the role of stock variables in economic behaviour.

5.3.3 Property income and asset accumulation

One motive behind the maintenance of asset inventories is that this allows the calculation of property income flows. The crucial importance of these flows in exchange-rate determination was indicated in Chapter 4. Furthermore, Easton (1985) demonstrates that abbreviated treatment of this issue can lead to a perverse response of property flows to interest-rate changes. In any policy study it is extremely important that the model used should not incorporate such perverse effects. Otherwise highly misleading conclusions might be reached about the feasibility of particular policies. We have therefore decided to impose the following property income equations, so as to maintain a satisfactory relationship between stock variables and property income payments.[6]

The overseas sector

Payments of property income abroad $(PAYF)$ depend on the home short-term (Treasury bill) rate (RTB) and on the long-term (consol) rate $(RCNS)$. 95 per cent of the home assets of foreigners (HAF) are assumed to be fixed rate, with the remaining 5 per cent floating rate. Capital inflows (FIN) enter into the equation because the interest earned on fixed rate assets depends on the ruling interest rate at the time the foreigners acquire home assets. Property income payments are given as

$$PAYF_t = PAYF_{t-1} + 0.05(RTB_{t-1} - RTB_{t-2})$$
$$\times HAF_{t-2}/400 + 0.05 \times RTB_{t-1} \times FIN_{t-1}/400$$
$$+ 0.95 \times RCNS_{t-1} \times FIN_{t-1}/400 \qquad (5.7)$$

Receipts ($RECF$) are earned on both private (FAP) and public (FAG) sector holdings of foreign assets. Private sector receipts are assumed to be 95 per cent fixed rate and 5 per cent floating rate, but we do not distinguish short from long foreign interest rates; instead we use the short rate (RUS) to represent both. The interest stream is therefore mainly determined as the cumulated product of the interest rate and capital outflow ($HOUT$). Income flows are revalued in the light of exchange-rate (EX) changes. Public sector foreign assets (FAG) are assumed to be entirely floating rate. Since the asset stock is revalued when the exchange rate changes, explicit flow revaluation is needed.

$$RECF_t = RECF_{t-1} \times EX_{t-1}/EX_t + RUS_{t-1} \times HOUT_{t-1}/400$$
$$+ 0.05 \times (RUS_{t-1} - RUS_{t-2}) \times FAP_{t-2} \times EX_{t-1}/(400 \times EX_t)$$
$$+ RUS_{t-1} \times FAG_{t-1}/400 \qquad (5.8)$$

Other variables are as defined in previous sections. The total net payment abroad is $PAYF_t - RECF_t$.

The public sector

The property income of the government on its foreign-exchange reserves is shown on the last line of (5.8). It is in fact

$$NPIGF_t = RUS_{t-1} \times FAG_{t-1}/400 \qquad (5.9)$$

The interest on the home debt, $NPIGH$, is[7]

$$NPIGH_t = NPIGH_{t-1} - 0.7 \times RCNS_{t-1}(BD_{t-1} - ZOF_{t-1} - \Delta D_{t-1})/400$$
$$- 0.3 \times RTB_{t-1}(BD_{t-1} - ZOF_{t-1} - \Delta D_{t-1})/400$$
$$+ 0.3 \times \Delta RTB_{t-1} \times (HAG_{t-2} + D_{t-2})/400 \qquad (5.10)$$

It reflects the fact that the change in interest receipts depends negatively on new interest-bearing sterling borrowing ($BD_{t-1} - ZOF_{t-1} - \Delta D_{t-1}$) and on the change in interest payments on the outstanding interest-bearing assets. This component is assumed to be 30 per cent of the total interest-bearing debt.

The private sector

The property income of the private sector (*NPIP*) is then found by adding up. It is

$$NPIP_t = RECF_t - PAYF_t - NPIGF_t - NPIGH_t \qquad (5.11)$$

The links to the rest of the model

These property income flows feed into the income-outlay accounts of each sector. In particular they affect the asset accumulation identities (5.1) and (5.2) in the following way. The budget deficit, which appears in both equations, depends on the excess of government expenditure over income (inclusive of government net property income). And the balance-of-payments surplus which appears in the second equation includes net property income receipts from abroad as well as the balance of trade on goods and non-factor services. There is feedback into both identities.

Property income flows are important from a policy point of view because (i) they influence private-sector income and wealth, thus driving consumption and (ii) they affect the current account of the balance of payments, and thus the exchange rate, with consequent impact on prices and expenditures in the economy. Neglect of these flows may lead to a mistaken treatment of both private-sector wealth and consumption, and the current balance of payments and the exchange rate. This can then lead to mistaken conclusions about the dynamics of the economy; indeed the effect of property income flows on the current balance was shown, in Chapter 4, to be destabilizing. This needs to be allowed for in policy design.

5.3.4 Capital gains and asset accumulation

The revaluation term applied to home assets of the government is calculated from the change in the price of consolidated loan stock. The change in the aggregate price index takes into account the fact that only 70 per cent of the interest-bearing debt ($HAG + D$) is assumed to be fixed-rate.

$$DG_t = 0.7 \times (HAG_{t-1} + D_{t-1}) \times RCNS_{t-1}/(RCNS_t \times HAG_{t-1}) \quad (5.12)$$

The private sector owns both government debt and private sector assets. There are two types of private-sector assets (consumer durables and investment goods; the latter are broadly defined to include stocks, work in progress and privately owned land as well as other capital goods). Consumer durables are not owned by foreigners investing in the UK. Revaluations to the stock of durable goods were dealt with in (5.1) and (5.2). The revaluation of other private-sector assets has to reflect both changes in the replacement cost of capital goods and changes in the valuation ratio.

$$DP_{1t} = Q_t \times PDK_t/(Q_{t-1} \times PDK_{t-1}) \quad (5.13)$$

The revaluation index to private and foreign sector home assets, excluding consumer durables (*HAP-SDUR* and *HAF*), is calculated by weighting together these two price indices, using weights (σ_1 and σ_2) which reflect the relative supplies of these assets:

$$\sigma_1 = -HAG_{t-1}/(Q_{t-1} \times PDK_{t-1}[K_{t-1} + S_{t-1} + LAND] - HAG_{t-1}) \quad (5.14a)$$

$$\sigma_2 = (Q_{t-1} \times PDK_{t-1}[K_{t-1} + S_{t-1} + LAND])/ \\ (Q_{t-1} \times PDK_{t-1}[K_{t-1} + S_{t-1} + LAND] - HAG_{t-1}) \quad (5.14b)$$

where

LAND – value of private sector land holdings (measured at 1980 'replacement cost' and treated as constant).[8]

The capital gains index applied to home assets (*HAP-SDUR* and *HAF*) is now given as

$$DP_t = \sigma_1 DG_t + \sigma_2 DP_{1t} \quad (5.15)$$

The capital gains index for foreign assets in foreign currency, DF_t, is exogenous. Their value in home currency also reflects the effects of exchange-rate changes. This can be seen in (5.2).

Correct monitoring of capital gains is important because they affect the asset accumulation equations (5.1) to (5.5) and so can have an influence on economic behaviour. The most important link to the rest of the economy is to be found in the consumption function (section 5.4.1), but capital gains also make their presence felt in the capital flow equations (section 5.3.5), since they lead to rebalancing of portfolios.

5.3.5   Asset prices and portfolio allocation

The previous two sections have discussed the evolution of quantities of asset stocks. We now turn to their pricing. The basic idea is very simple: given the supply of assets arising from the processes just described, and given the demands for them arising from portfolio allocation decisions, we solve for the prices at which the stocks of assets are willingly held.

The valuation ratio and the consol yield

The home asset groups include private-sector capital and the sterling national debt. The 'price' of private-sector capital is represented by the product of the replacement cost of capital goods and the ratio of the market value to replacement value of capital goods (the valuation ratio). Fluctuations in the price of the sterling national debt are tracked by means of variations in the price of consolidated loan stock. However, part of the debt is assumed to be floating-rate, and so the aggregate value fluctuates less than the consol rate (section 5.3.4).

As noted above, for the purpose of asset price determination, the assumption is made that all home assets are perfect substitutes (except currency and durable goods). This has the necessary implication that the expected return on any asset, inclusive of capital gains, is equal to the yield on Treasury bills which, as noted in the next section, is treated as administered by the authorities. For the purposes of simplicity it has been assumed that the major agents active in these markets pay tax at the same rates on income and on capital gains, so that taxes do not enter the arbitrage equations.

The yield on consolidated loan stock comprises only two components. A fixed coupon is paid and the expected future price may vary. This second component is assumed to adjust so that the expected sum of both components is equated to the bill yield. However, the equation is most conveniently expressed in terms of the consol yield (which is the reciprocal of the price).

The yield on private-sector capital comprises three components: (i) profits earned through the use of the capital stock (including stocks and work in progress) in generating output; (ii) nominal capital gains arising from changes in the replacement cost of capital goods and (iii) real capital gains arising from changes in the ratio of the stock exchange valuation of capital to the replacement cost. The arbitrage equation assumes that the third component is expected to adjust so that when added to the other two an expected return equal to the known return on Treasury bills is generated.

The arbitrage equations for the yield on consols and the stock exchange valuation ratio can therefore be written as

$$RCNS^e_{t+1} = RCNS_t/(1 + RTB_t - RCNS_t) \quad (5.16)$$

$$Q^e_{t+1} = (2 + RTB_t/400 - PDK_t/PDK_{t-1})Q_t$$
$$- PROF_t/\{PDK_t \times (K_t + S_t)\} \quad (5.17)$$

where

$RCNS_t$ – yield on consols (% pa)
RTB_t – Treasury bill yield (% pa)
$PROF_t$ – rent and profit accruing to capital

and other variables are defined above.[9]

If expectations are assumed to be model-consistent, it is necessary for the valuation ratio and the consol rate to converge to their respective steady-state values, on a path along which, at all times in the absence of any shocks, $RCNS_{t+1} = RCNS^e_{t+1}$ and $Q_{t+1} = Q^e_{t+1}$. For Q we have taken a steady-state value of 0.64 (which was the historical mean over the period).[10] For the consol rate, more simply, $RCNS = RTB$ defines the steady state. That is, that the yield gap between $RCNS$ and RTB is entirely due to changes in expected future short rates of interest. These disappear in the steady state. The convergence trajectory to the steady state will normally be saddlepath stable. In the case of the consol rate, the saddlepath is degenerate, in that a permanent step change in RTB leads to an equal permanent step change in $RCNS$. For Q, however, any change in the expected future path of the right-hand side variables in (5.17) may lead to a change in the capital gains required in each future period if expectations are to be fulfilled.[11] A 'jump' in Q is assumed to take place as a consequence of such a shock, leading to the establishment of a new asymptotic saddlepath. The determination of the jump in Q and the link with domestic investment is described in section 5.4.2.

If expectations are adaptive the solution technique is in one sense similar, in that the initial price settles at a level such that the expected value from the arbitrage equation equals the expected value generated by the expectations formation process. However, now we must substitute in the explicit adaptive process for expectations formation. We adopted the following simple form for Q.

$$Q^e_{t+1} = \alpha_1 Q_t + \alpha_2$$

Given this, Q^e_{t+1} can be eliminated by the use of the arbitrage equation to yield

$$Q_t = (\alpha_2 + PROF_t/[K_t + S_t]PDK_t)/$$
$$(2 - \alpha_1 + RTB_t/400 - PDK_t/PDK_{t-1}) \quad (5.18)$$

Thus with this particular regressive form of adaptive expectations, the valuation ratio depends only on the current rate of profit and the real rate of interest.

We tried to estimate a similar adaptive expectations equation for the consol rate of the form

$$RCNS^e_{t+1} = \beta_1 RCNS_t + \beta_2 + \text{terms in } RTB$$

but were unable to find a satisfactory result. We therefore simply adopted a form of an explicit equation for *RCNS* which has been in use in the Treasury model (HM Treasury, 1985). This represents the current consol rate directly as a function of the current Treasury bill rate and the past consol rate.

$$RCNS_t = \beta_1 RCNS_{t-1} + \beta_2 RTB_t \quad (5.19)$$

With $\beta_1 + \beta_2 = 1$ the consol rate and Treasury bill rate are brought into equality in the long run. This restriction in turn means, then, that expectations are fulfilled in the steady state (see (5.16)), and we impose it in our model. Our procedure implies after substituting (5.19) into (5.16) that, as we move along any path to a steady state,

$$RCNS^e_{t+1} = (\beta_1 RCNS_{t-1} + [1 - \beta_1]RTB_t)/(1 + RTB_t - RCNS_t) \quad (5.20)$$

Figure 5.1 shows the effect of a permanent 0.2 point reduction in the domestic short-term interest rate on the long rate, with both model-consistent and adaptive expectations. It can be seen that the effects are very much more powerful if expectations are model-consistent, because in this case the market knows that the arbitrage equations will have to be satisfied in future periods as well as in the present period. The consol rate moves to its steady-state value immediately if expectations are model-consistent, but only falls there gradually if they are adaptive.

The effects of an interest-rate change on the valuation ratio are not illustrated here but are described in section 5.4.2.

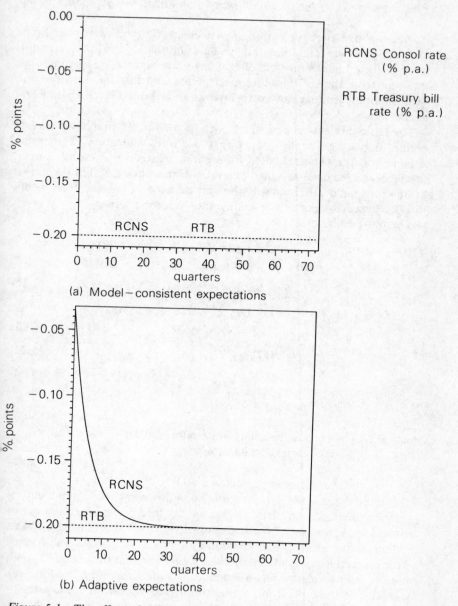

Figure 5.1   *The effect of a 0.2 point interest-rate decrease on the consol rate*

The exchange rate, international portfolio allocation and capital flows

As noted above, the assumption of perfect substitutability between home and foreign assets is not maintained. This implies that the joint determination of the exchange rate and of exchange-rate expectations is somewhat different from that of the other asset prices, and that the outcomes are in turn jointly endogenous with international portfolio allocation and capital flows.

The basic model is one in which each of the foreign and home private sectors adjusts gradually to a target portfolio allocation. The target depends on the expected yield differential between home and foreign assets. Since we have assumed perfect substitutability within those two groups this yield differential is the gap between home and foreign bill rates adjusted for expected exchange-rate appreciation.

The basic equations are:

$$HAP_t/NWPR_t = \lambda([HAP_{t-1} - SDUR_{t-1}] \times DP_t + [INV_t -$$
$$DEP \times K_{t-1} + SB_t] \times Q_t \times PDK_t + SDUR_t$$
$$+ BPS_t + BD_t)/NWPR_t + (1 - \lambda)(\theta_1 + \theta_2 Z_t) \qquad (5.21)$$

$$HAF_t \times EX_t/WW_t = \lambda \times DP_t \times HAF_{t-1} \times EX_t/WW_t$$
$$+ (1 - \lambda)(\theta_3 + \theta_4 Z_t) \qquad (5.22)$$

$$NWPR_t = HAP_t + FAP_t \qquad (5.23)$$

$$Z_t = (RTB_t - RUS_t)/400 + \Delta\log EX^e_{t+1} \qquad (5.24)$$

Here

$\Delta\log EX^e_{t+1}$ — expected exchange-rate appreciation
Z_t — excess yield on home assets

and the other variables are as defined above. [12]

In these equations λ represents an auto-regressive component of portfolio demand, so that $1 - \lambda$ can be interpreted as a speed of adjustment. θ_1 and θ_3 are the steady-state portfolio shares of home asset holdings in the portfolios of the domestic private sector and the foreign sector respectively, calculated on the assumption that the expected yields on home and foreign assets are equal. θ_2 and θ_4 represent the long-run sensitivity of these portfolio shares to an excess yield on home assets.

The model is one in which, for a given expected excess yield between home and foreign assets, the exchange rate adjusts so as to bring the supply and demand of home assets into balance. The constraint which must be met is (5.1).

$$HAP_t + HAF_t = (HAP_{t-1} + HAF_{t-1} - SDUR_{t-1}) \times DP_t$$
$$+ (INV_t - DEP \times K_{t-1} + SB_t) \times PDK_t \times Q_t$$
$$+ SDUR_t + BD_t - ZOF_t$$

Using this with (5.2) and (5.23), the reduced form for the exchange rate, EX, is as follows. (Recall that a rise in EX denotes an appreciation and that expectations enter through the variable Z.)

$$EX_t = \{(1 - \lambda)(DF_t[\theta_1 + \theta_2 Z_t] FAP_{t-1} \times EX_{t-1} + [\theta_3 + \theta_4 Z_t] WW_t)\} /$$
$$\{(1 - \lambda)(1 - \theta_1 - \theta_2)([INV_t - DEP \times K_{t-1} + SB_t] PDK_t \times Q_t$$
$$+ SDUR_t + BD_t + DP_t[HAP_{t-1} - SDUR_{t-1}]) - ZOF_t$$
$$+ HAF_{t-1}(1 - \lambda)DP_t - (\lambda + [1 - \lambda][\theta_1 + \theta_2 Z_t])BPS_t\} \quad (5.25)$$

It is clear that the exchange rate is increasing in both excess yield, Z_t, and in intervention, ZOF_t, as would be expected. The larger the capital substitution parameters, θ_2 and θ_4, the less powerful is intervention, as a policy to influence the exchange rate, relative to changes in the excess yield, brought about by changes in the interest rate.

Hicks (1939) pointed out that a necessary condition for market stability is that the response to an excess demand should be stabilizing. In this case a fall in the exchange rate should reduce the excess supply of the currency. Since the short-term trade elasticities incorporate the well-known *J*-curve effect, a fall in the exchange rate should generate a capital inflow more than large enough to offset the current account outflow it causes.

There are two mechanisms by which a fall in the exchange rate can generate a capital inflow. The first is a valuation effect. A fall in the rate leads to capital gains on foreign assets. These begin to take up a disproportionate amount of the portfolio, and so a 'reflux' of foreign investment takes place, reducing the excess supply of currency as required. This is often known as portfolio rebalancing.[13] The second mechanism, which is potentially much more powerful, is that a fall in the exchange rate may generate expectations of a rise. Then the further the fall the greater the capital inflow which can be so generated. It is now apparent that the sensitivity of the spot exchange rate to shocks in the capital account will depend on both the degree of capital mobility (the parameters θ_2 and θ_4) and the way in which expectations are formed.

Hicks' condition is met provided that a depreciation of the exchange rate leads to an expected appreciation of the exchange rate. This need not be the case with model-consistent expectations and imperfect substitutability (Christodoulakis, Meade and Weale, 1987), although in practice we find that it is (section 5.4.3). With adaptive expectations, Hicks' condition would not be met if the adaptive process were extrapolative. It must in fact be sufficiently regressive to offset the J-curve effect of the current balance.

If the adaptive function for $\Delta \log EX_t^e$ is written as $\Delta \log EX_{t+1}^e = -\phi \Delta \log EX_t$[14] then, provided ϕ is large enough, one obtains the regressive expectations formation as required. Using this one can eliminate $\Delta \log EX_{t+1}^e$ to obtain an equation in EX_t. However, the expression is somewhat complex analytically and in our model we find it more convenient to solve iteratively for EX_t without ever performing this substitution. The effects of an interest-rate change on the exchange rate and on portfolio allocation are shown empirically in section 5.4.3.

As noted above, the exchange rate is jointly determined with international portfolio holdings, as shown in equations (5.21)–(5.25). Private-sector capital flows are, in turn, calculated from the changes in asset stocks given by these equations after suitable adjustment for revaluations.

The foreign capital inflow (FIN) is given as

$$FIN_t = HAF_t - HAF_{t-1} \times DP_{t-1} \qquad (5.26)$$

and the outflow of domestic private sector capital ($HOUT$) is given as

$$HOUT_t = FAP_t - FAP_{t-1} \times DF_{t-1} \times EX_{t-1}/EX_t \qquad (5.27)$$

Official intervention (ZOF) is exogenous.

5.3.6 The rate of interest and the monetary base

The previous section discussed the determination of three key asset prices: the valuation ratio, the yield on consols and the exchange rate. All these asset prices are market determined: the asset prices adjust to bring supply and demand into balance. It is common (e.g. Tobin, 1969, 1982) to treat the determination of the short-term interest rate in the same market-determined way. The short-term interest rate is supposed to adjust to bring the demand for base money into balance with the supply.

This is not our approach. Rather we treat the short-term rate of interest as administered by the authorities. It is not exogenous but instead is driven by the control rules which we display in this book. This then means that the stock of non-interest-bearing money is demand-determined according to the portfolio preferences of the private sector and the interest rate which the authorities have fixed.

Modelling the demand for currency is straightforward. It is assumed to be a function of private sector home assets, money income, interest rates and capital gains. The function adopted is similar to that used by Weale (1986):

$$D_t/HAP_t = \Psi_1 + \Psi_2 RTL_t + \Psi_3 \log(HAP_t/GDP_t)$$
$$+ \Psi_4 D_{t-1}/(HAP_{t-1} \times DP_t) \quad (5.28)$$

where

D – private sector holding of currency and banking department deposits

DP – $1 + \%$ capital gain on home assets relative to previous period and other variables are defined as before

GDP – gross domestic product (current market prices)

RTL $= (RTB_t + RTB_{t-1})/2$

The sole role of this variable is, as noted above, in calculating the interest on the national debt. This was explained in section 5.3.3.

5.3.7 Taking stock

Asset prices are a key link in the mechanism by which monetary and fiscal policy affect economic activity. The determination of these prices has been the subject of section 5.3. As determinants of the value of wealth, these prices are an important influence on consumption; there are also good reasons to believe that the stock exchange valuation ratio drives domestic investment (Hayashi, 1982a), and of course the exchange rate is universally regarded as a major determinant of net foreign investment. These links in our model are considered in the next section.

5.4 STOCK EFFECTS AND AGGREGATE DEMAND

This section describes the ways in which the stock effects discussed above influence the various components of aggregate demand. Models are presented with the assumptions of both model-consistent and adaptive (regressive) expectations. When expectations are model-consistent, the text illustrates how unstable roots can be cleared by jumps in appropriate variables.

5.4.1   The consumption function

Theoretical models of consumers' expenditure tend to explain pure consumption (*CZ*). This differs from measured consumption because purchases of durable goods are replaced by income imputed from and depreciation of the stock of durable goods. The property income (gross of depreciation) generated by the stock of durable goods is also added on to disposable income where relevant. The calculations are described by Weale (1987).

Our basic consumption model is one in which consumers spend out of their current wealth and out of their expected future income over their lifetime. A particular problem, which arises in such a modelling of consumer behaviour, is made clear by any overlapping generations model. If the economy consists of a number of overlapping generations, any solution of the dynamics of income and wealth has as many roots as there are generations. It is not possible to estimate such a model empirically. Hall (1978) adopted the simplification that agents are effectively infinitely-lived. Such an assumption has the implication that each agent is at the same point in his life-cycle and thus aggregation poses no problems. The simplification of infinite life has to be justified by means of a bequest motive (Barro, 1974), whereby each agent shows the same concern for his descendants' welfare as he does for his own. However, Blanchard (1985) suggested a more satisfactory model, which does not run into aggregation problems. He assumed that each agent has a probability of death independent of age. This retains the feature that each agent is at the same point in the life-cycle but also preserves some of the Keynesian properties (non-neutrality of fiscal policy) which are lost in the case of infinite horizons. Weale (1987) finds that Blanchard's model is preferred to Hall's.

Blanchard's life-cycle model has sound origins based in microeconomic behaviour. The form used in our work assumes that consumption is derived from intertemporal optimization subject to a lifetime budget constraint. The consumer solves for the path implied by the Lagrangian

$$\text{MAX} \sum_{T=t}^{\infty} (1 - \alpha)^{T-t} U(CZ_T) +$$

$$\lambda \{ NWPS_{t-1} + H_{t-1} + N_{t-1} - \sum_{T=t}^{\infty} CZ_T / (1 + \mu)^{T-t} \} \quad (5.29)$$

where

CZ_t = pure consumption (adjusted to reflect consumption from the stock of durable goods)

$NWPS_t$ = real value of physical and net financial assets of personal sector at market prices $= NWPR_t/CPI_t$
H_t = capitalized expected future labour income (end period)
N_t = capitalized expected future grant income (end period)
α = rate of discount of utility
μ = rate of discount of consumption and income
$H_t + N_t$ = human capital
λ = Lagrange multiplier

If the utility function is assumed to be logarithmic, $U(CZ_t) = \log(CZ_t)$, the consumption rule is

$$CZ_t = \alpha(NWPS_{t-1} + H_{t-1} + N_{t-1}) \qquad (5.30)$$

In order to solve this model with model-consistent expectations, the method proposed by Hayashi (1982b) can be used. For

$$H_t = \sum_{k=1}^{\infty} YL^e_{t+k}/(1+\mu)^{k-1} \text{ and } N_t = \sum_{k=1}^{\infty} YG^e_{t+k}/(1+\mu)^{k-1}$$

where YL is labour income and YG is grant income. It now follows that

$$H^e_{t-1} = (1+\mu)(H_{t-2} - YL^e_{t-1}) \text{ and } N^e_{t-1} = (1+\mu)(N_{t-2} - YG^e_{t-1})$$

One may now use expected values to substitute out for H_{t-1} and N_{t-1} in (5.30) to obtain

$$CZ_t = \alpha NWPS_{t-1} + (1+\mu)(CZ_{t-1} - \alpha[YL_{t-1}$$
$$+ YG_{t-1}] - \alpha NWPS_{t-2}) + \varepsilon_t \quad (5.31)$$

where the error term ε_t includes the effects of errors in expectations of non-property income.

The econometric study in which the function was actually estimated (Weale, 1987) suggested that this function should be modified. The assumption that all households discount future utility at the same rate may be unrealistic. In particular, a slightly more general specification could be adopted in which there are two groups of households. The first group are assumed to discount their utility at the rate $\alpha < \mu$. The second group are assumed to discount their utility at a rate higher than μ. These households will try to own negative net wealth. If capital market imperfections imply that it is impossible to become a steady-state net debtor, such households will own no net wealth and spend all their income immediately. The aggregate consumption function, including the effects generated by the presence of such spendthrift households, is therefore

$$CZ_t = \alpha(NWPS_{t-1} + \lambda_2 H_{t-1} + \lambda_3 N_{t-1}) + (1 - \lambda_2) YL_t + (1 - \lambda_3) YG_t$$
$$(5.32)$$

where $(1 - \lambda_2)$ and $(1 - \lambda_3)$ are the fractions of labour and grant income accruing to spendthrift housholds. H_{t-1} and N_{t-1} can be eliminated as before, yielding

$$CZ_t = \alpha NWPS_{t-1} + (1 - \lambda_2) YL_t + (1 - \lambda_3) YG_t$$
$$+ (1 + \mu) \{ CZ_{t-1} - \alpha\lambda_2 YL_{t-1} - \alpha\lambda_3 YG_{t-1}$$
$$- \alpha NWPS_{t-2} - (1 - \lambda_2) YL_{t-1} - (1 - \lambda_3) YG_{t-1} \} \qquad (5.33)$$

The properties of this function are most simply illustrated by examining them in a framework in which the rate of return and both types of non-property income are constant. The equation for the evolution of wealth is then given, with interest rate RTB and prices fixed (so that RTB represents the real interest rate), as

$$NWPS_{t-1} = (1 + RTB)(NWPS_{t-2} + \lambda_2 YL_{t-1} + \lambda_3 YG_{t-1} - CZ_{t-1})$$
$$(5.34)$$

Substituting for $NWPS_{t-1}$ in the consumption function yields

$$\begin{bmatrix} CZ_t \\ NWPS_{t-1} \end{bmatrix} = \begin{bmatrix} 1 + \mu - \alpha(1 + RTB) & \alpha(RTB - \mu) \\ -1 - RTB & 1 + RTB \end{bmatrix} \begin{bmatrix} CZ_{t-1} \\ NWPS_{t-2} \end{bmatrix}$$
$$+ \text{ constants} \qquad (5.35)$$

The eigenvalues of the matrix are approximately

$$1 + RTB - \alpha + \alpha RTB(\mu - RTB)/(\alpha + \mu - RTB) \text{ and}$$
$$1 + \mu - \alpha RTB(\mu - RTB)/(\alpha + \mu - RTB)$$

The last term of each eigenvalue is very small (and would be zero if it were assumed that no property income was forgone on current consumption). The second eigenvalue is therefore greater than 1 provided μ is positive. The first is less than 1 if $RTB < \alpha$, which we assume.

Even if the propensity to consume out of wealth exceeds the long-run real rate of return, there is an unstable root. This has the implication that a disturbance would be cumulatively unstable. If labour or grant income rose, but no sudden change took place to consumption, savings would initially rise. The extra spending out of these savings is not, in itself, sufficient to stabilize the system. The feedback of consumption on itself means that consumption would remain too low to stabilize the system. It is as though unspent 'human capital' were accumulating without limit.

The instability can be removed by a jump in consumption. The single unstable root creates a stable saddlepath. If consumption is allowed to jump after some external disturbance, so as to alight on the new saddlepath, then the instability can be avoided. The assumption that such a jump takes place provides a useful means of modelling the behaviour of consumers as a response to changes in expectations about their future income.

For a growing economy, the condition for one stable root is that $\alpha > RTB - g$. The rate of discount must exceed the real rate of interest less the growth rate. It is also necessary that $\mu > g$. Otherwise capitalised labour income will have an infinite value.

The impact of an unanticipated shock to labour income, such as would arise from an unanticipated tax change,[15] can be shown diagrammatically. In Figure 5.2 we demonstrate the partial effects of a joint 2 point increase in the VAT rate and in the rate of employees' national insurance contributions. We choose these fiscal instruments because the composite fiscal instrument which we subsequently use in our control exercises is represented by equal changes in VAT and in employees' contributions. We take wages, the valuation ratio and the exchange rate as exogenous. A rise in taxes means that consumption will fall since the rate of discount of future income and consumption is higher than the real return on the national debt (Weale, 1987). It can be seen that, with model-consistent expectations, consumption reacts almost immediately to the tax change, moving to a value close to its steady-state level almost straightaway. Despite the fact that consumption does not depend on disposable income (Ando and Modigliani, 1963), in this case the two move almost exactly in step. The jump in consumption described above rose from the assumption that households form their behaviour in a manner consistent with the model and that, in response to a shock, they fix consumption at a level so that the economy converges to an equilibrium.

It is sometimes argued that fiscal policy is useless as a tool of economic stabilization. A combination of infinite horizons (with no risk of dying) and model-consistent expectations leads to such a conclusion. We have demonstrated, relying on work by Blanchard, that it is possible for fiscal

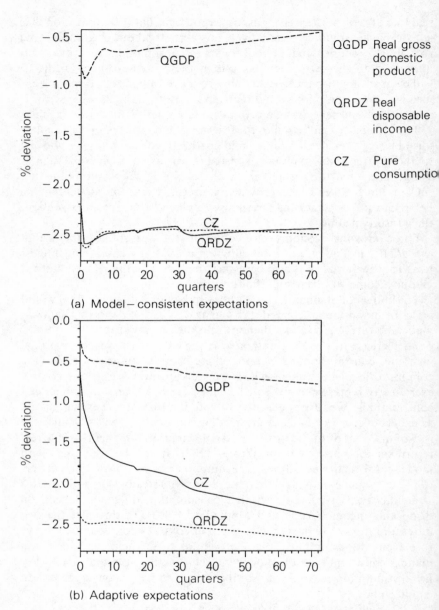

Figure 5.2 *The response of consumption to an increase in tax*

policy to be effective in a model-consistent expectations world. Such an effect is generated if the assumption of infinite horizons is dropped. It is augmented by the presence of spendthrift households. It does not, however, rely on households misunderstanding the fact that a budget deficit will imply future taxation.

If consumers did not form their expectations in the manner so described but were backward-looking, the consumption function would show spending out of current and past income and wealth. Logically there ought not to be significant effects for both wealth and property income, but the statistical evidence suggests that the most parsimonious representation is of the form

$$CZ_t = \beta_1 CZ_{t-1} + \beta_2 QRDZ_t + \beta_3 CG_t + \beta_4 NWPS_{t-1} + \varepsilon_t \quad (5.36)$$

where

$QRDZ_t$ – real disposable income (adjusted for durable good holdings)
CG_t – changes to real wealth not arising from current saving (real capital gains)

Since the saving housholds are now assumed to respond to current and lagged income it is no longer possible to distinguish them from spend-thrift households.

In a steady state the capital gains can be set to zero, so as to allow a study of the stability of the equation. Once the short-term dynamics have died out, we have

$$CZ_t = (\beta_2 QRDZ_t + \beta_4 NWPS_{t-1})/(1 - \beta_1)$$

Now

$$NWPS_t = QRDZ_t - CZ_t + NWPS_{t-1}$$
$$= (1 - \beta_2/[1 - \beta_1])QRDZ_t + (1 - \beta_4/[1 - \beta_1])NWPS_{t-1} \quad (5.37)$$

Disposable income includes a component arising from property, $RTB \times NWPS_{t-1}$. With prices stable, the dynamic equation for asset accumulation may therefore be written as

$$NWPS_t = (1 - \beta_2/[1 - \beta_1])RTB \times NWPS_{t-1}$$
$$+ (1 - \beta_4/[1 - \beta_1])NWPS_{t-1} + \text{other terms} \quad (5.38)$$

This is stable if $(1 - \beta_2/[1 - \beta_1])RTB - g < \beta_4/[1 - \beta_1]$. The requirement is less strong than the condition for there to be one rather than two unstable roots in the consistent expectations model,[16] because consumption takes place out of property income. The steady-state properties are similar to those of the consistent expectations function but, because there is no initial jump, the reaction to an exogenous change (such as tax increases) is normally slower (Figure 5.2).

5.4.2 Domestic investment

Domestic private investment can be broken down into four categories. First there is public-sector investment. The second is investment in stocks and work in progress. The third is investment in durable goods by consumers and fourthly there are private sector purchases of investment goods. In the model we have treated public-sector investment as exogenous, and have used the equations for the second and third as estimated by the National Institute. Stockbuilding is driven by what are essentially accelerator functions[17] and durable goods purchases are a dynamic function of personal disposable income. It would have been possible to modify these functions to represent adaptive or model-consistent behaviour more fully defined, but the effect on the overall properties of our model would probably have been small.

The role of clearly modelled expectational effects has therefore been left to the largest category, private-sector purchases of investment goods. A simple aggregate equation has been estimated showing how investment, measured as a fraction of the existing capital stock, depends on the valuation ratio (Tobin's Q). Similar models of investment by the manufacturing sector have been studied by Jenkinson (1981) and Oulton (1981). The practical advantage of aggregating all investment is that it is only necessary to model the evolution of one valuation ratio, but against this it is, of course, certain that some detail of the response of the disaggregate economy will be lost.

The key investment equation is

$$\Delta K_t / K_{t-1} = \lambda_4 (Q_t - Q_\infty) + g \qquad (5.39)$$

where g is the trend rate of growth and Q_∞ is the steady-state value of Q (see section 5.3.5). An investment function of this type can be justified by a quadratic cost of adjustment function. It is most easily understood in terms of constant returns to scale (Hayashi, 1982a), since in this case marginal and average Q are the same.[18]

The version of the NIESR model we are using does not have a fully articulated production function. We rely instead on employment functions which show substantial increasing returns to scale in the short and long run. The implication of this is that the capital stock plays a role in determining the rate of return through its influence as a denominator but not through any influence on the total level of profits. This may be seen below.

The investment equation interacts with the arbitrage equation (5.17)

$$Q_{t+1}^e = (2 + RTB_t/400 - PDK_t/PDK_{t-1})Q_t - PROF_t/\{(K_t + S_t) \times PDK_t\}$$

to give, with model-consistent expectations, a system which can, if expectations are fulfilled, be linearized in matrix form

$$\begin{bmatrix} K_t \\ Q_{t+1} \end{bmatrix} = \begin{bmatrix} \alpha_1 & \alpha_2 \\ \alpha_3 & \alpha_4 \end{bmatrix} \begin{bmatrix} K_{t-1} \\ Q_t \end{bmatrix} + \begin{bmatrix} 0 & 0 \\ \beta_1 & -\beta_3 \end{bmatrix} \begin{bmatrix} RTB_t \\ PROF_t \end{bmatrix} \tag{5.40}$$

The derivation of this linear form is presented by Christodoulakis and Weale (1987). They show that $\alpha_1 = 1$ and that the system then has one stable and one unstable root, provided that the condition, $\alpha_2\alpha_3 > 0$, is met, which it is. The instability generated by this is assumed to be removed by a jump in the valuation ratio on to a saddlepath so that the economy again converges to equilibrium.

The capital-stock/valuation ratio system is sensitive to both fiscal and monetary policy. A reduction in the tax rate increases the rate of return on capital. The arbitrage condition now requires that the valuation ratio should be falling. The rate of return can be brought back in line with the rate of interest by means of an increase in the capital stock. An upward jump in Q followed by a gradual fall will ensure that, except with the initial jump, the arbitrage condition is met and the capital stock is increased. A reduction in the real rate of interest requires that the valuation ratio be falling. Equilibrium can only be regained if the rate of return on capital is increased. These conditions are met by an upward jump in Q followed by a steady fall. Accumulation of capital takes place and eventually the rate of return is brought into line. Figure 5.3 shows the effect of a 0.2 point reduction in the interest rate, on the assumption that wages, human capital and the exchange rate are constant.

The valuation ratio influences investment directly and, through its effect on wealth, it also influences consumption. The impact on consumption dwindles over time for two reasons. First of all, the capital gains are gradually spent. And, secondly, the fall in the interest rate reduces the property income of the private sector. Although no consumption takes place out of this income directly, the fall in property income has an impact on saving and, therefore, in the longer term on wealth. The effects on consumption and investment are much more

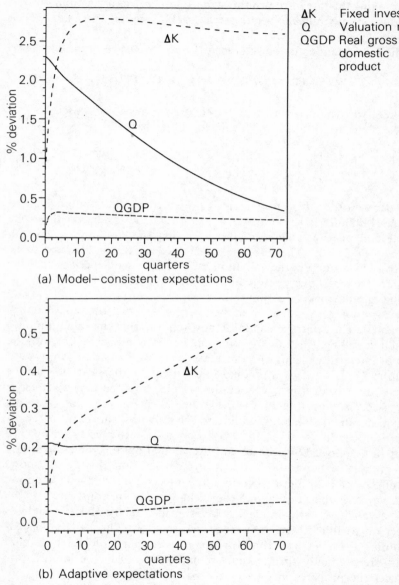

Figure 5.3   *The valuation ratio and investment: a 0.2% interest-rate reduction*

powerful than those found in other macroeconomic models (Easton, 1985). We attribute this to the role we have given to the valuation ratio which is, at present, unique to our model.

Although this system provides a coherent modelling of the investment sector with model-consistent expectations, it is not fully complete. As noted above, the model does not embody a conventional production function. The share of profit in national income is independent of the capital stock, since it is given by, in essence, a system of mark-up equations. Correction of this omission would probably have the effect of increasing the unstable root, and ensuring faster convergence of the system.

With adaptive expectations the investment function is unchanged. However, Q_t is given by adaptive equation (5.18). It can be seen in Figure 5.3 that whenever $Q_t > Q_\infty$ (the steady-state value) the capital stock is rising and so $Q_t > Q_\infty$ is falling. It is clear from this adaptive equation that, here, too, fiscal and monetary policy will both influence Q and thus have effects on aggregate demand through their consequences for fixed investment. The effect is very much smaller than with model-consistent expectations. The reason for this is that the effect of a permanent change in the interest rate on Q is very much reduced if expectations are adaptive rather than model-consistent. This can, in turn, be explained by the fact that Q is no longer a jumping variable. It is also worth noting that the decline in consumption appears much sooner than with model-consistent expectations. The reason for this is that the adaptive consumption function has a larger propensity to consume out of wealth.

5.4.3 Net foreign investment

The previous section has shown how the valuation ratio interacts with the capital stock. We set up a partial model which demonstrated how variations in the valuation ratio can drive the capital stock to an equilibrium in which, down to a risk-premium, the rate of return on fixed capital is the same as the rate of return on Treasury bills.

In the same way the real exchange rate interacts with the rate of net foreign investment. In Chapter 4 we demonstrated that there was an inherent instability in the stock of net foreign investment; we investigated whether the real exchange rate could move so as to clear this; in the unregulated economy we suggested that this was only possible if the real exchange rate was able to jump so as to clear the instability. On the other hand, in a model which does not have forward-looking expectations, it is perfectly possible to simulate an unstable model.

The results which we presented there were for an economy with perfect capital mobility between home and foreign assets, but we would not expect them to be greatly modified by high, but imperfect, capital mobility. Here we do not add to the analysis of Chapter 4 by presenting a new algebraic model with imperfect capital mobility, but we limit ourselves to a simulation of our model. The portfolio allocation aspect of this (equations (5.21) to (5.24)) is effectively an imperfect capital mobility variant of equation (4.19d).

The balance sheet structure which we have adopted (section 5.3.1) allows us to keep track of the stock of foreign investment, and the property income equations (section 5.3.3) ensure that interest payments and receipts are not neglected. The implications of changes in the real exchange rate for the value of net foreign assets in terms of the home product are also taken into account.

Version 7 of the National Institute model, in common with most other econometric models, shows the effects of the real exchange rate on imports and exports, identified by several broad sectors. In version 7 the Marshall–Lerner conditions scarcely hold. We have taken the view that these low elasticities may be due to aggregation bias, and instead have applied the much larger elasticities found by the disaggregate analysis of the Cambridge Growth Project model (Barker and Peterson, 1988; see Appendix to this chapter).

The basic idea of our model, in the absence of exchange-rate targeting and with model-consistent expectations, is that adjustments in the real exchange rate take place so as to clear stock instability arising from the cumulation of interest payments on net foreign assets.[19] This simulation corresponds to Regime 1 in section 4.5. In our simulation with model-consistent expectations, we impose the jump which is needed to make the model saddlepath stable. With adaptive expectations (section 4.5) we would expect the model to be unstable because the exchange rate cannot move to clear the instability due to the cumulation of foreign assets, but this is not in itself a barrier to simulation.

In Figure 5.4 we present simulations showing the effect of a 0.2 per cent fall in the home interest rate, holding the wage rate, the valuation ratio and human capital constant. The interest-rate reduction results in a downward jump in the exchange rate. This generates capital gains on private sector investment abroad. Foreign assets in the UK also rise initially because foreigners make gains on their non-UK assets and invest some of those gains in the United Kingdom. An adjustment process then takes place whereby each sector adjusts its portfolio towards the final equilibrium. The exchange rate continues to move so as to maintain

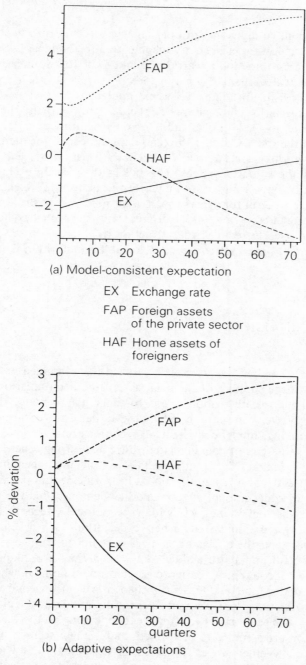

(a) Model-consistent expectation

EX   Exchange rate

FAP Foreign assets
      of the private sector

HAF Home assets of
      foreigners

(b) Adaptive expectations

*Figure 5.4   The exchange rate and foreign investment: a 0.2% point
reduction in the interest rate*

capital account equilibrium, and only reaches its final steady state very gradually. The lower net property income paid to foreigners, as a result of lower interest rates and a rearrangement of portfolios, means that the steady-state real exchange rate is appreciated relative to its reference level. This is visible in Figure 5.4(a) extrapolated.

When expectations are adaptive, there is no jump in the foreign exchange rate. Instead it falls steadily, again generating a current account surplus. In the short term the foreign sector appears to be increasing its holding of sterling assets despite the fall in the interest rate. This happens because of the valuation effect. The fall in the sterling exchange rate leads to a fall in the value of sterling assets measured in foreign currency, and in the short term foreigners top up their holdings. In the longer term the fall in the interest rate (taking account of the expected exchange-rate change) has clearly reduced the attraction of domestic assets, but the model probably does not converge to a stable equilibrium.

5.5 CONCLUSION

This chapter has had two purposes. First, it has examined in detail the evolution of the supplies of financial assets, the determination of their prices and the resulting implications for aggregate demand. These are shown to be very important. Secondly, it has shown the effects of forward-looking, model-consistent, expectations on aggregate demand. These two issues are of course related, since it is through their effects on asset quantities and prices that expectations influence expenditures. Our thorough treatment of asset effects has been an essential prerequisite to our study of expectational effects, and has demonstrated the means by which financial policy interacts with expectational effects to affect the real economy. We find that, when expectations are assumed to be model-consistent, the effects of changes in policy instruments are much more powerful and more sudden than when they are adaptive. This suggests that it could prove easier to regulate an economy in which policy rules are understood and believed, than it will in an environment in which expectations are formed from simple adaptive rules.[20] The response of the economy is very different depending on the way in which expectations are assumed to be formed, and it might seem to be an open question of whether we can succeed in designing rules which work independently of whether expectations are assumed to be adaptive or are assumed to be model-consistent. It is to this question that we now turn.

5.6 APPENDIX – MODEL PARAMETERS

5.6.1 Variable list

This list covers the variables referred to in the Appendix.

BD	budget deficit (current prices)
BPS	balance of payments surplus (current prices)
CDUR	purchases of consumer durables (current prices)
CPI	consumer price index
CZ	pure consumption, adjusted for durable goods (1980 prices)
D	monetary base (current prices)
DEP	Depreciation rate of fixed capital (1.2% per quarter)
DEPC	Depreciation rate of consumer durables (4% per quarter)
DF	1 + fractional capital gain on foreign assets
DP	1 + fractional capital gain on home assets
ECZ	stochastic term in consumption
EX	nominal exchange rate index (foreign currency/£)
EXA^e	expected exchange rate appreciation
FAP	foreign assets of private sector (current prices)
g	long-term real growth rate of the economy (per cent per quarter)
GDP	Money GDP (current market prices)
HAF	home assets of foreigners (current prices)
HAP	home assets of private sector (current prices)
INV	gross fixed investment (1980 prices)
K	capital stock (1980 prices)
NWPR	personal sector wealth (current prices)
NWPS	total personal wealth (1980 prices)
PDK	price of capital goods (1980 = 1)
PROF	profit and rent on private capital (current prices)
Q	valuation ratio
QRDZ	personal disposable income adjusted for durable goods (1980 prices)
RCNS	consol rate (% p.a.)
RTB	UK Treasury bill rate (% p.a.)
RTL	average of beginning and end period Treasury bill rates
RUS	foreign bill rate (% p.a.)
S_1, S_2, S_3 and S_4	seasonal dummies
S	private sector stocks and work in progress (current prices)
SB	private sector stock building (1980 prices)
SDUR	stock of consumer durable goods (current prices)
TIME	time trend

WW world wealth (current price indicator)
YG   grant income (1980 prices)
YL   labour income (1980 prices)

5.6.2 Stock and share prices

The dynamic adaptive process for Q is

$$Q^e_{t+1} = \alpha_1 Q_t + \alpha_2 \qquad (5.41)$$

This equation can be estimated by replacing the expected values by their
actual outturns. On estimation over the period 1973 IV to 1984 II it
turned out to be severely autocorrelated. A model with a longer lag was
found to be dynamically unstable when inserted in the full econometric
model; it developed autocorrelation if restricted to be stable. Instead of
introducing a longer lag the equation was therefore estimated on the
assumption that the residuals were autocorrelated. In an equation of this
form no common-factor restriction, of the type discussed by Hendry and
Mizon (1978), is required.

The actual value of Q is determined by the interaction of the arbitrage
and expectational equations, eliminating Q^e_{t+1}. The reduced form for Q
is therefore an equation in the rate of profit, the rate of interest and the
rate of inflation of capital goods. No numerical long-run value for Q can
be imposed without making some assumptions about the steady-state
values these other variables take. The reduced form (equation 5.18) is

$$Q_t = \{\alpha_2 + PROF_t/(PDK_t \times [K_t + S_t])\}/2 - \alpha_1$$
$$+ RTB_t/400 - PDK_t/PDK_{t-1}) \qquad (5.42)$$

If one assumes that in the steady state the rate of interest is 7 per cent, the
rate of inflation of capital goods is 2.8 per cent and the rate of profit 4.2
per cent per annum (which is broadly consistent with our perception of
the long-run steady state of the model), the condition on α_1 and α_2
needed to ensure Q takes a steady-state value of 0.64, its historical mean
is

$$0.64 = (\alpha_2 + 0.0105)/(1 - \alpha_1 + 0.0105) \qquad (5.43)$$

This condition is accepted ($t_{42} = 1.30$) and the final equation is

$$Q_{t+1}^e = 0.753 \times Q_t + 0.153 \qquad (5.44)$$
$$\phantom{Q_{t+1}^e = 0} (8.3) (8.3)$$

$$\rho = 0.49$$
$$(3.5)$$

$R^2 = 0.60$
Test for autocorrelation $F(4,34) = 1.83$
Test for stability on last 5 observations $F(5,41) = 4.4$
Estimation period 1973 IV to 1984 II
F-statistics are derived from χ^2 statistics using the small-sample adjustment suggested by Evans and Savin (1982). The stability test is accepted at a 2.5 per cent level, but not a 5 per cent level. Had more resources been available this problem would have been investigated in detail.

The expected future values for Q can now be eliminated and the resulting equations solved for the current values of Q:

$$Q_t = \{0.153 + PROF_t/(PDK_t \times [K_t + S_t])\}/(0.247$$
$$+ RTB_t/400 - PDK_t/PDK_{t-1}) \quad (5.45)$$

The current price of Q can be interpreted as adjusting so that expectations are consistent with the arbitrage equations. The expectations thus formed are, of course, not normally fulfilled.

We attempted to estimate a similar equation for the consol rate. However, the results implied that the rate moved one for one with the Treasury bill rate. It seemed to us that this implied excessive volatility of long-run expectations of future interest rates. We therefore imposed a modified version of an equation from the Treasury model (HM Treasury, 1985). The modification ensures that, in the steady state, the long and short interest rates are equal. With our assumption about perfect capital mobility, this then implies that expectations are fulfilled in the steady state.

$$RCNS_t = 0.831 \times RCNS_{t-1} + 0.169 \times RTB_t \qquad (5.46)$$

It is of course possible to calculate the expectational equation for the consol rate which, together with the arbitrage equation, implies this relationship for the actual rate.

5.6.3 The exchange rate

The exchange rate is determined by the capital flow model (section 5.3.5).
With model-consistent expectations the model is solved by, once again,
making the assumption that expectations are fulfilled. When expectations are adaptive, a suitable model of expectations-determination is
needed. Attempts to estimate such an equation were unsuccessful. They
suggested an extrapolative process. A fall in the exchange rate would lead
to expectations of a further fall and the market would not clear. It has
therefore been necessary to impose an adaptive equation

$$\Delta \log EX^e_{t+1} = -0.3 \ \Delta \log EX_t \tag{5.47}$$

5.6.4 Portfolio allocation

Considerable resources were devoted to the estimation of a model of
portfolio allocation, defining the choice between home and foreign assets
by the private and foreign sectors. The results implied a degree of capital
mobility very significantly below that generally believed to exist; we have
therefore had to use an equation for private sector portfolio allocation
which gives equal weight to the data and a strongly-held prior belief that
there is high substitutability between home and foreign assets. Since we
only use our model for the purposes of rerunning history and the
residuals are therefore added back, it has not been necessary to include a
dummy for the ending of exchange control.

The home assets of the private sector are a weighted average of a
component which is sensitive to expected yield differentials and the sum
of home assets in the previous period, appropriately revalued, and
current saving. Saving is measured as the sum of private sector investment (including stockbuilding and net durable goods purchases), the
budget deficit and the current account surplus. The weighting indicates a
speed of adjustment.

$$
\begin{aligned}
HAP_t/NWPR_t = 0.915(& [HAP_{t-1} - SDUR_{t-1}] \times DP_t \\
+ & [INV_t - DEP \times K_{t-1} + SB_t] \times Q_t \times PDK_t \\
+ & SDUR_t + BPS_t + BD_t)/NWPR_t + 0.085 \times \{0.873 \\
+ & 17.34 \times (0.0025 [RTB_t - RUS_t] + EXA^e_t)\} \quad (5.48
\end{aligned}
$$

The related stock variables (section 5.3.2) are maintained as:

$$NWPR_t = (HAP_{t-1} - SDUR_{t-1}) \times DP_t + FAP_t \times DF_t \times EX_{t-1}/EX_t$$
$$+ SDUR_t + (INV_t - DEP \times K_{t-1} + SB_t) \times Q_t$$
$$\times PDK_t + BD_t + BPS_t \tag{5.49}$$

$$K_t = (1 - DEP) \times K_{t-1} + INV_t \tag{5.50}$$

$$SDUR_t = (1 - DEPC) \times SDUR_{t-1} \times CPI_t/CPI_{t-1} + CDUR_t \tag{5.51}$$

$$FAP_t = NWPR_t - HAP_t \tag{5.52}$$

Coefficients in the foreign sector equation have been imposed so as to lead to the same absolute average currency flow as the domestic sector shows in response to an interest-rate change. No easy interpretation can be placed on the coefficients since WW is not measured in units of its own. The equation is

$$HAF_t = 0.915 \times HAF_{t-1} \times DP_t + 0.085 \times \{7.4 -$$
$$1000 \times (0.0025\,[RTB_t - RUS_t] + EXA_t^e)\} \times WW_t/EX_t \tag{5.53}$$

The demand for the monetary base is modelled using a form similar to that adoped by Weale (1986). It is expressed as a fraction of private sector home assets. This fraction depends on stock of home assets relative to a 'baseline' demand which is a function of Money GDP and the opportunity cost of holding the monetary base. It also depends on the interest rate and on the lagged ratio of monetary base to home assets, adjusted for average capital gains on all home assets. The estimated equation is

$$D_t/HAP_t = 0.0229 - 0.005 \log(HAP_t/GDP_t) - 0.00005\,RTL_t$$
$$\quad\;(2.85)\quad\;(2.65)\qquad\qquad\qquad\qquad(1.75)$$

$$+ 0.652 D_{t-1}/(HAP_{t-1} \times DP_t) - 0.00006 \times TIME \tag{5.54}$$
$$\quad(5.17)\qquad\qquad\qquad\qquad(3.42)$$

$$- 0.0007 S_1 + 0.0006 S_2 + 0.0002 S_3$$
$$\quad(3.52)\qquad(3.38)\qquad(0.89)$$

$R^2 = 0.98$

Test for autocorrelation up to four periods $F(4,28) = 0.65$
Test for stability on last five observations $F(5,30) = 1.8$
Estimation period 1973 IV to 1984 II

5.6.5   Consumers' expenditure

The consumption function with rational expectations is an estimated form of equation (5.33). The estimation technique takes account of the fact that the consumption function implies that moving average errors are present. The model is a restricted form of a much more general model. Weale (1987) presents the results of a full battery of test statistics, showing that the restrictions implied by the particular form of the consumption function can be accepted by the data. The model, parameter estimates and basic test statistics are set out below.

$$CZ_t = (-2760 \times S_1 + 606 \times S_2 + 651 \times S_3 + 1504 \times S_4)(1 + g)^t$$
$$\quad\ (34.3)\qquad\ (8.6)\qquad\ (8.1)\qquad\quad (20.4)$$

$$+\ 0.060 \times NWPS_{t-1} + (1 + 0.0104)(CZ_{t-1} - 0.006NWPS_{t-2}$$
$$\quad (5.4)\qquad\qquad\qquad (7.0)\qquad\qquad\ (5.4)$$

$$-\ 0.006(0.663\,[\,YL_{t-1} + YG_{t-1}]) + 0.337 \times (YL_t + YG_t)$$
$$\quad (5.4)\ \ (9.3)\qquad\qquad\qquad\qquad (4.7)$$

$$-\ (1 + 0.0104) \times 0.337 \times (YL_{t-1} + YG_{t-1}) + ECZ_t$$
$$\qquad (7.0)\qquad\quad (4.7)$$

$$-\ (1 + 0.0104)ECZ_{t-1} \qquad\qquad\qquad\qquad\qquad (5.55)$$
$$\quad (7.0)$$

The data are detrended before estimation, allowing the seasonal terms to be treated as constant seasonal dummies. During estimation due account is paid to the moving average nature of the error term.

Autocorrelation parameter -0.439 ($t_{36} = 2.7$)
Chow test (last 5 observations) $F(5,30) = 0.3$
Autocorrelation up to 4th order $\chi_4^2 = 0.55$
S.E. 200

The estimation is carried out using version 4.0 of TSP. The estimation period is 1974 III to 1984 II. The χ^2 statistics show the results of the Wald test.

In a purely adaptive expectation model, with no forward-looking behaviour, the consumption function is very simple. It is found to be

$$CZ_t = 0.108 \times QRDZ_t + 0.0028 \times NWPS_{t-1} + 0.013 \times CG_t$$
$$\quad (2.2) \qquad\qquad (2.7) \qquad\qquad (3.7)$$

$$+ 0.740 \times CZ_{t-1} - 4395 \times S_1 - 1095 \times S_2$$
$$\quad (8.8) \qquad\qquad (22.5) \qquad (7.9)$$

$$- 1173 \times S_3 + 4242 \qquad\qquad\qquad\qquad\qquad (5.56)$$
$$\quad (9.0) \qquad (3.8)$$

$R^2 = 0.965$
Test of autocorrelation of up to fourth order $F(4,26) = 0.22$
Chow test with split last five observations $F(5,29) = 1.27$
Estimation period 1974 I to 1984 II

The equation was estimated after scaling by disposable income.

The original NIESR equation is used to model purchases of durable goods. The stock of durable goods is maintained by means of a perpetual inventory (section 5.3.2), assuming a rate of depreciation of 4 per cent per quarter. Income is imputed to the stock of durable goods at a rate of 0.55 per cent per quarter (a rate equal to the average real return in the economy as a whole from 1974 to 1984).

5.6.6 Fixed investment

In order to produce a simple explanation of fixed investment the disaggregation present in the NIESR model has been suppressed. Aggregate gross private sector investment is modelled as a function of the valuation ratio

$$INV_t/K_{t-1} = 0.011(Q_t + Q_{t-1})/2 + 0.713 INV_{t-1}/K_{t-2} - (0.0030 S_1$$
$$\qquad (2.85) \qquad\qquad\qquad (5.65) \qquad\qquad (7.68)$$

$$+ 0.00104 S_2 + 0.00109 S_3) \qquad\qquad\qquad (5.57)$$
$$\quad (2.77) \qquad\quad (3.07)$$

$R^2 = 0.61$
Chow test with split after 31 observations $F(5,31) = 1.36$
Test for serial correlation of up to fourth order $F(4,28) = 0.64$
Estimation period 1974 II to 1984 II

This equation is multiplied up by the lagged capital stock for use in the model. It is also seasonally adjusted. When Q takes its equilibrium value INV_t/K_{t-1} will equal the aggregate rate of depreciation plus the expected (trend) rate of growth in the economy. The mean value of Q over the estimation period was 0.64. This was associated with gross investment of 1.9 per cent of the capital stock per quarter. The national accounts imply a depreciation rate of 1.2 per cent per quarter. The resulting growth rate in the capital stock is regarded as an equilibrium growth rate. The behaviour of this function is studied in detail by Christodoulakis and Weale (1987).

The link with the existing investment functions in the National Institute model has been made by replacing the existing aggregate, which is the sum of component parts with the value derived above. The disaggregate estimate for investment by the service sector is replaced by a balancing item, and the other parts operate as in the existing model.

5.6.7 Exports and imports

A feature of the National Institute model is that the Marshall–Lerner conditions hold at best weakly. The trade price elasticities are lower than those suggested by Barker's (1988a) survey. To attempt to investigate exchange-rate policies on such a model is not likely to prove fruitful. In such circumstances it would be necessary to restrict imports for balance-of-payments adjustment.[21]

The low sensitivity of trade flows to exchange-rate movements in the National Institute model comes about for three reasons. First, the price of exports is more sensitive to world prices and less sensitive to home prices than the mainstream of the estimates presented by Barker (1988b). Furthermore the price of manufacturing output sold domestically itself has a high sensitivity to import prices. The implication of this is that a 5 per cent depreciation leads to a fall in relative export prices in the long run of only 0.5 per cent even though the nominal wage is fixed. Secondly, the price elasticity of demand for exports is not large (see below). Thirdly, on the import side, again the elasticity of substitution is low. (The import price is not sensitive to domestic prices and this at least does enhance the effects of a depreciation compared with a model which attaches some weight to domestic prices. However, this enhancement is small since the weight on domestic prices is typically not very large.)

In the modified version of the model it has been decided to impose as long-run elasticities those offered by Barker (1988a) derived by aggregating disaggregate trade equations. Table 5.2 summarizes the changes

Table 5.2   Elasticity of demand with respect to relative prices

		NIESR	Barker	Share in Total
Exports	manufactures	0.90	0.59	0.53
	other goods	0.0	} 1.11 {	0.23
	service	1.20		0.24
	Total	0.59	· 1.01	1.0
Imports	manufactures	0.33	1.48	0.55
	other goods	0.11	} 0.34 {	0.21
	services	0.0		0.24
	Total	0.21	0.96	1.0

made. The elasticities are calculated in 1981 for those equations where they are not constant, in order to be comparable with Barker's (1988a) results.

In order to impose Barker's price elasticities on the model, the long-term manufacturing price elasticities are changed. The 'other goods' elasticities are kept as in the original NIESR model. The long-term export service price elasticity is set at 2.22, while the import service price elasticity is set at 1.29.

Barker's (1988b) estimates for the long-term sensitivity of export and import prices to home and foreign prices have also been imposed. The long-term sensitivity of domestic output prices to import prices and unit labour costs has been derived from the disaggregate estimate of Weale (1988). The import weight in this equation does not fall very far but this fall can have a marked impact on the overall effect of a trade depreciation. The change to price effects are summarized in Table 5.3. These

Table 5.3   Relative weights on home prices/costs

		NIESR	Barker/ Weale	Share in Total
Exports	manufactures	0.41	0.57	0.53
	other goods	0.54	} 0.53 {	0.23
	services	0.75		0.24
	Total	0.52	0.55	1.0
Imports	manufactures	0	0.13	0.55
	other goods	0	} 0.26 {	0.21
	services	0		0.24
	Total	0	0.19	1.0
Home sales	manufactures	0.38	0.45	

The weights on foreign prices are 1 − those on home prices.

long-run properties are imposed, where possible, by modifying 'catch-up' terms in model equations. Each coefficient on the relevant variable has been scaled appropriately. In the case of service imports where there was originally no price effect, the time path of the price response is assumed to be the same as that of the quantity response. The modified equations are available on request.

Chapter Six

Macroeconomic policy rules for economic stabilization

6.1 INTRODUCTION

In this chapter we demonstrate the working of policy rules designed to be capable of regulating the two policy targets which we use in our empirical study of New Keynesian economic policy; these targets are the level of nominal GDP and the level of real national wealth. The case for choosing these two variables as targets was set out in Chapter 1. Our policy rules are intended to be suitable for use independently of whether expectations are model-consistent or follow the adaptive processes described in Chapter 5. We also consider the problem of stabilizing an economy which suffers from strong cost-push linkages, and compare this with regulation of an economy in which wages are not linked to prices but respond only to excess demand and a core rate of inflation.

In our static analytic model in Chapter 2 we argued that the appropriate use of monetary or fiscal policy as a means of achieving both policy targets, what we called the appropriate instrument-target emphasis, depends on the relative strength of the effects of monetary and fiscal policy on each of the targets. We summarized this idea of relative strength by the concept of comparative advantage. We went on to argue that, because changes in taxes may influence wages, the pattern of comparative advantage, and thus the appropriate policy-target emphasis, was crucially dependent on the structure of the labour market as represented by the aggregate wage equation. If wages were fixed in terms of real take-home pay, then it was likely that monetary policy would have a comparative advantage in fighting inflation, while, if wages were negotiated in nominal terms in the face of demand pressures, it was more likely that fiscal policy would have a comparative advantage in fighting inflation. This would have immediate implications for the appropriate policy-target emphasis.

In Chapter 3 we turned to dynamics. We expressed monetary policy using a real exchange rate target and retained the use of taxes as a fiscal policy instrument. We looked at a particularly simple form of instrument-target emphasis, normally known as policy assignment, since an analytical treatment of the active use of both instruments to control both targets threatened to get out of hand. Our investigation of simple 'decoupled' policies was useful in indicating some of the problems faced by the use of fiscal policy to control inflation.

We complemented this dynamic analysis by an investigation of the pattern of comparative advantage, in both the short and the long term, of our two instruments, taxes and real exchange rate policy, in controlling two targets, the price level and, in Chapter 3, investment. We argued that in the simple case in which the pattern of comparative advantage is well defined and the desired form of policy rules is straightforward, the pattern of comparative advantage should be reflected in the control rules used to regulate the dynamic economy. Otherwise the control rules are likely to perform badly. This is simply a generalization of Mundell's Principle of Effective Market Classification (Mundell, 1962). In the more complicated case in which the pattern of comparative advantage changes over time, it is not possible to make general inferences about instrument-target emphasis from the pattern of comparative advantage. However, we suggested that it is still generally the case that the pattern of short-term comparative advantage will need to be reflected in the structure of the proportional components of the control rules. One would thus expect that a rule for stabilizing inflation in a cost-push economy would need to have a strong proportional component of monetary policy in the control of inflation. This chapter investigates whether these hypotheses, formed from a theoretical investigation, are borne out in our empirical model. We demonstrate that satisfactory policy rules can be found whose proportional components do reflect the pattern of comparative advantage, but we stress that these rules are representative and we do not claim to prove that, in our dynamic model, all possible satisfactory rules must reflect the pattern of comparative advantage.

Chapter 4 introduced the further dynamic complication of wealth accumulation. Again, we simplified the treatment of instrument-target emphasis by applying it in its extreme form. We assumed that each instrument was applied to the control of only one target. This allowed us to investigate problems of stock instability, but did not make any further contribution to our knowledge of appropriate instrument-target emphasis.

For reasons which will now be obvious, after some preliminary definitions we proceed to examine the behaviour of the wage equation in our simulation model, and look at the influence of wage indexation on the pattern of comparative advantage of our policy instruments in controlling our target variables. We then present representative rules which reflect the pattern of comparative advantage, and study their properties by looking at some simulations.

6.2 THE TARGET VARIABLES DEFINED

We must now give precise definitions to the target variables which we adopt in our empirical work.

6.2.1 Money GDP

Money GDP is defined at factor cost, so as to remove the direct effects of any indirect tax changes on the price level.

6.2.2 National wealth

The definition of national wealth which we have adopted is

Private sector capital stock (including land and stocks and work in progress) valued at actual (or in the case of land a notional) replacement cost × the ratio of home assets of the private sector at market prices (excluding consumer durables) to all net home assets (excluding consumer durables) at market prices
PLUS
Foreign assets of the private sector at market prices
PLUS
Net foreign assets of the government

The first term attempts to allocate the domestic private capital stock, adjusted, as far as possible, for denationalization, so as to produce a consistent series, at replacement cost between home and foreign investors on the basis of their overall holdings of claims on capital goods. Only the share allocated to the domestic private sector is included in national wealth. The remainder, which is allocated to the foreign sector, is not part of the wealth of the nation. On the other hand, having excluded foreign claims on domestic capital, we must aim to include domestic claims on foreign assets. Private sector foreign assets are included at market prices because there is no obvious way of measuring them at replacement cost. Finally, even if the government never intervenes it may own some net foreign assets and these have to be included.

The statistics from which we have calculated this aggregate are probably less reliable than many. We have, for example, had to interpolate within annual estimates in estimating the components which go into these aggregates. And we have had to make use of variables such as trade credit, which are themselves unreliable. Nevertheless we have been able to produce an aggregate which represents a particular definition of national wealth. As far as is possible, it is measured at replacement cost rather than at market prices and it excludes a number of items which could reasonably be included. The most important of these is the public sector capital stock. A second is the value of unextracted natural resources, and a third is the value of the stock of consumer durable goods.

We measure national wealth at replacement cost rather than at market value (stock market valuation) because, in our model, fluctuations in the valuation ratio about its equilibrium are temporary. To value wealth at market prices would encourage the use of policy instruments which manipulate the stock exchange valuation of capital in the short term. This would have, if anything, an adverse effect on national saving, because a high valuation ratio would be induced if wealth were low. This high valuation ratio would encourage consumption rather than increased saving. To value wealth at market prices would also mean that our policy instruments would respond to noise in the valuation ratio; this is in itself undesirable. These arguments point, very much, to a replacement cost valuation; we value foreign assets at market price only because it is not possible to measure a replacement cost valuation.

In the 1980s there has been a dispute about the quality of much public sector investment. We have left public sector capital out of the measure of national wealth, not because we believe that public sector capital goods, such as hospitals, are in any sense less useful than private sector goods, such as casinos, but because we do not wish to become embroiled in this debate. Instead we have, in our simulations of Chapters 8 and 9, adopted separate exogenous trajectories for public sector investment.

We exclude the stock of unextracted natural resources for reasons of measurement. The stock of consumer durables is left out for much the same reason as the public sector capital stock. Many people would find it hard to describe an economy as making prudent provision for the future by increasing its purchases of consumer durables.

We do not claim a cast-iron case for any of these exclusions, and we could imagine that the pragmatic economist would want to run several wealth targets in parallel (although they might not all be attainable). But we are confident that our results would not be changed significantly by a slightly different approach.

6.3   ENDOGENOUS WAGES

In Chapter 5 we set out the basic stock-flow relationships of the model which we use for an empirical analysis of macroeconomic policy. Now we discuss the wage equations which we use in our analysis. We have three different equations. The major distinction is between our 'unreformed wage' economy, in which we use a realistic wage equation, with wages indexed to prices, based on one which has been econometrically estimated, and our 'reformed wage' economy in which wages are set with reference to the core rate of inflation and to unemployment terms, but without any direct indexation or 'real wage catch-up' terms.

With unreformed wages, expectations of consumer price inflation play an important role; we distinguish the case in which these are model-consistent from that in which they are adaptive. With reformed wages, expectations of consumer price inflation do not affect wage behaviour, and so there is no difference between the model-consistent and adaptive cases. Despite the fact that we have four types of simulation, we have therefore only three wage equations.

We take the wage equation in version 7 of the NIESR model as our starting point. It is

$$\Delta \ln WAGERATE_t = 0.307 - 0.138RTT_{t-3} + 0.759\Delta \ln CPI_t^e$$
$$- 0.00651\Delta AVHMF_t - 0.00268AVHMF$$
$$- 2.72\Delta^2 UPC_{t-1} - 2.43\Delta UPC_{t-3} - 0.262UPC_{t-4} \qquad (6.1)$$

where

$WAGERATE$	— wage rate
$AVHMF$	— average hours worked in manufacturing
UPC	— unemployed/labour force
RTT	— real earnings aspiration gap defined as
RTT	$= \ln AVEARN/(CPI \times 0.976 \times (1.00554)^t)$
$AVEARN$	— average earnings
CPI	— consumer price index
$\Delta \ln CPI_t^e$	— expected rate of inflation, determined adaptively with
$\Delta \ln CPI_t^e$	$= 0.75\Delta \ln CPI_{t-1} + 0.15\Delta \ln CPI_{t-2} + 0.10\Delta \ln CPI_{t-3}$

Equation (6.1) implies a target rate of growth in the real wage of 2.2 per cent per annum. The effect of the terms in manufacturing hours is small. We set the level of *AVHMF* to 100 (which is the base value) and the change to zero. The equation as it stands suggests that only 76 per cent of expected price increases are reflected in wage demands. More recent work (Layard and Nickell, 1986) tends to impose the restriction that wage increases are fully indexed to price increases. However we wish to consider the effects of different degrees of indexation rather than settle on only one value. We also wish to investigate the effects of changes in the cost-push parameters. In order to do both of these we modify the NIESR equation to give an equation more like that used in our analytic work of Chapter 3.

$$\Delta\ln WAGERATE_t = 0.039 - 0.138\nu RTT_{t-3} + \nu\Delta\ln CPI_t^e$$
$$- 2.72\Delta^2 UPC_{t-1} - 2.43\Delta UPC_{t-3} - 0.262 UPC_{t-4} + (1 - \nu)\dot{p}^* \quad (6.2)$$

where $\dot{p}^*$ is the authorities' target rate of inflation.

We can allow the indexation parameter, ν, to take values between 0 and 1,[1] although in fact we focus on the two extreme cases of $\nu = 0$ and $\nu = 1$. Note that the value of ν also affects the strength of the catch-up term, *RTT*, as well as the extent of direct wage indexation. The coefficient on UPC_{t-4} corresponds to α_1 in equation (3.1). It shows that a one percentage point increase in the unemployment rate will cause roughly 0.25 per cent reduction in the quarterly rate of wage inflation, or a 1 per cent reduction in the annual rate of wage inflation. This equation is more general than that of Chapter 3 in that it contains quite large hysteresis terms in ΔUPC and $\Delta^2 UPC$, which increase the effect of increases in unemployment in reducing inflation but have the opposite effect when unemployment falls and have no effect unless the level of unemployment is changing.

If the model is to be solved with model-consistent expectations we assume that $\Delta\ln CPI_t^e = (\Delta\ln CPI_t + \Delta\ln CPI_{t-1})/2$, a simplifying assumption that wages are set at the beginning of the current period on the basis of the average of the past and the correctly foreseen current inflation rate. This assumption avoids the need to use Taylor's (1979) overlapping contracts framework at the cost of assuming that wage contracts only last one period and that actual prices are not distinguished from expected prices. This expression is open to the criticism that it gives a strong instantaneous wage-price loop which makes inflation easy to control.

If the model is solved with adaptive expectations we use the expression in the original NIESR equation, shown above. It implies a slower adjustment of wages to inflation than in the previous case, but is not otherwise very different.

6.4   THE EFFECT OF TAXES ON MONEY GDP AND ON PRICES

In our reformed wage case the parameter v is set equal to zero, while with unreformed wages v is set equal to 1. Our analysis of Chapter 3 suggests that the response of wages and prices, and therefore of Money GDP, to a fiscal change will depend crucially on that value taken by v, at least in the case in which the fiscal policy instrument is a tax variable.

We regard this case as empirically relevant. There is every reason to assume that the fiscal instrument is a tax variable; some types of government spending can be varied at short notice, but these are typically transfer payments and we do not regard it as politically feasible to use transfer payments as instruments of macroeconomic policy.

Previous research (Vines *et al.*, 1983) suggested that VAT and employees' national insurance contributions were feasible fiscal instruments which could be used for fine-tuning on a quarterly basis. A compound fiscal variable consisting of equal percentage point movements in the VAT rate and the rate of employees' national insurance contributions seems to be the most broadly-based fiscal instrument available.

With $v > 0$ our fiscal instrument certainly has a cost-push effect on wages. However, our equation suggests, somewhat illogically, that wage claims are affected by indirect tax increases which affect the price of consumer goods, but not by direct tax increases which affect take-home pay, a property which we have retained because it is a common feature of UK wage equations. It may, then, be the case that our equation understates the cost-push effect of our fiscal instrument when wages are indexed. This has to be borne in mind in interpreting the results.

We now present graphs showing the effects of a permanent 0.2 percentage point increase in the VAT rate and in employees' national insurance contributions on our targeted variable, Money GDP. We also indicate the effect of this tax increase on the GDP deflator. The simulations are carried out on the assumption that the real exchange rate is held constant.[2] Figure 6.1(a) shows the effects of the tax increase on Money GDP and on the deflator when expectations are model consistent with unreformed wages ($v = 1$). Figure 6.1(b) shows the response when expectations are assumed to be adaptive. Figures 6.2(a) and (b) show the effects of the tax increase when wages have been reformed ($v = 0$) and expectations are assumed to be model-consistent and adaptive respectively.[3]

It can be seen from these graphs that our wage equation interacts with the rest of the model so as to produce a system in which, with unreformed wages, tax increases are cost-push in the short to medium

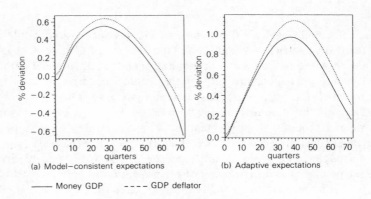

Figure 6.1   The effect of a tax increase with unreformed wages

term. In the long term the effect becomes demand-pull with model-consistent expectations within the time-horizon of our simulation. With adaptive expectations it remains cost-push, but the demand-pull influences are clearly growing and would dominate over a longer time-horizon. With unreformed wages the use of fiscal policy to control inflation must therefore be handled carefully so as to take account for this.

With reformed wages (Figure 6.2), not surprisingly, a tax increase is

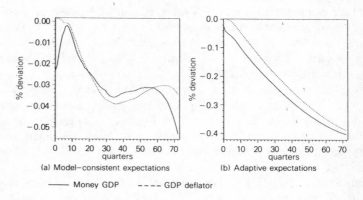

Figure 6.2   The effect of a tax increase with reformed wages

unambiguously deflationary. The effect is much weaker with model-consistent expectations than with adaptive expectations because the tax increase depresses demand and squeezes wages. This has a positive short- to medium-term effect on profits which more than offsets the effect of reduced demand and leads to an upward jump in the valuation ratio. As a consequence investment rises adding to demand. The dynamics of the process induce cycles.

6.5 THE COMPARATIVE ADVANTAGE OF MONETARY AND FISCAL POLICY

We now look empirically at the comparative advantage index, ω, in our model for the two extreme values of ν, 0 and 1, which interest us. As in Chapter 3 we define our monetary policy instrument to be the real exchange rate since this corresponds closely to the way in which we use the real exchange rate as an intermediate target variable in our subsequent policy rules.[4]

Table 6.1 presents the value of the comparative advantage parameter, ω, calculated both 12 periods and 72 periods after the use of each instrument. Each period is one quarter. The index is calculated as in Chapter 3, but is defined with reference to the two policy targets which we adopt in our empirical work, national wealth and Money GDP, rather than the targets we used in our simplified analytical model of Chapter 3.

The comparative advantage indices are defined as $\{(\partial z/\partial S)/(\partial n/\partial S)\}/\{(\partial z/\partial A)/(\partial n/\partial A)\}$ in our standard notation. This is calculated at 12 and at 72 periods. With model-consistent expectations the 12-period results are calculated on the assumption that the step changes to S and A are only expected to last 12 periods. The 72-period results are calculated on the assumption that they are expected to last for 72 periods.

We can see from the table that the pattern of comparative advantage depends on both the way in which expectations are formed and on the

Table 6.1 Comparative advantage indices in our empirical model

	Model-consistent Expectations		Adaptive Expectations	
	Unreformed Wages ($\nu = 1$)	Reformed Wages ($\nu = 0$)	Unreformed Wages ($\nu = 1$)	Reformed Wages($\nu = 0$)
12 periods	1.45	-0.53	0.88	-1.14
72 periods	-0.15	-0.01	0.57	-1.06

value of ν. But within this there are a number of important patterns. First we note that, with unreformed wages, the short-term comparative advantage indices are close to or above 1. This suggests that, for short- to medium-term control of the model, cases (c) and (d) of Table 3.2 will be relevant. In the longer term case (b) appears relevant with model-consistent expectations and case (c) with adaptive expectations. But we may infer, from Figure 6.1(b), that, had we been able to run our model for more than 72 periods, we would have eventually found that a tax increase with unreformed wages and adaptive expectations would eventually reduce Money GDP, making case (b) relevant. Secondly, with reformed wages the parameter is negative in both the short and the long term, making cases (a) and (b) relevant. Although (a) implies that emphasis should be put on demand-pull fiscal policy to control inflation, while (b) implies that monetary policy should be emphasized, it can be seen from Table 3.2 that both these cases imply the same pattern of signs for the parameters.

In both unreformed and reformed wage cases we hope to see these values of the comparative advantage parameter reflected in the instrument-target emphasis of our policy rules.

6.6   THE DESIGN OF ECONOMIC POLICY

6.6.1   Simultaneous rules and lagged rules

Our analytical model was set out in continuous time. It did not, therefore, allow us to distinguish policy rules which respond simultaneously with current events from those which can only respond with a lag. Lags may arise for two possible reasons. First of all, some instruments can be adjusted frequently, while others cannot. For example, the rate of interest can be adjusted on a day-to-day basis while fiscal policy probably cannot be adjusted so frequently. Secondly, some targets can be monitored regularly, while others can only be observed infrequently. Daily information accrues on the exchange rate and on the level of the foreign-exchange reserves, while information on Money GDP and on national wealth is at present only available quarterly, and only accrues with a lag.[5]

In our analytical model, economic policy responded immediately new information became available about the state of the economy, and it was therefore possible in section 3.5 to eliminate the target exchange rate from the dynamic model by substitution. In a discrete time model in which some information becomes available with a lag, the role of the target exchange rate as a guide to monetary policy is more obvious. If a target exchange rate regime were adopted, both the target exchange rate and fiscal policy could only be set on the basis of Money GDP and national wealth data which became available only infrequently. Until new information became available both fiscal policy and the target exchange rate would be held constant. However, the target exchange rate would be used to determine short-term monetary policy (alterations in the interest rate and foreign-exchange intervention). If the actual exchange rate strayed from its target value then appropriate adjustments to the short-term interest rate and to intervention could be made very quickly, i.e. effectively simultaneously.

This approach should be contrasted with one in which the interest rate is set directly on the basis only of lagged information about the level of Money GDP and the level of national wealth. In such a framework the exchange rate could move to an inappropriate level for quite a long time building up future difficulties for economic management, without leading to the required policy response. Those difficulties could be partly avoided if, as we suggested in Chapter 1 (section 1.5), the exchange rate were held close to an appropriate target value by means of short-term monetary policy,[6] and that is what we suppose in what follows.

The basic structure for our policy rules is therefore to set the fiscal variable and the target real exchange rate on the basis of past values of Money GDP and national wealth, while the interest rate is set on the basis of the deviations of the actual real exchange rate from its current and past target values. With a high degree of capital mobility, such as is present in our model, foreign-exchange intervention turns out to be of little value. But it could be set by a simultaneous rule on the same criteria as the interest rate and also taking into account the size of the foreign-exchange reserves.

The structure of economic policy, as we suggest it, is set out in Figure 6.3. The rules for short-term monetary policy can be described as 'simultaneous rules', while the rules for setting fiscal policy and the target exchange rate are 'lagged rules'. In principle any lag structure would be possible. However, the simplest specification includes proportional and integral components only, giving rules in the following form

$$\Delta S_t = a_{11}\Delta(z_{t-1} - z_{t-1}^*) + a_{12}(z_{t-1} - z_{t-1}^*)$$
$$+ b_{11}\Delta(n_{t-1} - n_{t-1}^*) + b_{12}(n_{t-1} - n_{t-1}^*) \quad (6.3a)$$

$$\Delta a_t^* = a_{21}\Delta(z_{t-1} - z_{t-1}^*) + a_{22}(z_{t-1} - z_{t-1}^*)$$
$$+ b_{21}\Delta(n_{t-1} - n_{t-1}^*) + b_{22}(n_{t-1} - n_{t-1}^*) \quad (6.3b)$$

$$\Delta R_t = c_{11}\Delta(a_t - a_t^*) + c_{12}(a_t - a_t^*) \quad (6.3c)$$

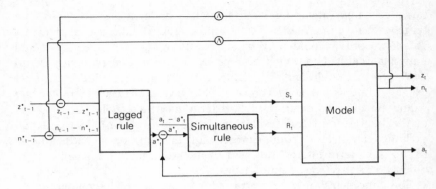

z_t log Money GDP at end of period t
n_t log national wealth at end of period t
S_t fiscal variable in period t
a_t log actual real exchange rate in period t
R_t nominal interest rate
*   indicates a target value
Λ lag operator

Figure 6.3   The structure of economic policy with simultaneous and lagged rules

The proportional component of a rule of this type ensures a rapid response to any disturbance, but cannot eliminate the effects of disturbances completely. The integral component guarantees that, provided the system is stable, the final targets are actually met, but needs in general to be weak so as to avoid introducing cycles or complete instability. Without the proportional component any disturbance would persist for a long time before sufficient offsetting action was taken. Thus to ensure both that responses are rapid and that targets are finally attained, control rules need at least proportional and integral components.

One of our aims is, then, to produce simple policy rules. A second aim is to try to produce rules which are robust across a range of model specifications. The analysis of Chapters 3 and 4 indicates that the way in which expectations are formed might not have a major effect on model stability or on the pattern of comparative advantage, whilst the structure of the wage equation is likely to have an important impact on both stability and the pattern of comparative advantage in the model. It is therefore likely to have a profound influence on the form of well-designed policy rules. This suggests that, while it may well be possible to find a simple rule which is robust to the way in which expectations are formed, it may not be possible to find a rule which works for all values of the indexation parameter between 0 and 1 in the wage equation (6.2).

In practice, just as we are not able to consider all possible types of expectations formation, so too we cannot consider all possible values of ν, the indexation parameter. We therefore proceed to present policy rules for the two extreme cases; we present each case with both model-consistent and adaptive expectations. The 'unreformed' case has $\nu = 1$, while the 'reformed' wage case has $\nu = 0$.

6.6.2 The design of policy rules

There are a wide variety of techniques available which we could have adopted in order to design effective financial policies. In particular, we could have designed 'optimal control' policies on the model directly using non-linear optimizing techniques. However, we wished to investigate systematically the use of 'simple' feedback rules of the type set out in Figure 6.3, that feed back only on the final values of the target variables and the exchange rate. As we made clear in Chapter 1 and discuss again in Chapter 11, such simplicity seems to us to be a helpful property of policy rules. Even so, it would have been possible to derive 'optimal' simple feedback rules that minimized a representative welfare loss function directly, as demonstrated by Westaway (1986). However, there is no guarantee that the resulting rules will be stable, since there is nothing in the optimization process to ensure this. Moreover, it is not straightforward to design optimal simple rules which are robust across model specification, although we note that Becker *et al.* (1986) have made some progress in this area. We have therefore chosen to design our simple proportional plus integral feedback rules in a different way.

We design our policies with the aid of a linear representation of the model. This has several advantages. First, it is invaluable in enabling the designer to obtain a 'feel' for the model properties in an accessible manner which is difficult to do with a non-linear simulation model. Secondly, we can evaluate the stability of the rules by evaluating the roots of the model under control directly. We reject unstable rules without further consideration on the grounds that they are not sustainable. No such simple stability check can be made on the non-linear model. Finally, we can investigate the performance of our control rules in great detail.[7] These issues are discussed in more detail in Chapter 11.

To be able to proceed in this way, we must have a good linear representation of the model which we can be reasonably certain has retained the properties of the original model. A structural linearization would be tedious to calculate, particularly as we are concerned only with the input-output properties of the model. The method we have instead adopted is computationally much simpler but the final form is essentially the same sort of linear representation. The technique, outlined by Maciejowski and Vines (1984), is known as balanced realization. It is very efficient in reproducing the original model's responses. Chapter 10 shows how this powerful method can be used when the model contains model-consistent expectations.

We thought it helpful to adopt a set of simultaneous rules common to both 'unreformed-' and 'reformed-wage' economies. In order to do this, we used rather crude target exchange-rate and tax-rate rules, and then designed simultaneous rules that gave acceptable variation in the interest rate in reruns of history for both wage equations. The basic requirement of the simultaneous rules was that they generally achieved good exchange-rate targeting performance. The resulting set of simultaneous rules was then retained and the quarterly rules were then redesigned. In doing this we followed the informal approach adopted by Edison *et al.* (1987); we were mainly influenced by the ability of our rules to deliver satisfactory step increases in Money GDP and national wealth (Figures 6.4–6.11). Our design technique could almost be regarded as an informal search for rules which deliver low quadratic losses on these step changes (Tables 6.2 and 6.3)[8] and we paid more attention to the losses with model-consistent expectations than with adaptive expectations. It should also be noted that with reformed wages we were influenced by a desire to keep the real exchange rate reasonably stable. We also ensured that our rules could rerun history satisfactorily, which was sometimes a severe constraint. However, we then pursued the important second step of checking these rules for asymptotic stability on our linear model.

The linear model fulfils another important role, at least when we solve our simulation model with model-consistent expectations. When the model is solved in this way it is necessary to find values for the 'forward-looking' variables, human capital, the consol rate, the stock exchange valuation ratio and the exchange rate. These are assumed to jump so as to cancel the unstable roots in the manner discussed in Chapter 5. Using the linear model it is possible to identify the initial values for these 'jumping' variables, so as to ensure that the unstable root is in fact removed. Without the linear model it would be necessary to adopt a shooting solution (Lipton *et al.*, 1982). This solution depends on the terminal conditions which are adopted and there is no guarantee that the solution path identified does in fact cancel the unstable roots (see section 7.2).

The use of the linear model in policy design is described fully in Chapter 11 and the role of the linear model in computing the solution trajectories is described in Chapters 7 and 10.

6.7 POLICY RULES FOR AN UNREFORMED WAGE EQUATION

We are able to design the following representative rule for the economy with wages fully indexed to prices.

$$\Delta S_t = -0.6\Delta(z_{t-1} - z_{t-1}^*) + 0.03(z_{t-1} - z_{t-1}^*)$$
$$- 1.1\Delta(n_{t-1} - n_{t-1}^*) - 0.03(n_{t-1} - n_{t-1}^*) \quad (6.4a)$$

$$\Delta a_t^* = 1.6\Delta(z_{t-1} - z_{t-1}^*) + 0.1(z_{t-1} - z_{t-1}^*)$$
$$- 0.6\Delta(n_{t-1} - n_{t-1}^*) + 0.01(n_{t-1} - n_{t-1}^*) \quad (6.4b)$$

$$\Delta R_t = -0.45\Delta(a_t - a_t^*) - 0.03(a_t - a_t^*) \quad (6.4c)$$

This rule has the following six features:

(1) It is not diagonal: both instruments respond to both targets.

(2) The real exchange rate target exercises the major control over inflation: a 1 per cent rise of Money GDP above its target causes a 1.6 per cent appreciation of the real target exchange rate, i.e. a 0.6 per cent appreciation of the nominal exchange rate if the rise in Money GDP is due to a rise in prices.

(3) Fiscal policy controls wealth (slowly), but a rise of Money GDP above its target also leads to a 'cost-push' cut in taxes.

(4) The interest-rate rule is strong: a 1 per cent fall of the real exchange rate below target causes a 0.45 per cent rise in the (nominal) interest rate.

(5) The proportional components of the policy rules (i.e. the terms $\Delta(z_{t-1} - z_{t-1}^*)$ and $\Delta(n_{t-1} - n_{t-1}^*)$ have broadly the signs and emphasis which we would expect from our analysis of comparative advantage. Monetary policy is emphasized in controlling inflation and fiscal policy in controlling wealth. In fact the rules reflect a combination of cases (c) and (d) of Table 3.2. This is because, in the very short term, $\omega > 1$ with both types of expectations formation. After 12 periods (Table 6.1) $\omega = 1.45$ with model-consistent expectations (case (d)) and $\omega = 0.88$ (case (c)) with adaptive expectations. With both, ω is falling over time, so that case (c) becomes increasingly relevant. The rules mean that the exchange rate is appreciated if Money GDP is rising, and that taxes are raised and the exchange rate is appreciated if wealth is falling. All these are implied by case (c) $(0 < \omega < 1)$. The one influence of case (d) $(\omega > 1)$ is that a satisfactory rule is found to need a cost-push reduction in taxes in response to a rise in Money GDP.

(6) The integral components of the policy rules, i.e. the terms in $(z_{t-1} - z_{t-1}^*)$ and $(n_{t-1} - n_{t-1}^*)$, have all of the signs which we would expect, and the expected emphasis, for a comparative advantage para-

meter in the range $0 < \omega < 1$ (see case (b) of Table 3.2). This is the case with model-consistent expectations after 72 periods and would probably be the case for adaptive expectations after a longer period (see Table 6.1). Thus the integral control terms show the exchange rate appreciated but taxes raised if Money GDP is too high, and the taxes raised but exchange rate depreciated if wealth is too low, with monetary policy emphasized in the control of inflation.[9]

The choice of parameters for this rule was severely constrained by the requirement that it should produce a satisfactory rerun of history (see Chapter 8 below). In particular the integrators are all much smaller than

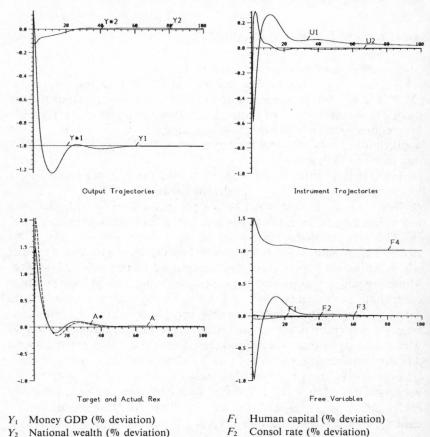

Y_1	Money GDP (% deviation)	F_1	Human capital (% deviation)
Y_2	National wealth (% deviation)	F_2	Consol rate (% deviation)
A	Real exchange rate (Rex) (% deviation)	F_3	Valuation ratio (% deviation)
A^*	Target real exchange rate (% deviation)	F_4	Nominal exchange rate (% deviation)
U_1	Tax variable (deviation)	U_2	Treasury bill rate (deviation)

Figure 6.4 Money GDP -1% with model-consistent expectations and unreformed wages

the initial design of rules on the linear model on its own would have suggested to be feasible,[10] and the magnitude of the proportional term linking taxes to Money GDP is smaller than appeared desirable, since without the last adjustment VAT would become negative in the rerun with model-consistent expectations. And the proportional term linking the interest rate to the deviation of the real exchange rate from target was reduced in order to prevent the interest rate becoming negative in the model-consistent simulation.

Figures 6.4 and 6.5 show the outcome of attempting to use a rule of this type to reduce Money GDP by 1 per cent. In Figure 6.4 expectations are assumed to be model-consistent, while in Figure 6.5 they are taken to

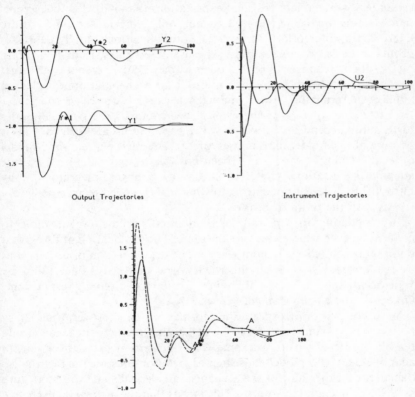

Output Trajectories   Instrument Trajectories

Target and Actual Rex

Y_1	Money GDP (% deviation)	A^*	Target real exchange rate (% deviation)
Y_2	National wealth (% deviation)	U_1	Tax variable (deviation)
A	Real exchange rate (Rex) (% deviation)	U_2	Treasury bill rate (deviation)

Figure 6.5 Money GDP -1% with adaptive expectations and unreformed wages

be adaptive. Time is measured in quarters.[11] In both cases the response is very considerably slower than that found by Vines, Maciejowski and Meade (1983). We can identify two reasons for this. The first and more important reason is that they treated wages as a control variable, while we have worked from an estimated wage equation slightly modified. This has a much slower response of wages. The second reason is that the modifications which we have made to the consumption and investment functions have the effect of making demand less sensitive to current income than it was in their model.

In both cases the target real exchange rate appreciates and the tax rate is reduced so as to cut Money GDP. The actual real exchange rate moves rather less with model-consistent expectations than with adaptive expectations, because it has to reflect not only current but also future interest-rate differentials. In both cases the deflation initially depresses profits and this, together with the rise in interest rates, leads to a slump on the stock exchange. In both models Money GDP overshoots its target value. We have found this to be a useful feature when our policy rules are applied to rerunning history, perhaps because historical disturbances tend to die away slowly. The cyclical behaviour of the two economies turns out to depend on the way in which expectations are formed. This is because the short-term responses of the adaptive expectations model differ markedly. It would have been possible to damp the cycles in the adaptive expectations model by means of stronger integrators or by introducing differential control. But both of these led to unsatisfactory results with the rerun of history.

By simulating for an additional hundred periods, we are able to confirm that the steady states are the same. The explanation of this is that both 'real economies' are homogeneous of degree zero in prices. In both cases the steady state is one in which wages and prices have fallen by 1 per cent and the nominal exchange rate has risen by 1 per cent. Otherwise there is no change.

With both types of expectations formation the short-term monetary policy rule is found to be effective at keeping the actual exchange rate reasonably close to its target value. The rule is in fact less effective with adaptive than with model-consistent expectations despite the fact that in the latter case the value of the exchange rate depends on expected future as well as current interest rates. This means that the actual real exchange rate will jump in response to a shock; the real exchange rate target is not a jumping variable and so, with model-consistent expectations, will be left behind by a jump in the actual real exchange rate. In fact the jump in the real exchange rate (Figure 6.4) is such that the nominal exchange rate overshoots its final value, a phenomenon first explained by Dornbusch (1976).

Figures 6.6 and 6.7 show the consequences of using the same rules to raise national wealth by 1 per cent of its value. The adjustment to real national wealth is in both cases very much slower than was the adjustment of nominal national income. This is not very surprising.

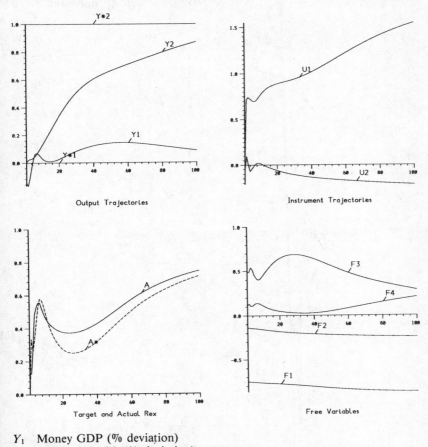

Y_1 Money GDP (% deviation)
Y_2 National wealth (% deviation)
A Real exchange rate (Rex) (% deviation)
A^* Target real exchange rate (% deviation)
U_1 Tax variable (deviation)
F_1 Human capital (% deviation)
F_2 Consol rate (% deviation)
F_3 Valuation ratio (% deviation)
F_4 Nominal exchange rate (% deviation)
U_2 Treasury bill rate (deviation)

Figure 6.6   National wealth +1% with model-consistent expectations and unreformed wages

Changes in national wealth can only be achieved by means of variations in the rate of national saving (apart from valuation effects on foreign assets). Money GDP can be varied by means of policies which affect the price level, and this can partly be achieved – especially with forward-looking expectations – by means of changes which do not have much

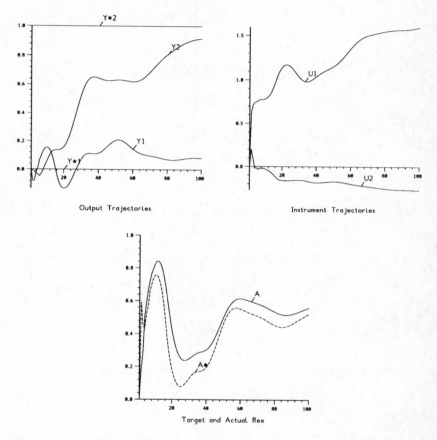

Y_1 Money GDP (% deviation)
Y_2 National wealth (% deviation)
A Real exchange rate (Rex) (% deviation)
A^* Target real exchange rate (% deviation)
U_1 Tax variable (deviation)
U_2 Treasury bill rate (deviation)

Figure 6.7   National wealth + 1% with adaptive expectations and unreformed wages

effect on people's real behaviour. As explained in Chapter 1, we are not unduly worried by the fact that prompt control of national wealth is not possible.

Our model in Chapter 4 suggests that increased wealth will be associated with a tighter fiscal position and with a higher real exchange rate. We observe this in Figures 6.6 and 6.7 and also note that, because our analytical model has imperfect capital mobility, this increased wealth (which includes accumulation of net overseas assets) is associated with a lower interest rate. The economy moves gradually towards this new steady state. In particular the higher tax rate means that the economy is doing more saving despite the fact that the real exchange rate is raised during the transition as well as in the steady state. This raised real exchange rate has the effect of suppressing the inflationary effects of higher taxes on Money GDP. Nevertheless the two models do not show the same steady states in this case. The reason is that the two consumption functions have different steady-state properties.

The effects of the rules may be summarized in Table 6.2 showing quadratic losses arising from use of the policy rules.

Table 6.2   Quadratic losses with unreformed wages

		Loss
Model-consistent expectations	Money GDP reduced	1.589
	Nat. wealth raised	11.97
Adaptive expectations	Money GDP reduced	5.752
	Nat. wealth raised	14.35

The loss function is $W = \Sigma_{t=1}^{100} 0.9975^t [(z_t - z_t^*)^2 + (n_t - n_t^*)^2]$, implying an (annual) discount rate of a little over 1 percent.

The rules we have presented are efficient at avoiding large interactions between Money GDP and wealth. When Money GDP is reduced, wealth is disturbed by no more than 0.5 per cent in the adaptive expectations case and by no more than 0.12 per cent in the consistent expectations case. Similarly policy-induced changes to wealth do not disturb Money GDP by more than 0.2 per cent in either case. These desirable properties can only be achieved by placing the right emphasis on monetary policy relative to fiscal policy in the control of each target. As already noted, the regulation of GDP is much easier than the regulation of wealth. This happens because changes in GDP can be achieved by means of changes in prices, while real wealth (apart from valuation effects on foreign investment) can only be varied by influencing national saving.

6.8 POLICY RULES FOR A REFORMED WAGE EQUATION

The analysis of Chapter 2 and sections 3.8 and 6.3–6.5 leads us to expect that if a reform of pay bargaining were to lead to a value of $v = 0$, then the pattern of comparative advantage of monetary and fiscal policy would be altered and, as a consequence the instrument-target emphasis of good policy rules would change. We find that the following policy rules are satisfactory, whether expectations are model-consistent or adaptive

$$\Delta S_t = 1.0\Delta(z_{t-1} - z_{t-1}^*) + 0.04(z_{t-1} - z_{t-1}^*)$$
$$- 1.25\Delta(n_{t-1} - n_{t-1}^*) - 0.05(n_{t-1} - n_{t-1}^*) \quad (6.5a)$$

$$\Delta a_t^* = 0.7\Delta(z_{t-1} - z_{t-1}^*) + 0.03(z_{t-1} - z_{t-1}^*)$$
$$+ 1.3\Delta(n_{t-1} - n_{t-1}^*) + 0.02(n_{t-1} - n_{t-1}^*) \quad (6.5b)$$

and the rule for short-term monetary policy is as before

$$\Delta R_t = -0.45\Delta(a_t - a_t^*)10.03(a_t - a_t^*) \quad (6.5c)$$

Note four features of this rule:
(1) It is not diagonal.
(2) The interest-rate rule is as before.
(3) The proportional components of the policy rules give emphasis to demand-pull effects of fiscal policy in the control of inflation. Table 6.1 predicts this as being a desirable property with adaptive expectations but suggests that emphasis should be placed on monetary policy with model-consistent expectations. Our empirical examination confirmed that this gave better results, but we avoided it because we wanted to produce rules which avoided excessive movement in the real exchange rate.[12] The integral terms reflect Table 6.1 more faithfully. They emphasise monetary policy in the control of inflation. In fact the long-run comparative advantage parameter of Table 6.1 is between -1 and 0, making case (b) relevant.
(4) The signs of the components of the fiscal and exchange rate policy rules – both proportional and integral – are exactly what one would expect as long as $\omega < 0$ (see Table 3.2, cases (a) and (b)). As shown in Table 6.1, this is true for both kinds of expectation formation, in both the short and the long term.

These rules, then, are intended to provide a compromise between Williamson and Miller's (1987) proposals that fiscal policy should be used to control inflation, and the need, dictated by the value of the comparative advantage parameters, to make reasonable use of monetary policy in the control of inflation (see also Tirelli, 1988).

Figures 6.8 and 6.9 show the results of using these rules to reduce Money GDP by 1 per cent. In Figure 6.8 expectations are assumed to be model-consistent, while in Figure 6.9 they are assumed to be adaptive. The time profile of Money GDP is not very different from that which was found with unreformed wages. The deflation is generated by an increase in taxes and much less use is made of interest rates. Nevertheless the real

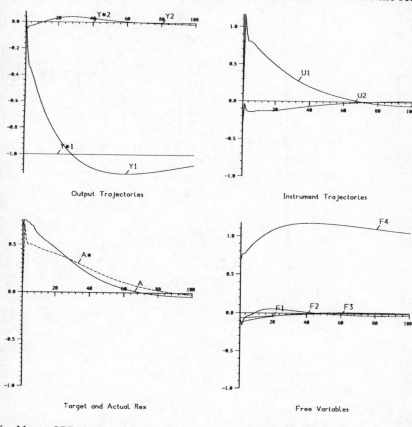

Y_1	Money GDP (% deviation)	F_1	Human capital (% deviation)
Y_2	National wealth (% deviation)	F_2	Consol rate (% deviation)
A	Real exchange rate (Rex) (% deviation)	F_3	Valuation ratio (% deviation)
A^*	Target real exchange rate (% deviation)	F_4	Nominal exchange rate (% deviation)
U_1	Tax variable (deviation)	U_2	Treasury bill rate (deviation)

Figure 6.8 Money GDP − 1% with model-consistent expectations and reformed wages

exchange rate is not constant in the adjustment process: it appreciates by about one half of the appreciation needed with unreformed wages. Indeed it is difficult to see how an initial rise of over 0.5 per cent in the real exchange rate could be avoided, since the nominal exchange rate jumps close to its new equilibrium (which is an appreciation of 1 per cent) almost immediately. Control is rather more precise with model-consistent expectations than in the case with adaptive expectations. The

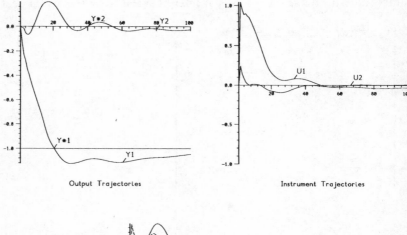

Output Trajectories   Instrument Trajectories

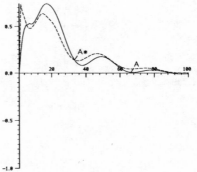

Target and Actual Rex

Y_1 Money GDP (% deviation)
Y_2 National wealth (% deviation)
A Real exchange rate (Rex) (% deviation)
A^* Target real exchange rate (% deviation)
U_1 Tax variable (deviation)
U_2 Treasury bill rate (deviation)

Figure 6.9   Money GDP − 1% with adaptive expectations and reformed wages

main reason for this is that, in this model, consumption depends not only on current but also on expected future taxation. As a consequence the effect on demand of the tax rule is much more sudden with model-consistent than with adaptive expectations. This is reflected in the jump

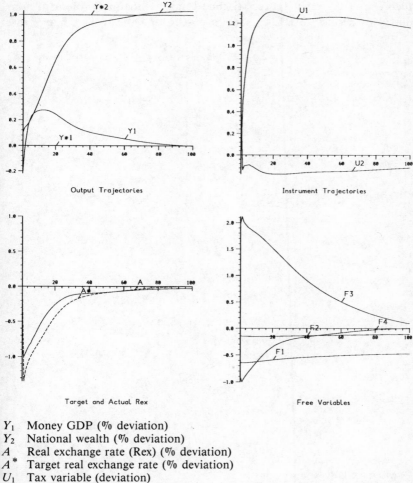

Y_1　　Money GDP (% deviation)
Y_2　　National wealth (% deviation)
A　　　Real exchange rate (Rex) (% deviation)
A^*　　Target real exchange rate (% deviation)
U_1　　Tax variable (deviation)
F_1　　Human capital (% deviation)
F_2　　Consol rate (% deviation)
F_3　　Valuation ratio (% deviation)
F_4　　Nominal exchange rate (% deviation)
U_2　　Treasury bill rate (deviation)

Figure 6.10　National wealth　+1% with model-consistent expectations and reformed wages

in human capital. Overall the control of Money GDP with model-consistent expectations is worse in this reformed-wage case than in the cost-push case. There are two reasons for this. First, the wage reform has broken the cost-push wage-price loop and slowed the rate at which prices can be changed by currency appreciation. Secondly, we avoided too much use of currency appreciation and have deliberately tolerated poor control of Money GDP in order to ensure that the real exchange rate

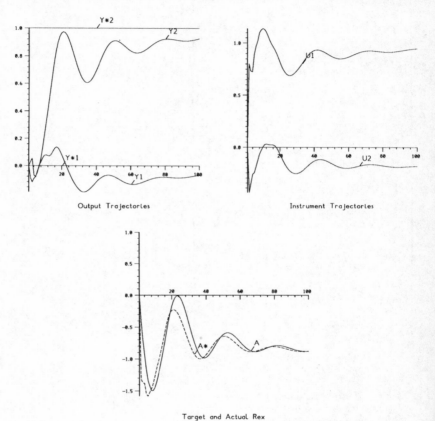

Output Trajectories   Instrument Trajectories

Target and Actual Rex

Y_1 Money GDP (% deviation)
Y_2 National wealth (% deviation)
A Real exchange rate (Rex) (% deviation)
A^* Target real exchange rate (% deviation)
U_1 Tax variable (deviation)
U_2 Treasury bill rate (deviation)

Figure 6.11   National wealth +1% with adaptive expectations and reformed wages

should be reasonably stable in our simulations in Chapter 9. On the other hand, the control of Money GDP with adaptive expectations is much better in this reformed wages case than with unreformed wages. The reason for this is that the lagged response of wages to prices (equations 6.1 and 6.2) became a source of cyclical disturbances in the unreformed wage model with adaptive expectations. Their absence facilitates the control problem of the economy with reformed wages.

These rules regulate the stock of wealth in the economy with reformed wages rather more promptly than was possible with unreformed wages. Figure 6.10 shows a 1 per cent increase in wealth with model-consistent expectations and Figure 6.11 shows the same change with adaptive expectations. One feature of these simulations is difficult to explain. The real exchange rate is depreciated after the increase in wealth, while we might have expected it to be appreciated on account of property income effects. The best explanation we can offer is that the pattern of demand has changed as a consequence of the increase in wealth, shifting demand towards import-intensive sectors. Such an effect was not apparent in the case of unreformed wages, because in the unreformed economy the higher level of taxes restricts labour supply. This reduces output and imports and enables a higher real exchange rate to be maintained. By contrast, in the reformed wage economy, labour supply is independent of the tax rate. Output is not restricted and imports are higher. This requires a lower real exchange rate.

The results may again be summarized in Table 6.3. These values again show that the economy is easier to regulate with model-consistent expectations than with adaptive expectations. This is much more marked in controlling wealth than in controlling Money GDP, because in the former case our rules exploit the forward-looking nature of the consumption function. We have already observed that the control of Money GDP with model-consistent expectations is worse in the reformed wage case than with unreformed wages, but that with adaptive expectations it is better in this reformed wage case than it was with unreformed wages. The control of wealth is better in this case with both types of expectations.

Table 6.3   Quadratic losses with reformed wages

		Loss
Model-consistent expectations	Money GDP reduced	2.886
	Nat. wealth raised	5.459
Adaptive expectations	Money GDP reduced	3.021
	Nat. wealth raised	7.147

The loss function is $W = \Sigma_{t=1}^{100} 0.9975^t [(z_t - z_t^*)^2 + (n_t - n_t^*)^2]$

6.9   THE RESPONSE TO OTHER DISTURBANCES

In the sections above we have illustrated the ability of our representative
rules to control Money GDP and national wealth. But they will also have

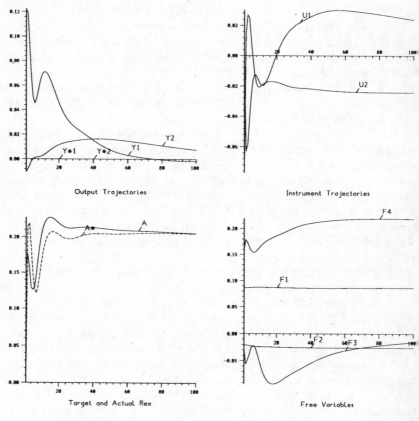

Y_1 Money GDP (% deviation)
Y_2 National wealth (% deviation)
A Real exchange rate (Rex) (% deviation)
A^* Target real exchange rate (% deviation)
U_1 Tax variable (deviation)
F_1 Human capital (% deviation)
F_2 Consol rate (% deviation)
F_3 Valuation ratio (% deviation)
F_4 Nominal exchange rate (% deviation)
U_2 Treasury bill rate (deviation)

*Figure 6.12   World   trade   + 1%   with   model-consistent   expectations   and
unreformed wages*

to cope with a variety of disturbances to exogenous variables. We therefore present Figures 6.12–6.27, which show the responses of each of our four models (unreformed wages: model-consistent or adaptive expectations; reformed wages: model-consistent or adaptive expectations) to each of four shocks (world trade, world prices, the foreign interest rate and a shock to wages).

We find that shifts in world trade and world prices have relatively little effect on the economy. A favourable shift in world trade leads to a higher

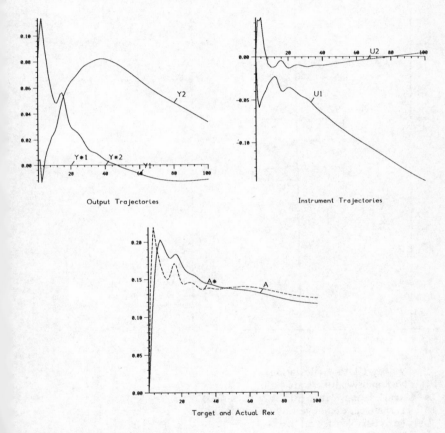

Y_1 Money GDP (% deviation)
Y_2 National wealth (% deviation)
A Real exchange rate (Rex) (% deviation)
U_1 Tax variable (deviation)
U_2 Treasury bill rate (deviation)
A^* Target real exchange rate (% deviation)

Figure 6.13   World trade +1% with adaptive expectations and unreformed wages

real exchange rate. With model-consistent expectations and unreformed
wages (Figure 6.12), a higher tax rate is also needed so as to damp
economic activity and there is a favourable effect on human capital. The
numbers differ but the same sort of pattern is observed with reformed

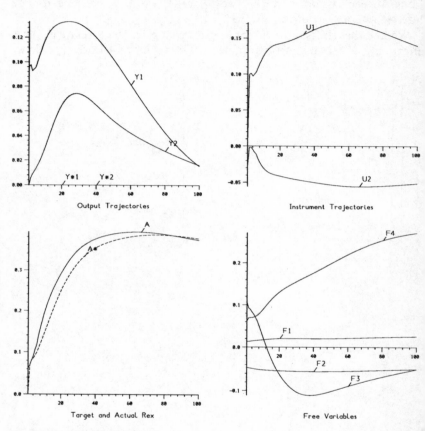

Y_1 Money GDP (% deviation)
Y_2 National wealth (% deviation)
A Real exchange rate (Rex) (% deviation)
A^* Target real exchange rate (% deviation)
U_1 Tax variable (deviation)
F_1 Human capital (% deviation)
F_2 Consol rate (% deviation)
F_3 Valuation ratio (% deviation)
F_4 Nominal exchange rate (% deviation)
U_2 Treasury bill rate (deviation)

*Figure 6.14   World   trade   +1%   with   model-consistent   expectations   and
reformed wages*

wages for both types of expectation (Figures 6.14 and 6.15). The general uniformity is broken only in the case of adaptive expectations and unreformed wages. In this case the absence of any anticipatory rise in consumption means that national saving, and so national wealth, increases by so much as to force a reduction in taxes during the simulation period.

A disturbance to the world price level has almost no effect in our

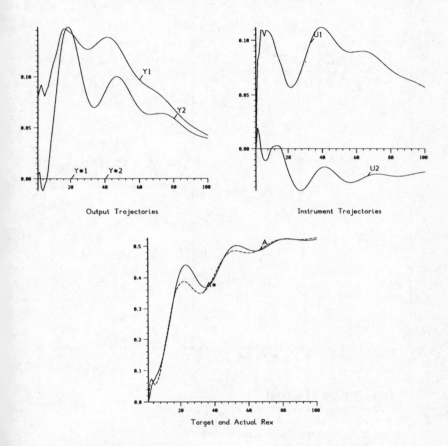

Output Trajectories   Instrument Trajectories

Target and Actual Rex

Y_1 Money GDP (% deviation)
Y_2 National wealth (% deviation)
A Real exchange rate (Rex) (% deviation)
U_1 Tax variable (deviation)
U_2 Treasury bill rate (deviation)
A^* Target real exchange rate (% deviation)

Figure 6.15   World trade + 1% with adaptive expectations and reformed wages

consistent expectations model (Figures 6.16 and 6.18). The reason for this is that the nominal exchange rate jumps to its new level almost immediately; there is some small effect because of lags in the trade and price equations. But the disturbance is minimal. However, a curious

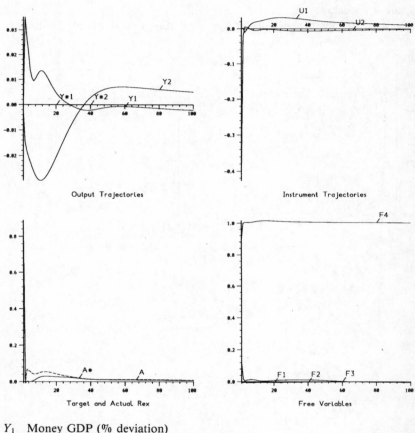

Y_1 Money GDP (% deviation)
Y_2 National wealth (% deviation)
A Real exchange rate (Rex) (% deviation)
A^* Target real exchange rate (% deviation)
U_1 Tax variable (deviation)
F_1 Human capital (% deviation)
F_2 Consol rate (% deviation)
F_3 Valuation ratio (% deviation)
F_4 Nominal exchange rate (% deviation)
U_2 Treasury bill rate (deviation)

Figure 6.16   World prices +1% with model-consistent expectations and unreformed wages

feature of this result is that a change in expectations of the future world price level turns out to be a very important source of disturbance in the model even if that change does not in fact materialize. The reason for this is that if future world prices are expected to move, the nominal exchange rate will jump almost immediately to the new steady state. [13] Expected future changes in the world price level can thus be a very powerful source of disturbance to the real exchange rate and to the real

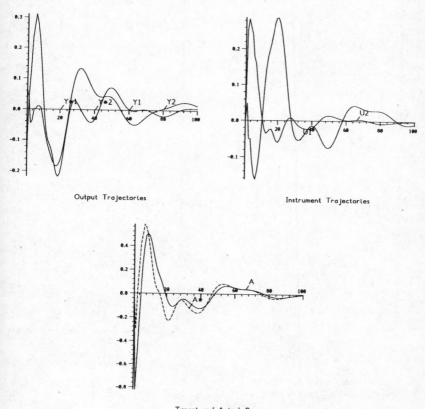

Output Trajectories

Instrument Trajectories

Target and Actual Rex

Y_1 Money GDP (% deviation)
Y_2 National wealth (% deviation)
A Real exchange rate (Rex) (% deviation)
U_1 Tax variable (deviation)
U_2 Treasury bill rate (deviation)
A^* Target real exchange rate (% deviation)

Figure 6.17 World prices +1% with adaptive expectations and unreformed wages

economy. With adaptive expectations the adjustment processes are
slower and we find, particularly with unreformed wages (Figure 6.17)
that the effects of the world price shock are longer-lasting, although there
are, of course, no expectational effects of the type mentioned above.

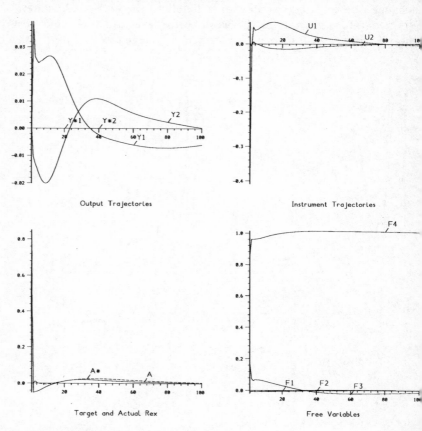

Y_1 Money GDP (% deviation)
Y_2 National wealth (% deviation)
A Real exchange rate (Rex) (% deviation)
A^* Target real exchange rate (% deviation)
U_1 Tax variable (deviation)
F_1 Human capital (% deviation)
F_2 Consol rate (% deviation)
F_3 Valuation ratio (% deviation)
F_4 Nominal exchange rate (% deviation)
U_2 Treasury bill rate (deviation)

*Figure 6.18   World   prices   +1%   with   model-consistent   expectations   and
reformed wages*

On the other hand, permanent movements in the foreign (real) interest rate turn out to be a major source of disturbance to the economy if expectations are model-consistent and to do much less damage if they are adaptive. The reason for this is seen in Figure 5.3 of Chapter 5. A permanent change in the interest rate has a much larger short-term effect on the valuation ratio with model-consistent expectations than with adaptive expectations, because it is, with model-consistent expectations,

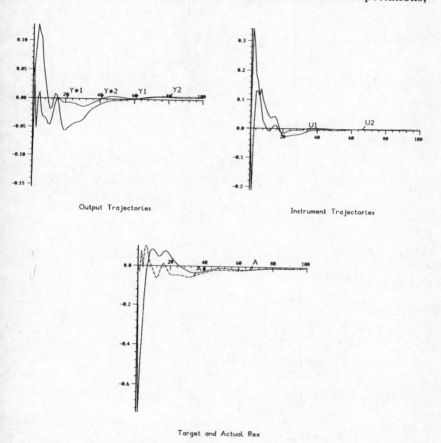

Output Trajectories

Instrument Trajectories

Target and Actual Rex

Y_1 Money GDP (% deviation)
Y_2 National wealth (% deviation)
A Real exchange rate (Rex) (% deviation)
U_1 Tax variable (deviation)
U_2 Treasury bill rate (deviation)
A^* Target real exchange rate (% deviation)

Figure 6.19   World prices + 1% with adaptive expectations and reformed wages

a forward-looking variable. This disturbance to the valuation ratio affects consumption and investment demand in the manner which we describe. In the long run the home interest rate rises by less than the shift in the foreign interest rate. The reason for this is as follows. An increase

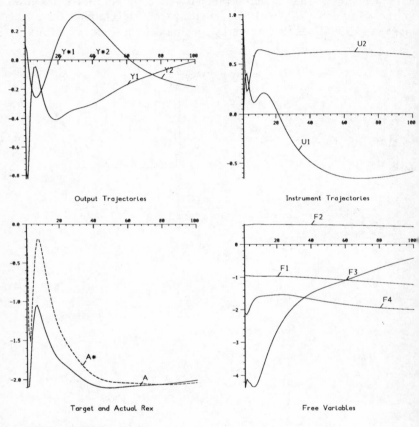

Y_1 Money GDP (% deviation)
Y_2 National wealth (% deviation)
A Real exchange rate (Rex) (% deviation)
A^* Target real exchange rate (% deviation)
U_1 Tax variable (deviation)
F_1 Human capital (% deviation)
F_2 Consol rate (% deviation)
F_3 Valuation ratio (% deviation)
F_4 Nominal exchange rate (% deviation)
U_2 Treasury bill rate (deviation)

Figure 6.20   Foreign interest rate + 1% with model-consistent expectations and unreformed wages

in the home interest rate means that the capital stock is reduced, since in equilibrium changes in the interest rate are reflected in changes in the rate of profit. With a fall in the domestic capital stock, national wealth can only be maintained by the extra accumulation of foreign assets. As a result foreign assets command a risk premium relative to home assets, and so the home interest rate rises by less than the foreign interest rate. This effect is particularly marked with model-consistent expectations,

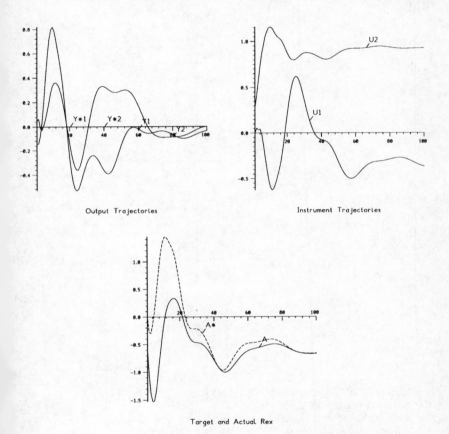

Output Trajectories   Instrument Trajectories

Target and Actual Rex

Y_1 Money GDP (% deviation)
Y_2 National wealth (% deviation)
A Real exchange rate (Rex) (% deviation)
U_1 Tax variable (deviation)
U_2 Treasury bill rate (deviation)
A^* Target real exchange rate (% deviation)

Figure 6.21   Foreign interest rate +1% with adaptive expectations and unreformed wages

and once again the result differs from the adaptive expectations case because the consumption functions differ. The disturbance to Money GDP is particularly acute with reformed wages; this is because our policy

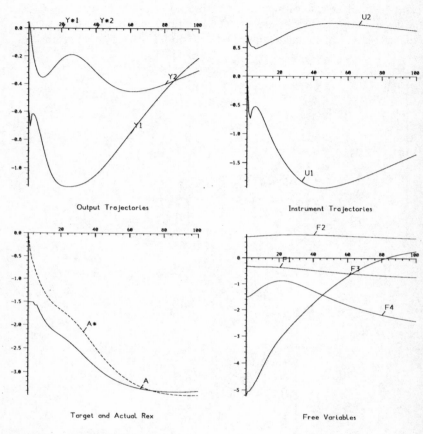

Y_1 Money GDP (% deviation)
Y_2 National wealth (% deviation)
A Real exchange rate (Rex) (% deviation)
A^* Target real exchange rate (% deviation)
U_1 Tax variable (deviation)
F_1 Human capital (% deviation)
F_2 Consol rate (% deviation)
F_3 Valuation ratio (% deviation)
F_4 Nominal exchange rate (% deviation)
U_2 Treasury bill rate (deviation)

Figure 6.22   Foreign interest rate + 1% with model-consistent expectations and reformed wages

rules deliberately put up with poor control of Money GDP in order to purchase a stable real exchange rate.

The final set of graphs (Figures 6.24–6.27) demonstrate the reaction of the system to a situation where Money GDP and wealth are on target but the wage rate is initially too high. This high wage rate introduces upward pressure on prices, and so Money GDP will rise. We see that with unreformed wages the shock is rapidly damped, mainly by means of an

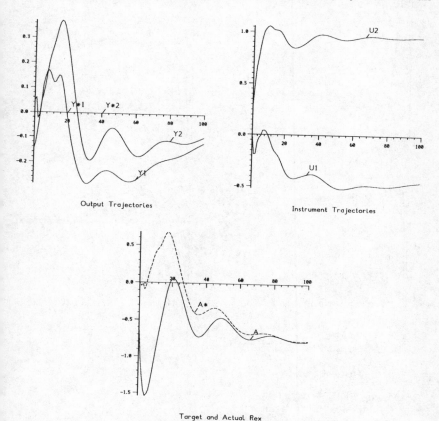

Y_1 Money GDP (% deviation)
Y_2 National wealth (% deviation)
A Real exchange rate (Rex) (% deviation)
U_1 Tax variable (deviation)
U_2 Treasury bill rate (deviation)
A^* Target real exchange rate (% deviation)

Figure 6.23   *Foreign interest rate +1% with adaptive expectations and reformed wages*

appreciation of the real exchange rate. Initially taxes are cut so as to generate a favourable cost-push effect and help damp the shock. These two together bring down Money GDP, but have an unfavourable effect on wealth, and in the longer run taxes have to be raised to offset this.

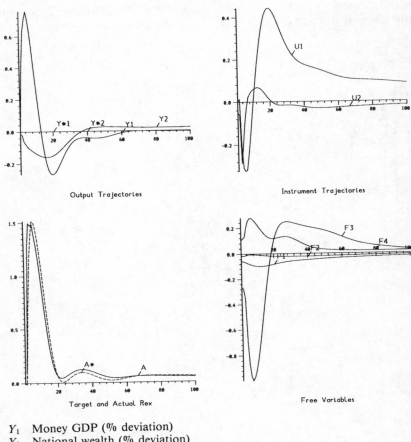

Y_1 Money GDP (% deviation)
Y_2 National wealth (% deviation)
A Real exchange rate (Rex) (% deviation)
A^* Target real exchange rate (% deviation)
U_1 Tax variable (deviation)
F_1 Human capital (% deviation)
F_2 Consol rate (% deviation)
F_3 Valuation ratio (% deviation)
F_4 Nominal exchange rate (% deviation)
U_2 Treasury bill rate (deviation)

Figure 6.24 Wage rate + 1% with model-consistent expectations and unreformed wages

This process works faster with model-consistent expectations (Figure 6.24) than with adaptive expectations (Figure 6.25), because in the former case there is almost no lag in the response of wages to prices. With reformed wages (Figures 6.26 and 6.27) the complete absence of the wage-price spiral means that the shock is damped more slowly, but on the other hand the real exchange rate is much more stable. In the early part

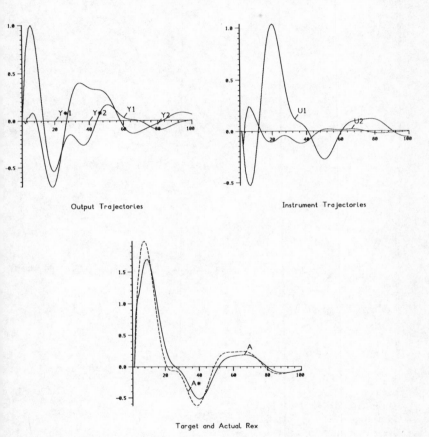

Output Trajectories

Instrument Trajectories

Target and Actual Rex

Y_1 Money GDP (% deviation)
Y_2 National wealth (% deviation)
A Real exchange rate (Rex) (% deviation)
U_1 Tax variable (deviation)
U_2 Treasury bill rate (deviation)
A^* Target real exchange rate (% deviation)

Figure 6.25   Wage rate + 1% with adaptive expectations and unreformed wages

of the period taxes rise by more than in the unreformed case, but the interaction with wealth is much less and taxes are reduced sooner.

There is one general point which can be noticed in these simulations. The control of the models with adaptive expectations is, in general, more

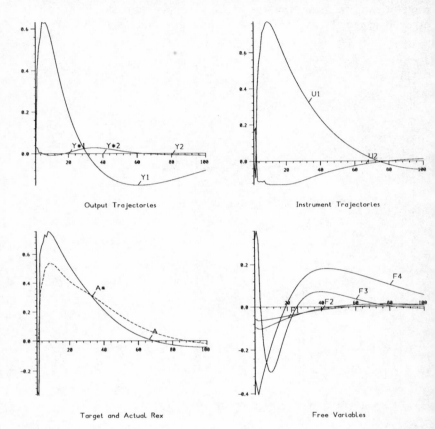

Output Trajectories   Instrument Trajectories

Target and Actual Rex   Free Variables

Y_1 Money GDP (% deviation)
Y_2 National wealth (% deviation)
A Real exchange rate (Rex) (% deviation)
A^* Target real exchange rate (% deviation)
U_1 Tax variable (deviation)
F_1 Human capital (% deviation)
F_2 Consol rate (% deviation)
F_3 Valuation ratio (% deviation)
F_4 Nominal exchange rate (% deviation)
U_2 Treasury bill rate (deviation)

Figure 6.26   Wage rate + 1% with model-consistent expectations and reformed wages

prone to cyclical disturbances than is the control of the models with model-consistent expectations. This is a consequence of the fact that our control of Money GDP with adaptive expectations is itself more cyclical than our control of the economy with model-consistent expectations.

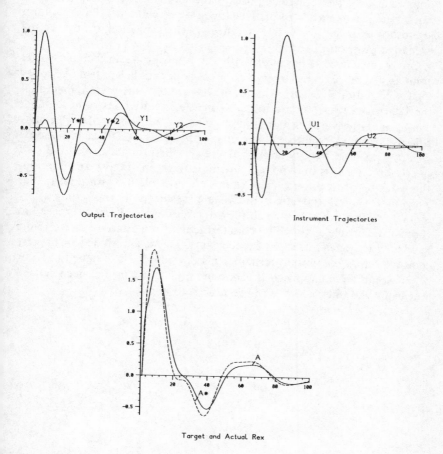

Y_1 Money GDP (% deviation)
Y_2 National wealth (% deviation)
A Real exchange rate (Rex) (% deviation)
U_1 Tax variable (deviation)
U_2 Treasury bill rate (deviation)
A^* Target real exchange rate (% deviation)

Figure 6.27   Wage rate +1% with adaptive expectations and reformed wages

6.10   CONCLUSION

In this chapter we have shown how the joint use of monetary and fiscal policy allows the authorities to achieve an investment or wealth target as well as a target level of Money GDP (or target price level). At the same time we have demonstrated empirically the way in which monetary policy can be guided by means of an exchange-rate target, with the short-term interest rate being set with reference to the deviation of the actual exchange rate from its target.

Our main concern has been with the appropriate instrument-target emphasis to place on monetary and fiscal policy in the control of Money GDP and national wealth. The results have shown the great impact that the degree of wage indexation has on the required instrument-target emphasis. However, it is not enough to assess the impact of each policy rule by its ability to effect a step change in Money GDP or in national wealth (or even by its ability to reject disturbances, as discussed in section 6.6). It is only possible to come to a general assessment about the working of our policy rules (and only possible to form a particular judgement about the effect of wage indexation in this context) by simulating the model for which they were designed. We now proceed to discuss the problems posed by counterfactual simulation of an economic model with model-consistent expectations. This is a prelude to Chapters 8 and 9, where we present reruns of history which are designed to show what would have happened if economic policy had in fact been carried out using the rules which we have described above.

Chapter Seven

Counterfactual simulation with forward-looking expectations

7.1 INTRODUCTION

An important part of our work has been to test the working of various policies over a historical period by means of counterfactual simulation. The purpose of this exercise is to show the performance of each set of policy rules in the face of historical shocks. These historical shocks come from two sources. In the first place, exogenous variables, such as world trade and the foreign interest rate, are not fixed. They move around and so disturb the domestic economy. Our policy rules are intended to damp the effects of such disturbances. Secondly, the econometric equations which comprise the model do not fit history exactly. There are residuals, representing disturbances in each of these equations. These residuals can also blow the model off course; our policy rules are also intended to suppress the effects of events such as wage explosions, which occurred in some historical periods but are not necessarily predicted by the econometric equations of the model.

It is possible to carry out a counterfactual simulation of a model with backward-looking expectations without a great deal of difficulty. In each period the model is solved on the basis of the current and past values of the exogenous and endogenous data. The effects of the second type of shock are represented by adding on the residuals from the econometric equations to the results generated by the simulation of the model, and the policy instruments are set endogenously by means of the policy rules. The model moves from one period to the next and the solution does not depend in any way on anticipations of future events. The simulations with adaptive expectations, which we present in Chapters 8 and 9, are carried out in this way. The only exception we make to the principle of adding back the residuals in the econometric equations is that we do not add back the residuals which would be found if the reformed-wage equation were used in an attempt to track history. The reason for this is clear. The reformed-wage equation is meant to be counterfactual. To add back the residuals which would make it track history would not give a realistic representation of the residuals which would be found if this equation had been estimated on an economy with a reformed labour market.

Counterfactual simulation with forward-looking expectations raises difficulties of quite a different nature. The essence of forward-looking models is that current variables are affected by expectations of future events, whether those future events actually materialize or not. The manner in which these expectations affect current events depends on the expected future values of the policy instruments. This in turn depends on the control rules which are adopted. This chapter is devoted to explaining first how we use expectations of future exogenous variables in our model, and secondly how we construct those expectations of future events.

7.2 POSSIBLE APPROACHES TO THE PROBLEM

There are two possible approaches to the problem of solving models with forward-looking expectations. Both of them offer ways of determining the values to be taken by the free or 'jumping' variables; these values are dependent on expected future events as well as on variables endogenous to the model. The first and more widely used approach involves setting terminal conditions for the model, at some point far in the future. An iterative technique is then used to find starting values for the jumping variables so that they describe trajectories over which expectations are fulfilled and so that the terminal conditions are satisfied. This method is described by Lipton *et al.* (1982). It has the advantage that it produces a trajectory on which expectations are fulfilled almost exactly (down to the convergence criteria set by the user) and this probably explains its popularity.

Nevertheless there are a number of features which make the technique unsuitable for use in our case. First of all, the solution trajectory is sensitive to the terminal conditions which are inevitably somewhat arbitrary. Lack of sensitivity is only found when the technique is used on a model in which expectational variables are inherently unimportant.

Secondly, in order to solve a rerun of history in which expectations of future events change from one period to the next, it would be necessary to solve a complete trajectory so as to find the initial position at the start of that trajectory for each period. It is as though a solution for n^2 rather than n periods were required. This is computationally very expensive. It would not be a problem for individual solutions, but it would make the development stage of any piece of work very difficult. This is no doubt one reason why the technique has, to our knowledge, only been applied on the assumption that expectations of future events were not revised or revised infrequently (e.g. Hall, 1987).

The alternative available to us is to use the linear representation of our model so as to provide an analytical solution for the response of the economy to revisions in expectations of future events. This solution is calculated using the technique described by Blanchard and Kahn (1980). It produces values for the free variables as deviations from the equilibrium of the economy, as described in section 11.2.2. We explain below how it is possible to derive estimates for the levels rather than the deviations of these variables. The values of the jumping variables can then be used as exogenous inputs into the non-linear model. The need to solve for a complete trajectory is replaced by the need to use the linear model in each iteration of the non-linear model. Since a number of variables are exogenous, the solution of the non-linear model proceeds more rapidly than it would when those variables are endogenous, and this compensates to some extent for the need to use the linear model in each iteration. The main advantage of this method is computational.

However, there is also a theoretical advantage. The first solution relied on the adoption of an arbitrary end-point. The choice of this may influence the out-turn. The second solution produces a trajectory which converges asymptotically to a steady-state path. Of course, this trajectory depends on the expected trend paths of the exogenous variables; in addition, terminal conditions are still needed, but they are not arbitrary. This is explained below.

The main disadvantage of the technique arises from the fact that a linear approximation is used. As a consequence, even if there were no revision to expectations from one period to the next, the model solution would be one in which expectations were only approximately fulfilled. Since, in our reruns, we do allow for expectations to be revised from one period to the next, we are unable to determine how approximate this approximation is. A second disadvantage arises from the fact that in our non-linear model there are over a hundred exogenous variables. Our linear model is unable to handle all of these (and it would be difficult to monitor revisions to expectations of all of these). In our linear model we are forced to identify a small number of key exogenous variables to which expectational shocks can occur. These are the level of world trade, import prices in foreign currency, the foreign interest rate and government expenditure on goods and services.[1] We make the assumption that these are the key exogenous variables which drive our model.

7.3   THE INFLUENCE OF EXPECTED FUTURE EVENTS IN THE LINEAR MODEL

7.3.1   Exogenous variables

In Chapters 10 and 11 (sections 10.6 and 11.2) we set out formally how expectations of future events can influence the jumping variables and so affect the current state of the real economy. We assume that economic agents treat our key exogenous variables as having an expected trend running from a perceived initial value and that there may, in the short term, be easily identifiable deviations from this trend line. Using our linear model we can then calculate reaction functions, showing how our jumping variables are influenced by each of (i) a change in the expected trend value, (ii) a change in the perceived base value and (iii) a change in the one-period deviation from trend any number of periods ahead. We can cumulate the effects of these three types of disturbance to show the total effect of unanticipated changes in exogenous variables on the jumping variables.

7.3.2   The target trajectories

We also show in section 11.2 that a change in the target trajectory will have an identifiable effect on the current values of the jumping variables, even if that change lies some way in the future. This would seem to imply that we should use our target trajectories in some way in calculating the values taken by the jumping variables.

However, the real side of our model is homogeneous of degree zero in prices; the model is long-run inflation-neutral. We assume that the target path for Money GDP does not in itself affect the rest of the economy. This assumption is justified provided that the target is credible, which we assume in our simulations; credibility is in any case much more plausible if the target trajectory does not imply any sudden change in the rate of growth of Money GDP – and our target trajectory (equation 8.2) meets that condition. It means, in effect, that we are treating the target path of Money GDP as influencing the particular integral of the difference equations which describe our system (see Chapter 10). The difference equations can be interpreted as describing disturbances around any long-run equilibrium path and, given the price homogeneity of our model, it is sensible to take the Money GDP path as defining the particular integral path, or equilibrium trajectory, rather than inducing deviations from that equilibrium. The fact that the money GDP trajectory is different from history does not on its own affect the model.

In interpreting the target trajectory for wealth we face a problem to which there is no easy solution when working from a largely ready-made econometric model. This is that the long-run steady-state growth paths of real variables are not all the same. It is a situation which often arises when some of the relationships, such as trade equations, imply non-unit long-term quantity elasticities.

We have simply assumed that the long-term growth in output in our non-linear model in each of the reruns represents growth on the fundamental trajectory, and that wealth grows at the same rate along its fundamental trajectory. In the unreformed wage simulation that rate of growth is 2 per cent per annum, while with reformed wages it is 2.8 per cent per annum.

This assumption is of much less concern than might be thought. The purpose of this analysis of the effects of disturbances in the exogenous variables or in the target trajectories is to allow the calculation of the jumping variables from the linear model. A constant non-zero time-trend would induce a constant shift in the jumping variables. But, as we explain in section 7.6, our use of terminal conditions ensures that the effects of constant shifts of this type are taken care of. It would not therefore matter if the 'true' rate of growth of the quantity variables in our model were different from that which we have identified.

These assumptions mean that the target trajectories enter very simply. Both are treated as coinciding with the fundamental trajectory of the linear model. Thus in fact neither trajectory enters visibly into the linear model.

We now proceed to explain how we calculate the values taken by the jumping variables in the non-linear model. First we describe how equilibrium trajectories, or particular integrals, are calculated down to some constant value. Then we explain how the effects of expectational shocks are calculated in practice. These allow us to calculate the jumps in the jumping variables from one period to the next. Finally we explain how terminal conditions are used to calculate the absolute values of the jumping variables.

7.4 EQUILIBRIUM TRAJECTORIES FOR THE JUMPING VARIABLES

The equilibrium values, or fundamentals, which have to be calculated, are derived on an *ad hoc* basis which reflects the special characteristics of each variable.

7.4.1 The valuation ratio

For the valuation ratio there is no problem. In the steady state it takes a value of 0.64 (section 5.3.5).

7.4.2 The exchange rate

The treatment of the exchange rate is only a little more complex. Our linear model calculates both target and actual values for the real exchange rate, measured as disturbances from a rest state. The percentage gap between the two is independent of the absolute value of the target real exchange rate. Fortunately this target real exchange rate is a backwards-looking variable, which is directly identifiable in the non-linear model. The deviation of the actual real exchange rate from its target value, found in the linear model, can simply be added back to give an absolute value for the real exchange rate. This is then inflated up without any difficulty to give the nominal exchange rate by multiplying by the ratio of home to foreign unit labour costs. In effect we exploit the simple fact that, in equilibrium, the actual real exchange rate is the same as its target value.

7.4.3 The consol rate

The calculation of the fundamental trajectory for the consol rate is slightly more difficult. We assume that the steady-state real rate of interest ($\tilde{R}_\infty$) is 4 per cent per annum. To this we have to add the rate of inflation implied by the target path for Money GDP. This is equal to the target growth rate of Money GDP ($\hat{z}_t^*$) less the trend rate of growth of productivity (q). The one-period rate of interest on the fundamental trajectory is therefore $\tilde{R}_\infty + \hat{z}_t^* - q$ and, exploiting the perfect substitutability of short and long assets, we find

$$1/RCNS_t = \sum_{T=t}^{\infty} \prod_{\tau=t}^{T} \frac{1}{(1 + \tilde{R}_\infty + \hat{z}_\tau^* - q)}$$

It may be checked that, if $\hat{z}^*_{t+j}$ is constant, $\hat{z}^*_t$, so that nominal interest rates are expected to remain constant on the equilibrium trajectory, then $RCNS_t = \tilde{R}_\infty = \hat{z}^*_t - q$. Except in this special case, the fundamental value will change as a consequence of movement in $\hat{z}^*_t$ even if $\tilde{R}_\infty$ is constant. For example, if the rate of inflation of Money GDP along its target path is projected to decline over time, then the consol rate too will fall.

7.4.4 Human capital

The fundamental trajectory for human capital is the hardest to identify. We have noted (section 6.2), that the original wage equation implies a target rate of growth of the real wages of 2.2 per cent per annum. It is therefore sensible to take human capital as growing at this rate. In addition to identifying the trend rate of growth of human capital, it is necessary to know the level of the trajectory at any one point so as to determine the whole path. Fortunately the correct level can be identified by the use of terminal conditions as described below.

7.5 EXPECTED FUTURE VALUES OF EXOGENOUS VARIABLES: EFFECTS ON JUMPING VARIABLES

We now discuss how we identify expectational shocks and calculate their effects on the jumping variables. It is an essential feature of our simulations that we do not wish to make the assumption that expectations are never revised. Rather we wish to find what was expected for the evolution of these exogenous variables at each point in time, and then to study the effects of revisions to these expectations from one period to the next. As a consequence we have to produce some estimate of expected values of exogenous variables. There are a variety of ways in which this could have been done.

7.5.1 World trade

We have chosen to take the projected values for world trade from the *National Institute Economic Review* as indicating the path that it was expected to follow. The projected trajectories are shown in Figure 7.1(a).

We must now convert these projections into expected deviations of world trade from its perceived equilibrium trajectory in each period. It is then necessary to identify shifts in each of the three types of disturbance mentioned in section 7.3 from one period to the next.

We have assumed that the long-term expected rate of growth of world trade is 5 per cent per annum, and that this is constant. There are therefore no expectational shocks of the first type arising from trend changes.

This long-term growth rate gives the slope of the trend line for world trade. We assume that this trend line passes through the furthest actual data projection given in the *National Institute Economic Review*. The initial value of the trend line is now given by extrapolating the trend line (equilibrium trajectory) through this furthest projection back to the present. Upward or downward shifts in the trend line from one period to the next are expectational disturbances of the second type.

The values of one-off disturbances j periods ahead are then deviations of the *Review's* projections from the current trend line; views on these may change from one period to the next, affecting the values of the jumping variables.

7.5.2 World prices in foreign currency

The long-term rate of inflation of foreign currency prices is taken to be the long-term nominal rate of interest (see below) less 4 per cent per annum, which is taken to be the real rate of interest. This long-term inflation rate gives a trend line for world prices. Its slope changes from one period to the next as the long-term interest rate changes. These changes in slope are disturbances of the first type.

We tried using the same approach as with world trade, of assuming that this trend line passed through the furthest projection point identified by the *National Institute Economic Review* (see Figure 7.1(b)), but found that this led to a very volatile initial value, suggesting unreasonably large disturbances of the second type. We therefore smoothed the initial values using a 5-period moving average filter (Kendall and Stuart, 1981) and used changes in these to identify disturbances of the second type.

For the period for which published projections are available we once again set the one-off shocks j periods ahead to be the deviations of those projections from the current trend line. However, the smoothing process means that the last published projection, n periods ahead, no longer lies on the trend line. We assumed that the shift occasioned by the smoothing process decays linearly between n and 20 periods ahead (n is between 6 and 9 depending on the forecast available). This gave us values for disturbances of the third type for 20 periods ahead.

7.5.3 Foreign interest rates

We assume that there are no trends in equilibrium interest rates. Disturbances of the first type are absent.

Expected foreign interest rates are not calculated from published forecasts; the *National Institute Economic Review* does not give projections of these. Instead we have used short and long rates of interest for Germany (as representative of the hard currency countries) and the United States in order to derive a projected term structure of interest rates. For each country we have assumed that there is a constant rate of convergence of short and long rates to steady-state values. This, combined with the expectations hypothesis of the term structure of interest rates, allows the expected pattern of short-term interest rates in each country to be calculated. This is shown in Figure 7.1(c). The deviations from the steady state for the world interest rate are then taken to be the arithmetic mean of the figures for these two countries. These deviations are then hung from our estimate of the world short-term interest rate (which was in fact a wealth-weighted mean of the rates in the United States, Germany, Japan and France – data problems prevented us calculating long rates on the same basis).

The method used is that described by Frankel (1982). It is assumed that the gap between the short-term interest rate and its steady-state value decays at a constant rate (which is here assumed to be 15 per cent per annum). Algebraically, the long-term interest rate is given as R_∞^F, where R_∞^F is the root of the equation

$$\prod_{j=0}^{9} (1 + R_\infty^F + [R_1^F - R_\infty^F].0.85^j) = (1 + R_{10}^F)^{10} \qquad (7.1)$$

This method is not ideal. Leaving aside the shortcomings of the model, data problems mean that it is not possible to take the coupon effect (Schaefer, 1981) into account. But it does provide a means of inferring the long-term interest rate, R_∞^F.

Long-term interest rates are calculated separately for Germany and the United States, and then averaged. The difference between this average long-term rate and the average of their short-term rates is then added on to our world average short-term rate, to give a world long-term rate of interest. Changes in this from one period to the next represent disturbances of the second type.

The expected deviation of the nominal short-term interest rate from its current level, j periods in the future, is then given as

$$E(R_j^F) = (R_1^F - R_\infty^F)(1 - 0.85^j)$$

These deviations are measured relative to the world short-term interest rate in the data base, which is a weighted average of the rates in the United States, Germany, France and Japan. Changes in these represent disturbances of the third type.

7.5.4   Government spending

This is an exogenous variable of a different type from the other three, since it is policy-determined rather than truly exogenous. In our simulations (sections 8.4.3 and 9.4) we adopt smooth trajectories with the aim of removing a source of historical disturbance to the economy.

With unreformed wages we keep the level of government consumption and investment constant. We assume that it is expected to resume growth at the fundamental rate (taken to be 2 per cent) five years from the end of each current period. Since this rate is constant, there are no disturbances of the first type but, since the equilibrium growth rate is not achieved, there are disturbances of the second and third types.

Using the long-run growth rate we can calculate the shift in the trend line (equilibrium trajectory) implied in each period.[2]

However, we also assume that the private sector is expecting five years of no growth in government spending. This means that actual government spending is at the same value as its expected level in five years, and is therefore well above the trend line, although the gap narrows to nothing over the five-year horizon. These disturbances of the third type do not change from one period to the next. They affect the initial values of the jumping variables but they do not induce shocks during the simulations.

With reformed wages we find that the economy is able to afford growth in public consumption and investment at what we have identified as the fundamental growth rate of the reformed-wage economy (2.8 per cent per annum). There are therefore no unanticipated changes in government spending on goods and services at any point in the rerun.

7.6 A TERMINAL CONDITION

The fundamental trajectories of the jumping variables can be added to the values calculated in section 7.4 to determine absolute values of the jumping variables based on the premise that the model is at rest at the start of the simulation. Some way must be found of correcting for the fact that the underlying premise is undoubtedly false.

Our simulation covers a long period in which the economy is subjected to shocks, but we include several periods of smooth evolution at the end of the simulation. During these periods of smooth evolution the linear model continues to produce values of the jumping variables. These should be on deterministic saddlepaths. The joint assumptions of consistent expectations and the absence of further shocks mean that, during this period of smooth evolution, values of the jumping variables can also be identified in the non-linear model. The terminal conditions which we impose are nothing more than that changes in the jumping variables in the linear and non-linear models should coincide, down to some acceptable convergence criterion, in the last period of our simulations. These terminal conditions mean, in effect, that the starting values of the jumping variables are calculated without reference to the level of the fundamental trajectory of each. As a consequence our model solution is independent of constant displacements in the fundamental trajectories of section 7.4.

The nature of the condition can be described by a simple example. Suppose that the exchange rate starts off too low relative to its target value. Interest rates will then be too high, and the non-linear model will be projecting depreciations which do not take place. This cannot be identified during the noisy period of the simulation, when expectations are not normally fulfilled. But during the period of smooth evolution the inconsistency will be apparent. An upward jump in the initial value of both nominal and real exchange rates will mean that interest rates are lower throughout the simulation, and a value of the jump can normally be found which will deliver consistency of expectations between the linear and non-linear models in the absence of shocks. The values of the jumps could no doubt be found by an algorithm, but we found the solution manually.

We do not claim that this method gives an exact solution to the problem of simulation of a consistent expectations model. But we attach considerable importance to the fact that it allows us to make the realistic assumption that expectations keep changing. And we are glad to avoid producing a solution which hinges on an arbitrary terminal condition.

7.7 EXPECTATIONS AND REALITY

The graphs we present opposite show the actual trajectories for the key exogenous variables shown by the solid lines, together with the expected future trajectories, shown by each dotted line. As can be seen from the graphs, if expectations of future events have any significant influence on the determination of current economic variables, then the assumption that the future was foreseen correctly would lead to quite different results from the assumption which we use, that expectations were as represented by the projections in the *National Institute Economic Review*. Figure 7.1(a) displays actual and expected values of world trade. Its main features concern the recovery of world trade after the first oil crisis, and its subsequent slowdown and contraction in the aftermath of the second oil crisis. The solid line shows the path which was actually traced by world trade, and each dotted line shows the expected trajectories, starting from the observed points on the solid line. We can see that the recovery in 1976/7 came as a surprise. During the late 1970s world trade grew steadily, and could therefore be projected reasonably accurately. However, the downturn in the early 1980s was not foreseen, nor was the subsequent recovery in the mid 1980s.

The behaviour of world prices, in Figure 7.1(b), shows some similarities. In the period 1976–8 world inflation was reasonably smooth and easily predictable. The second oil crisis led to a rapid and unexpected increase in prices. Inflationary expectations, as represented by the slopes of the dotted lines, increased in this period. No one foresaw the stagnation in world prices in the period 1981–3. This was partly caused by the fall in oil and other raw materials prices (see Beckerman and Jenkinson, 1986). But people went on expecting prices to rise, and towards the end of the period they started to do slightly better in their forecasts, because prices did actually recover.

In Figure 7.1(c) we assess the performance of forecasts which are actually 'observed' in the market. In the late 1970s long-term interest rates were considerably higher than short-term interest rates and we infer from this that short rates were expected to rise, even though for a period of 4 years they did not actually do so. The sudden rises in short rates in 1980 and 1981 did not lead to corresponding rises in long rates. During this period interest rates were expected to fall. Finally from about the middle of 1982 the market seems to have become convinced that high short-term interest rates were there to stay, and went on expecting short-term rates to rise to the region of 11–12 per cent per annum, even though actual short-term rates seemed to stay considerably below this.

The expectations shown in these three graphs are, of course, not the

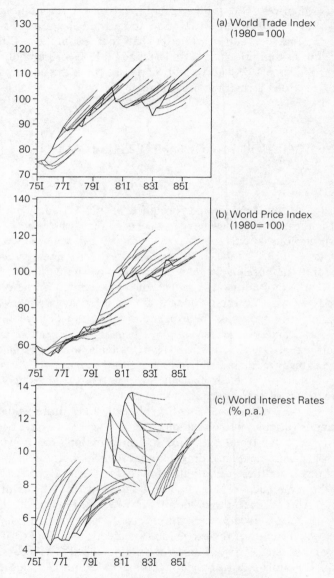

130 —

120 —

110 —

100 —

90 —

80 —

70 —

75I   77I   79I   81I   83I   85I

(a) World Trade Index
(1980=100)

140 —

120 —

100 —

80 —

60 —

75I   77I   79I   81I   83I   85I

(b) World Price Index
(1980=100)

14 —

12 —

10 —

8 —

6 —

4 —

75I   77I   79I   81I   83I   85I

(c) World Interest Rates
(% p.a.)

Figure 7.1   Expectations and reality

only possible series which we could have derived. But where expectations cannot be observed directly it does not seem unreasonable to use the projections of a prominent forecaster. We have done this for world trade and world prices. Our third expectational series, for nominal interest rates, is derived from an assumption about the behaviour of the money and bond markets, and is no better than that assumption. But we note that similar assumptions have underpinned other work on bond markets such as Shiller's (1979) study, and we do not think the underlying model will be regarded as highly unreasonable.

7.8 EXOGENOUS SHOCKS TO THE JUMPING VARIABLES

In order to simulate the performance of the economy with model-consistent expectations we have to take account of the effects of changes in expectations about the future levels of the genuinely exogenous variables (which we take to be world prices in foreign currency, world trade and the foreign interest rate). In any simulation with model-consistent expectations the effect of movements in these variables depends on whether these changes are expected to last. Movements in expected future values of the exogenous variables will have an effect on the current values of the free variables, even if no disturbance takes place to their actual values. Equation (11.6) explains how disturbances to the free variables are calculated from shocks to the exogenous variables. The basic result is that the current values of the free variables depend on all future values of the exogenous variables.

We cannot, of course, identify all expected future values of the exogenous variables but, as explained in section 7.5, we have been able to identify expected trend paths for the three major exogenous variables and for government spending. We have also been able to identify deviations from these trend paths for up to 20 periods ahead.

In the remainder of this chapter we describe the effects of expectational disturbances to the economy in two ways. First of all, we present tables of multipliers indicating the effects of 1 per cent or 1 point shifts in the expected trends of the exogenous variables of shifts in their expected levels and of one-off disturbances one period ahead. These correspond to the three types of disturbance identified in section 7.3, although, for reasons of brevity alone, we only display the effects of one-off disturbances one period ahead.

Secondly, we display graphically the impact effects of disturbances in the exogenous variables on the jumping variables during the course of our rerun. We use the values for the disturbances which we have identified through the procedures described in section 7.6, taking account of one-off expected disturbances for up to 20 periods ahead.

These graphs do not display any impact from expectational shocks to government spending. With unreformed wages the only shock to government spending is a shift in the expected base value of the trend line from one period to the next. This shift is the same in every period and so only induces a constant disturbance in the jumping variables. But our use of terminal conditions (section 7.6) ensures that nothing is lost by neglecting a constant shift. With reformed wages there are no expectational shocks and so nothing is omitted.

We present multiplier tables and graphs first for our controlled economy with unreformed wages and secondly for our controlled economy with reformed wages.

7.8.1   The controlled economy with unreformed wages

We find the following responses in the jumping variables to trend changes in each of our three exogenous variables and government spending.

We first identify the effects of changes in the trend rate of growth of our exogenous variables on the jumping variables. We display results even for variables such as the foreign interest rate which we assume cannot be trended. This is done for completeness.

Table 7.1   *The controlled economy — unreformed wages*
(a) 1 per cent or 1 point per cent per quarter trend

Jumping Variable	World Trade	World Prices	World Interest Rates	Government Spending
Human Capital	7.48	5.47	− 112	− 35.1
Consol Rate	− 2.31	− 2.82	43.7	− 9.10
Valuation Ratio	− 0.342	19.2	− 108.0	− 4.52
Nominal Exch. Rate	3.04	8.66	− 57.9	− 9.92

These effects are very powerful indeed. This is not surprising. A trend of 1 per cent per quarter rapidly becomes an extremely powerful deviation.

We now look at a step change of 1 per cent or 1 point.

Table 7.1   (cont.) The controlled economy — unreformed wages
(b) 1 per cent or 1 point step change

Jumping Variable	World Trade	World Prices	World Interest Rates	Government Spending
Human Capital	0.086	− 0.006	− 0.942	− 0.559
Consol Rate	− 0.022	− 0.011	0.628	− 0.167
Valuation Ratio	− 0.028	0.123	− 4.38	− 1.01
Nominal Exch. Rate	0.161	0.891	− 2.10	0.151

Disturbances to foreign interest rates are very important, and we also note the impact of a change in the world price level on the nominal exchange rate. Since the model is homogeneous of degree one in prices, a 1 per cent change in the world price level causes, with no other disturbance, a 1 per cent change in the nominal exchange rate in the long run. We see that 89 per cent of this shift is achieved immediately.

Tables 7.1(a) and 7.1(b) do offer one useful check. The world real interest rate can be changed either by a change in the trend in world prices, or by a change in the level of the world interest rate with no change in prices. We would not expect the two to have exactly the same effect, because their short-term consequences are different. But the jumps they induce should not be very different. We can see that the effect of a 1 per cent per quarter trend in prices is roughly minus 4 times the effect of a 1 per cent point per annum increase in the nominal interest rate. Our linear model suggests that real interest changes have much the same effect whether they are induced by inflation or by interest-rate changes. This validates our model.

Lastly we may see the effects of an expected 1 per cent or 1 point disturbance one period in the future, but lasting only for one period. The impact of this is found to be as shown in Table 7.1(c).

Table 7.1   (cont.) The controlled economy — unreformed wages
(c) 1 per cent or 1 point shock 1 period ahead

Jumping Variable	World Trade	World Prices	World Interest Rates	Government Spending
Human Capital	0.0007	− 0.003	0.0054	− 0.0079
Consol Rate	0.0011	0.0079	0.0023	0.0019
Valuation Ratio	− 0.017	− 0.106	− 0.024	− 0.104
Nominal Exch. Rate	0.022	0.139	− 0.205	0.068

The impact of one-period shocks further ahead is calculated using equation (11.6). The resulting impact is generally lower, in absolute magnitude, than the multipliers of Table 7.1(c). The reason for this is that the effects of expected one-period disturbances increase the closer they loom to the present.

The actual disturbances to the free variables come from two sources. In addition to those arising from movements in the exogenous variables, which we have studied in Tables 7.1(a–c), deviations of Money GDP or national wealth from their target paths lead to policy reactions and thus affect the free variables. Since we calculate the values of the free variables on the basis of our linear model, as can be seen from (11.6), we may consider the two sorts of disturbance quite separately, and then simply add them together.

This makes it worthwhile to study the effects of disturbances in the three exogenous variables on the free variables, while neglecting the effects of deviations from target paths. We simply multiply each of the multipliers in Table 7.1 by the appropriate disturbances for each period, and are then able to calculate the change in each free variable relative to

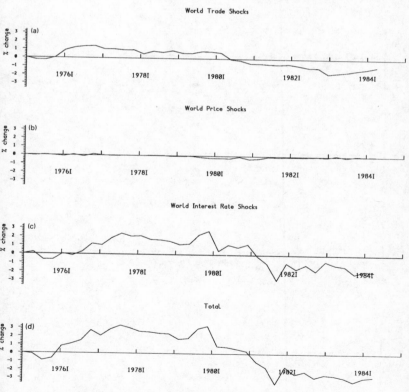

Figure 7.2 Unreformed wages: human capital

the previous period, which is occasioned by each exogenous variable. Finally we combine all the disturbances, so as to show the overall effect of the exogenous shocks on each of the free variables. The results of this are displayed graphically in Figures 7.2–7.5. These graphs (and Figures 7.6–7.9 which relate to the reformed-wage economy) run from the period from 1975 I to 1984 II, and thus cover the period for which we have a full data set. Our simulations in Chapters 8 and 9 run from 1975 I to 1989 IV, but the simulations from 1984 III are constructed using projections for some or all data items and do not take account of the effects of revisions to expectations of our key exogenous variables. This is explained in more detail in Chapter 8; it does have the implication that the graphs in this chapter cannot run beyond 1984 II.

Looking first at human capital (Figure 7.2), we can see that, without any wage reform, the major disturbances arise from shocks to world trade and to world interest rates. During the first part of our period

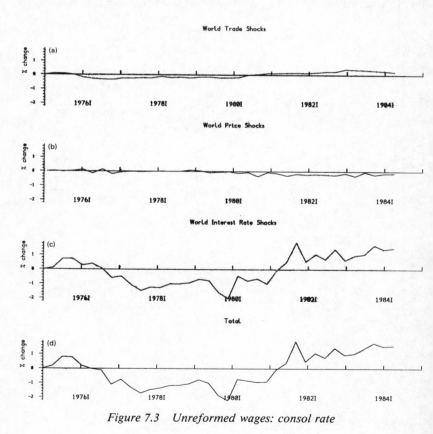

Figure 7.3   Unreformed wages: consol rate

world trade did better than had been expected looking ahead from 1975, and interest rates were lower. These effects both work in the same direction, raising human capital above its initial value. From 1980 onwards we have a period of underperforming world trade and higher-than-expected interest rates, and so human capital is depressed below its initial value.

Given the high level of capital mobility, one would expect the consol rate to be sensitive mainly to the foreign interest rate, with other variables having much less effect. This is shown in Figure 7.3. Interest rates also have a powerful effect on the valuation ratio but, as the arbitrage equation (5.17) implies, profits are also important. Figure 7.4 suggests that in fact interest rates are also by far the dominant force on the valuation ratio, although changes in prices are, because of their impact on profits, also of some importance.

Finally in Figure 7.5 we can observe the effect of shocks on the

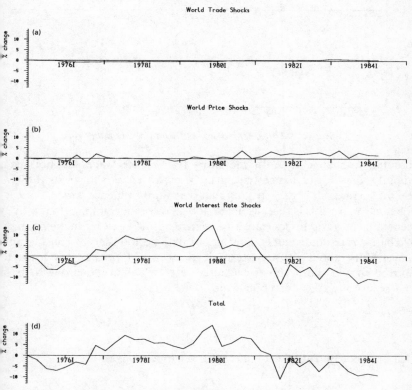

Figure 7.4   Unreformed wages: valuation ratio

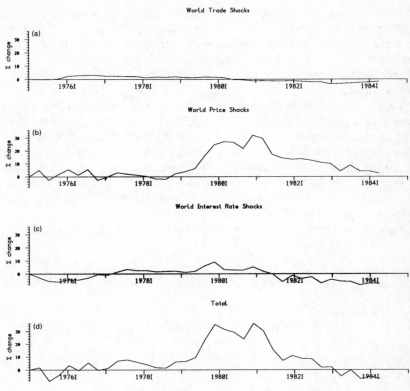

Figure 7.5   Unreformed wages: nominal exchange rate

nominal exchange rate. In the short term, since wages do not reac
rapidly, these disturbances can also be regarded as shocks to the rea
exchange rate.[3] It is very striking that the major influence is world prices
The reason for this is that, as noted above, our model implies that a 1 pe
cent shift in world prices leads to a change of 0.89 per cent in the nomina
exchange rate immediately. During our data period there is considerabl
uncertainty about the long-term level of world prices; this leads t
movements in the nominal exchange rate[4] which could prove to be a
major problem for our policy rules.

7.8.2 The controlled economy with reformed wages

The responses of the jumping variables in the controlled economy wit
reformed wages are given in Table 7.2.

Table 7.2   The controlled economy — reformed wages
a) 1 per cent or 1 point per quarter trend

Jumping Variable	World Trade	World Prices	World Interest Rate	Government Spending
Human Capital	2.23	2.12	− 49.4	− 46.1
Consol Rate	− 3.32	− 3.87	57.4	− 9.99
Valuation Ratio	4.7	23.8	− 186	− 19.0
Nominal Exch. Rate	0.435	5.47	− 13.7	− 0.49

Table 7.2   (cont.) The controlled economy — reformed wages
b) 1 per cent or 1 point step change

Jumping Variable	World Trade	World Prices	World Interest Rate	Government Spending
Human Capital	0.0132	− 0.0682	− 0.322	− 0.669
Consol Rate	− 0.0468	− 0.0132	0.817	− 0.186
Valuation Ratio	0.106	0.175	− 5.23	− 0.37
Nominal Exch. Rate	0.062	0.853	− 1.51	− 0.162

These numbers are obviously not the same as those with unreformed wages, but the magnitudes of the various multipliers are broadly similar. One important point to note is that the jump of the nominal exchange rate in response to a world price shock is much the same in both cases. In the reformed-wage economy much less weight is placed on the exchange rate and on monetary policy for the purpose of controlling inflation, but this does not affect the fact that, in response to a world price shock, the nominal exchange rate jumps to close to its final position. We also note that the consol rate responds rather less with unreformed wages than with reformed wages, to a disturbance to the world interest rate. The reasons for this are explained in Chapter 6.

Once again we observe that the effect of a 1 per cent per quarter trend in world prices is roughly minus 4 times the effects of a 1 per cent point per annum increase in the world interest rate. This again validates our model.

Table 7.2   (cont.) The controlled economy — reformed wages
c) 1 per cent or 1 point temporary disturbance 1 period ahead

Jumping Variable	World Trade	World Prices	World Interest Rate	Government Spending
Human Capital	− 0.00015	− 0.00137	0.00342	− 0.0095
Consol Rate	− 0.00017	0.0079	0.00128	− 0.0047
Valuation Ratio	− 0.00334	− 0.09471	− 0.0231	0.0090
Nominal Exch. Rate	0.0090	0.131	− 0.206	− 0.0253

The effects of temporary disturbances are again found to be mu
smaller than those of disturbances which are expected to be permanen

Figures 7.6–7.9 show the effects of the disturbances in the expecte
values of the exogenous variables on the jumping variables in th
economy with reformed wages. The effect of changing expectations o
the path of world prices on the value of human capital (Figure 7.
provides the most dramatic demonstration that the impact of shoc
depends on the policy regime in force. With unreformed wages pri
shocks had almost no effect on human capital, while now they are
major depressing influence. The reason for this is that a world pri
shock, combined with a slowly moving target for the real exchange rat
has an inflationary impact on the domestic price level (even though it
substantially damped by movement in the nominal exchange rate). Fisc
control of inflation implies a loss of human capital in the adjustme

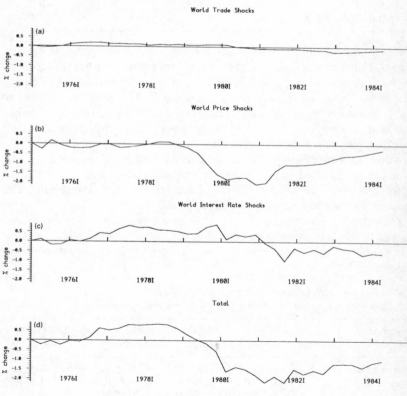

Figure 7.6   Reformed wages: human capital

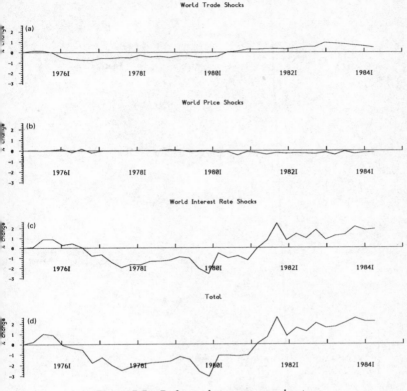

Figure 7.7 Reformed wages: consol rate

rocess, while monetary control of inflation clearly does not. The effect f interest rate disturbances on human capital is in the same direction as efore, but it is much weaker. World trade shocks, too, play much less of role in disturbing human capital.

The main influence on the consol rate (Figure 7.7) remains the world nterest rate, but the effect of shocks to world trade is enhanced in the eformed wage economy. The valuation ratio (Figure 7.8) is more ffected by interest-rate shocks than with unreformed wages. But erhaps the most interesting distinction is that the impact of trade hocks, while still small, is now in the opposite direction from that of igure 7.4. This happens because growth in world trade leads to higher rofits, which raise the valuation ratio. But there is also a policy esponse. The higher level of demand is inflationary. With unreformed vages, interest rates are raised. This depresses the valuation ratio. With eformed wages the inflation is controlled by means mainly of tax

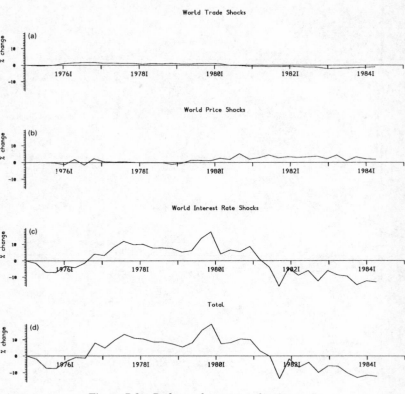

Figure 7.8   Reformed wages: valuation ratio

changes. The valuation ratio is less sensitive to these, and the valuation ratio remains above its initial position.

The behaviour of the nominal exchange rate (Figure 7.9) is once more dominated by the effects of changes in the expected level of world prices. The uncertainty about this is likely to prove a major obstacle to exchange rate stabilization.

7.9 CONCLUSION

This chapter has described how a linear representation of an economic model can be used as an aid to counterfactual simulation of that model. Without its help, it would not be possible to calculate the impact of

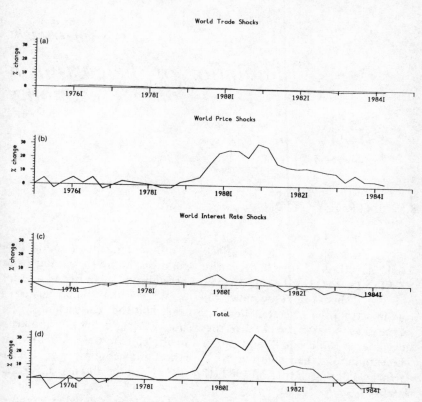

Figure 7.9   Reformed wages: nominal exchange rate

disturbances of various types in the exogenous variables. Nor would it be practical to run a counterfactual simulation of any length in which expectations were revised in every period. The linear model forms the basis not only for the stability test of policy rules, but also, when expectations are assumed to be model-consistent, for their simulation.

In this chapter, then, we have set up the basic infrastructure which we need to run a counterfactual simulation with model-consistent expectations. We now proceed, in Chapters 8 and 9, to apply this technology so as to rerun history on the assumption that economic agents are forward-looking and understand the underlying economic model. We contrast these simulations with others carried out on the assumption that expectations are purely adaptive and that the economy is not directly sensitive to changing expectations of future events.

Chapter Eight

A simulation of the cost-push economy

8.1 INTRODUCTION

This chapter shows what the effects of our policy rules (section 6.7) would have been if they had been in operation during the period from 1975 I to 1987 II. During this period the economy was exposed to a series of external shocks, and the policy rules would have had to play an active role in setting the tax rate, the interest rate and the real exchange rate target so as to damp the effect of these shocks on the economy, and keep the values of Money GDP and national wealth close to their target paths. The simulations then continue to show how the economy would have performed during the period 1987 III to 1989 IV in the absence of further shocks.

We present two simulations in both this and the following chapter. The first simulation shows the projected behaviour of the economy on the assumption that expectations are model-consistent. The second simulation shows the behaviour of the economy on the assumption that expectations in the financial markets follow the adaptive mechanism which we identified in Chapter 5, and that consumption does not depend on model-consistent expectations of future income.

We have carried out the first simulation using a new model-solution technique, which was described in Chapter 7. This technique takes as an input the projections for certain key exogenous variables (world trade, world prices, the foreign interest rate and government spending) which are given in the *National Institute Economic Review* for the relevant period, or were derived in other ways which we described in Chapter 7. The effect of these projected events on the free, or jumping, variables is calculated using the linearized model which we describe in Chapters 10 and 11, and is recalculated in each new period of the solution. This means that full account can be taken of revisions to expectations as represented by changed projections for the exogenous variables. As such ur simulation reflects expectations of the key variables as we think they were believed to be, and independently of whether these expectations were rational or not. The second simulation does not have any forward-looking variables, and does not require any special simulation technique.

In our simulations we subject our model to historic shocks by adding back the single-equation residuals which the model generates. When expectations are assumed to be model-consistent, we must also include shocks arising from revisions to expectations, or from reality turning out differently from expectations.[1] The simulation from 1975 I to 1984 II is carried out using a full data set. For the period from 1984 III to 1987 II our data set is less complete, and for most data we make smooth projections from the 1984 II figures. However, we ensure that historic shocks in our main output variables are nevertheless present, by adding back the residuals in the equations for these variables. From 1987 III we make smooth projections of all the variables. This does lead to abrupt changes in slope for some variables (e.g. Figure 8.1(d)) and in no sense reflects actual history. The residuals needed in order to ensure that the model equations are satisfied in this period also evolve smoothly; there are no further disturbances to the model. These two break points are clearly marked on our graphs.

.2 THE UNREFORMED WAGE EQUATION

n this chapter the simulations are carried out on the assumption that wage-setting behaviour has not been reformed. This is what we mean by . 'cost-push' economy. The wage equation we use is (6.2) with the cost-push parameter, v, set to 1.

$$\Delta \ln WAGERATE_t = 0.039 - 0.138 RTT_{t-3} + \Delta \ln CPI_t^e$$

$$- 2.72 \Delta^2 UPC_{t-1} - 2.43 \Delta UPC_{t-3} - 0.262 UPC_{t-4} \quad (8.1)$$

where $WAGERATE$ –   wage rate
    UPC –   unemployed/labour force
    RTT –   real earnings aspiration gap defined as
    RTT = $\ln AVEARN / \{ CPI \times 0.976 \times (1.00554)^t \}$
    $AVEARN$ –   average earnings
    CPI –   consumer price index
    $\Delta \ln CPI_t^e$ –   expected rate of inflation
With model-consistent expectations we assume

$$\Delta \ln CPI_t^e = 0.5(\Delta \ln CPI_t + \Delta \ln CPI_{t-1})$$

and with adaptive expectations the NIESR model gives

$$\Delta\ln CPI_t^e = 0.75\Delta\ln CPI_{t-1} + 0.15\Delta\ln CPI_{t-2} + 0.10\Delta\ln CPI_{t-3}$$

Equation (8.1) shows wages as responding to expectations of inflati
and to lagged unemployment terms. There is also a term in the level
the real wage, which can be taken, in conjunction with the unemplo
ment terms, as representing a rising labour supply curve. This term
trended, indicating that the real wage associated with a given labo
supply rises at 0.554 per cent per quarter. We assume that labo
productivity grows at the same rate; otherwise there would be no stab
long-term trajectory for the economy (Meade, 1981).

8.3   THE TARGET TRAJECTORIES

The dynamic path of the economy depends not only on the structure
the economy and the policy rules used to regulate it, but also on t
target trajectories which are adopted. We have illustrated this in a simp
way in Chapters 2 and 3.

It is important to stress that policy rules which may be perfec
satisfactory for one set of target trajectories, could yield unsatisfacto
results in other cases. For example, it would be possible to imagi
trajectories which required large tax cuts or very low interest rate
Taken to an extreme, either of these variables might be forced to
negative. A negative tax rate is perhaps imaginable, but in an econor
with circulating currency a negative interest rate is much harder
imagine, and a rule which wanted to deliver this would be invalidated
a particular target path. On the other hand, a trajectory which requir
very rapid growth in wealth would also require very high tax rates. This
the fault of the target trajectory and not of our policy rules. In fact th
second point is nothing more than a conclusion to be drawn fro
Chapter 2. But it must be borne in mind in interpreting our simulatior
The choice of target path for Money GDP might be expected to ta
into account any costs of changing the rate of inflation as well as co
imposed by a particular rate of inflation. The choice of wealth target
determined by the issues identified in the literature on optimal savi
(Meade, 1966b). We do not discuss the calculation of the optimal targ
trajectories in this book. The purpose of our study is to show how simp
policy rules can be used in order to steer the economy back on to
target trajectory after some disturbance has blown it off course. V
therefore take plausible target trajectories as given.

8.3.1 Money GDP

The target path for Money GDP has to reflect the fact that, at the start of our simulation period, inflation was rapid. The rate of growth of Money GDP was around 20 per cent per annum or 5 per cent per quarter. We have assumed that the policy target was to reduce this rate of growth of Money GDP to 1.25 per cent per quarter. This reduction in the rate of nominal growth is assumed to be asymptotic, and we have found that a target trajectory of the form

$$Z_t^* = Z_0.\{1.05^t.e^{-0.04t} + 1.0125^t(1 - e^{-0.04t})\} \qquad (8.2)$$

where Z_0 is the value of Money GDP in 1974 IV, gives a trajectory on which the rate of growth of Money GDP is brought down to 1.25 per cent per quarter with a faster rate of disinflation than occurred historically. This can be seen in Figure 8.1(a), which shows the historical, target and simulation paths of Money GDP. The choice of a low-inflation trajectory allows us to demonstrate the working of our rules rather more clearly than would be possible if we aimed to follow a path close to the historical trajectory.[2]

8.3.2 National wealth

The choice of wealth target is rather more difficult. There is a strong case for saying that the target rate of growth of national wealth should reflect the long-term rate of growth of the economy, at least in the absence of knowledge about the nature of economies of scale or capital-saving technical progress. However, we are unable to identify that long-term growth rate precisely. We have chosen a target rate of growth of national wealth of 2 per cent per annum. This is below the target rate of growth of real wages, and therefore below the value of long-run productivity growth which we have assumed. But it is above the rate of growth which the economy delivers in the reruns of history with unreformed wages and could be regarded as consistent with a modest estimate of long-term economic growth. We start with the wealth target at the initial (1974 IV) estimate of actual national wealth. We have, as noted in Chapter 6, excluded the public sector capital stock from the wealth target (with, as

far as possible, suitable adjustments for denationalization). We regulate
the size of the public sector capital stock by keeping the level of public
sector investment constant in volume terms (see section 8.4.3).

8.4   HISTORICAL DISTURBANCES

8.4.1   Types of disturbance

The purpose of rerunning history is to demonstrate how the controlled
economy is able to respond to and damp down the effects of shocks
which impinge on it. As noted in Chapter 7, two types of shocks happen
in every quarter, whether expectations are adaptive or model-consistent.
The estimated regression equations have residuals which have to be
added back so as to ensure that, if the exogenous variables take their
historical values, a rerun of history would reproduce history. These
behavioural shocks reflect the fact that people's behaviour cannot be
precisely modelled by regression equations. Our control rules have to be
able to cope with the possibility that the economy may diverge from a
particular trajectory because of disturbances of this type.

The second type of shock arises from shifts in exogenous variables. A
change in the level of world demand will have implications for UK export
demand and thus for the balance of payments, Money GDP and national
wealth. Unless offset by the exchange rate, a movement in world prices is
also likely to have consequences for Money GDP[3] and national wealth.
Other disturbances to exogenous variables will also influence Money
GDP and require offsetting action by the policy rules.

In the case of the simulation with model-consistent expectations, there
is a third category of disturbance which has to be considered. For with
model-consistent expectations the current values of the freely-floating
(jumping) variables (the exchange rate, the valuation ratio, the consol
rate and human capital) depend on the expected future values of the
exogenous variables in a manner which depends on the structure of the
controlled economy (see Chapters 7 and 11). Therefore revisions to
expectations of future events cause changes to the current values of the
jumping variables. The policy rules also have to offset the effects of these
on the targeted variables.

It is obviously not possible to discuss all possible shocks which
impinged on the economy during the period under consideration. We
first highlight some of the major disturbances, so as to be able to discuss

the policy response to these when presenting the simulations. We then also discuss the effects of disturbances in the exogenous variables on the jumping variables.

8.4.2 Shocks to residuals and to exogenous variables

Our reruns start in the first quarter of 1975. At this time the inflation rate was close to its modern peak, as the inflationary consequences of the oil crisis and the commodity price boom spread throughout the economy. However, our target trajectory is designed to accommodate the historical rate of inflation at the start of the rerun, and so this high initial rate of inflation does not actually imply a deviation of the economy from its target path. Indeed, as Figure 8.1(a) shows, until 1978 the target and historical trajectories of Money GDP moved closely in step.

The first major disturbance which the economy faced was the sterling crisis of 1976. Large capital outflows led to a rapid fall in the nominal exchange rate. Concern over the possible inflationary consequences of this led to an attempt to stem and reverse the decline by means of high short-term interest rates. These capital outflows appear as shocks of the first type, and might well be faced by an economy even with our policy regime in force. They provide a useful laboratory to test our interest-rate rule which is designed to keep the exchange rate close to its target value.

The sterling crisis was reversed by early 1977. The government first attempted to peg sterling at a level some 10 per cent above the low of 1976, by means of intervention and low interest rates. However, at the end of 1977 interest rates were raised again and sterling was allowed to float upwards. This was probably at least in part due to movement in capital flows which is not explained by the interest-rate differentials ruling at the time. Such capital flows will also test our exchange-rate policy rule.

In 1978 inflation fell to its lowest level since before the oil crisis, helped by the incomes policy which had been in operation since the summer of 1975. However, the incomes policy had become rather unpopular; arguably it failed to bring workers' aspirations in line with the reality of the fall in national income that the 1974 oil crisis had caused. Wage demands, motivated by the desire to restore real incomes to aspirations based on pre-oil crisis experience, were made.

At the same time as these inflationary pressures were gathering in the labour market there came the second oil crisis. Even net of North Sea oil profits, this raised Money GDP because, in our model, prices are set as a mark-up on costs including imports and domestically produced inputs.

All of this inflationary pressure is present in the simulations in this chapter and without any wage reform it feeds into the wage-price loop and produces a sharp rise in Money GDP. In fact, the main effort of our policy rules, during the whole of the rerun, goes into offsetting this inflationary burst which appeared in 1979.

A Conservative Government came to power in 1979. On the one hand, it made clear that it was prepared to tolerate large pay increases. This probably had the effect of exacerbating the upward pressure on wage rates, with which we have to deal in our reruns. On the other hand, the new government raised interest rates to record levels so as to achieve monetary targets. The exchange rate rose, perhaps partly as a consequence of high interest rates, reaching a peak in real terms in mid 1981. From then until late 1986, the exchange rate (nominal and real) declined. Interest rates were raised on occasions, such as late 1981, late 1982 and late 1985 when the decline seemed to be precipitate. All these fluctuations in the exchange rate can only be partly explained by our portfolio balance model of the exchange rate (see Chapter 5), and the balance must therefore be attributed to capital account shocks or, with model-consistent expectations, to uncertainty about the world price level (see Chapter 7). These shocks remain present in our reruns, even though they may have been partly induced by the historical policy regime in force. They provide further tests of the ability of our policy rules to stabilize the economy against the effects of capital account disturbances.

The economic policies of the early 1980s were only one of the factors leading to a severe contraction of the economy. Unemployment rose sharply in 1981/2 and continued to rise to a peak in 1986.[5] Exogenous causes of the contraction include sharp reductions in stockbuilding during the period. Although these may have an economic explanation in terms of expectations of future demand (Hall and Henry, 1985), from the point of view of our model they are treated as purely exogenous disturbances, with which our policy rules have to cope.

Once the contraction was over, the economy grew steadily, although unemployment continued increasing until 1986. However, the miners' strike in 1984/5 had a depressing effect on output and therefore on Money GDP. Rising real wages were to some extent supported by a fall in raw material prices (Beckerman and Jenkinson, 1986) and the consequent favourable exogenous movement in the terms of trade. But the most substantial external shock of this period came from the sharp fall in the oil price in 1985–6. This raised real incomes at a time when asset prices were also buoyant. The two effects together led to a considerable consumer boom which was substantially responsible for an increase in the growth rate of the economy in 1986 and 1987, leading to a marked fall in unemployment which was, however, only beginning at the end of our data period.

8.4.3 Budgetary shocks

The above shocks, whether external or arising from model residuals, represent the sort of hazard with which our policy rules would have to cope. Since some of them may have been induced by erratic policies, we may have in fact made our task more difficult than it would have been in our stable policy regime. But there is one category of shock which we have deliberately taken out of our rerun. During the period there were a number of adjustments to tax rates. Changes to planned rates of government expenditure were also made from time to time. On some occasions, such as at the time of the 1976 sterling crisis, these changes were an *ad hoc* policy response to an outside factor. On other occasions, such as the 1979 budget which raised VAT and reduced income tax, they may have been genuinely exogenous disturbances.

We see no point in presenting reruns of history in which our policy rules are used to unwind policy-induced shocks. This makes it desirable to allow government spending to proceed along a smooth trend path. We note that from 1975 to 1986 total government purchases of goods and services were more or less unchanged in total, and think it sensible to impose this on our simulations of the unreformed economy. We therefore keep both government consumption and public investment constant throughout the period of our simulation; this in fact implies more public investment and less public consumption than was in fact observed historically. We have thus deliberately chosen to follow the received wisdom of the period, that private consumption is preferred to public consumption, and that the economy was overstocked with public sector capital goods (which we exclude from our wealth target – see section 6.2). In the end one would imagine that public consumption and investment would have to increase at the same trend rate as real GDP, but we place this change in the trend of government demand beyond the period of our rerun of history. Our assumption in fact makes our 2 per cent target growth in national wealth feasible without the very high tax rates which would be needed to finance growth in the public sector capital stock. In this important respect our simulations present an optimistic picture of the British economy.

8.4.4 Disturbances to jumping variables

Our new method of solving economic models with model-consistent expectations makes it possible to identify the effects of disturbances in the exogenous variables on the free, or jumping, variables; study of these can shed some light on the behaviour of the economy during our simulations, because they are imposed as shocks to the free variables in our simulation of the forward-looking economy.

The four Figures 7.2–7.5 in Chapter 7 show the effects on the jumping variables of disturbances in the exogenous variables. These graphs in fact indicate what would have been the disturbances to the jumping variables in each period, as a consequence of each shock, if nothing else were to have happened to the model. The component parts, arising from each exogenous variable, are shown together with the overall total. The graphs do not indicate the actual deviations of the jumping variables from their steady-state path; that also depends on the history of the economy, and on previous shocks. But they play a useful role in indicating the importance of expectational disturbances to these variables and, in the case of the exchange rate, shed an interesting light on the history of the period.

The effects of the disturbances which we identify are discussed in detail in Chapter 7. Of these the main shock we would highlight is that to the nominal exchange rate (Figure 7.5), arising from disturbances to the expected world price level. In the long term homogeneity ensures that the nominal exchange rate moves one-for-one in response to a permanent change in the world price level. And 89 per cent of this shift takes place immediately (Table 7.1(b)).

In the period 1979–81 the long-term level of world prices was expected to be considerably higher than it had been expected to be before the oil crisis of 1979, or than it was expected to be later on, after it became clear that foreign governments were committed to fighting inflation. On the other hand, we assume that the market continued, all the time, to believe our commitment to the Money GDP target, and thus our commitment to low inflation. As a consequence the nominal exchange rate faced considerable upward pressure in 1979–81. In this simulation this turns out to be helpful. At a time of domestic inflationary pressure it delivers a deflationary increase in the real exchange rate which would otherwise have to be delivered by a substantial increase in interest rates.

8.5 A SIMULATION WITH MODEL-CONSISTENT EXPECTATIONS

The most striking feature of the behaviour of Money GDP (Figure 8.1(a)) during the first five years or so of our simulation is the close match between the rerun and the historical trajectory. In 1977 and 1978 the rerun falls below the historical path because our simulation avoids the inflationary effects of the 1976 sterling crisis. But the gap is not large. Then in 1979 both history and the rerun diverge from the target. The main reason for this is that at the start of 1979 there was an inflationary burst. As explained above, we treat this as an exogenous disturbance with which our rules have to deal. Historically wages rose by 19 per cent between 1978 IV and 1979 IV. In our rerun this explosion is reduced slightly, but there is still an increase of 15 per cent, at a time when the target for Money GDP only grows by 10 per cent. The inflationary effects of the oil price increases of 1980 compound this domestic inflationary shock, and Money GDP rises by 20 per cent in 1979 and 15 per cent in 1980.

This inflationary burst triggers an immediate policy response. The VAT rate (Figure 8.2(a)) is reduced by 3 per cent in 1979 III (at the same time as the standard VAT rate was actually raised from 8 per cent to 15 per cent). This cost-push fiscal policy is complemented by a tightening of monetary policy. The target real exchange rate is raised in 1979 III by 11 per cent (Figure 8.1(c)), and is further raised in 1980. The actual real exchange rate is driven up alongside this.

Despite this policy reaction, the rerun economy is in this period apparently suffering from worse inflation of Money GDP than did the historical economy (even though, on account of tax cuts, the rate of consumer price inflation is lower, Figure 8.2(c)). In 1981 III GDP is over 2 per cent above its historical level and over 16 per cent above the target path. The reason for this underperformance relative to history merits some investigation. VAT has been reduced to almost nothing by late 1980, but the real exchange rate is, despite our cost-push rule, depreciated by 15 per cent relative to its historical level. Our policy rules moderate the currency appreciation of the early 1980s. The cost-push effects of the two (historic and simulation) combinations of taxes and the real exchange rate are probably broadly equivalent. There is a demand-pull stimulus, and as a consequence unemployment rises less fast in the early 1980s than it did historically. But the starting point is higher and in fact the level of unemployment does not drop perceptibly below the historical figure at any point in the rerun.

The apparent failure to control inflation during this period does not mean that the rules have failed. Historically there was a large appreciation of the real exchange rate for reasons which are not perfectly understood. On replacing a freely-floating exchange rate by a policy rule working through a target exchange rate, increases of this type are partially damped.[6] It just so happens that the historic exchange-rate shock coincided with inflationary pressures, and damped those pressures in a manner that was more immediately successful than our policy rule.

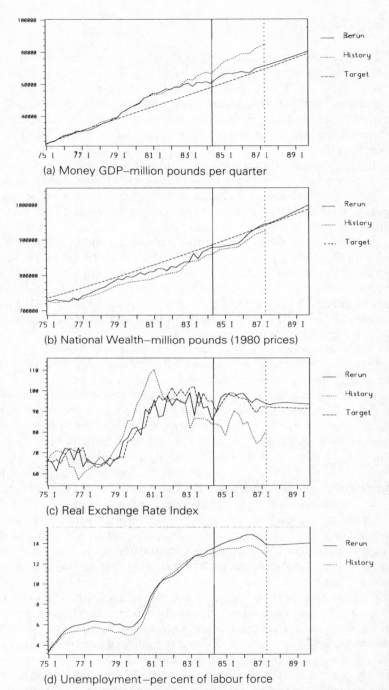

(a) Money GDP—million pounds per quarter

(b) National Wealth—million pounds (1980 prices)

(c) Real Exchange Rate Index

(d) Unemployment—per cent of labour force

Figure 8.1   The UK economy 1975–89: unreformed wages and model-consistent expectations

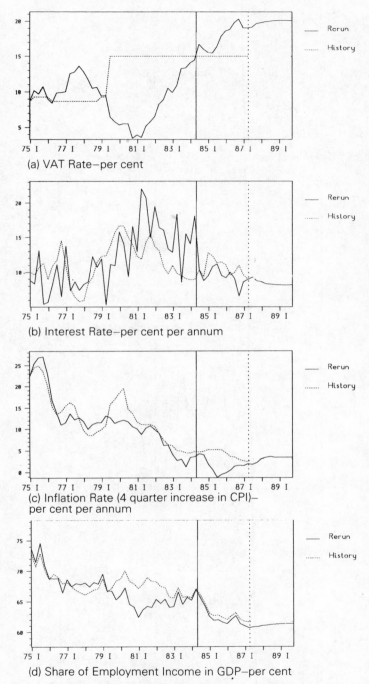

(a) VAT Rate—per cent

(b) Interest Rate—per cent per annum

(c) Inflation Rate (4 quarter increase in CPI)—
per cent per annum

(d) Share of Employment Income in GDP—per cent

*Figure 8.2   The UK economy 1975–89: unreformed wages and
model-consistent expectations (contd)*

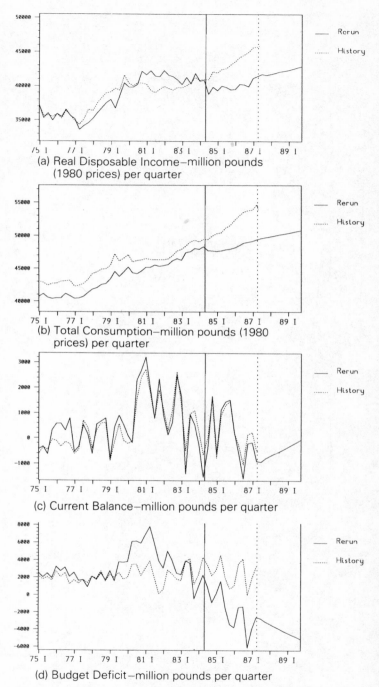

Figure 8.3   The UK economy 1975–89: unreformed wages and
model-consistent expectations (contd)

While the performance of Money GDP in 1981 seems to be worse than the historical out-turn, this is not true of national wealth (Figure 8.1(b)). The reason for this is that, at the start of the simulation, there is a 7 per cent downward jump in human capital. This leads to a reduction in consumption and an increase in saving. The consequent fall in demand is probably the main factor causing higher unemployment in the early stages of the rerun (Figure 8.1(d)).

During the period after 1982 the policy rules are very effective at bringing inflation down (Figure 8.2(c)), and taking Money GDP away from the historical path towards its target value. This is achieved through the cost-push effect of the lower VAT rate during 1980/1 working through the system. The real exchange rate (Figure 8.1(c)) catches up with its historical value in 1981. For the rest of the rerun it remains at or above this value (apart from short-period disturbances), and it is then no longer a source of inflationary pressure relative to history.

As the labour market disturbances of 1979–80 fade away, and with wealth being in 1982/3 below its target, the VAT rate is raised close to its historic 15 per cent by the end of 1983. The upward trend continues, although in 1984 a further surge in Money GDP leads to temporary reductions in VAT. But overall, towards the end of the period the VAT rate stops rising and then turns down slightly. This reflects the fact that wealth has overshot its target slightly and is above its historic value by 15 per cent of annual GDP by the end of the simulation.

These movements in tax rates are the main causes of deviations in real disposable income from its historical values (Figure 8.3(a)), although one also has to bear in mind that we suppress the direct tax cuts which took place between 1978 and 1988. We see that real disposable income 'does well' in the period of very low taxes in 1981/2, but badly during the periods of high taxes before and after this. Is this a demonstration that our rules are less satisfactory than historical muddling through? The answer is emphatically no. If we had chosen a lower rate of growth of national wealth, keeping closer to the historical trajectory (Figure 8.1(a)), we would have been able to deliver a level of disposable income similar to the historical value in the last few years of the period. It is not our policy rules but our wealth target which leads to the underperformance of disposable income.

In Figure 8.3(b) we show total national consumption, adding together that of the public and private sectors. This allows us to look at the overall resources available for consumption independently of the division between public and private sectors (an issue with which our policies are not concerned). We see that throughout the simulation this is lower than it was historically, reflecting the fact that the historical levels of consumption are inconsistent with constant public investment and 2 per cent growth in national wealth.

The fluctuations in tax are observed in the budget deficit (Figure 8.3(d)). This is much bigger in 1980/2, when taxes are low in order to buy off inflation. But long-term concern with the level of national wealth, and the fact that the government is prepared to save when the private sector does not, means that, once the inflationary bubble has burst, the budgetary position becomes very favourable, with large surpluses developing. This happened historically in the late 1980s.

These fluctuations in the budget deficit are not reflected in the current balance (Figure 8.3(c)) which remains close to its historical value. In particular, the large budget surplus at the end of the simulation reflects the fact that the wealth target is being achieved at least partly by means of high public saving. On the other hand, domestic (private) investment has risen enough to absorb the saving needed to achieve the wealth target[7] and the current balance (foreign investment) is therefore unchanged.

Our policy rules succeed in keeping the real exchange rate to within 10 per cent of its target value in all periods except 1977 I, 1979 II, 1981 II, 1983 II and 1984 II. Despite the fact that monetary policy is given an important role in the control of inflation and although we do not adopt exchange-rate stability as an aim, we note that the real exchange rate does not breach a Williamson and Miller (1987) target zone centred on a mid-value index of 95 and with a width of 10 per cent after 1980 III.

We present summary statistics for the volatility of major economic variables in Chapter 9 (section 9.8), so as to facilitate comparison between the effects of the two wage equations on the economy. Overall, as we see in Table 9.2, the real exchange rate is more volatile than it was historically, but this is a consequence of short-term movement arising from volatility in expectations. Long periods of misalignment are avoided.

The price for keeping the exchange rate reasonably close to its target is a high degree of interest rate volatility (Figure 8.2b and Table 9.2). The violence of these movements may be seen as a major disadvantage of our policy framework. However, we note that the parts of the private sector most affected by this volatility would be able to make arrangements to borrow at rates which could be fixed for several years so as to avoid this volatility. This would have no implications at all for the working of our control rules in our model, since we have assumed that all home assets are, in any case, perfect substitutes. Furthermore there is always the possibility that expectations were less volatile than those we observed in the *National Institute Economic Review*; this would imply less volatile interest rates and smaller deviations in the real exchange rate about its target path. The reason for believing this is that our policy rules have made both interest rates and the exchange rate more volatile than they were historically, a result which would probably be difficult to achieve using the same expectations as those to which markets actually reacted. The results of this rerun may be summarized as follows:

i) We have shown that our policy rules may be used to control inflation and to guide national wealth towards a target path. Our policy targets have been more stringent than those which the economy has followed during the historical period of our simulation: we have imposed more severe control of inflation, and we have required that national wealth should grow faster than it did historically. Both objectives were broadly achieved by the end of the simulation.

ii) We have not been able to do anything about unemployment (and indeed a price for higher saving and lower inflation is slightly higher unemployment), but we have not claimed and do not believe that financial policy, on its own, can have a lasting effect on unemployment (Friedman, 1968). In order to do better here, some sort of supply-side reform is needed.

iii) The exchange rate has been kept reasonably close to its target value, but this target value has needed to be manipulated substantially in order to control inflation. The policy rules are certainly outside the spirit of Williamson's target-zones proposal, but it is also worth noting that, for the period 1981−9, they conform to the letter of Williamson's proposal. Our rules deliver a surprising degree of real exchange-rate stability despite the use they make of monetary policy in fighting inflation.

iv) The policy rules require substantial fluctuations in both the tax rate and the exchange rate target (and indeed our cost-push use of the tax rate has been curtailed by the requirement that the tax rate must remain positive throughout the simulation). These fluctuations are very different from what was observed historically and also very different from what we would expect to observe when simulating an economy with a reformed labour market.

It is, of course, possible to quantify the performance of the controlled economy by means of various numerical indicators. However, we defer this until the next chapter, so as to be able to consider the unreformed and reformed wage economies side by side.

8.6 A SIMULATION WITH ADAPTIVE EXPECTATIONS

We now present the same rerun of history, but making the assumption that expectations are adaptive rather than forward-looking. The results of this are presented in Figures 8.4–8.6. The most important difference from the previous simulation arises because the favourable effect of a jump in human capital is no longer available as a means of influencing wealth. The work which was done by this in the previous simulation must now be achieved by a mixture of tax changes and exchange-rate changes. We see in Figures 8.4(a) and 8.4(b) that Money GDP follows much the same path as in Figure 8.1(a), being slightly worse controlled, but that wealth is much worse controlled (Figure 8.4(b)). The use of cost-push means to buy off inflationary pressures during the period 1980/2 means that the current balance does no better than it did historically, and wealth accumulation is correspondingly depressed. It is only later in the period, once the inflationary problems have been overcome, that the economy is able to turn its attention to maintaining the stock of national wealth. After 1985 the tax rate (Figure 8.5(a)) passes its historic level, and then this high tax rate leads to high public-sector saving (Figure 8.6(d)) which finds its outlet largely in the current account surplus (Figure 8.6(c)). This high surplus finally brings wealth towards its target value with an overshoot at the end of the period (Figure 8.4(b)).

One problem, particularly visible in this simulation, arises from the valuation effects of changes in the real exchange rate on national wealth. In the period 1982–4 a very high real exchange rate is needed to damp inflation. This reduces the value of net foreign assets, and taxes have to rise to increase saving. But once inflation is brought under control the real exchange rate can be allowed to fall, raising foreign assets and national wealth. This is one reason for the sharp rise in wealth at the end of the simulation.

As we noted above, the different consumption function affects the pattern of demand. Broadly speaking we now find that unemployment is higher than its historical value when the tax rate is above the historical trajectory, and that lower taxes are associated with lower unemployment, whereas with model-consistent expectations consumption depended less on current income and so this was not true. But perhaps the most visible effect of the different consumption function and its implications for the tax rate, is seen in the pattern of disposable income. The model with adaptive expectations in fact places a greater weight on public sector saving than on private sector saving if the wealth target is to be achieved. This public sector saving can only be achieved by high taxes. Consumption (Figure 8.6(b)) is depressed and the budget is in surplus. But only if we had ignored the wealth target, or had set a much lower target trajectory, would it have been possible to achieve the historical levels of disposable income and consumption. The outcome is a consequence of the target and not of the policy rules.

The real exchange rate shows less short-term volatility than it did in the

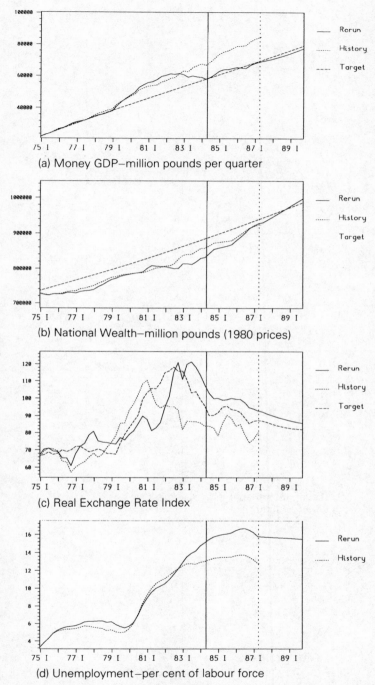

(a) Money GDP—million pounds per quarter

(b) National Wealth—million pounds (1980 prices)

(c) Real Exchange Rate Index

(d) Unemployment—per cent of labour force

Figure 8.4   The UK economy 1975–89: unreformed wages and adaptive expectations

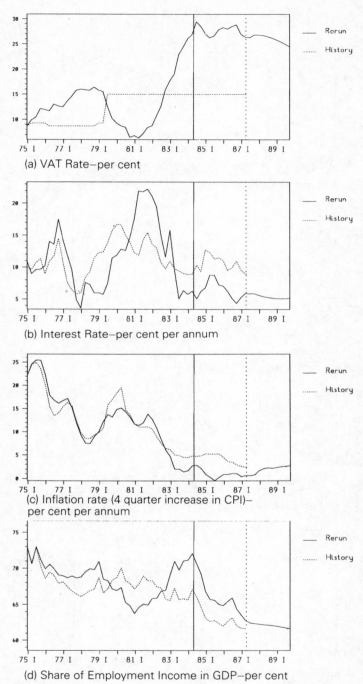

(a) VAT Rate–per cent

(b) Interest Rate–per cent per annum

(c) Inflation rate (4 quarter increase in CPI)–
per cent per annum

(d) Share of Employment Income in GDP–per cent

Figure 8.5   The UK economy 1975–89: unreformed wages and adaptive expectations (contd)

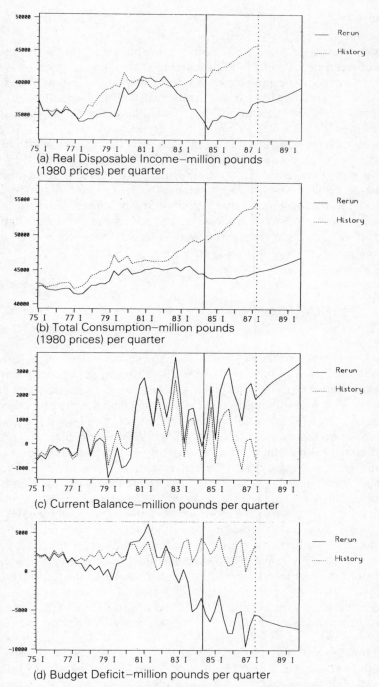

(a) Real Disposable Income—million pounds
(1980 prices) per quarter

(b) Total Consumption—million pounds
(1980 prices) per quarter

(c) Current Balance—million pounds per quarter

(d) Budget Deficit—million pounds per quarter

Figure 8.6   The UK economy 1975–89: unreformed wages and
adaptive expectations (contd)

model-consistent simulation. This is probably explained by the absence of expectational shocks in this simulation. With the exception of 1980–1 we do succeed in keeping the exchange rate within 10 per cent of its target value, by means of an interest rate which is less volatile than with model-consistent expectations, but more volatile than it was historically. However, the different properties of the model now mean that, although the short-term volatility is reduced, long-term movements, which mirror changes in the exchange-rate target, are more marked than they were with model-consistent expectations, and the outcome is less consistent with a Williamson-type target zone. The reason for this is, broadly speaking, that, with adaptive expectations, the effects of policy instruments on the economy are weaker, at least in the short term, and so larger movements are required in both taxes and in the real exchange-rate target in order to control both inflation and wealth.

8.7 CONCLUSION

In this chapter we have demonstrated that our rules can be used to control inflation and to guide national wealth towards a target path. The broad features of the outcomes and the implications for the policy instruments were summarized in the four points at the end of section 8.5. The same rule works with both model-consistent and adaptive expectations, although we have seen that Money GDP is easier to control and national wealth is much easier to control when expectations are model-consistent. The main reason for this is that, as noted in Chapter 6, our policy rules were designed more with reference to the economy with model-consistent expectations than with reference to the economy with adaptive expectations; the model-consistent expectations economy is in any case easier to control. Our controlled economy was required to do considerably better than history in terms of inflation, particularly during the period 1980–2. We also do considerably better in terms of national wealth but, particularly with adaptive expectations, the public sector is required to do much of the extra saving, and this means that tax rates are high and disposable income is depressed towards the end of the period. The unemployment position is worse than it was historically because of the emphasis we have placed on fighting inflation and on growth in national wealth. In order to do better with unemployment, some sort of supply-side reform is needed, and in the next chapter we demonstrate the benefits of this.

Chapter Nine

The controlled economy with reformed wages

9.1 INTRODUCTION

In the previous chapter we demonstrated how control rules could be used
to achieve target paths for Money GDP and for national wealth. In those
simulations we were broadly successful at delivering our two policy
targets, but we also demonstrated that, once attention was paid to
national wealth as well as to Money GDP, the unemployment record was
likely to be even worse than historically. Here we show the effect of
controlling an economy in which the labour market has been reformed;
we demonstrate that we are able to achieve a similar record on inflation,
but faster real growth in output and in national wealth. Much better
results are obtained for both real disposable income and unemployment,
and all this can be delivered at the same time as rapid growth in
public-sector demand for goods and services. In short, while the previous
chapter discussed the UK economy as it is, here we demonstrate how, by
changing one key equation of the model, we are able to deliver something
of an economic miracle. A basic property of our model, and, we believe,
of the UK economy, is that better long-run performance on unemployment can only be achieved by means of a supply-side reform. The
purpose of this chapter, then, is not to claim that any particular reform
of the labour market is necessarily feasible. What we do is to show what
a particular supply-side reform could achieve, taken within the context
of a New Keynesian strategy of maintaining an announced target path
for the growth in Money GDP.

We regulate the economy using the representative rule for reformed
wages, which was presented in section 6.8. This rule uses taxes in a
demand-pull rather than a cost-push fashion, and gives relatively more
weight to the use of fiscal policy in the control of Money GDP than did
the rule which we used in Chapter 8. It would be hoped that such a rule

would result in a more stable real exchange rate than we had in Chapter 8, but the truth of this can in fact only be established by a second counterfactual simulation.

9.2   THE TARGET TRAJECTORIES

We use the same trajectory for Money GDP as in Chapter 8 (equation 8.2). This implied a gradual reduction in the rate of growth of Money GDP from the rate of around 5 per cent per quarter at the start of 1975 when the policy is assumed to be introduced, to a target rate of growth of 1.25 per cent per quarter. The target trajectory asymptotically converges on this target rate of growth of Money GDP.

Early experimentation with simulation of the reformed wage economy showed that it was able to deliver more rapid growth of real GDP than had been possible without the wage reform, and it therefore seemed essential that national wealth should be targeted to grow at the same trend rate as real GDP, so as to avoid implying a falling wealth to output ratio. This implied a target rate of growth of real national wealth of 2.8 per cent per annum.[1]

9.3   THE REFORMED WAGE EQUATION

The basic wage reform which we require is that wages should become insensitive to prices, changing only with reference to unemployment. We achieve this by setting the parameter, v, in (6.2) to zero. But there is a separate problem which we have to face up to in our reformed wage simulation. At the start of the rerun the share of wages in the national product was abnormally high. The historical trajectory of the wage share in Figure 9.2(d) displays this. We have seen in Chapter 6 (Figure 6.26) that with reformed wages the suppression of a shock of this type is a lengthy process. It requires a sustained deflation. We found that our policy rules delivered VAT rates of around 40–50 per cent and induced considerable fluctuations in Money GDP as they attempted to correct this problem arising from the abnormally high share of wages. This suggests that 1975 I would have been an inauspicious time at which to introduce the wage reform we have in mind.

If our wage reform had been introduced in the 1960s or 1950s the share of wages would not have risen to an unsustainable level. We therefore take steps to correct the wage share in the economy by means other than our policy rules, and interpret the result as resembling more closely what would have happened if the wage reform had taken place well before 1975. We could have assumed a step reduction in wage rates, and therefore in the wage share, at the start of the simulation. But a sudden reduction in wages would have introduced dynamic disturbances all of its own. We have instead achieved a gradual reduction in the wage share, by assuming a core rate of wage inflation which is, at the start of the simulation, below the core-target rate of inflation of Money GDP, but tends to it asymptotically. In our target path for Money GDP, the rate of Money GDP inflation falls asymptotically from 5 per cent per quarter to 1.25 per cent per quarter. In the wage equation we use the same asymptotic rate of core inflation and the same rate of convergence, but we use an initial core inflation rate of only 2.5 per cent per quarter.

$$\Delta \ln WAGERATE_t = 1.572 - 2.72\Delta^2 UPC_{t-1}$$
$$- 2.43\Delta UPC_{t-3} - 0.262UPC_{t-4}$$
$$+ 0.025 \times e^{-0.04t} + 0.0125(1 - e^{-0.04t}) \quad (9.1)$$

where $WAGERATE$ – wage rate
UPC – unemployed as per cent of labour force

This equation, then, shows wages responding to the level of and changes in unemployment. The natural rate of unemployment, determined by the constant and the coefficient on the level of unemployment, is 6 per cent. On top of this, wages increase at the core rate of inflation, which declines over time.

9.4 BUDGETARY POLICY

We have followed the same principle as in Chapter 8, of keeping the income tax rate constant, and of keeping government demand (both consumption and investment) on smooth target paths. This means that our policy rules do not have to fight 'artificial' disturbances created by erratic changes in tax rates or in government demand.

In the previous chapter we were unable to allow for any real growth in government demand over the whole 15-year period of our simulation. To have done so would have required higher taxes by the end of the period.

Our restriction meant that, by the end of the period, a substantial reduction in the share of government demand in the economy had taken place. In our reformed wage economy we are able to allow for public-sector demand to grow at our perceived long-run rate of growth for the economy as a whole (2.8 per cent per annum). This means that, by the end of our simulation, public provision of goods and services is 51 per cent higher than it was in our simulations in Chapter 8. In this chapter, as in Chapter 8, we have avoided any sort of discretionary intervention by means of variations in public consumption and investment. This is not because we think that discretionary intervention is in itself a bad thing, but because we want to demonstrate what our rules can achieve without any extra help.

9.5 HISTORICAL DISTURBANCES

The genuinely exogenous disturbances, which we described in section 8.4, also, of course, affected the economy during this simulation. Events in the rest of the world are assumed to be unaffected by the policy regime in force in the United Kingdom. With one exception, we have again added in the historical residuals to the behavioural relationships of our model. That exception is to the reformed wage equation. It would fit history very badly − it is not in any sense estimated. To add back the historical residuals would have the effect of putting back much of the inflation which our wage reform is supposed to have taken out. We therefore do not add any residuals back into the wage equation.

Despite the fact that the genuinely exogenous variables are assumed to behave in the same way as in Chapter 8, their impact on the jumping variables differs, and it differs both because different policy rules are in place and because the change to the wage equation alters the structure of the model. The impact effects of the exogenous shocks are shown in Figures 7.6–7.9.

Once again the dominant disturbance is the behaviour of the nominal exchange rate in the period 1979–81. The reasons for this are the same as before (section 8.4.4). A permanent change in the world price level leads to an equal change in the long-run nominal exchange rate. Even with our reformed wage economy policy rules, 85 per cent of this change takes place immediately (Table 7.2(b)). But in an environment which places much less emphasis on monetary policy for fighting inflation, these world price shocks may turn out to be less helpful than they were in Chapter 8.

9.6   A SIMULATION WITH MODEL-CONSISTENT EXPECTATIONS

The simulation begins with an attempt to generate growth in Money GDP of 5 per cent per quarter. In the opening quarters of this simulation the target is in fact undershot. The main cause of this is the slow growth in nominal wages because, for the reasons given in section 9.3, we require wages to start off by growing at well under the target rate of growth of Money GDP.

There are, in addition, two important influences on real demand which have to be considered. These work in opposite directions although, on balance, they turn out to be expansionary. Both of them arise from the anticipation of the very marked shift in the distribution of income from labour to capital (Figure 9.2(d)). The consequent increase in profits means that the return to capital, measured at net replacement cost, is much increased. This leads to an upward jump in the valuation ratio, in the first period of 26.5 per cent (compared with only 9 per cent with unreformed wages). This increases both investment and, through the wealth effect, consumption.

At the same time human capital becomes less valuable, because expected future wages are lower. There is a downward jump of 10 per cent in human capital which depresses consumption, an effect which is augmented by the reduction in consumption financed directly out of wages. The overall effect is to depress consumption but to raise investment. Overall real GDP is increased, which is why unemployment falls to 2 per cent at the start of 1980. But the effect of real GDP on Money GDP is more than offset by the relative reduction in the GDP deflator occasioned by the slow growth of nominal wages.

Our policy rules react to the underperformance of Money GDP and also to the fact that wealth (Figure 9.1(b)) is below target. The VAT rate is reduced mainly because Money GDP is too low. The target exchange rate is reduced because GDP is too low but also, and more importantly, because wealth is below target.

Money GDP returns to its target in 1978, but the economy is now subjected to disturbances from two directions. First, there is a burst of inflation in 1979 which drives Money GDP above its target path. This burst is not as severe as we found in Chapter 8. The reason is that on this occasion its sole origin is a sudden rise in raw material prices, which are marked up, leading to increased profits. Figure 9.2(d) shows a sudden fall in the share of labour income at this stage. In Chapter 8 this imported inflation was enhanced by the wage-price spiral. There were

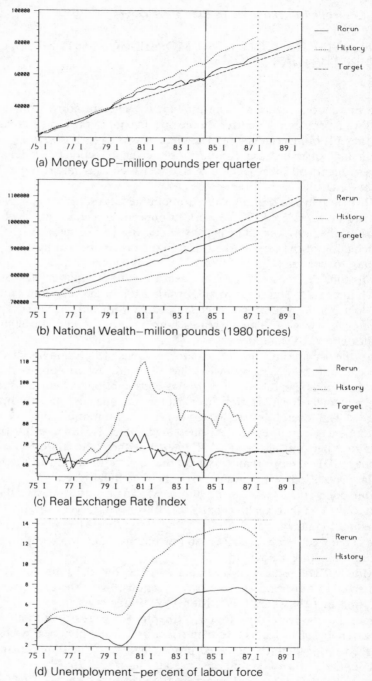

(a) Money GDP—million pounds per quarter

(b) National Wealth—million pounds (1980 prices)

(c) Real Exchange Rate Index

(d) Unemployment—per cent of labour force

Figure 9.1   The UK economy 1975–89: reformed wages and model-consistent expectations

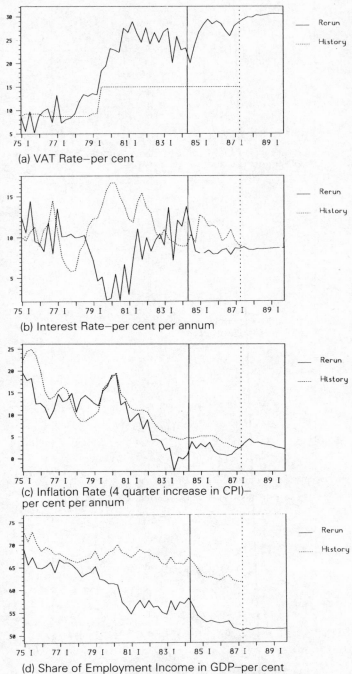

(a) VAT Rate–per cent

(b) Interest Rate–per cent per annum

(c) Inflation Rate (4 quarter increase in CPI)–
per cent per annum

(d) Share of Employment Income in GDP–per cent

*Figure 9.2   The UK economy 1975–89: reformed wages and model-
consistent expectations (contd)*

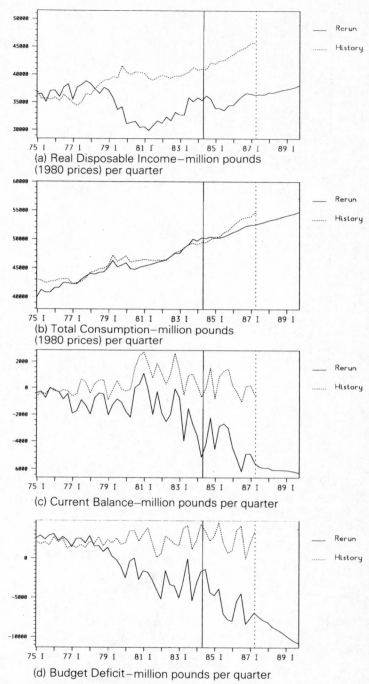

Figure 9.3   The UK economy 1975–89: reformed wages and model-consistent expectations (contd)

also separate disturbances originating in the labour market and represented by residuals in the wage equation. These are suppressed by our wage reform.

The policy response to this inflationary burst is to raise the VAT rate, to 28 per cent by 1981, and to raise the target exchange rate slightly, from 62 in 1978 to 68 in 1981. Paradoxically this monetary tightening is associated with a period of low nominal interest rates (Figure 9.2(b)). The reason for this is that, in the early 1980s, our expectational series suggest that it was believed that there had been a permanent upward shift in world prices (section 7.8 and Figure 7.9), but that this shift would not happen to the price level in the United Kingdom. As a result the long-run level of the nominal exchange rate rose, and, even with our reformed wage policy rules, 85 per cent of that change in the long-run exchange rate occurs immediately. In 1979 III the real exchange rate rises, as a consequence of this, to nearly 15 per cent above its target level. This unwanted appreciation helps bring Money GDP back towards its target (Figure 9.1(a)) but, on the other hand, it drives wealth slightly further away from its target (Figure 9.1(b)).

Despite this exchange-rate appreciation, Money GDP proves difficult to bring under control. There are periods, in 1983 and 1984, when Money GDP touches its target path, but in the main it seems to run parallel to, and above, the target. In such circumstances the proportional components of the policy rules are not doing any work in bringing Money GDP towards its target. It is the integral components which ensure that Money GDP finally meets its target instead of choosing a parallel trajectory. These integral components are weak and, as we can see from Figure 6.8, our policy rules can allow Money GDP to move almost parallel to its target for a very long time, converging only slowly. While this could seem to be a weakness of our rules, it is unlikely to be a cause for any grave concern. The growth rate in Money GDP is much the same as it would be if Money GDP were moving along, instead of parallel to its trajectory. The control of wealth works reasonably smoothly (Figure 9.1(b)). Although it is generally rather below its target path, this gap is never very great and, at the end of the simulation, it is clearly being closed.

The policy regime also works well at delivering a stable real exchange rate (Figure 9.1(c)). It is true that the actual real exchange rate is up to 15 per cent above its target in the period 1979 II to 1981 I and as much as 12 per cent below its target in the period 1982 I to 1984 III. These deviations reflect the expectational effects shown in Figure 7.9. The tracking of the actual exchange rate to its target appears to work better from late 1984 onwards. But this is only because our full data set ends in 1984 II. We project no further disturbances, and so the exchange rate stays close to its target. We could have achieved a better performance by means of a more powerful interest-rate rule. But, with the external shocks as we have identified them, a significantly more powerful rule would have required a negative nominal interest rate at some stage in our subsequent adaptive expectations rerun.

As in the first rerun of the previous chapter, we see that interest rates are volatile. They reflect the magnitude of the expectational shocks to the exchange rate. Once again, we suspect that our simulation shows greater exchange rate volatility and greater interest volatility (both are quantified in section 9.8) either because our expectational series are too volatile or because markets did not, historically, behave in the sort of forward-looking manner which we have represented here. Either of these problems would explain both the high nominal interest rates in the period 1981–4 and the fact that the real exchange rate is well below its target value.

The outstanding success of our reformed wage economy is shown in Figure 9.1(d). Unemployment varies between 2 and 8 per cent of the workforce during the rerun. At the end of the simulation it is very close to the natural rate of 6 per cent which we have built into the model. We stress yet again that this performance is not caused by any particular assignment of any one instrument to any one target, or indeed by financial policy at all. The target rate of growth of Money GDP is the same as it was in Chapter 8. We represent what a supply-side reform of the labour market could achieve.

The behaviour of unemployment draws attention to a second interesting point. It can be seen that the profiles of historical and rerun unemployment are very similar, although historical unemployment rose by 9 per cent of the labour force between 1980 and 1986, while rerun unemployment rose by only 6 per cent in the same period. We may conclude from this first of all that the major part of the historical rise cannot have been caused by inflationary wage pressure. Our rerun does not have any. Secondly, it cannot have been caused by any sudden policy change in 1979. Once again, our rerun does not have any such discontinuity. This suggests the inevitable conclusion that a significant part of the rise in unemployment was caused either by residuals in the model (such as labour productivity rising faster than the model predicted) or by other exogenous factors and unexplained residuals.

The reformed wage economy is, even more than that of Chapter 8, one in which the private sector does not do all the saving which is needed to meet the wealth target. There are two reasons for this. First, the wealth target is in itself more ambitious. Secondly, the capital gains made from the effect of the shift to profits on the valuation ratio are themselves spent off. For both these reasons a considerable amount of saving has to be done by the public sector. The high tax rates persist (Figure 9.2(a)) and personal disposable income stagnates (Figure 9.3(a)). But there is an important difference from Chapter 8. There we had current account balance; the accumulation of wealth broadly financed the domestic investment. Here we have a large current account deficit. The reason for this is that the high valuation ratio induces very high domestic investment. The flow of domestic saving, despite being enhanced by high tax rates, is not sufficient to finance this investment, and the economy has to resort to borrowing from abroad.

Finally, it is important to note that total consumption (Figure 9.3(b)) is scarcely below its historical level, while with unreformed wages (Figure 8.3(b)) there was a much more substantial shortfall. Moreover, since this reformed wage economy seems to have an underlying growth rate of 2.8 per cent per annum, we can be confident that, despite the widening gap at the end of the simulation, consumption in the reformed wage economy will eventually overtake its historical counterpart. These facts, and the much lower level of unemployment, demonstrate clearly the benefit of wage reform.

We may summarize the results of this simulation:

i)   The reform of the labour market means that a better than historical out-turn for unemployment can be delivered. Unemployment varies between 2 and 8 per cent of the labour force, compared with 3.5 and 16 per cent with unreformed wages. The 'price' for this lower unemployment is a lower share in labour income in the national product. We discuss this in section 9.8.2.

ii) The economy is able to deliver 50 per cent more public consumption and investment than it could without wage reform. This is made available on account of increased output arising from a combination of lower unemployment and economies of scale.

iii) Tax rates are considerably higher than in our unreformed economy. The final VAT rate is 30 per cent as compared with 21 per cent there. But with a much higher level of public spending, there is plenty of scope for having lower taxes and a lower, but still generous, provision of public goods and services. We have not done this solely because we want to demonstrate the working of the policy rules without any other policy intervention.

iv) Inflation control still requires the use of monetary as well as fiscal policy. This does have the implication that the real exchange rate will be allowed to rise in order to damp an inflationary burst, but the effect is much weaker than in the cost-push economy.

v)   It proves possible to deliver a much higher terminal value of wealth than seemed possible in the cost-push economy. The reason for this

      is that control of wealth is easier with wage reform, and that more
resources are available. However, higher taxes are still needed.

vi) The real exchange rate has been kept within 10 per cent of its target
for most of the period, but our policy rules are still outside the
spirit of Williamson's target-zone proposal. We thus think it likely
that a stable target real exchange rate would be incompatible with
any policy which allowed prompt control of inflation (since this
'reformed wage' scenario is the most optimistic one could imagine
on this score). Nevertheless it is also the case that our policy rules
keep the real exchange rate within a band 20 per cent wide for
nearly a decade.

9.7   THE REFORMED WAGE ECONOMY SIMULATED WITH ADAPTIVE EXPECTATIONS

In Figures 9.4–9.6 we present simulations of the same policy rules, on
the assumption that expectations are adaptive rather than model-consistent. The main differences arise from the fact that there are no initial
jumps in human capital and in the stock exchange valuation ratio in this
model. This means, first of all, that the effects of a very high valuation
ratio are not present, and secondly that consumption does not adjust to a
level which reflects the policies intended to achieve the wealth target.

During the initial stages of the rerun this means that the depressing
effect on nominal GDP of slow growth in nominal wages is present, and
it is not offset by high real demand arising from the behaviour of the
jumping variables. We therefore see that during the early part of the
rerun the undershoot in Money GDP (Figure 9.4(a)) is more severe than
with model-consistent expectations. And the level of unemployment is
higher.

Inflationary pressures again drive Money GDP above its target path in
1980–1. Without the presence of expectational shocks the real exchange
rate (Figure 9.4(c)) is kept much closer to its target. The unplanned rise in
the actual real exchange rate, which we had with model-consistent
expectations, is now absent, and the tax rate is used to fight the inflation
(Figure 9.5(a)). It reaches much the same level as in the previous rerun
because, although the deflationary effect of the exchange rate rise is
absent, so too is the expansionary effect of the jump in the valuation
ratio.

The much reduced scale of the investment boom can be seen most

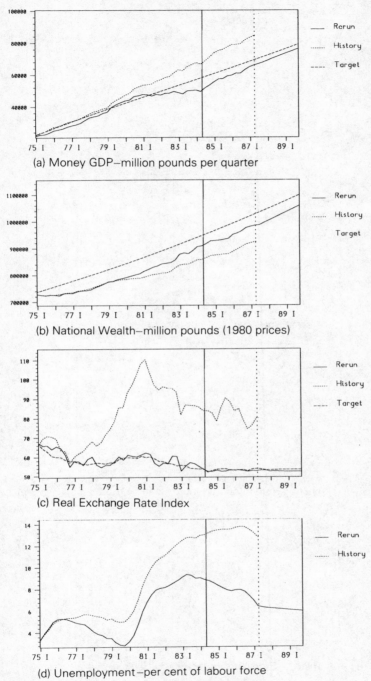

(a) Money GDP—million pounds per quarter

(b) National Wealth—million pounds (1980 prices)

(c) Real Exchange Rate Index

(d) Unemployment—per cent of labour force

Figure 9.4   The UK economy 1975–89: reformed wages and adaptive expectations

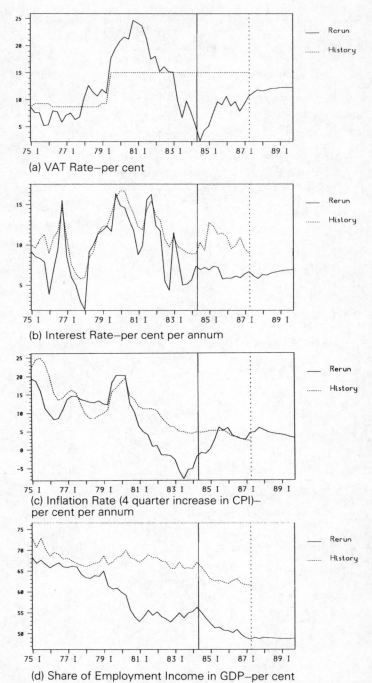

Figure 9.5   The UK economy 1975–89: reformed wages and adaptive expectations (contd)

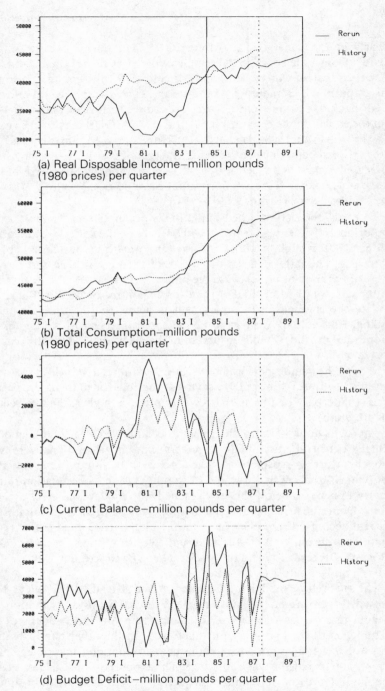

(a) Real Disposable Income—million pounds
(1980 prices) per quarter

(b) Total Consumption—million pounds
(1980 prices) per quarter

(c) Current Balance—million pounds per quarter

(d) Budget Deficit—million pounds per quarter

*Figure 9.6   The UK economy 1975–89: reformed wages and
adaptive expectations (contd)*

clearly in the behaviour of Money GDP and unemployment (Figure 9.4(d)) from 1982 onwards. Unemployment rises higher than it did with model-consistent expectations and Money GDP this time falls below its target path. The remainder of the rerun is spent trying to take Money GDP back to its target path. Taxes are reduced between 1981 and 1984, but the shocks to the economy mean that Money GDP falls further below its target. From 1985 onwards the gap starts to narrow, and the proportional component of the tax rule then leads to the tax rate being increased again. The behaviour of the tax rate is mirrored in real disposable income (Figure 9.6(a)), total consumption (Figure 9.6(b)) and the budget deficit (Figure 9.6(d)).

Towards the end of the simulation we can observe a number of important differences from the consistent-expectations simulation. Money GDP is slightly below its target and wealth is considerably below its target. The latter reflects the fact that saving has been too low for most of the simulation, because the policy rules have devoted more effort to the control of Money GDP than to the control of wealth. But at the end of the simulation unemployment is below the natural rate and is falling. This will allow taxes to be increased further without depressing Money GDP and should ensure that the deficiency in wealth can be corrected.

Wealth has underperformed because, with relatively low tax rates designed to raise Money GDP, saving is too low for most of the period. The counterpart of this is that consumption is higher. This is seen in Figure 9.6(b).

The behaviour of both the current balance (Figure 9.6(c)) and the budget deficit (Figure 9.6(d)) are less extreme than they were with model-consistent expectations. The absence of the jump in the valuation ratio means that, even at the end of the simulation, the valuation ratio is nearly 15 per cent below the level reached with model-consistent expectations. Domestic investment is much lower, and so there is no counterpart current account deficit. The fact that the budget is in small deficit rather than large surplus reflects the failure of wealth to meet its target. Once Money GDP recovers, and the VAT rate can be raised, one would expect a large budget surplus to appear.

The theoretical models of Chapters 3 and 4 lead us to believe that, provided there are no cost-push terms in the labour supply equation, the steady-state values of the real exchange rate are independent of the parameters of the consumption function.[2] On the other hand, the final value of the tax rate does depend on the consumption function as well as the parameters of the wage equation. These observations suggest that, if the final periods of our simulations are anywhere near a steady state of the economy, they should have much the same real exchange rate, even though they may have rather different tax rates. The real exchange rates are in fact rather different, and this is probably because, even at the ends of the simulations, the two models are quite a long way from their respective steady states.

The two simulations of the reformed wage economy differ more than do those of the cost-push economy. In particular, Money GDP overshoots with model-consistent expectations, and undershoots with adaptive expectations. The main reason for this is that, with model-consistent expectations, there is a large jump in the valuation ratio reflecting the increased profits arising from the reduced wage share. This leads to an investment boom which persists throughout the simulation period. With adaptive expectations the adjustment of the capital stock to the higher share of profits is much slower (Figure 5.3). Real demand is weaker throughout the simulation and therefore Money GDP is considerably lower.

9.8 A COMPARISON OF THE UNREFORMED AND REFORMED WAGE ECONOMIES

9.8.1 Summary performance statistics

We begin our assessment of the relative perfomance of the four economies which we have simulated, by presenting a variety of summary measures of economic performance. First, we present statistics for growth in real GDP, growth in real national wealth and growth in the consumer price index. These do not themselves feature in our control rules, but a consideration of them is obviously of crucial importance in evaluating our controlled economies and comparing them with the historical out-turn.

Table 9.1 *Growth rates of key variables (per cent per annum)*

	History	Unreformed		Reformed	
		Model-Consistent	Adaptive	Model-Consistent	Adaptive
Real GDP	1.8	1.7	1.5	2.9	3.0
Real Wealth	1.9	2.1	2.2	2.7	2.5
CPI	8.1	7.1	7.2	6.8	5.8

We see from Table 9.1 that the comparison between the historic and the unreformed economy shows that our control rules lead to a better performance on wealth but a slightly worse performance on real GDP. We have aimed for faster growth in wealth, so as to ensure that it grows in line with a modest estimate of the long-term potential growth of real GDP. Our target rate of growth of national wealth is in fact below the long-term rate of productivity growth which we have inferred from the wage equation (section 8.2). We claim that our controlled economy offers a more satisfactory outcome because it pays due regard to future as well as current needs. But independently of this, there is no doubt that our controlled economy has been able to offer a better out-turn on inflation.

Compared with either the historic or the unreformed economies, our simulations of the economy with reformed wages appear to offer something of an economic miracle. We can deliver faster growth in real GDP and real national wealth together with lower inflation. This is not, of course, a consequence of our particular control rules, but rather reflects the benefits of a reformed labour market. We have argued throughout this book that the structure of the labour market imposes a crucial constraint on the pattern of economic policy which can be adopted. In the simulations of the reformed wage economy we can also see that labour market structure has major implications for the medium-term growth of the economy.

So far we have looked at the performance of variables which could be regarded as important indicators of economic welfare. But it is also important to assess the rules in their own terms, looking at the question of whether the rules were able to keep the controlled variables close to their targets. We may summarize the performance of the control rules in each simulation by means of the quadratic sums of the logarithmic

Table 9.2   *Quadratic losses and sums of movements*

	History	Unreformed		Reformed	
		Model-Consistent	Adaptive	Model-Consistent	Adaptive
$\Sigma \log(C_t + G_t)$	647	644	642	647	648
$\Sigma(z_t - z_t^*)^2$	–	4172	5294	1535	2590
$\Sigma(n_t - n_t^*)^2$	–	209	984	571	1495
$\Sigma \Delta a_t^2$	1205	1861	1173	1421	1723
$\Sigma \Delta a_t^{*2}$	–	883	607	111	107
$\Sigma \Delta R_t^2$	109	826	277	359	395
$\Sigma \Delta S_t^2$	49	65	95	417	229

Variables are defined in the notation table (see p. xxi).

deviations of the out-turns from their targets, and by the sums of the squared movements in the instruments. We also look at a 'utility index' calculated as the sum of the logarithms of total (private + public) consumption during the rerun, $\Sigma \log(C_t + G_t)$. This does not take account of the terminal value of wealth, but it does summarize the behaviour of consumption during each simulation.

The distinction between the quadratic loss of Table 9.2 and the entries of Table 9.1 illustrates an important point about the interpretation of the performance indicators of Table 9.2. By almost any reasonable measure of welfare (such as our utility index in the top line of Table 9.2) the reformed wage economy is to be preferred to the unreformed economy. Some of the variables show higher quadratic losses, but the quadratic losses are measured on variables which we would not expect to enter into anyone's utility function and it would be a mistake to interpret these as costs of economic policy operation.

We note from this that the control of Money GDP is better with model-consistent expectations than with adaptive expectations. This is to be expected from the simulations of Chapter 6. Table 9.2 also shows that the control of wealth is much better when expectations are assumed to be model-consistent than when they are assumed to be adaptive. We have already noted that the distinction between the two consumption functions offers an explanation of this.

We can see from the summary table that, when the model is simulated with adaptive expectations, interest rates are more volatile than they were historically, while the real exchange rate shows less short-term volatility. On the other hand, with model-consistent expectations both the interest rate and the real exchange rate are more volatile than they were historically. Looking back at the relevant graphs (Figures 8.1(c) and 9.1(c)), it is apparent that the volatility is generated by short-term fluctuations. There are a number of possible explanations of this high volatility of both the interest rate and the real exchange rate. Of these the two most plausible are (i) that the expectational series which we have used (see Chapter 7) is more volatile than expectations were in practice and (ii) that expectations were historically not model-consistent.

An alternative way of looking at exchange-rate volatility is to consider long-term fluctuations. If we look at the gap between the highest and lowest values of the real exchange rate, measured as a percentage of the mid-point of the gap, we find values of 64 per cent for the historical economy, 46 per cent for the unreformed economy with model-consistent expectations and 68 per cent for the unreformed economy with adaptive expectations. With reformed wages the figures are 26 per cent with model-consistent expectations and 25 per cent with adaptive expectations. So, despite the higher short-term volatility, we can see that all policies of using the real exchange rate as an intermediate target (except with unreformed wages and adaptive expectations) have the effect of reducing long swings in the real exchange rate, and that our reformed wage economy does better at avoiding long swings than does our unreformed economy. This is only to be expected; with reformed wages less use has to be made of monetary policy in fighting inflation.

9.8.2   The distribution of income

One important feature of our simulations is that the wage reform leads to a substantial fall in the share of pre-tax wages in national income. This can be seen by comparing Figures 8.2(d) and 8.5(d) with 9.2(d) and 9.5(d). With unreformed wages the share of labour income stays at over 60 per cent of Money GDP, while with reformed wages it falls to 50 per cent or below.

Our model is one in which domestic prices are set partly with reference to costs of production and partly with reference to the price of competing imports. This means that the lower real exchange rate in the simulations with reformed wages, relative to that in the simulations with unreformed wages, raises the share of profits in the value added of domestic sales for two reasons. First of all, the import component of costs rises and the mark-up is calculated with reference to this imported component of costs. This means that profits rise as a share of value added. Secondly, the increase in the price of competing imports means that the mark-up itself rises.

The effect is enhanced by the behaviour of export prices. These are fixed with rather more reference to world prices and rather less reference to home costs than are domestic prices. A fall in the real exchange rate, therefore, leads to a rise in the profit margin on exports larger than the rise in the margin on home sales.

For both these reasons, then, a fall in the real exchange rate is associated with a fall in the share of wages in value added. Our simulations suggest that this is a very significant effect. It does draw attention to one of the problems which would be raised by a wage reform of the type which we describe.[3]

9.9   CONCLUSION

The reruns of history have illustrated a number of key points which we made in the theoretical section of this book. First, we have demonstrated that it is possible to control an economy by means of simple policy rules, and to do so over a 15-year period without any other form of intervention. Secondly, we have demonstrated that these rules have a structure which is crucially dependent on the structure of the wage equation. Thirdly, we have shown how the exchange rate can be used as a guide for short-term monetary policy, although our demonstration has been positive rather than normative. Fourthly, we have suggested that assignment of particular instruments to particular targets oversimplifies economic policy. Our rules have to be cross-linked to be effective. Fifthly, we have shown that, although the short-term behaviour of the economy is dependent on expectational effects, it is quite possible to design rules which work independently of the way in which expectations are formed.

Our simulations also draw attention to some important features of the economy. First of all they suggest that, if policies are adopted which ensure adequate provision for the future by recognizing a sensible target for national wealth, a higher than historic level of employment is associated with a lower than historic share of wages in the economy. This result is not a consequence of our policy rules, but follows from the underlying implicit production function in the model, and the assumption that there is not perfect substitutability between export goods and goods sold in the home market. It could be altered only if policies were identified which changed that underlying production function. Secondly, we see that private-sector saving is unlikely to be adequate to allow wealth to grow in line with output. This means that a structural budget surplus will tend to result. This, on its own, serves to demonstrate the dangers of adopting the budget surplus or the stock of national debt as a final target of economic policy.

Part III
Method

Chapter Ten

The derivation and use of a linear model

10.1 INTRODUCTION

In Chapters 6 to 9 we studied empirically the workings of various policy rules on the economy. The following chapter describes, in technical detail, how policy rules, such as those used in this book, can be tested and implemented in an empirical non-linear model. In our work on policy design we have attempted to place rather less emphasis on 'optimality' than is usual. We presented reasons for this in Chapter 1 and discuss the issue further in Chapter 11. On the other hand, we have placed a great deal of stress on stability, because we would not want to recommend policies which appeared to be unstable in the long run, however desirable their properties might appear to be over some finite horizon. [1]

In order to examine the stability of our policies we make use of a linear representation of our economic model. This linear representation also proves to be invaluable for solving our non-linear model with model-consistent expectations. This chapter discusses the 'linear reduction algorithms' used to produce the linear model and in particular discusses in detail for the first time how these can be used when there are forward-looking expectations. It develops ideas presented by Christodoulakis, Vines and Weale (1986), Blake (1988) and Christodoulakis (1989). Section 10.2 describes the approach we have adopted to linearize our empirical model. Section 10.3 describes particular problems which arise in the present context, in particular unstable uncontrolled models and consistent expectations. The following two sections outline methods for dealing with both of these. Sections 10.6 and 10.7 show how consistent expectations solutions can be found when the model is subject to a variety of disturbances, and outlines how the linear model can be used in consistent expectations reruns of history. A final section gives exact details of the methods used to derive the linear models used in this book.

10.2 LINEAR REDUCTIONS OF LARGE MODELS

We present here the basic properties of the linearization algorithm, which can be used for any large non-linear model of the economy. We then discuss how this is applied in models with expectational variables where expectations are either adaptive or model-consistent.

In this chapter we depart from the notation given at the beginning of this book. We use capital letters for vectors of variables of the original non-linear economic model, while lower-case letters are used to denote their counterparts in the linear reduction.

A dynamic economic model includes in general the following categories of variables:

U_t: Vector of r policy instruments determined either exogenously or through specified control rules.

V_t: Vector of l exogenous variables impinging upon the economy.

P_t: Vector of m endogenous variables which are not pre-determined and, thus, are free to react to unanticipated changes of the economic environment.

P_{t+1}^e: Vector of expectations of the next-period value of P_t, formed at the preceding date t.

Z_t: Vector of dimension N which includes all the endogenous variables of the model, the modelled disturbances and the lags that appear in the model up to period $(t - \tau + 1)$ where τ indicates the maximum order of lags in the model. For purposes of generalization we specify Z_t to include the vectors U_t, V_t, P_t and P_{t+1}^e through simple identities. Vector Z_{t-1} then includes all the lags that appear in the model either on endogenous or exogenous variables.

The non-linear time-varying model is described by a vector function of difference equations:

$$f_t(Z_t, Z_{t-1}, P_{t+1}^e, P_t, U_t, V_t, t) = 0 \qquad (10.1)$$

In a policy exercise we are interested in a number of q variables Y_t which are either selected from vector Z_t or formed as combinations of them:

$$Y_t = \Gamma Z_t \qquad (10.2)$$

where Γ is a constant selection operator.

We first solve model (10.1) over an 'equilibrium' trajectory, along which all volume variables grow at one particular rate, all price variables grow at another rate and all ratio variables are constant.[2] It may be necessary to add in single-equation residuals, so as to ensure that all output variables change at the appropriate rates. This solution along the equilibrium trajectory in effect calculates those single-equation residuals. Allowing for these constant adjustments by the single-equation residuals the equilibrium trajectory is given by:

$$f_t(\overline{Z}_t, \ \overline{Z}_{t-1}, \ \overline{P}_{t+1}^e, \ \overline{P}_t, \ \overline{U}_t, \ \overline{V}_t, \ t) = 0 \qquad (10.3)$$

for $t = 0, 1, ..., T$.

When expectations are assumed consistent, the above solution should satisfy the consistency condition $P_{t+1}^e = P_{t+1}$ for every period.

Our next step is to obtain a satisfactory linear and time-invariant approximation of the non-linear model described in (10.1). The linear model may be used to represent the dynamics of the observed variables Y_t and the non-predetermined variables P_t as they respond to policy instruments and exogenous shocks. It measures their path relative to an equilibrium trajectory for the economy.

The reduced linear model serves two purposes:

(a) It allows a thorough analysis of the dynamic properties of any set of control rules. In particular, it enables us to test control rules for asymptotic stability. Unstable rules are rejected on the grounds that they are not sustainable (see Vines, Maciejowski and Meade, 1983).

(b) When the model is to be solved with the assumption of consistent expectations, the linear model can be used to obtain analytic saddlepath solutions for the non-predetermined variables by using the well-known method of Blanchard and Kahn (1980). As explained later, these linear solutions provide approximate solution paths for the non-linear model and can be used instead of, or to improve the performance of, the computer-intensive methods typically employed in solving the large models.

The linearization algorithm is based on the balanced realization technique which has long been used in engineering applications of modelling. Kung (1978) has devised an algorithm for discrete-time systems and Maciejowski and Vines (1984) have implemented the algorithm so as to give linear systems with impulse responses closely approximating the dynamic multipliers of variables Y_t from a temporary shock on the exogenous variables U_t and V_t.

Details of the algorithm can be found in the work mentioned above; here we merely outline the approach. The linearization relies on the singular value decomposition of the Hankel matrix, which is constructed by the time responses $\hat{Y}_t(i, j)$ of output i at time t in response to an impulse perturbation of input j. A circumflex is used to express level or proportional deviations from equilibrium trajectories as:

$$\hat{Y}_t = (Y_t - \overline{Y}_t)/\overline{Y}_t \qquad \text{or} \qquad \hat{Y}_t = (Y_t - \overline{Y}_t) \qquad (10.4)$$

The Hankel matrix is defined as

$$H = \begin{bmatrix} [\hat{Y}_1(i,j)] & [\hat{Y}_2(i,j)] \dots & [\hat{Y}_T(i,j)] \\ [\hat{Y}_2(i,j)] & [\hat{Y}_3(i,j)] \dots & 0 \\ \vdots & \vdots & \vdots \\ [\hat{Y}_T(i,j)] & 0 & 0 \end{bmatrix} \qquad (10.5)$$

where $[\hat{Y}_t(i,j)]$ denotes the matrix with elements $\hat{Y}_t(i,j)$. Note that the impact multipliers are not part of the Hankel matrix.

A linear time-invariant state-space model is of the form:

$$x_{t+1} = Ax_t + B\begin{bmatrix} u_t \\ v_t \end{bmatrix} \qquad (10.6)$$

$$y_t = Cx_t + D\begin{bmatrix} u_t \\ v_t \end{bmatrix} \qquad (10.7)$$

Here the input variables u_t and v_t correspond to the appropriately defined perturbations of U_t and V_t in equation (10.1) and x_t is a vector of state variables. The impulse responses for such a model are given by D for $t = 0$ and $CA^{t-1}B$ in all subsequent periods. By decomposing the Hankel matrix an approximate linear representation of the non-linear model that takes this form can be found. See Maciejowski and Vines (1984) for the details of the procedure.

Singular value decomposition is generally known to be more robust than the corresponding eigenvalue decomposition against parameter changes in a matrix. As a consequence, the linear model of the approximation remains robust when small parameter changes are considered in the non-linear model. This property is particularly important as it implies that minor time-dependency in the model does not seriously affect the dynamics of the approximation.

The order of the reduction in the linear approximation is chosen so as to achieve an acceptable discrepancy between the time responses of the linear and the non-linear system. Denoting the state-space matrices of the linear system as $(A_L B_L C_L D_L)$, the order n is selected by looking at the error[3] of the approximation:

$$\varepsilon = \sum_t \sum_i \sum_j |\hat{Y}_t(i,j) - y_t(i,j)|^2 \qquad (10.8)$$

where y_t is the observed outcome of the linearized model:

$$x_{t+1} = A_L x_t + B_L \begin{bmatrix} u_t \\ v_t \end{bmatrix} \tag{10.9}$$

$$y_t = C_L x_t + D_L \begin{bmatrix} u_t \\ v_t \end{bmatrix} \tag{10.10}$$

The responses of the linear reduction are then D_L for $t = 0$ (which is exactly equal to D) and $C_L A_L^{t-1} B_L$ for $t \geq 0$.

State vector x_t is a compressed expression of the endogenous vector of the non-linear model, and therefore it bears no apparent economic interpretation. Following the analysis of Moore (1981), the state vector x_t may in fact be seen as the vector of principal components of the original system.

It can be shown that the following are basic properties of the reduced linear model:

i) The order of the linear system is minimal in the sense that it does not include superfluous dynamics; (see Kailath (1980, section 2.4)).

ii) The linear system is balanced in the sense that the controllability and the observability matrix are full-rank and their Grammians are equal.

iii) The transition matrix A_L of the linear approximation has by construction singular values less than unity, and therefore is asymptotically stable since all eigenvalues will be strictly within the unit circle. The method is, thus, appropriate for non-linear models which are themselves asymptotically stable, i.e. the solution Y_t returns gradually to the base trajectories after any exogenous impulse perturbation is over.

10.2.1 A method for approximating step multipliers

In practice, it may be more desirable to approximate step rather than impulse multipliers, as this will help to 'average' any time-variance of the model, as well as modelling the types of disturbances that are of most interest. By applying permanent changes to the exogenous variables U_t and V_t we obtain the step multipliers $\hat{Y}_t(i, j)$. If the non-linear model is asymptotically stable, then the long-run solution $\hat{Y}_\infty$ is finite and the deviations from this long-run

$$\tilde{Y}_t = \hat{Y}_\infty - \hat{Y}_t \tag{10.11}$$

are asymptotically vanishing. Long-term multipliers to unit changes are given by the matrix:

$$J_\infty = \hat{Y}_\infty(i, j) \begin{bmatrix} \hat{U}(1) & & & & \\ & \ddots & & & \\ & & \hat{U}(r) & & \\ & & \hat{V}(1) & & \\ & & & \ddots & \\ & & & & \hat{V}(l) \end{bmatrix}^{-1} \tag{10.12}$$

where $\hat{U}(j)$ and $\hat{V}(j)$ represent permanent shocks of the various exogenous inputs. Step changes in linear inputs u_t and v_t are set equal to the changes of input variables $\hat{U}_t$ and $\hat{V}_t$ respectively and therefore (10.12) is written in vector form as:

$$\tilde{Y}_t = J_\infty \begin{bmatrix} u_t \\ v_t \end{bmatrix} - \hat{Y}_t \tag{10.13}$$

Following the algorithm of Maciejowski and Vines (1984) mentioned in the previous section, a linear model may now be constructed so as to approximate the decaying responses $\tilde{Y}_t$ in the sense of equation (10.8). Inputs to this linear system are now the corresponding deviations $\tilde{U}$ and $\tilde{V}$ from their permanent changes. They are easily modelled as impulse shocks at $t = 0$ and are therefore represented as first-order differences (Δ) of the changes in U_t and V_t. The state-space equations are written as:

$$\tilde{x}_{t+1} = A_L\tilde{x}_t + B_L\begin{bmatrix} \Delta u_t \\ \Delta v_t \end{bmatrix} \tag{10.14a}$$

$$\tilde{y}_t = C_L\tilde{x}_t + D_L\begin{bmatrix} \Delta u_t \\ \Delta v_t \end{bmatrix} \tag{10.14b}$$

A linear representation in this form is asymptotically stable by construction.

Considering the auxiliary state variables in transposed form

$$\xi_t' = [u_{t-1}' \; v_{t-1}'] \tag{10.15}$$

we form the augmented system:

$$\begin{bmatrix} \tilde{x}_{t+1} \\ \xi_{t+1} \end{bmatrix} = \begin{bmatrix} A_L & -B_L \\ 0 & 0 \end{bmatrix}\begin{bmatrix} \tilde{x}_t \\ \xi_t \end{bmatrix} + \begin{bmatrix} B_L \\ I \end{bmatrix}\begin{bmatrix} u_t \\ v_t \end{bmatrix} \tag{10.16a}$$

$$\tilde{y}_t = [C_L \quad -D_L]\begin{bmatrix} x_t \\ \xi_t \end{bmatrix} + D_L\begin{bmatrix} u_t \\ v_t \end{bmatrix} \tag{10.16b}$$

Linear approximations y_t of the step responses $\hat{y}_t$ are obtained in a way similar to (10.13) as:

$$y_t = J_\infty \begin{bmatrix} u_t \\ v_t \end{bmatrix} - \bar{y}_t \qquad (10.17)$$

Defining the augmented state vector $x_t' = [\bar{x}_t' \; \xi_k]$ we finally obtain the linear system:

$$x_{t+1} = Ax_t + B \begin{bmatrix} u_t \\ v_t \end{bmatrix} \qquad (10.18a)$$

$$y_t = Cx_t + D \begin{bmatrix} u_t \\ v_t \end{bmatrix} \qquad (10.18b)$$

where:

$$A = \begin{bmatrix} A_L & -B_L \\ 0 & 0 \end{bmatrix} \qquad B = \begin{bmatrix} B_L \\ I \end{bmatrix}$$

$$C = [-C_L \quad D_L], \qquad D = J_\infty - D_L$$

The impact multipliers of the linear model are given by matrix D. They are chosen accurately to represent the impact multipliers of the non-linear model $\hat{Y}_0$ by simply setting

$$D_L = J_\infty - \hat{Y}_0 \qquad (10.19)$$

Matrix A is asymptotically stable, since A_L is such. Letting t go to infinity and $x_{t+1} \to x_t$ we easily verify that:

$$y_\infty = J_\infty \begin{bmatrix} u_\infty \\ v_\infty \end{bmatrix} = \hat{Y}_\infty \qquad (10.20)$$

Therefore the long-term multipliers[4] of the linear model are always equal to those of the non-linear model. As the impact and long-term multipliers are accurately represented by the linear model, independently of the order of the linear reduction, the number of state variables is chosen satisfactorily to approximate the intermediate-run multipliers.

10.3 'INSTABILITY' PROBLEMS

However desirable the properties of the methods just described might be, it is the requirement of asymptotically vanishing multipliers which

severely limits the practical applicability of the algorithm to large
economic models. The reasons for asymptotic instability may be any of
the following:

(a) The existence of particular non-linearities that produce asymptotic
offsets to temporary shocks. For example, consider the simple non-
linear structure

$$\frac{Y_t - Y_{t-1}}{Y_{t-1}} = \lambda \frac{U_t - U_{t-1}}{U_{t-1}} + \text{(other terms)} \qquad (10.21)$$

When a temporary proportional shock is applied to U_t we have:

$$\hat{U}_0 = \varepsilon \, \bar{U}_0, \; \hat{U}_t = 0 \text{ for } t \geq 1$$

Working with proportional deviations $\hat{Y}_t = (Y_t / \bar{Y}_t - 1)$ the following
formula is obtained by subtracting from (10.21) its base counterpart

$$\hat{Y}_t = \hat{Y}_{t-1} + \lambda \frac{\bar{U}_t / \bar{U}_{t-1}}{\bar{Y}_t / \bar{Y}_{t-1}} (1 + \hat{Y}_{t-1}) \frac{\hat{U}_t - \hat{U}_{t-1}}{1 + \hat{U}_{t-1}} \qquad (10.22$$

with responses:

$$\hat{Y}_0 = \varepsilon \lambda \gamma_0$$

$$\hat{Y}_1 = \varepsilon \lambda \left[\gamma_0 - \frac{\gamma_1 + \varepsilon \lambda \gamma_0 \gamma_1}{1 + \varepsilon} \right] \neq 0$$

$$\hat{Y}_t = \hat{Y}_{t-1}, \text{ for every } t \geq 2$$

where for simplicity we set $\gamma_t = (\bar{U}_t / \bar{U}_{t-1}) / (\bar{Y}_t / \bar{Y}_{t-1})$.

If base trajectories are such that $\gamma_0 \neq \gamma_1$, the above equations result
in serious steady-state offsets for deviations $\hat{Y}_t$. Even when $\gamma_0 = \gamma$
offsets will still be present, though of an order ε^2.

Observe that these offsets are generated without the system being
necessarily unstable. But they may render the linearization algorithm
useless as they introduce persistent error terms in equation (10.8).

In contrast, step changes in input variables do not generate offsets.
Given that the non-linear model is not explosive, we set $\hat{U}_t = \varepsilon \, \bar{U}_t$ for
every t and obtain from (10.22) the finite responses:

$$\hat{Y}_0 = \varepsilon \lambda \gamma_0$$

$$\hat{Y}_t = \hat{Y}_{t-1} \text{ for every } t \geq 1$$

Modelling the impulse multipliers might introduce serious inade quacies into the results. This is because when the impulse multipliers are asymptotically vanishing, they are significant mainly at the beginning of the solution period and, as a consequence, do not adequately capture the behaviour of the model in later periods. As a consequence they cannot properly represent the response of the observed Y_t to permanent shocks in exogenous variables. A more appropriate choice, which does capture this behaviour, is to consider the step multipliers showing the observed response of Y_t to permanent shocks to the exogenous variables. This is particularly important if the policy rules are to cope with permanent disturbances to the exogenous variables. And it has added emphasis with model-consistent expectations, when current responses will depend on such permanent shocks.

(b) A second cause of instability is the presence of integrators in the model. These typically occur with a simple stock-adjustment process such as

$$Y_t = Y_{t-1} + \text{(flows)} \tag{10.23}$$

When the stock variable does not interact sufficiently strongly with the rest of the model, its behaviour becomes border-line stable, and a permanent deviation appears after only a temporary shock is applied. Step changes in exogenous variables generate ever-rising responses of Y_t. If the flows themselves respond positively to Y_t then the problem is aggravated. There will be a clear case of instability. We have shown, in Chapter 4, that this instability is likely to be found in models of an open economy, as a consequence of stock-flow interactions.

(c) A third cause of instability is rapid response of the price mechanism to shocks. For example, in Version 7 of the NIESR model the wage equation produces unstable simulations when the control-free model is subject to shocks, even though all expectations are formed adaptively. This happens because a rise in wages leads to a fall in the real interest rate. This fall in the real interest rate stimulates an increase in demand, which leads to a rise in prices and so to a further fall in the real interest rate. The process is unstable.[5]

(d) When models are solved with model-consistent expectations, each expectational variable, P_{t+1}^e, is equated to the actual out-turn, P_{t+1}, always provided that expectations of exogenous events have not changed. This normally introduces an unstable root into the model. The usual way of solving such a model is to assume that the current value of the variable, P_t, is not constrained by its past values, but is free to 'jump', so as to cancel the unstable root; the model then converges to its equilibrium along a saddlepath. As we make clear in section 10.6, the magnitude of the jump in each free variable depends on the structure of the policy regime in force. This is an example of the Lucas critique (Lucas, 1976). This poses a problem. Without the jump the model is unstable and cannot be linearized. With the jump the model is stable, but the magnitude of the jump depends on the policy regime in force. But the policy cannot be tested for stability without already having done the linearization.

The first type of 'instability' can be removed simply by using step rather than impulse multipliers and provides a further rationale for adopting this approach. The remaining types need to be removed before we can use either of our linearization procedures. In order to remove the second and third types of instabilities, simple stabilization rules to change instruments U_t according to the behaviour of the observed variables Y_t can be used. If the model is thus stabilized a linear approximation can be obtained. These *ad hoc* rules may either be taken out in the linear model, or amalgamated with the policy rules which are to be devised for the instruments. The issue of *ad hoc* rules is discussed in section 10.4. The fourth type, caused by expectations, is removed by renormalizing the model prior to linearization. This is explained in section 10.5.

10.4   THE OPERATION OF *AD HOC* STABILIZATION RULES

When a non-linear model produces explosive simulations to step perturbations of exogenous variables, a simple rule for the instruments must be found before the linearization procedure is applied. We call these rules *ad hoc*. Policy rules pursue well-defined economic targets. *Ad hoc* rules are introduced solely to obtain an asymptotically stable model before linearization.

A simple way of devising and operating the *ad hoc* rule is to think of the policy instrument as 'split' into two parts, $U_t = H_t + W_t$. The first part H_t is used for the *ad hoc* rule, while the second is devoted to the policy task.

A linear *ad hoc* rule would preferably operate only on variables represented in the linear model; it is then possible to unwind it, if necessary, at the later stage of policy design and recover a linearization of the original model as it would have been without the simple rule in place. The simplest case would be to consider proportional *ad hoc* rules with no instrument lags, i.e. $H_t = K_1 Y_t$. To unwind this rule one has only to set

$W_t = -K_1 Y_t + \tilde{W}_t$ and then immediately recover the original instrument U_t as input to the model, since $U_t = \tilde{W}_t$. If a linear system (A, B, C, D) is obtained with W_t as an input, it takes only a few matrix manipulations to establish the following linear approximation of the original system (10.1) with U_t as an instrument:

$$x_{t+1} = (A - B_1 K_0 C)x_t + [B_1 K_0 \quad B_2 - B_1 K_0 D_2]\begin{bmatrix} u_t \\ v_t \end{bmatrix} \quad (10.24a)$$

$$y_t = (C - D_1 K_0 C)x_t + [D_1 K_0 \quad D_2 - D_1 K_0 D_2]\begin{bmatrix} u_t \\ v_t \end{bmatrix} \quad (10.24b)$$

where $K_0 = (I + K_1 D_1)^{-1}$ and B_1, B_2, D_1 and D_2 are appropriate partitions of B and D. A similar equation is derived in the case where expectations are to be treated as consistent.

There might be cases, however, where a proportional-only rule is not capable of stabilizing the model, and higher lags need to be used. In this situation, the policy rule must be combined with the *ad hoc* rule. An example of such a rule could be:

$$H_t = \theta_1 U_{t-1} + K_1 Y_t \quad (10.25a)$$

with θ_1 a diagonal and K_1 possibly non-diagonal constant matrices. Suppose now that during the policy design another dynamic rule has been found for the other part W_t:

$$W_t = \theta_2 W_{t-1} + K_2 Y_t \quad (10.25b)$$

with θ_2 a diagonal and K_2 possibly non-diagonal constant matrices. Using the diagonal lag-operator to write $LX_t = X_{t-1}$ we can put both rules into the equation:

$$\begin{bmatrix} H_t \\ W_t \end{bmatrix} = \begin{bmatrix} \theta_1 L & \theta_1 L \\ 0 & \theta_2 L \end{bmatrix}\begin{bmatrix} H_t \\ W_t \end{bmatrix} + \begin{bmatrix} K_1 \\ K_2 \end{bmatrix} Y_t \quad (10.26)$$

This is a system of linear operational equations and its solution is:

$$H_t = (I - \theta_1 L)^{-1}(I - \theta_2 L)^{-1}[(I - \theta_2 L)K_1 + \theta_1 L K_2]Y_t \quad (10.27a)$$

$$W_t = (I - \theta_1 L)^{-1}(I - \theta_2 L)^{-1}(I - \theta_1 L)K_2 Y_t \quad (10.27b)$$

Original instruments are then found as:

$$U_t = (I - \theta_1 L)^{-1}(I - \theta_2 L)^{-1}[(I - \theta_2 L)K_1 + K_2]Y_t \quad (10.28)$$

Rearranging the matrix inverses we arrive at the following combination of *ad hoc* rules and policy rules in the non-linear model:

$$U_t = (\theta_1 + \theta_2)U_{t-1} - \theta_1\theta_2 U_{t-2} + (K_1 + K_2)Y_t - \theta_2 K_1 Y_{t-1} \quad (10.29)$$

Observe that the complete rule is not obtained by simple superposition of the control matrices Θ_i and K_i, because the *ad hoc* rule operates on the total instrument U_t.

10.5 EXPECTATIONS

We now consider the treatment of expectations in the linearization procedure. We wish our investigation of economic policy to take place with a number of possible assumptions about the way in which expectations are formed and, in our text, have emphasized the two cases of adaptive and model-consistent expectations. When expectations are regressive, there are only predetermined variables in the model, P_t. The fact that the current value of a variable may depend on its expected future value does not matter, provided that the expected future value only depends on past history. We therefore demonstrated, in Chapter 5, how we were able to eliminate expected future variables, P_{t+1}^e, by simple transformation.

In the linearization procedure, we have invalidated the consistency condition solely for the purposes of deriving the linear model. We treat the jumping variables, P_t, as though they were exogenous, and analyse the effects of step changes in these exogenized variables. The expected future values, P_{t+1}^e, are treated as normal variables, i.e. as endogenous outputs.[6]

Handled in this way, the model, although invalid, is likely to be stable, since the unstable roots are usually associated with the expectational equations and the consistency of expectations. If not, further *ad hoc* stabilizing rules should be adopted as described in the previous section. Thus, a linear reduced approximation may now be obtained without any specific assumption about expectations. The desired assumptions about expectations can be imposed at will later on. In particular, consistency of expectations in the linear model is imposed by simply setting $p_{t+1}^e = p_{t+1}$. This endogenizes p_t, and the Blanchard–Kahn formula can then be used to solve the model.

This treatment of expectational variables is particularly helpful when the system is to be investigated with different assumptions about expectations. We have so far focused on consistent expectations, but any adaptive process of the form

$$P_{t+1}^e = \sum_j \beta_j P_{t-j}$$

can be easily incorporated and analysed. Further technical details of the handling of expectational variables in simulating our model are given in the following sections. But first we must show explicitly how to handle expectational variables during linearization.

10.5.1 The treatment of consistent expectations during linearization

As mentioned in section 10.2, the state vector represents a compressed expression of vector Z_t in the original model, with no easy economic interpretation. It is a predetermined vector with initial conditions $x_0 = 0$. The standard form for a state-space rational expectations model with expectations of future values of endogenous variables is:

$$\begin{bmatrix} x_{t+1} \\ p_{t+1}^e \end{bmatrix} = A \begin{bmatrix} x_t \\ p_t \end{bmatrix} + B \begin{bmatrix} u_t \\ v_t \end{bmatrix} \tag{10.30a}$$

$$y_t = C \begin{bmatrix} x_t \\ p_t \end{bmatrix} + D \begin{bmatrix} u_t \\ v_t \end{bmatrix} \tag{10.30b}$$

By exogenizing the current value of an expectational variable p_t and using this as an input to the linearization with its expectational counterpart observed, the linear approximation would give the state-space system:

$$x_{t+1} = \tilde{A} x_t + \tilde{B} \begin{bmatrix} u_t \\ v_t \\ p_t \end{bmatrix} \tag{10.31a}$$

$$\begin{bmatrix} y_t \\ p_{t+1}^e \end{bmatrix} = \tilde{C} x_t + \tilde{D} \begin{bmatrix} u_t \\ v_t \\ p_t \end{bmatrix} \tag{10.31b}$$

Partitioning the matrices $\tilde{B}$, $\tilde{C}$ and $\tilde{D}$ conformably, the same form as (10.30) would now be obtained by setting:

$$A = \begin{bmatrix} \tilde{A} & \tilde{B}_3 \\ \tilde{C}_2 & \tilde{D}_{23} \end{bmatrix} \tag{10.32a}$$

$$B = \begin{bmatrix} \tilde{B}_1 & \tilde{B}_2 \\ \tilde{D}_{21} & \tilde{D}_{22} \end{bmatrix} \qquad (10.32b)$$

$$C = [\tilde{C} \qquad \tilde{D}_{13}] \qquad (10.32c)$$

$$D = [\tilde{D}_{11} \qquad \tilde{D}_{12}] \qquad (10.32d)$$

This basic form for a linearized consistent expectations model is the one employed in our work.

10.6 CONSISTENT SOLUTIONS IN THE LINEAR MODEL

By setting $p_{t+1} = p^e_{t+1}$ a saddlepath solution for the free variables may now be obtained through the method of Blanchard and Kahn (1980). The diagonalization of matrix A in equation (10.30) yields:

$$A = T^{-1} \begin{bmatrix} \Lambda_1 & 0 \\ 0 & \Lambda_2 \end{bmatrix} T \qquad (10.33a)$$

$$T = \begin{bmatrix} T_1 \\ T_2 \end{bmatrix} = \begin{bmatrix} T_{11} & T_{12} \\ T_{21} & T_{22} \end{bmatrix} \qquad (10.33b)$$

with Λ_2 denoting the Jordan block of unstable eigenvalues and the eigenvector matrix T being conformably partitioned. When the number of unstable roots (i.e. with magnitude exceeding unity) equals the number of free variables, then the unique solution of the reaction function is given by:

$$p_t = -(T_{22}^{-1} T_{21}) x_t - T_{22}^{-1} \Lambda_2^{-1} \sum_{j=0}^{\infty} \Lambda_2^{-i} T_2 B \begin{bmatrix} u^e_{t+j} \\ v^e_{t+j} \end{bmatrix} \qquad (10.34)$$

Partitions corresponding to the matrices of system (10.31) are:

$$A = \begin{bmatrix} A_{11} & A_{12} \\ A_{21} & A_{22} \end{bmatrix} \text{ and } B = \begin{bmatrix} B_{11} & B_{12} \\ B_{21} & B_{22} \end{bmatrix}$$

The state vector and the endogenous variables are then given as:

$$x_{t+1} = A_{11} x_t + A_{12} p_t + [B_{11} \quad B_{12}] \begin{bmatrix} u_t \\ v_t \end{bmatrix}, \quad x_0 = 0 \qquad (10.35a)$$

$$y_t = C\begin{bmatrix} x_t \\ p_t \end{bmatrix} + [D_1 \quad D_2]\begin{bmatrix} u_t \\ v_t \end{bmatrix} \qquad (10.35b)$$

Expression (10.34) may now be used to obtain analytic solutions for the effects on the free variables of specific kind of shocks. In section 7.3.1 we identified three types of shocks, whose impact we wished to study. These were (i) the effects of shocks to the trend growth of the exogenous variables, (ii) the effects of level changes (shifts in the trend lines) of the exogenous variables and (iii) the effects of specific one-off deviations in the exogenous variables expected to take place j periods in the future. We now present the effects of the three types of disturbance on the jumping variables, with the assumption that x_t is zero.

i) Trends
Putting $u^e_{t+j} = \hat{u}j$ and $v^e_{t+j} = \hat{v}j$ for every $j = 0, 1, 2, \ldots$ we may use the standard formula for the sum of a trended geometric progression to give

$$p_t = - T_{22}^{-1}\{\Lambda_2(\Lambda_2 - I)^{-2} - (\Lambda_2 - I)^{-1}\}T_2 B\begin{bmatrix} \hat{u} \\ \hat{v} \end{bmatrix} \qquad (10.36)$$

ii) Permanent changes
Putting $u^e_{t+j} = u_t$ and $v^e_{t+j} = v_t$ for every $j = 0, 1, 2, \ldots$ the series of discounted expectations is explicitly summed to give:

$$p_t = - T_{22}^{-1}(\Lambda_2 - I)^{-1} T_2 B\begin{bmatrix} u_t \\ v_t \end{bmatrix} \qquad (10.37)$$

iii) Temporary changes
We may now measure the effects of one-off disturbances relative to the trend line as $\bar{u}^e_{t+j} = u^e_{t+j} - u_t - \hat{u}j$ and $\bar{v}^e_{t+j} = v^e_{t+j} - v_t - \hat{v}j$. We may use (10.34) directly, but we apply it to the one-off components not covered by the trend and level terms to give

$$p_t = - T_{22}^{-1}\Lambda_2^{-1} \sum_{j=0}^{\infty} \Lambda_2^{-j} T_2 B\begin{bmatrix} \bar{u}^e_{t+j} \\ \bar{v}^e_{t+j} \end{bmatrix} \qquad (10.38)$$

Since any shock to any exogenous variable can be broken down into a trend change, a level shift and a series of one-off disturbances, it is possible to use these equations to work out the effects of shifts in the exogenous variables on the jumping or free variables. In Chapter 7 we give an account of the way in which observed expectational series can in practice be broken down in this way. Each component of the value of each jumping variable can be calculated, and they are simply added up to give the overall value. A non-zero value of x_t is taken account of, by adding on to the cumulated effects of the three types of disturbance $-(T_{22}^{-1} T_{21})x_t$ from equation (10.34).

We now proceed to explain how the resulting values for the jumping variables can be used in the calculation of the solution of the non-linear model.

10.7 PSEUDO-CONSISTENT SOLUTIONS FOR THE NON-LINEAR MODEL

10.7.1 The simple case

We use the linear solutions (10.36–38) in order to solve the non-linear model with consistent expectations, making the assumption that the policy regime has not changed from the base run. Then a solution of the full model is obtained in which free variables remain exogenized and are set using the values of the linear solution (10.36–38) and adding on the effects of non-zero x_t (equation 10.34) to give an overall value for the deviation of the jumping variable, p_t. This is then added back to the value of the jumping variable in the base run to give an absolute value for the jumping variable

$$P_t = p_t + \bar{P}_t \qquad \text{or} \qquad P_t = (1 + p_t)\bar{P}_t$$

depending on whether the deviations are additive or proportional in form. The expectational variables P_{t+1}^e are determined endogenously.

This solution will be considered as approximately-consistent whenever P_{t+1}^e emerge very close to the exogenously set P_{t+1} in all time periods $t \geq 0$.[7]

The solution technique which we have set out above allows us to calculate the effects of a disturbance on a non-linear model which was previously at rest and on which the same policy rules are used as were in place on the base run from which the linear model was built. We explain below how we are able to generalize this approach to the more general problem of rerunning history.

10.7.2 The role of terminal conditions in other solution methods

Unlike our approach, other common solution methods for consistent-expectations models (see, for example, Minford and Peel, 1983) impose arbitrary terminal conditions. They specify that jumping variables should finally reach either:

i)   a constant level,
ii) a constant growth rate, or
iii) a given fixed value at the terminal period

and the non-linear techniques of Lipton *et al.* (1982) or Fisher *et al.* (1985) determine the initial jump which is compatible with these. There are certain shortcomings in these approaches. First, there is no economic justification for choosing any particular value for condition (iii). The first two conditions are more general, but they both assume that the model has reached its long-term stage within the specified solution period. When the model is characterized by slow dynamics (see for an example Christodoulakis and Weale, 1987), there is no reason to assume that this is actually the case.

In contrast, the linear solutions obtained as in (10.36−38) are by construction stationary in the long run. Assuming that the base trajectory of (10.3) is long-run stationary, it follows that perturbed simulations of the non-linear model using the pseudo-consistent solutions above are also stationary. The terminal value $P_T^c = \bar{P}_T^c + p_T^c$ in this solution is justified on the grounds that it belongs to a stationary trajectory of an approximate solution of the non-linear model. This provides a justification for the solution which is not present with other methods.

10.7.3   Solutions in a rerun of history

The above procedures are adequate if the base run is treated as an equilibrium trajectory and seeks to examine a change relative to that base. For they assume, first, that the model is initially at rest ($x_0 = 0$); this is only justifiable if disturbances are considered relative to an equilibrium base. Secondly, they assume that the same policy rules are in place in the base run and in the perturbed run.

Neither of these assumptions are justified in the reruns of history which we carry out in Chapters 8 and 9. Here the starting position of the model is clearly well off the base path, and, in any case we want to look at the effects of changes to the policy regime. We can, and in Chapter 7 do, identify equilibrium trajectories for the jumping variables, so we can relate the divergences to these instead of to the base run. But we cannot identify the appropriate value of x_0 since we do not know the history of the model before the rerun. All we can do is to identify the effects of changes in the expected values of the exogenous variables on the jumping variables from one period to the next on the assumption that $x_0 = 0$ an in subsequent periods x_t takes the values given by the linear mode (10.35a). Given this information, and our knowledge of the equilibriun trajectories, we can identify the changes in the jumping variables fron one period to the next. But we cannot identify the appropriate startin point.

The solution we adopt to this problem is to simulate the model beyon the end of our historical data so as to study its evolution in the absenc of further shocks. Over this period we can study the evolution of th jumping variables in both the linear and non-linear models. We impos initial jumps in the free variables so as to ensure that, at the end of th run, and in the absence of shocks, the rates of change of the expecta tional variables in the linear and non-linear models coincide with a acceptable degree of accuracy. An example of how an initial jump ca ensure such convergence was given in Chapter 7.

This solution method is not ideal. It will not give exactly the sam results as would be found if the correct starting value of x_0 were known But we do claim that it offers a more satisfactory approach than is give by reliance on arbitrary terminal conditions.

10.8 PRACTICAL ASPECTS OF LINEARIZATION

This section describes the approach we have adopted to the linearizatior of our non-linear model. The possible problems that the previou: sections raised are dealt with in a number of ways.

One point to note is that the linearization of step rather than impulse responses has been adopted throughout. This not only improves the quality of the linearizations in terms of 'goodness-of-fit'; it has removec the potential problem raised in section 10.3 of spurious offsets in the impulse multipliers. A second important feature is that the long-rur properties of the model responses can be accurately monitored.

Two linearizations were used, one for the adaptive and one for the consistent expectations variants. For both, the inputs had to include the policy instruments (interest rates and our composite tax variable) and the outputs the policy targets (nominal GDP and wealth) as well as the real exchange rate, our intermediate target. Wages were used as an additional exogenous input to both these linearizations. This meant the same linearization could be used in the creation of both the reformed and unreformed wage linear models. As a bare minimum, the outputs must therefore include the consumer price index and the unemployment rate to allow the wage equations to be constructed. Our treatment of wages as exogenous in the linearization also removes the possibility that there will be any instability in the wage-price loop, as mentioned in section 10.3. The unstable root associated with wealth accumulation remains. This was dealt with by an *ad hoc* stabilizing rule, with taxes feeding back on wealth with a coefficient of 0.5 (see section 10.4). [8] This was confirmed as just stabilizing by simulating the model over an extended base.

Further inputs to both models are the exogenous variables described in Chapter 7, and used in the consistent-expectations reruns of history as sources of expectational disturbances.

The two linearizations treat expectations in different ways. For the adaptive model the expectational equations for the valuation ratio and the consol rate were 'switched in' except for the non-linear model simulations. Thus there is no need to treat these expectational equations differently from the other equations of the model. The expected nominal exchange rate was kept exogenous and used as an input. A regressive form of an adaptive expectations-formation mechanism was then closed in the linear model, in the same way as with the wage equation. This allowed easy experimentation with the degree of regressiveness. A final output for the adaptive model was therefore the nominal exchange rate.

With the consistent expectations model, the four forward-looking variables (see Chapter 6) were each kept exogenous and used as inputs to the linearization, and the expected future values used as outputs. This meant that there were three more inputs and outputs than in the adaptive case, since, as noted above, exchange rate expectations were treated as exogenous in that case. A fourth extra input was the domestic capital stock, which is endogenized to ensure that Q returns to the base level.

The linearizations in the form (10.18) were chosen to be of order 25 for the adaptive model and 27 for the consistent expectations model with the

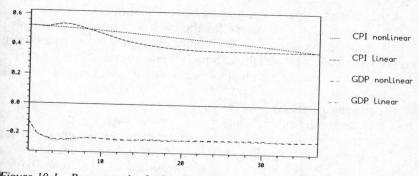

Figure 10.1   Responses in the linear and non-linear models: a 1% tax increase with exogenous wages

greater number of inputs and outputs. Figure 10.1 shows two representative trajectories for the adaptive model with exogenous wages and
expected nominal exchange rate, and with the *ad hoc* stabilizing rule in
place.

An additional point is that whilst step responses remove many of the
problems that linearizing over a finite base trajectory poses, there is still a
problem of ensuring that the long-run multipliers are the equilibrium
responses of the model. The historical data base over which the
simulations were run is only 37 periods. It was clear that some of the
responses had not reached their long-run values. Using a simple extrapolative procedure this time-horizon was extended to 55 periods. However, a simple extrapolation does not ensure that the constraints which
the model imposes on the equilibrium relationships will hold. In general,
we do not have strong prior views about the equilibrium of our model.
As with all large macroeconometric models less is known about its
aggregate steady-state properties than would be desirable. However,
there is one important property which we regard as essential in a model
used for policy analysis. This is that the real economy should be long-run
homogeneous of degree zero in prices. Despite being unable to run the
non-linear model for long enough to determine whether this feature is
present or not, we would have no great confidence in policy rules
designed on a linear model from which price homogeneity is absent. It
was therefore imposed on the linear model.[9] This means that the
multipliers in some cases have to be extrapolated to a 'fixed point' at
which two sets of conditions are satisfied. A unit increase in the wage rate
combined with a unit fall in the exchange rate must lead to unit changes
in prices and no changes in quantity variables. And a unit rise in the
exchange rate combined with a unit rise in world prices must have no
effects on quantities or home currency prices. These conditions were
imposed by first extrapolating the model to the extended time-horizon
and then adjusting the resulting long runs to ensure homogeneity.

This is particularly important for the consistent expectations model,
where small anomalies can lead to unwanted offsets in the equilibrium
responses of the free variables. Small alterations to the extrapolated
values ensured that the nominal exchange rate in particular held to the
expected values.

The two linearizations were then augmented to allow for the effects of
trends in the exogenous variables,[10] the relevant wage equation and the
endogenous expectations. For the adaptive model, the last simply meant
closing up the nominal exchange rate equation, but the model-consistent
expectations model required the forward-looking variables to be
included in the state-vector and the capital stock to be endogenized. This
makes the largest of the linear models the model-consistent expectations

unreformed wage case, with 53 state variables. Rather than reproduce the models here, all four linear models are available from the authors on request.

10.9 CONCLUDING REMARKS

This chapter has demonstrated how linear reduction algorithms can be used on models which have free or jumping variables, whose values depend on expectations of future events rather than solely on the history of the model. The resulting linear models can be used in order to provide an analytical solution for the behaviour of the models in response to any disturbance. Unlike other solution techniques used with such models, this solution does not rely on arbitrary terminal conditions. The solution can be used to solve for consistent expectations trajectories of the non-linear model; it requires terminal conditions but they are not arbitrary.

The linear models which we construct allow us to examine the effects of policy rules quickly and easily. In Chapter 11 we describe how we use our linear models in the process of policy design.

Chapter Eleven

The Design of Economic Policy Rules

11.1 INTRODUCTION

This book has studied the use of simple policy rules to steer the economy towards an inflation target and a wealth target using the instruments of fiscal and monetary policy. In the implementation of these rules there is also a real exchange rate intermediate target.

The basic structure of these rules was presented in section 1.7 of Chapter 1 and their precise form was displayed in Chapter 6. In that latter chapter we showed the performance of the rules in the face of shocks to the targets. Good performance in this context is, as we shall see, the main criterion we have used in policy design. Chapter 6 also showed how good the rules are at rejecting the effects on the economy of a variety of exogenous disturbances. The rules were then put through their paces in historical reruns in Chapters 7, 8 and 9.

In this chapter we return to the fundamental methodological question: how can one design simple feedback rules that perform adequately? The reader will see that we do not have a hard-and-fast answer. Much of what is required seems to be 'merely' enlightened trial-and-error. But we will explain what we have done, and sketch out how the methodology might be further developed.

Before proceeding, the reader should note that there is an extensive and lucid account of the application of feedback control methods to economic policy problems in Part IV of Vines, Maciejowski and Meade (1983). This exposition shows how the early insights of Phillips (1954, 1957) might be carried forward in the light of modern developments in multivariable control theory. A second key reference is Westaway (1985). He explains in detail how the process of trial-and-error searching for simple rules – particularly those relying on proportional integral and derivative terms – can be guided by a number of formal control theory methods which are not normally familiar to economists. A limitation of both of these references is that they do not consider the case where economic agents have forward-looking expectations. Christodoulakis (1984) and Blake (1988) have developed techniques for use with model-consistent expectations and we have built on their work.

The chapter proceeds as follows. In the first section we present a straightforward motivation for using rules containing only proportional and integral feedback components. We have relied almost entirely on such rules. Then we discuss the design of our policy rules and show how the use of such rules influences the final form and solution of our linear model from Chapter 10.

11.2 THE CONTROLLED ECONOMY

11.2.1 Feedback rules

We now proceed to a technical discussion of policy rules, and demonstrate their effects on the linear model discussed in Chapter 10. A simple dynamic feedback rule takes the form:

$$u_t = \theta u_{t-1} + K y_{t-1} + E y_t + M y_t^* + N v_t \qquad (11.1)$$

In this expression K and E denote the *feedback* from lagged and current values of the target variables, M represents the influence of their desired levels, and N is a form of *feedforward* action undertaken as soon as external shocks appear in the economic environment. The diagonal matrix θ is discounting the past behaviour. With $\theta = 0$, policy action does not depend on the actions of the past (u_{t-1}), so this rule might be considered as less prone to reneging. In contrast, $\theta = I$ gives a rule where there is full integration of past behaviour into the present.

To investigate the properties of rule (11.1), we assume that the government wishes to achieve asymptotically the target trajectories, y_t^*, and the economy is subjected to disturbances v_t. In the general case, when $\theta \neq I$, the necessary conditions are somewhat complex. If $\theta = I$, which we assume, the rule then becomes

$$\Delta u_t = K y_{t-1} + E y_t + M y_t^* + N v_t$$

We suppose that the target trajectory, y_t^*, is a constant. Then, if the is to be achieved even if the shocks are permanent, we must have

$$K + E + M = 0$$
$$N = 0$$

Only with these restrictions can we be sure that the instruments, u_t, will be changing unless the target, y_t^*, is reached. When these conditions are imposed the rule takes on the simple proportional-plus-integral form:

$$\Delta u_t = -K\Delta y_t - M(y_t - y_t^*) \tag{11.2}$$

Observe that in this form no feedforward action N is permitted.[1] This rule has the property that it will achieve the target trajectory at least if the target trajectory is constant. We also note that, if the target trajectory required a growth rate different from the trajectory of the uncontrolled economy, then the proportional-plus-integral rule would not achieve that target even asymptotically. More complex structures would be required.

In order to show the impact of proportional-plus-integral control, we substitute (11.2) into (10.30) to give:

$$
\begin{bmatrix} x_{t+1} \\ p_{t+1}^e \\ y_t \\ u_t \end{bmatrix} = \begin{bmatrix} A - B_1 K_0 (K+M)C & B_1 K_0 K & B_1 K_0 \\ C - D_1 K_0 (K+M)C & D_1 K_0 K & D_1 K_0 \\ -K_0(K+M)C & K_0 K & K_0 \end{bmatrix} \begin{bmatrix} x_t \\ p_t \\ y_{t-1} \\ u_{t-1} \end{bmatrix}
$$
$$
+ \begin{bmatrix} B_1 K_0 M & B_2 + B_1 K_0 D_2 \\ D_1 K_0 M & D_2 + B_1 K_0 D_2 \\ K_0 M & K_0 D_2 \end{bmatrix} \begin{bmatrix} y_t^* \\ v_t \end{bmatrix} \tag{11.3}
$$

where $K_0 = [I + (K + M)D_1]^{-1}$.

11.2.2 The consistent expectations solution

The consistent expectations solution now follows in precisely the same way as in (10.34). Free variables p_t react to unanticipated changes in targets y_t^*, and also to external shocks v_t. There are two important differences from the uncontrolled economy (equation (10.30)). First, the target variables now enter into the model, and secondly the dynamics of the reaction function have changed because of the introduction of the policy regime (11.3). This effect can be usefully exploited in the design of control rules. A choice of K and M which results in larger unstable eigenvalues than are found in the uncontrolled economy will result in heavier damping of shocks arising from changes in expectations about the future values of the exogenous variables.

We express the target trajectory as a trend from a base value

$$y_{t+j}^* = y_t^* + \hat{y}_t^* j$$

and shocks to the exogenous variables in the same form as in section 7.5, identifying a trend, a level term and one-off disturbances about the trend line

$$v_{t+j}^e = \hat{v}_t j + v_t + \bar{v}_{t+j}^e$$

Since all variables are measured in logarithms y_t^* represents a constant percentage shift in the target for y^* relative to the equilibrium trajectory and $\hat{y}_t^*$ represents a change in the target rate of growth relative to the equilibrium trajectory. In the same way $\hat{v}_t$ represents a change in the trend of the exogenous variables, and v_t a shift in the level, and expected deviations from the new trajectory are shown by $\bar{v}_{t+j}^e$. The trend and level variables are measured relative to the base run.

We may now write down the deviations of the jumping variables from their equilibrium path, p_t, using the expression given by Blanchard and Kahn (1980). We write (11.3) as

$$\begin{bmatrix} x_{t+1} \\ y_t \\ u_t \\ p_{t+1}^e \end{bmatrix} = A \begin{bmatrix} x_t \\ y_{t-1} \\ u_{t-1} \\ p_t \end{bmatrix} + B \begin{bmatrix} y_t^* \\ v_t \end{bmatrix} \qquad (11.4)$$

We diagonalize the matrix A in (11.4) as $A = T\Lambda T^{-1}$ where T is the matrix consisting of the eigenvectors of A and Λ is the matrix whose diagonal is the eigenvalues of A, and whose off-diagonal elements are all zero. We now partition the matrices T and Λ in the manner described in Chapter 10 (section 10.6), as

$$T = \begin{bmatrix} T_{11} & T_{12} & T_{13} & T_{14} \\ T_{21} & T_{22} & T_{23} & T_{24} \\ T_{31} & T_{32} & T_{33} & T_{34} \\ T_{41} & T_{42} & T_{43} & T_{44} \end{bmatrix} \qquad \Lambda = \begin{bmatrix} \Lambda_1 & 0 & 0 & 0 \\ 0 & \Lambda_2 & 0 & 0 \\ 0 & 0 & \Lambda_3 & 0 \\ 0 & 0 & 0 & \Lambda_4 \end{bmatrix}$$

It is then possible to write down the values for the jumping variables, p_t, as linear functions of the lagged values of the endogenous variables, x_t, y_t

and u_t, and as functions of the expected future shocks, v_t^e, and the target trajectory, y_{t+j}^*.

$$p_t = -T_{44}^{-1}(T_{41} \quad T_{42} \quad T_{43}) \begin{bmatrix} x_t \\ y_{t-1} \\ u_{t-1} \end{bmatrix}$$

$$- T_{44}^{-1}\Lambda_4^{-1} \sum_{j=0}^{\infty} \Lambda_4^{-j}(T_{41} \quad T_{42} \quad T_{43} \quad T_{44})B\begin{bmatrix} y_{t+j}^* \\ v_{t+j} \end{bmatrix} \quad (11.5)$$

We can, as in section 10.6, then use the standard results for the summation of infinite series in (11.5) on splitting y_{t+j}^* and v_{t+j} into their component parts. This gives

$$p_t = -T_{44}^{-1}(T_{41} \quad T_{42} \quad T_{43}) \begin{bmatrix} x_t \\ Y_{t-1} \\ U_{t-1} \end{bmatrix}$$

$$- T_{44}^{-1}\{\Lambda_4(\Lambda_4 - I)^{-2} - (\Lambda_4 - I)^{-1}\}(T_{41} \quad T_{42} \quad T_{43} \quad T_{44})B\begin{bmatrix} \hat{y}_t^* \\ \hat{v}_t \end{bmatrix}$$

$$- T_{44}^{-1}(\Lambda_4 - I)^{-1}(T_{41} \quad T_{42} \quad T_{43} \quad T_{44})B\begin{bmatrix} y_t^* \\ v_t \end{bmatrix}$$

$$- T_{44}^{-1}\Lambda_4^{-1} \sum_{j=0}^{\infty} \Lambda_4^{-j}(T_{41} \quad T_{42} \quad T_{43} \quad T_{44})B\begin{bmatrix} 0 \\ \hat{v}_{t+j}^e \end{bmatrix} \quad (11.6)$$

The first term in (11.6) shows the effects of the history of the model on the jumping variables. The feedback nature of the control rules mean that historical values of y and u, as well as the values of x, influence the jumping variables. We then see the effects of the three types of disturbances in the exogenous variables, trends, levels and one-off deviations from the trend line. There are assumed to be no one-off disturbances to the target variables.

11.2.3 Solution of the controlled non-linear model

We use the above expression to calculate the effects of expectational disturbances on the non-linear model, as described in Chapter 7. The basic method is as set out there and in section 10.7. The main point to note is that we cannot identify fundamental trajectories for the exogenous variables with respect to which expectations are to be measured, i.e.

we cannot identify v_0, $\hat{v}_0$ and $\bar{v}_{0+j}$ exactly. The consequence of this is that we have to measure shifts in trends and in levels relative to the first period of the simulation so as to work out the change in the deviation from base from one period to the next. This, together with any changes in the base values implied by the fundamental trajectories of the jumping variables (section 7.4), allows us to calculate the change in each jumping variable from one period to the next. But it does not locate the appropriate starting values for the jumping variables. We do this using terminal conditions as discussed in sections 7.6 and 10.7.3.

We also note here that the above solution is the solution to the auxiliary equation of the full linear difference equation which represents the model. This equation could hold true round any suitable particular integral. For the reasons given in section 7.3.2, we think it appropriate to treat the target trajectories as influencing the particular integral and not the solution to the auxiliary equation. This has the implication that the target paths do not enter into our calculation of the appropriate jumps.

11.3 POLICY DESIGN

The success of a particular economic policy is often assessed by means of a quadratic loss function. This loss function tends to penalize extreme values of, or rapid changes in, policy targets and/or policy instruments. It can be used simply in order to provide statistics which summarize the degree to which policy targets have been met. We do that in Chapters 6 and 9.

However, loss functions are often used formally to calculate optimal policies which minimize the value of the loss function. These policies are called optimal despite the fact that the arguments of a loss function may be included solely for technical reasons; there is usually no obvious connection between the quadratic loss functions used in such exercises and any normal welfare function.

Three issues are involved in this procedure, no matter how expectations may be formed. The first issue is a practical point. The trajectory produced by constrained optimization, y_t, may be a long way from the target trajectory, y_t^*. This has often been regarded as undesirable, and Rustem *et al.* (1979) suggest an iterative technique for 'tuning' the penalty matrices, Q and R, so that the optimal solution trajectories are reasonably close to the target path. These results may look very satisfactory, but they are no longer the outcome of any genuine process of constrained optimization.

A second, related, problem arises. In order to produce any sort of plausible solution it is often necessary to include a surprisingly wide range of variables in the objective function. The use of policy instruments will be penalized, although it is not clear why a variable like the interest rate *per se* should be penalized, since it is hard to imagine it entering directly into the utility function of a representative agent. More generally, it is often difficult to relate the sort of cost function which is actually used to any sort of plausible social welfare function. Practitioners of this approach often state openly that certain variables are included in loss functions purely for technical reasons, inducing results that are 'acceptable'.[2]

The third issue is of great concern. The control rules which give the 'optimal' trajectory may produce solutions with poor dynamic performance. In an extreme case, with strong discounting or a short horizon, the controlled model may be dynamically unstable. This means that the control rules could not be sustained. To obtain a controlled system with robust operating characteristics, Doyle and Stein (1981) suggest the use of the penalty matrices as instruments which are determined during the design procedure. In this case too, penalty matrices do not embody any economic or political judgement, and the solution is not optimal in any genuine sense.

A fourth problem arises because minimization of a loss function over a finite time-horizon produces a feedback policy with an order equal to the order of the whole economic model. Such a policy rule will inevitably be highly complicated.

In view of these four problems with 'optimal' control techniques, we choose to design policy rules that are simple rather than optimal and that have good dynamic properties. Feedback rules can be selected which both give satisfactory dynamics to the controlled economy and at the same time ensure that the desired values of the target variables are eventually met. These rules do not have to be of high order. Having a parsimonious structure, these rules can be easily administered by the authorities. The loss function is then used as an *ex post* measure to compare alternative selections of desired trajectories, or the operation of alternative policy regimes.

Notice that, assessed by a quadratic loss function, simple feedback rules perform less well than do optimal rules designed to minimise that loss function. But this apparent argument in favour of optimal rules is in fact illusory. Uncertainty, either parametric or with regard to exogenous variables, may mean that it is no longer true that optimal rules will outperform simple rules, even when performance is measured by the loss function.[3]

For example Christodoulakis and Levine (1987) juxtaposed simple rules for fiscal and monetary policy, relying only on feedback on output and prices, against the full optimal structure designed with regard to the same welfare objectives. They found that the difference, as measured by the different loss functions, between the simple rule and optimal control outcomes was much reduced by unforeseen changes in the economic environment. Indeed, in some cases the simple rule produced a better result than the optimal rule, as indicated by the very loss function used in the design of the optimal rule.

This outcome is in fact quite likely to occur in practice because optimal rules tend to exploit fine details of the model being controlled. This can lead to large and undesirable movements if the characteristics of the economy change. Simple rules normally avoid this problem.

Both optimal control and our alternative simple rules can be applied straightforwardly to the traditional case where expectations are adaptive, since the policy structure is simply 'superimposed' on the dynamics of the model. However, when expectations are assumed model-consistent, there are two further and related problems for the optimal control methodology. These concern the credibility and intelligibility of the policy regime that is announced by the authorities. For policies to work as intended with consistent expectations they must be believed by the private sector. To this end, the government (i) must convince the economic agents that they will in fact be pursued and (ii) must ensure that they can be understood.

The first problem arises, because there is always a temptation for a policy-maker to create an expectation that he will behave in a certain way and then do something different. For the manipulation of expectations about the future value of each policy variable then offers an instrument over and above the actual value to which the authorities set that policy instrument, at least if the current values of economic variables depend partly on the expected future values of the policy instruments. If the government is constrained to keep its word it has less room for manoeuvre than if it feels able to ignore previous promises.[4] The second problem arises because, as noted above, policy rules could be highly complex. This could be a source of confusion to the private sector.

In what follows we briefly examine the credibility issue, and we also argue that simple policy structures might be preferred to complicated optimal alternatives, not only for the reasons discussed above, but also on grounds of administrability and comprehensibility.

11.3.1 Credibility

The minimization of a loss function with the assumption of consistent expectations with a model such as (10.30) is now commonplace in the literature; see, for example, Driffill (1982) for deterministic models, and Levine and Currie (1987) for systems with stochastic disturbances. The optimal rule is time-inconsistent in the sense that the government might have an incentive to re-optimize the loss function in each period (see Miller and Salmon, 1985). When the private sector is aware of the incentive to abandon the announced policy rule, it may well not believe the announcement in the first place. The authorities have to precommit themselves to keep to the time-inconsistent policies if they wish to ensure that the private sector reacts as they would hope. The time-inconsistent rules operate only with the assumption that the private sector believes that the government means to follow specific policy prescriptions despite the motivation it has to renege on them. Kydland and Prescott (1977) suggested that economic policy should not be used to optimize a specific welfare function, but rather should adopt fixed rules that can be correctly perceived by the private sector.

Recent economic literature is now in a position to offer solutions which are optimal and time-consistent. These policies are often called 'non-reputational'. The criticism of Kydland and Prescott does not, as they thought it did, have to lead to the rejection of active policy intervention; see, for example, Holly and Zarrop (1983), Buiter (1984) and Levine and Smith (1987) for methods of applying Bellman's optimality principle to ensure time-consistency. However, the requirement that policy should be easily understood and monitored by the private sector does remain true.

In a survey on time-inconsistency Holly and Levine (1987) point out that a government may keep to its policies even when they are time-inconsistent, because the government may well need to use its policy rules on future occasions. The argument runs as follows. Optimal time-consistent policies are derived by imposing on the optimizing process the constraint that there is never any incentive to renege. Such a constraint may make the resulting policies very suboptimal, in the sense that instrument movements tend to be larger and the damping of disturbances tends to be less efficient.[5,6] In such circumstances what Barro and Gordon (1983) describe as the 'temptation' for the government to break its promises, is much reduced.

If the government uses some simple rather than optimal rules to control the economy, then it is true that it could gain, on a one-off basis, by breaking its policy rule. But the loss of credibility in doing this means that the government will be in a worse position to take steps to damp any future disturbance. Even though the policies are not optimal, the argument about why the government might not wish to renege on them is the same as in the previous paragraph.

This argument has been used by many to justify the design of time-inconsistent policies when carrying out optimal control exercises (see Levine and Currie, 1987). We extend this argument to our analysis of simple economic policies even though our policy rules include integral terms. These imply a commitment to correct for past errors and Whiteman (1986) implies that such rules are an obstacle to credibility for this reason. But we assume that our structure is credible for the above reasons. Throughout this book we assume that the private sector believes that the policies will in fact be carried out.

11.3.2 Intelligibility

The issue of policy intelligibility is very straightforward. A policy rule must be believed in order to have the desired effect on people's expectations. In order to be believed it must first be understood – this is much more likely if the control structure is simple. The policy rules which result from an optimal control exercise are likely to be highly complicated. This is an argument against the use of optimal control as a technique of policy design.

11.4 THE DESIGN OF SIMPLE RULES

As already stated, our aim has been to find simple policy rules which can be used to steer Money GDP and national wealth towards their target values. As we made clear in Chapter 6 we have done this by using a target real exchange rate as a guide to short-term monetary policy. But taking this as given, the question arises as to the criteria which we have used to choose the coefficients of our policy rules.

First of all we have been keen to avoid rapid movements for our policy instruments. This has meant we have been forced to rely solely on proportional and integral components for our policy rules. Differential terms lead to excessive volatility.[7] Being restricted to proportional and integral terms, we then looked for coefficients in the policy rules which led to satisfactory behaviour in response to step changes in our target variables (Money GDP and national wealth). Vines, Maciejowski and Meade (1983) demonstrated that policy rules which deliver satisfactory step changes will also be successful at damping the effects of other types of disturbances – a basic result in control theory. This is the justification we offer for designing policies on the basis of responses to step changes in targets.

Starting points for the proportional elements of the policy rules can be found by studying the pattern of short-term comparative advantage. For reasons discussed extensively in Chapters 1 to 4 and Chapter 6, one would expect this to be a good guide to the instrument-target emphasis which our rules should have. We have found this to be the case: it guides the relative strength of the proportional components of the policy rules which link our policy instruments to our policy targets. The absolute strength of the proportional components was restricted by the need to avoid, on the one hand, too slow a response, and on the other hand, too rapid a response in reacting to divergences of each policy instrument from its desired value. Too slow a response means that, for long periods of time, the targets will diverge from their desired values. Too rapid a response leads to overshooting of targets, rapid movement in the instruments and cyclical convergence of the economy. We found in practice that we were able to remove disturbances to Money GDP reasonably rapidly, but that the response of wealth was inevitably slow. For the reasons given in Chapter 1, this did not concern us unduly.

These three considerations:

- relative strength of response of instruments to desired changes in policy targets,
- desired speed of suppression of disturbances in targets,
- the avoidance of excessive instrument movement,

were a sufficient starting point to guide the choice of all four proportional components linking Money GDP and national wealth to the tax rate and to the exchange rate intermediate target. These criteria gave us initial reference points from which to experiment.

Starting points for the integral components of policy rules were found from the pattern of long-term comparative advantage. Again, for the reasons discussed in Chapters 1 to 4 and 6, one would expect this to be some guide to the integral components of our policy rules, and we have found that to be the case. It is a basic result in control theory (see Vines, Maciejowski and Meade, 1983, Part IV, and Westaway, 1985) that, in order to avoid instability, the size of the integral components of control rules should be much smaller than the size of the proportional components. Again, this initial guidance as to both instrument-target emphasis and required absolute size provided the starting point for further experimentation.

We next tried to find a rule for the interest rate that achieved acceptable variations of the exchange rate about the intermediate target trajectory.

The question then arises of 'tuning' the policy rules. We have done this visually, studying the step responses and adjusting the coefficients of the rules so as to reduce the quadratic deviations of the target variables from their desired paths, and with the aim of avoiding excessive cyclical behaviour.[8] In this process we have paid more attention to achieving a good performance on the models with model-consistent expectations than on the models with adaptive expectations. This is reflected in the quadratic losses which we tabulate in Chapters 8 and 9. But we have also ensured that our rules will work in the adaptive expectations case by checking to ensure that the linear model is stable in the cases of adaptive expectations as well as being saddlepath stable with model-consistent expectations. We have also, as noted in section 6.8, tolerated a 'sub-optimal' performance with reformed wages so as to avoid excessive use of the target real exchange rate in damping inflationary bursts.

The rules which we have produced are 'illustrative' rather than in any sense optimal. But the basic criterion which we have used has been an informal minimization of the quadratic losses in the step responses shown in Figures 6.4–6.11, subject to the requirements that the control instruments should be well behaved in the reruns of history and that, with reformed wages, the use of monetary policy to control inflation should be restricted.

It would be desirable that this procedure should be formalized. Blake (1988) sets out the results of some preliminary steps in this direction, and it should be noted that he reports that a formal procedure does not reduce the value of the loss function much below what can typically be achieved by the steps set out above. Christodoulakis, Gaines and Levine (1989) also provide guidance for further progress in this area.

11.5 CONCLUDING REMARKS

This chapter has described the methodology behind our use of simple feedback control rules. We have produced rules which are 'representative' rather than meeting any clear 'optimum' criterion. But we see a number of points justifying our approach as an alternative to conventional optimization. First,. we can test our rules to ensure that they are dynamically stable. This is not possible if optimal control is carried out on the non-linear model. Secondly, the rules we produce are simple feedback rules of a type that are easily understood and which one could easily see imposed in practice. For this reason they are more plausible than are optimal rules. Finally, they are clearly, if informally, defined with reference to step changes in targets, instead of relying on a welfare function which has no real economic meaning.

The procedure which we have adopted is capable of further development and formalization. Blake (1988) has set out some of the initial steps in developing this approach into a precise technical method.

Part IV
Conclusion

Chapter Twelve

Summary of results and conclusions

12.1 NEW KEYNESIAN POLICY

This book has provided a coherent structure for the analysis of economic policy.

12.1.1 Money GDP

We have not proposed the conventional Keynesian approach, that either monetary or fiscal policy should be used with the aim of maintaining a high level of employment and real output. Instead, in our New Keynesian framework, it is the task of these policies to promote steady growth in the level of total money expenditure. The supply side of the economy, and in particular the labour market structure, then determines how this nominal expenditure is split between output on the one hand and wages and prices on the other.

12.1.2 National wealth

But we have argued that that financial policy ought also to ensure that an adequate proportion of the nation's output is devoted to capital accumulation or, in other words, to ensure that adequate national saving takes place. This is necessary so as to ensure that the financial authorities do not attempt to 'buy off' inflationary wage demands by means of lax fiscal and tight monetary policy, at the expense of future living standards. It may also be important for offsetting the effects of any private sector 'spending spree'.

12.1.3 Two policy instruments

We have noted that, with two targets for financial policy (Money GDP and national wealth), two instruments are required (taxes and the interest rate). Much of this book has concerned the appropriate emphasis which ought to be placed on one or other policy instrument in the pursuit of each of the policy targets.

12.1.4 Instrument-target emphasis

The appropriate instrument-target emphasis is shown to depend on the underlying structure of the economy, and this is, in turn, crucially dependent on the structure of the labour market as summarized by the aggregate wage equation. If wages are strongly indexed to prices it is almost certain that prompt control of Money GDP and therefore of inflation can only be achieved by emphasizing the use of monetary policy in the control of inflation. Some perverse (or cost-push) short-run use of fiscal policy may also be helpful. Even if wages are not indexed to prices, we find that good control of Money GDP still requires considerable reliance on monetary policy.

12.1.5 A target real exchange rate

We have argued that monetary policy can include the use of a target exchange rate. This can help to protect the economy from speculative bubbles and other disturbances in the foreign-exchange market. We have shown carefully how such an exchange-rate intermediate target could work. In particular, we have noted that this target should not be fixed, either in nominal or in real terms, for any length of time, but should itself evolve so as to help ensure that the main targets of financial policy (Money GDP and national wealth) are met. We have also shown in a manner which does not seem to depend crucially on any particular assumption about the formation of expectations, how the interest rate can be used to steer the exchange rate towards its intermediate target.

12.2   THEORETICAL ARGUMENTS

The theoretical underpinning of our proposals was set out in Part I. Chapter 1 explained the overall structure of the proposals and the subsequent chapters explored detailed aspects of them. Chapter 2 set out a simple static model, in order to demonstrate formally how the emphasis on particular instruments required in order to achieve particular policy targets is not a matter of choice. It is determined by the structure of the underlying model, and is in particular dependent on the degree of indexation in the wage equation. The same question was explored in a dynamic model in Chapter 3. We also looked there at the role of the exchange rate as an intermediate policy target. Chapter 4 showed how the dynamics of wealth accumulation can be a source of instability. It set out the implications for economic policy of this particular problem.

12.3   EMPIRICAL ANALYSIS

Part II of the study contains a thorough empirical investigation of our proposals for the United Kingdom, although we are confident that the results would be similar for any small open economy.

12.3.1   A coherent econometric model

For the purposes of our investigation we developed our own econometric model from Version 7 of the NIESR model. Our model incorporated a number of important features absent from the other econometric models of the United Kingdom. In particular it paid proper attention to stock-flow effects and it treated expectations with a coherence lacking in other econometric models of the United Kingdom. The structure which it adopted may perhaps be of interest outside the confines of this study.

12.3.2   Policy rules

Chapter 6 presented the actual policy rules which we have designed for this model. The two sets of policy rules presented there show how, in this particular model, fiscal and monetary policy can be combined in the pursuit of targets for Money GDP and national wealth, in the presence of an exchange-rate intermediate target. These rules were presented in sections 6.7 and 6.8. With wages fully indexed to prices, we found a rule in which the real exchange rate intermediate target exercises the major influence over inflation and the tax rate exercises the major influence over national wealth. Importantly, however, we found that good control could only be obtained, within the confines of a simple rule structure, if both instruments (monetary policy through the medium of a target real exchange rate and fiscal policy) were assigned to the control of both targets. With a reform of wage bargaining, which removed the indexation of wages to prices, we found that much more weight should be given to fiscal policy in the control of inflation. But it was still necessary to assign both instruments to both targets. The chapter showed in a series of experiments how these rules were capable of steering the policy target variables towards their desired values. And it also showed that these rules can satisfactorily remove the influence on the economy of a series of exogenous shocks. A fundamental implication of this chapter was that, with either indexed or unindexed wages, a system of fixed exchange rates, set out either in real or in nominal terms, was likely to perform badly.

12.3.3 Reruns of history

Chapters 7 to 9 presented the results of applying these rules to the UK economy. Counterfactual reruns of history were described, so as to show how our approach to policy might work in practice. In Chapter 7 we described the solution we adopted to the difficult problem of counterfactual simulation of an economy with model-consistent expectations.

12.3.4 The unreformed economy

In Chapter 8 we described the results of reruns of history with the wage equation as it is believed to be in practice. We identified the following points as summarizing the effects of the simulation with model-consistent expectations.

  i) Our policy rules were used to control inflation and to guide national wealth towards a target path. Our policy targets were more stringent than those which the economy had followed during the historical period of our simulation: we imposed more severe control of inflation, and we required that national wealth should grow faster than it did historically. Both objectives were broadly achieved by the end of the simulation.

ii) We could not do anything about unemployment (and indeed a price for higher saving and lower inflation was slightly higher unemployment), but we did not claim, and do not believe, that financial policy, on its own, could have a lasting effect on unemployment. In order to do better here, some sort of supply-side reform is needed.

iii) The exchange rate was kept reasonably close to its target value, but this target value needed to be manipulated substantially in order to control inflation. The policy rules were certainly outside the spirit of Williamson's (1985) target-zone proposal, but it is also worth noting that, for the period 1981–9, they conformed to the letter of Williamson's proposal. Our rules delivered a surprising degree of real exchange-rate stability despite the use they made of monetary policy in fighting inflation. This, perhaps, implies that almost any sensible form of exchange-rate targeting will improve on history.

iv) The policy rules required substantial fluctuations in both the tax rate and the exchange rate target (and indeed our cost-push use of the tax rate was curtailed by the requirement that the tax rate had to remain positive throughout the simulation). These fluctuations were very different from what was observed historically and also very different from what we would expect to observe when simulating an economy with a reformed labour market.

The conclusions we found were broadly similar with adaptive expectations, although the long-term movement in the real exchange rate appeared to be greater.

12.3.5 The reformed wage economy

Chapter 9 showed the results of the same exercise, but on the assumption that wage reform had removed all indexation of wages to prices, and had established a natural rate of unemployment of 6 per cent. We summarized the main conclusions with model-consistent expectations as;

i) The reform of the labour market meant that a better than historical out-turn for unemployment could be delivered. Unemployment varied between 2 per cent and 8 per cent of the labour force, compared with 3.5 per cent and 16 per cent with unreformed wages. The 'price' for this lower unemployment was a lower share in labour income in the national product.

ii) The economy was able to deliver 50 per cent more public consumption and investment than without wage reform. This was made available on account of increased output arising from a combination of lower unemployment and economies of scale.

iii) Tax rates were considerably higher than in our unreformed economy. The final VAT rate was 30 per cent as compared with 21 per cent there. But with a much higher level of public spending, there was plenty of scope for having lower taxes and a lower, but still generous, provision of public goods and services.

iv) Inflation control still required the use of monetary as well as fiscal policy. This did have the implication that the real exchange rate would be allowed to rise in order to damp an inflationary burst, but the effect was much weaker than in the cost-push economy.

v) It proved possible to deliver a much higher terminal value of wealth than was possible in the cost-push economy. The reason for this was that real income was higher and that control of wealth was easier with wage reform. Also the high tax rates, which were caused by the need to control Money GDP, helped with the tracking of wealth.

vi) The real exchange rate was kept within 10 per cent of its target for most of the period, but our policy rules were still outside the spirit of Williamson's target-zone proposal. We thus think it likely that a stable target real exchange rate would be incompatible with any policy which allowed prompt control of inflation (since this 'reformed wage' scenario is the most optimistic one could imagine on this score). Nevertheless it is also the case that our policy rules kept the real exchange rate within a band 20 per cent wide for nearly a decade.

With adaptive expectations we found that Money GDP tended to undershoot. This meant that taxes were held down and, as a result, the control of wealth was worse. But these differences are of minor importance.

12.3.6   Major conclusions of our empirical work

We can identify the following major conclusions from our empirical work:

i) With the production function as it is in our model, labour market reform is necessary for a sustained reduction in unemployment.

ii) The economy can be regulated perfectly satisfactorily, over a long and difficult period, by means of simple feedback policy rules.

iii) The structure of suitable feedback rules depends on the structure of the wage equation.

iv) The exchange rate can be treated as an intermediate target within the overall framework of economic policy.

v) Policy instruments must be cross-linked for satisfactory control of the economy. This implies that the real exchange-rate target must be flexible. Policy rules relying on fixed target exchange rates, nominal or real, are unlikely to be very successful.

vi) The way in which expectations are formed does not have a major effect on the stability, and therefore feasibility, of policy rules, but it does affect their impact on the economy.

vii) Our model implies that a lower level of unemployment will be associated with a lower share of wages and a higher share of profits in the economy. This identifies one of the major difficulties which will have to be faced if the United Kingdom is to return permanently to full employment.

viii) Private saving is not adequate to allow wealth to grow in line with medium- to long-term output. A structural budget surplus appears to be necessary. This highlights the danger of adopting a budgetary target rather than a wealth target.

12.4   METHODOLOGY

Part III of the book was devoted to explaining the methodology which we adopted for policy design. It depended on the use of a linear representation of our model. Chapter 10 explained how that linearization was obtained and how it could be used in order to solve an uncontrolled economic model with model-consistent expectations. In Chapter 11 we extended this new result to a linear model of a controlled economy, and we discussed the techniques which we used in order to design our representative policy rules. These were principally to rely on an informal optimization of the ability of our model to deliver step changes in the target variables, although we also paid attention to a number of other issues.

12.5   FUTURE WORK

This book points the way for further research in a number of important directions. Working still at the level of a single small open economy, it would be desirable to know whether our results about assignment are sensitive to the structure of the production function and the nature of competition in the goods market.[1] Secondly, it would be highly desirable to investigate the extent to which our analysis, using wealth targets and set out in terms of comparative advantage, also proves helpful in a multilateral framework. James Meade, in a preliminary version of Meade and Vines (1988), has provided some preliminary results and set out a basis for extending this work. Andrew Blake and Martin Weale hope to extend this study and to investigate the problems of international policy co-ordination using the approach set out here. Thirdly, it is highly desirable that our approach to policy design, relying on the tuning of step changes rather than on the conventional methods of optimal control, should be developed further. We note that Blake (1988) has already made some developments in this area.

1 A NEW KEYNESIAN FRAMEWORK FOR MACROECONOMIC POLICY

[1] We have excluded the publicly owned capital stock from this target, partly for statistical convenience, but with no great confidence that it is necessarily the best thing to do.

[2] Such a potential instability is analysed by Cagan (1956), and is explored by us in Chapter 3.

[3] We are in no way abashed by the silly criticism that this is 'merely an as-if exercise'. Of course it is. Indeed the whole of our work or anyone else's work on policy design consists of as-iffery. We attempt to see how the experience of the years 1975–89 might have been different if different policy strategies had been adopted. Why should we not also attempt to see how the experience would have been different if different wage arrangements had been adopted? All analyses of alternative policies and institutions are merely as-if exercises.

[4] One form of proposals for a Target Zone arrangement is discussed at length by Edison, Miller and Williamson (1987). A rule for the use of the rate of interest to keep the rate of exchange within a Target Zone might take the form of $\Delta R = -r_e([E - E^*]/\bar{E})^n$ where E^* is the central value of the exchange rate within the Target Zone, $\bar{E}$ is half the range of the Target Zone, and n is an odd integer >1 (an odd number being needed to preserve the correct sign). Thus the rate of interest is reduced at a speed which increases as the actual exchange rate appreciates beyond its Central Target Value, E^*. The higher the power n, the more restricted is the action of monetary policy as long as E remains within its Target Zone, but the more ferocious the monetary policy becomes if the exchange rate strays outside the Target Zone. Edison-Miller-Williamson use a value $n = 3$.

[5] Official intervention in the foreign exchange market (i.e. by the sale or purchase of foreign exchange from the central bank's official foreign exchange reserves) may be used as a supplementary tool to monetary policy for the management of the exchange rate. But foreign exchange reserves are not unlimited and for this reason, if for no other, the rate of interest must be regarded as the basic instrument for keeping the exchange rate on or near its target level.

[6] This is not to say that we regard the MTFS as a close substitute for our strategy. In particular we see three faults in the use of a PSBR target rather than our wealth target. First, it allows the target to be achieved by crediting the proceeds of denationalization and taxes on exhaustible resources, rather than by a genuine adjustment in national saving. Secondly it leaves the level of national wealth as a residual, rather than as the conscious outcome of any policy decision. And thirdly, as we demonstrate in Chapter 4, if pursued rigidly, its stability is dependent on the way in which expectations are formed.

[7] We do not propose to carry ease of understanding to the extent of assigning each

instrument of policy (S and R) exclusively to only one target (Z or N), i.e. to rule that fiscal policy should be planned solely to control Z and monetary policy (through E) solely to control N, or *vice versa*. We design rules for appropriate combinations of fiscal and monetary policy to cope with whatever combination of simultaneous adjustments is desired to GDP and national wealth, though, as appears in later chapters of this book, important questions arise as to which policy instrument should be the more emphasized in the control of which policy objective.

[8] Crockett and Goldstein (1987) give an exactly opposite view, arguing that the need for exchange-rate targets to be internationally compatible will persuade policy-makers to focus on the short-term consistency of economic policy. Their argument, then, sees target zones as part of a global economic system which requires centralized economic management.

2   THE LINKAGES BETWEEN FINANCIAL WEAPONS AND FINANCIAL TARGETS: A COMPARATIVE STATIC ANALYSIS

[1] In what follows the variables which are barred (such as $\bar{I}$) are assumed to remain constant throughout.

[2] Equations (2.3), (2.6) and (2.7a) assume that all taxation takes the form of a direct proportionate tax on all incomes. It would be simple to represent taxation as a single rate of indirect tax on all purchases by replacing $(1 - S)$ with $1/(1 + S')$ where S' was the equivalent rate of indirect tax. In this case in (2.7a), while P would measure the factor-cost price of output, $P(1 + S')$ would measure the market-price of output, i.e. the cost of living.

[3] In passing one may note a very important dynamic property implied by the distinction between these two 'cost-push' elements. The upward cost-push effects on money costs and prices due to a high rate of tax will be greater during the process of raising the tax than it will be subsequently when the rate of tax is stabilized at the higher level and the β_5-effect will have fallen to zero. This difference becomes important in Chapter 3.

[4] From the values for σ_p, σ_i, and σ_b in (2.11) it can be shown that $|\omega| = |\sigma_p//\sigma_i| = (1 - x_1[1 - S])(1 - \beta_7/\beta_6\mu x_1 Y)/\nu$ and $|\omega| = \sigma_p/\sigma_b = Sx_1(1 - \beta_7/\beta_6\mu x_1 Y)/(1 - x_1 - \nu)$.

[5] The need for a correct instrument-target emphasis is much more obvious in the case of a comparison between diagrams (a) and (b) of Figure 2.2 where the equilibrium points are far apart with a change of sign than in the case of diagrams (c) and (d) where the equilibrium points are close together without any change of signs. Nevertheless correct instrument-target emphasis remains important as may be suggested by the following parable in which we examine the case of what may be called 100% instrument-target emphasis with each control instrument being assigned completely to the control of one objective without any cross linkage to the other objective together with a dynamic process of interplay between the two controllers. Suppose the Bank of England operates R to control inflation and the Treasury operates S to control investment, each authority operating without thought about the repercussion of its action on the problem facing the other authority. The Bank of England is instructed to change $\hat{P}$ by an amount $(\delta\hat{P})^*$ and the Treasury to keep I unchanged. In terms of the parameters of matrix (2.10) this leads to the following stages of adjustment:

Stages: 1   2   3   4

$$\delta R = \frac{(\delta\hat{P})^*}{p_r} \to \delta I = (\delta\hat{P})^* \frac{i_r}{p_r} \to \delta S = -(\delta\hat{P})^* \frac{i_r}{p_r i_s} \to \delta\hat{P} = -(\delta P)^* \frac{p_s}{p_r} \cdot \frac{i_r}{i_s}$$

The Bank alters R as in stage 1 in order to change $\hat{P}$ by $(\delta\hat{P})^*$. This causes I to change as in stage 2. The Treasury responds as in stage 3 in order to offset the change of I of stage 2. In stage 4 the change of S of stage 3 gives rise to the need for secondary action by the Bank of

England in order to offset a secondary change in $\hat{P}$ which in absolute size is $|\sigma_p/\sigma_i|$ times the desired change in $(\delta P)^*$. The process will converge if $|\sigma_p/\sigma_i| < 1$ and will explode if $|\sigma_p/\sigma_i| > 1$. Thus the control of $\hat{P}$ should be assigned to the Bank of England if $|\sigma_p/\sigma_i| < 1$; and by a similar analysis it can be seen that it should be assigned to the Treasury if $|\sigma_p/\sigma_i| > 1$. The final adjustment would, of course, be achieved more directly and smoothly if suitable cross linkages were employed which implied that each authority was concerned also with what was the primary objective of the other authority; but it would still be essential to get the instrument-target emphasis correct in the use of each instrument of control. We do not advocate the use of 100% instrument-target emphasis for actual policy design nor do we consider that any dynamic process of the simple kind described in this parable is likely to occur in the real world. These features are introduced only to provide an intuitive understanding of the importance of paying regard to the correct instrument-target emphases in cases of the kind described in diagrams (c) and (d) of Figure 2.2.

[6] Except in the extreme case in which $\beta_7 = 0$ in which case the Y- and $\hat{P}$-contours have the same slope.

[7] From (2.37) we can obtain $p_s = -\beta_6 \varkappa_1(\bar{Y} - [\iota + \theta]R)\mu^2 + \beta_7(1 - \psi\eta\mu)$ where $\bar{Y} - (\iota + \theta)R > 0$ is the multiplicand. It follows that $\delta p_s/\delta\mu < 0$. Since μ will $\to \infty$ as S is decreased without limit, there must in the open economy as in the closed economy be a limit to the possibility of reducing $\hat{P}$ by reducing S. The demand-pull effect will ultimately be dominant in the open economy as it was shown to be in the closed economy in the discussion of equations (2.15) to (2.19).

[8] This is not impossible if the volume of the country's exports and the elasticity of the foreign demand for them are sufficiently small.

[9] It is, of course, possible in an international setting for the various countries to co-operate on choice of national financial targets which they will seek to attain. Such agreements could very materially affect their emphases on monetary and fiscal policies for the control of inflation and wealth.

3 THE DYNAMICS OF PRICE STABILIZATION

[1] Since the analytic model does not cumulate stocks we are obliged to limit ourselves to a target expressed in terms of the flow of investment.

[2] Notice that setting the real interest-rate and real exchange-rate terms in equation (3.5) equal to ι' and ε' respectively implies that, in equation (3.8), (i) we assume that the interest rate has no effect on domestic consumption and (ii) we assume that the 'impact' effect of the real exchange rate on aggregate demand is the same as that on the trade balance.

[3] Notice the absence of any time trend in this equation. If there were a time trend in l^s in the labour supply equation – due to the growth in workers' aspirations – and a time trend in labour productivity, then prices would rise or fall without limit unless the effects of these terms were brought into equality. One would then need to study the process by which that happened, but modelling that would introduce an extra dynamic equation into our system. We abstract from all of this.

[4] The position can be understood in the following way. Suppose S to be raised with R and a held constant. The rise in S would lead to a decrease in Y which in turn would cause (i) a decrease in I because of the accelerator effect and (ii) a rise in $(X - M)$ because of the reduced demand for imports. We are assuming that effect (ii) outweighs effect (i), so that there is a net increase in $J = I + X - M$. With R constant it would be necessary to appreciate in order to reduce the increase in $(X - M)$ to the extent necessary to keep $I + (X - M)$ constant. This is the end of the story as far as Figure 3.1 is concerned; for J to remain constant when S rises, there must also be a rise in a. There would of course remain some net increase in $X - M$ sufficient to offset the accelerator decrease in I. This increase in the current account balance needs to be financed. With the perfect unlagged substitutability between home and foreign assets of Chapter 3, this flow of capital funds needs no change in

R. But in the short-period model of Chapter 2 in equation (2.29) it is assumed that the increased outflow of capital funds would need a reduction in the rate of interest. If the change in the rate of interest had no effect on *I*, that would be the end of the Chapter 2 story. If *J* is to be kept constant, the rise in *S* would require the same rise in Chapter 2 as it does in Chapter 3, the only difference being that this must be associated with a constant rate of interest in Chapter 3 and a lower rate of interest in Chapter 2. But in so far as the reduction in *R* leads to an increase in *I*, there will be a need for a smaller increase in $(X - M)$ in order to keep *J* constant, and this will require a higher value of *a* to be associated with a given rise in *S* in Chapter 2 than in Chapter 3. Thus if it were drawn in both cases in the $S-a$ plane, the *j* curve would slope upwards in both cases, but rather more steeply upwards in Chapter 2 than in Figure 3.1.

[5] This corresponds to the problem raised in Chapter 2, relating to policies designed to reduce the rate of price inflation without changing the level of the investment target.

[6] In our empirical work $a \rightarrow a_\infty$ only as a result of 'integral control' in the policy feedback rules rather than as a result of setting *a* directly with reference to a_∞. But to add integral control would add another differential equation to our analytical model, which would not be helpful.

[7] In our empirical work $S \rightarrow S_\infty$ only as a result of integral control. See note 6.

[8] This is possible because the evolution of investment does not affect the dynamics of our system, given that stock effects are neglected and given our simplifying assumption that the level of investment does not feed back in to the determination of $\dot{p}$ or *a*. It is not possible in our empirical work.

[9] This is the result identified by Fischer (1988) – that 100 per cent accommodation of inflation by the real exchange rate ($k_1 = 0$) leads to price indeterminacy, but that 99 per cent accommodation does not.

[10] This is true however large the short-run cost-push effect β_3 of a tax increase.

[11] i.e. regimes in which both instruments are used to look after both targets.

[12] Proportional components relate the change in a policy instrument proportional to the change of the deviation of a target variable from its desired value. Integral components relate the change in a policy instrument to the level of the deviation of a target variable from its desired level. And derivative components relate the change in an instrument to the second difference of the deviation of a target variable from its desired level.

[13] This contrasts with the analysis of Boughton (1988). In his case it is almost certain that monetary policy has a comparative advantage in dealing with inflation. This is because his second target is a current account target rather than an investment target. As a result the reduction in imports following an interest-rate rise work to cancel the fall in net exports arising from the resulting currency appreciation. This means that monetary policy may have almost no effect on the current account and almost certainly gives it a comparative advantage in dealing with inflation. Here this presumption is less strong.

4   WEALTH TARGETS, STOCK INSTABILITY AND MACROECONOMIC POLICY

[1] The most straightforward function is $U(C) = \log(C)$.

[2] Except that the stability of the economy might be greatly affected if the tax rate could increase to the point at which the post-tax real rate of return became negative.

[3] Ideally we would investigate the working of a target exchange rate which was infrequently adjusted, and see whether this could be used to exert a stabilizing influence. This in fact raises the whole question of policy design when different instruments can be adjusted with different frequencies. It is an issue which we regard as very important, but not one on which we have made much progress.

[4] With $U_0 = 0$ the reader can determine, by examination of (4.70), that there is one stable root and one zero root.

5   A STOCK-FLOW MODEL WITH MODEL-CONSISTENT OR REGRESSIVE EXPECTATIONS

[1] The current state of this art was discussed at a recent conference organized by the National Institute of Economic and Social Research (Britton, 1988). That conference produced an opportunity for reflecting on the progress which has been made since a similar meeting held ten years earlier (Posner, 1978). In 1978 much emphasis was placed on a comparison of 'multiplier properties', showing the response of economic models to isolated shocks to policy instruments and exogenous variables. In 1988 people focused on the simulation of endogenous policy responses (i.e. on policy regimes) and the way in which the effects of these are influenced by forward-looking expectations. These themes are at the heart of the exercises which we describe in the subsequent chapters.

[2] We had originally intended to study the sensitivity of our results to the degree of substitutability between home and foreign assets. But it became apparent that the issues raised by the nature of the wage equation were of much greater interest, and we did not in the end study the effects of changes in other parameters such as this substitution parameter.

[3] We treat durable goods as perfect substitutes for other types of asset, as determinants of consumption and for the purposes of studying the portfolio allocation between home and foreign assets. However, we do not concern ourselves with the fact that our consumption function may not ensure that the implicit yield on durable goods is brought into equality with that on other assets.

[4] The reason for this is that we leave public sector capital out of our wealth target in Chapters 6–9. Its inclusion here would then be an unnecessary complication.

[5] The net asset position of the government is therefore negative, but the amount of negative interest-bearing assets which it owns is reduced by the extent to which it can issue non-interest-bearing debt (the monetary base). This explains why the government's interest-bearing net asset position is shown as $HAG + D$.

[6] In many econometric models (including version 7 of the NIESR model), property income flows are econometrically estimated. But that can end up with a violation of the implied logic of the balance sheet identities.

[7] The minus signs in this equation are present because an increased budget deficit reduces the government's net property income.

[8] The 'replacement cost' of land is calculated by dividing the market value of land holdings by the end-1980 valuation ratio.

[9] Depending on the timing of each period, the arbitrage equation for Q could be interpreted as backward-looking in expectations of changes in the price of capital goods. However, we thought it best to avoid introducing a variable to represent the expected future price of capital goods. The problem would, in any case, disappear in continuous time.

[10] The corporation tax system explains, at least partly, why Q was often below 1. Also, the stock market was, from the perspective of longer-term history, very depressed during the period.

[11] A unique solution exists because it is calculated for a linear reduction of the model. It is of course possible that multiple paths with this property may exist in the non-linear model.

[12] In order to satisfy the Lucas critique fully, our model would need two features which we have, for reasons of simplicity, omitted. First, expected future rather than lagged stocks should enter the portfolio allocation equations. And secondly, the sensitivity of portfolio allocation to expected yield should depend on the variance of that excess yield.

[13] The effect would work in the opposite direction if the private sector were a foreign currency debtor. Such a situation can lead to a 'debt trap' (Christodoulakis, Meade and Weale, 1987).

[14] In Chapters 3 and 4 we used a specification in which the expected change in the nominal exchange rate took account of core-target inflation. There is no historical value for core-target inflation, since we do not know what sort of normal rate of inflation people had in mind. It is difficult therefore to adopt a specification which both allows single-equation residuals to be used as a source of noise, and takes account of core-target inflation in its

determination. We have given priority to the calculation of single-equation residuals to the exchange rate over an adjustment for core-target inflation.

[15] Or of course a tax change resulting from a known policy response to an unforeseen shock.

[16] The other unstable root in the consistent expectations model arose from the interaction with human capital. Such an effect is not present here.

[17] We are aware that more recent versions of the National Insitute model take account of the effect of expected future changes in output on stockbuilding.

[18] The conventional view that marginal Q is relevant need not hold. If investment consists substantially of setting up new firms then average Q will be relevant even though there may be increasing returns within each firm (Christodoulakis and Weale, 1987).

[19] In the extreme case of perfect capital mobility no steady state would exist unless the home real interest rate were the same as the foreign real interest rate (see equation (4.20c)).

[20] This is the opposite of the conclusion that some people draw from the assumption of rational or model-consistent expectations. The reason, of course, is that we have not made the implausible assumptions necessary for the labour market to clear instantaneously, see Chapter 1.

[21] The General Agreement on Trade and Tariffs authorizes the use of import restrictions in this case.

6 MACROECONOMIC POLICY RULES FOR ECONOMIC STABILIZATION

[1] In the notation of Chapter 3, the wage equation has $\alpha_2 = \nu$ and $\alpha_4 = 1 - \nu$.

[2] In order to hold the real exchange rate constant, the interest rate is adjusted to clear the foreign exchange market. With model-consistent expectations the valuation ratio, human capital and the consol rate are allowed to jump to clear instabilities in their trajectories. This does raise a problem of the interpretation of the trajectories in the model-consistent case. Nevertheless the dynamics of the wage-price loop, which these graphs illustrate, seem to be relatively insensitive to the initial jumps in these variables, provided that jumps which lead to clear instability are rejected. An incorrect jump in the valuation ratio turns out to be the most important source of such instability.

[3] The same wage equation is used in both of the cases of Figure 6.2, but other aspects of the models differ, of course.

[4] Ideally we would have embedded our interest-rate policy rule, which we present in section 6.7, into our model and then treated the target real exchange rate as our instrument of monetary policy. But this raised problems in finding the necessary stabilizing jumps in our non-linear model with model-consistent expectations. We therefore settled on using the actual real exchange rate as the instrument for the purpose of the calculation of comparative advantage.

[5] McKay (1987) has investigated ways in which timely estimates of Money GDP can be produced. We have assumed, in setting out our policy rules here, that his preliminary estimates of Money GDP are available at the end of each quarter and that similar preliminary estimates of national wealth exist.

[6] This argument has two parts. First it relies on the assumption that a 'correct' exchange rate with an 'inappropriate' interest rate is much less damaging to the the economy than an 'incorrect' interest rate with an 'appropriate' exchange rate. We are confident that this is true for a country such as the United Kingdom, although we do not necessarily claim that it is universally true. Secondly, it supposes that the effects of an incorrect exchange rate on Money GDP or wealth are lagged, and that collecting data on these variables takes time, so that setting the interest rate with respect only to those targets would not call forth immediate corrective action in response to an incorrect rate.

[7] In principle the frequency domain methods described by Maciejowski and Vines (1984) could be used to assess the robustness of our rules. But we have not yet succeeded in extending these techniques to models of the complexity required for our consistent expectations solution. See Chapter 11.

[8] This is a procedure which Blake (1988) goes some way to formalizing. We hope to build on his results. See Chapter 11.

[9] It would have been possible to produce stable rules which did not conform to the pattern of comparative advantage. In fact we do this for a particular reason in regulating the reformed wage economy. But failure to follow the structure of comparative advantage makes the control less precise and more likely to be cyclical.

[10] See Blake, Vines and Weale (1988) for an illustration of rules which are not constrained by the requirements of counterfactual simulation.

[11] The linear model which we use with model-consistent expectations models directly the behaviour of the jumping variables. The reason for this is explained in Chapter 10. These variables can therefore be displayed graphically. With adaptive expectations we use a simpler model structure which does not allow us to display the same variables.

[12] This does not, of course, conflict with our point in Chapter 2 that the required instrument movements are determined by the choice of targets. Here we are tolerating poor short-run control of a target in order to avoid excessive short-term movement in an instrument. That possibility was explicitly allowed for in our discussions in Chapters 2 and 3.

[13] This is in fact the mirror image of the process identified by Buiter and Miller (1983) in which an expected reduction in the long-term domestic price level has an immediate effect on the nominal and real exchange rates.

7 COUNTERFACTUAL SIMULATION WITH FORWARD-LOOKING EXPECTATIONS

[1] Of course, tax rates are also exogenous. But, with the exceptions of those tax rates which are affected by our policy rules, we hold these constant throughout our conterfactual simulation.

[2] Since the private sector is expecting 2 per cent per annum growth which has not happened, this shift is 0.5 per cent per quarter.

[3] In fact, since we have defined the real exchange rate in terms of domestic and foreign unit labour costs with a lag of one period, the movements of the measured real exchange rate are exactly the same. But this lag of one period is introduced for statistical reasons, and the 'true' real exchange rate would not move in exactly the same way.

[4] The effects of these disturbances are very similar to those identified by Buiter and Miller (1983). But Buiter and Miller were discussing the effects of changing perceptions about the long-run level of home prices, while the problem which we are identifying concerns uncertainty about the long-run level of foreign prices.

8 A SIMULATION OF THE COST-PUSH ECONOMY

[1] In particular, we do not follow the much less realistic approach suggested by Hall (1987). He derives expectational series from the historical data set by fitting time-series models, and assumes that expectations are not revised.

[2] We could have equally well demonstrated this by a high-inflation trajectory, but this could have led to the misunderstanding that the high inflation was caused by our policy rules and not by the target path.

[3] Even though the price of imports does not enter into the GDP deflator directly, a change in import prices is likely to influence wages and profits, through mark-up and cost-push effects.

[4] The beneficial effects of this incomes policy on inflation during 1976 and 1977 are treated as negative inflationary shocks during this simulation. They facilitate the control of inflation during this period, in a fashion which could be regarded as 'illicit'.

[5] In our model we have attempted to standardize our measure of unemployment at the measure used in 1984, and our results therefore show the historical peak at considerably higher than the current published figures.

[6] Although we have noted that even with our policy rule, a substantial nominal appreciation takes place as a result of an upward shift in the perceived long-run price level.

[7] Our model suggests an estimate for the valuation ratio over 10 per cent above the long-run norm lasting for most of the 1980s. This figure, which is much the same as the historic value at the end of our data period, leads to a domestic investment boom. One explanation of this may be simply that the depressed valuation ratio of the 1970s led to a build-up of profitable investment opportunities which could be exploited once the problems of the 1970s had been overcome.

9   THE CONTROLLED ECONOMY WITH REFORMED WAGES

[1] This trend rate of growth of 2.8 per cent is actually slightly below the growth rate of 2.9–3 per cent which our model delivers. But, as we note when discussing the pattern of unemployment, there were, during the simulation period, gains in productivity which were unexplained by our model. It therefore seemed sensible to use a trend slightly below the actual growth rate of Money GDP, but faster than the long-term trend growth in real wages (2.2 per cent per annum) implied by the unreformed wage equation (9.1).

[2] For example, in equation (3.18b), one may set the term $\beta_6 = 0$, in order to consider the steady state without cost-push terms. It then follows that the multiplier parameter, $x_1{}'$, which reflects the propensity to consume out of income, cancels. And in (4.20), which assumes the absence of a cost-push term, the steady-state real exchange rate depends only on the value of (external) wealth, and not on the consumption function parameters.

[3] Meade (1985) suggests some possible solutions to this dilemma.

10   THE DERIVATION AND USE OF A LINEAR MODEL

[1] If the model is not saddlepath stable with consistent expectations there are additional solution problems.

[2] It would be possible to use a historical trajectory instead, but this introduces non-linearities which can confuse the subsequent identification of the response of the model to step-changes in key variables.

[3] In this aggregate form approximation errors of weak responses may be neglected, so the algorithm will produce good approximations for the strong responses only. To overcome any resulting problems input-output scaling can be used to balance the power of each response $\Sigma_t |\hat{Y}_t(i,j)|^2$.

[4] When the solution period T is not long enough to obtain steady-state values for $\hat{Y}_\infty$, a simple extrapolative procedure may be used to generate the long-term values.

[5] Recall that we are trying to linearize the uncontrolled economy in which the interest rate is an instrument; the instability would not normally be present in a model with a fixed money supply, but we are not interested in such a model. One of the tasks of our policy rules is to remove this instability.

[6] An alternative procedure which uses expectations as inputs and current values as outputs could also be adopted (see Christodoulakis, 1989).

[7] If a fully consistent solution were sought for the non-linear model, the linear expressions (10.36–38) could be used to supply the terminal conditions for the non-predetermined variables. Then, computer-intensive methods based on the shooting technique (Lipton *et al.*, 1982), or on full-period iterations (Fisher *et al.*, 1985) could be used to determine the initial jump that is compatible with the terminal specifications. In addition the starting position for the application of the shooting algorithm could be based on (10.34). The full model could then be solved as before.

[8] It should be noted that the policy rules were designed including the stabilizing rule, which meant that the rule had to be chosen very carefully.

[9] We are grateful to John Flemming for stressing the importance of this to us. It draws attention to an unsatisfactory aspect of optimal control exercises carried out over a finite horizon on a non-linear model. Such exercises will inevitably exploit implausible features of the model on which they are performed. Price inhomogeneity is one of those implausible features.

[10] This was necessary to enable the model solution techniques described in Chapter 7 and sections 10.7 and 11.2 to be used.

11 THE DESIGN OF ECONOMIC POLICY RULES

[1] Any feedforward control would have to be proportional and not integral (since otherwise the targets would not be met). But we have not used it in our study.

[2] This obviously means such results are no longer 'optimal'.

[3] Indeed, while it may be possible to quantify some types of uncertainty, that of the 'who could have known what a year would have brought' type cannot be quantified. The presence of such uncertainty makes the notion of optimality, except with reference to certain well-defined issues, meaningless.

[4] The simplest example of this dynamic or time inconsistency is given by considering a government (or indeed any economic agent) who borrows money. It is only possible to borrow by creating the expectation that the debt will be repaid. But, having borrowed, the government can improve its position by deciding not to repay, at least if it does not expect to want to borrow again.

[5] In our borrowing example of note 4, no borrowing could take place.

[6] The reason for this may be explained simply. The government may be able to reduce inflation simply by reducing future expectations of the price level, and thereby reduce the expectational cost-push in the Phillips curve. If the government is not credible it cannot do this, and must instead rely on deflation.

[7] For example, a differential rule which appeared satisfactory on our linear model led to the VAT rate moving from 3 per cent to 40 per cent between succesive quarters in a rerun.

[8] As noted above, Westaway (1985) describes some guidelines for formalizing this process of tuning 'by hand and eye'.

12 SUMMARY OF RESULTS AND CONCLUSIONS

[1] Richard Green, a postgraduate student in Cambridge, has begun to work in this area.

Bibliography

Adams, C. and Gros, D. (1986), 'The Consequences of Real Exchange Rate Rules for Inflation: Some Illustrative Examples', *IMF Staff Papers*, vol. 33, pp. 439–76.

Ando, F. and Modigliani, F. (1963), 'The Life-cycle Hypothesis of Saving: Aggregate Implications and Tests', *American Economic Review*, vol. 53, pp. 55–84.

Artis, M. J. and Currie, D. A. (1981), 'Monetary Targets and the Exchange Rate: a Case for Conditionality', in W. Ellis and P. Sinclair (eds), *The Money Supply and the Exchange Rate* (Oxford: Oxford University Press), pp. 176–200.

Baas, H. J. (1987), Review of *Demand Management*, Vol. II, *New Zealand Economic Papers*, vol. 21, pp. 138–40.

Barker, T. S. (1988a), 'Exports and Imports' in Barker and Peterson, op. cit.

Barker, T. S. (1988b), 'Export and Import Prices' in Barker and Peterson, op. cit.

Barker, T. S. and Peterson, A. W. A. (eds) (1988), *The Cambridge Multisectoral Dynamic Model of the British Economy* (Cambridge: Cambridge University Press).

Barro, R. J. (1974), 'Are Government Bonds Net Wealth?', *Journal of Political Economy*, vol. 82, pp. 1095–1118.

Barro, R. J. and Gordon, D. B. (1983), 'Rules, Discretion and Reputation in a Model of Monetary Policy', *Journal of Monetary Economics*, vol. 12, pp. 101–21.

Becker, R. G., Dwolatsky, B., Karakitsoz, E. and Rustem, B. (1986), 'The Simultaneous Use of Rival Models in Policy Optimisation', *Economic Journal*, vol. 96, pp. 425–48.

Beckerman, W. and Jenkinson, T. (1986), 'What Stopped the Inflation? Unemployment or Commodity Prices', *Economic Journal*, vol. 96, pp. 39–54.

Blake, A. P. (1988), 'Linearisation and Control of a Large-Scale Non-Linear Rational Expectations Macroeconomic Model', Ph.D. Thesis submitted to University of London.

Blake, A. P. and Weale, M. R. (1988), 'Exchange Rate Targets and Wage Formation', *National Institute Economic Review*, no. 123, pp. 48–64.

Blake, A. P., Vines, D. A. and Weale, M. R. (1988), 'Wealth Targets, Exchange Rate Targets and Macroeconomic Policy', in Britton, op. cit.

Blanchard O. and Kahn, C. (1980), 'The Solution of Linear Difference Models under Rational Expectations', *Econometrica*, vol. 48, pp. 1305–11.

Blanchard, O. J. (1985), 'Debt, Deficits and Finite Horizons', *Journal of Political Economy*, vol. 93, pp. 223–47.

Blinder, A. and Solow, R. (1973), 'Does Fiscal Policy Matter', *Journal of Public Economics*, vol. 2, pp. 319–37.

Boughton, J. M. (1988), 'Policy Coordination with Somewhat Flexible Exchange Rates'. Mimeo. International Monetary Fund.

Britton, A. (1983), *Employment, Output and Inflation* (London: Heinemann).

Britton, A. (ed.) (1988), *Policymaking with Macroeconomic Models* (Aldershot: Gower Press).

Buiter, W. H. (1980), 'The Macroeconomics of Dr Pagloss: A Critical Survey of the New Classical Macroeconomics', *Economic Journal*, vol. 90, pp. 34–50.

Buiter, W. H. (1983), 'Optimal and Time-Consistent Policies in Continuous Time Rational Expectations Models', London School of Economics, Discussion Paper no. A39.

Buiter, W. H. (1984), 'Saddlepoint Problems in Continuous Time Rational Expectations Models: A General Method and Some Macroeconomic Examples', *Econometrica*, vol. 52, pp. 665–80.

Buiter, W. H. and Miller, M. H. (1982), 'Real Exchange Rate Overshooting and the Output Cost of Bringing Inflation Down', *European Economic Review*, vol. 18, pp. 85–124.

Buiter, W. H. and Miller, M. H. (1983), 'Changing the Rules: Economic Consequences of the Thatcher Regime', *Brookings Papers in Economic Activity*, pp. 305–80.

Cagan, P. (1956), 'The Monetary Dynamics of Hyperinflation' in Friedman, op. cit.

Christodoulakis, N. (1984), Ph.D. Thesis submitted to University of Cambridge.

Christodoulakis, N. (1989), 'Extensions of Linearisation to Large Econometric Models with Rational Expectations'. *Computers and Mathematics with Applications* (forthcoming).

Christodoulakis, N., Gaines, J. and Levine, P. (1989), 'Macroeconomic Policy Design Using Large Econometric Rational Expectations Models: Methodology and Applications'. *Oxford Economic Papers* (forthcoming).

Christodoulakis, N. and Levine, P. (1987), 'Linear Rational Expectations Models: A Frequency-domain versus Optimal Control Approach to Policy Design', Department of Applied Economics, Cambridge. Mimeo. To be published in B. Martos, and M. Ziermann (eds), *Modelling and Control of National Economies* (Pergamon Press).

Christodoulakis, N., Meade, J. E. and Weale, M. R. (1987), 'Exchange-Rate Systems and Stock Instability', Department of Applied Economics, Cambridge, Mimeo.

Christodoulakis, N. and van der Ploeg, F. (1987), 'Macrodynamic Policy Formulation with Conflicting Views of the Economy: A Synthesis of Optimal Control and Feedback Design', *International Journal of System Science*, vol. 9.

Christodoulakis, N., Vines, D. A. and Weale, M. R. (1986), 'Developments in New Keynesian Policy Formation', *Journal of Economic Dynamics and Control*, vol. 10, pp. 185–9.

Christodoulakis, N. and Weale, M. R. (1987), 'The Stock Exchange in a Macroeconomic Model', *Economic Modelling*, vol. 4, 3, pp. 341–54.

Courakis, A. S. (1988), 'Modelling Portfolio Selection', *Economic Journal*, vol. 98, pp. 619–42.

Crockett, A. and Goldstein, M. (1987), 'Strengthening the International Monetary System: Exchange Rates, Surveillance and Objective Indicators', IMF Occasional Paper.

Currie, D. (1985) ,'Macroeconomic Policy Design and Control Theory – A Failed Partnership?', *Economic Journal*, vol. 95, pp. 285–306.

Davidson, J. E. H., Hendry, D. F., Srba, F., and Yeo, S., (1978), 'Econometric Modelling of the Aggregate Time-Series Relationship Between Consumers' Expenditure and Income in the United Kingdom', *Economic Journal*, vol. 88, pp. 661–92.

Davis, E. P. (1987a), 'A Stock-flow Consistent Macroeconometric Model of the UK Economy Pt I', *Journal of Applied Econometrics*, vol. 2, pp. 111–32.

Davis, E. P. (1987b), 'A Stock-flow Consistent Macroeconometric Model of the UK Economy Pt II', *Journal of Applied Econometrics*, vol. 2, pp. 259–308.

Dornbusch, R. (1976), 'Expectations and Exchange Rate Dynamics', *Journal of Political Economy*, vol. 84, pp. 1161–76.

Doyle, J. and Stein, G. (1981), 'Multivariable Feedback Design: Concepts for a Classical/Modern Synthesis', *Institute of Electrical and Electronic Engineers, Trans. AC*, vol. AC-26, no. 1, pp. 4–16.

Driffill, E. J. (1982), 'Optimal Money and Exchange Rate Policies', *Greek Economic Review*, vol. 3, pp. 261–83.

Easton, W. W. (1985), 'The Importance of Interest Rates in Five Macroeconomic Models', Bank of England Discussion Paper no. 24.

Edison, H., Miller, M. and Williamson, J. (1987), 'On Evaluating and Extending the Target Zone Proposal', *Journal of Policy Modelling*.

Edmunds, J. (1979), 'Control System Design and Analysis using Closed-loop Nyquist and Bode Arrays', *International Journal of Control*, vol. 30, no. 5, pp. 773–802.

Evans, G. B. A. and Savin, N. E. (1982), 'Conflict among the Criteria Revisited: The W, LR and LM Tests', *Econometrica*, vol. 50, pp. 737–48.

Fischer, S. (1988), Comment on Williamson and Miller, *European Economic Review*, vol. 32, no. 5, pp. 1048–51.

Fisher, P., Holly, S. and Hughes-Hallet, A. (1985), 'Efficient Solution Techniques for Dynamic Nonlinear Rational Expectations Models', London Business School, Discussion Paper No.145.

Frankel, J. A. (1982), 'A Technique for Extracting a Measure of Expected Inflation from the Interest Rate Term Structure', *Review of Economics and Statistics*, vol. 54, pp. 135–42.

Friedman, M. (1953), 'The Case for Flexible Exchange Rates' in M. Friedman, *Essays in Positive Economics* (Chicago: University of Chicago Press).

Friedman, M. (1956), 'The Quantity Theory of Money: A Restatement', in M. Friedman (ed.) *Studies in the Quantity Theory of Money* (Chicago: University of Chicago Press).

Friedman, M. (1968), 'The Role of Monetary Policy', *American Economic Review*, vol. 53, pp. 1–17.

HM Treasury (1985), *Macroeconomic Model Manual* (London: HMSO).

Hall, R. E. (1978), 'Stochastic Implications of the Life-cycle Permanent Income Hypothesis: Theory and Evidence', *Journal of Political Economy*, vol. 86, pp. 971–87.

Hall, S. G. (1987), 'Analysing Economic Behaviour 1975–85 with a Model Incorporating Consistent Expectations', *National Institute Economic Review*, no. 120, pp. 75–80.

Hall, S. G. and Henry, S. G. B. (1985), 'Rational Expectations in an Econometric Model: NIESR Model 8', *National Institute Economic Review*, no. 114, pp. 58–68.

Hayashi, F. (1982a), 'Tobin's Marginal q and Average q; A Neoclassical Interpretation', *Econometrica*, vol. 50, pp. 213–22.

Hayashi, F. (1982b), 'The Permanent Income Hypothesis: Estimation and Testing by Instrumental Variables', *Journal of Political Economy*, vol. 90, pp. 895–916.

Hendry, D. F. and Mizon, G. E. (1978), 'Serial Correlation as a Convenient Simplification, Not a Nuisance; A Comment on a Study of the Demand for Money by the Bank of England', *Economic Journal*, vol. 88, pp. 537–48.

Hicks, J. R. (1939), *Value and Capital* (London: Oxford University Press).

Holly, S. and Levine, P. (1987), 'The Issue of Time-Inconsistency in Rational Expectational Models: A Survey', London Business School, Discussion Papers.

Holly, S. and Zarrop, M. (1983), 'On Optimality and Time-Consistency when Expectations are Rational', *European Economic Review*, vol. 20, pp. 23–40.

Jenkinson, N. H. (1981), 'Investment, Profitability and the Valuation Ratio', Bank of England. Mimeo.

Kailath, T. (1980), *Linear Systems* (Englewood Cliffs, NJ: Prentice Hall).

Kendall, M. and Stuart. A. (1981), *The Advanced Theory of Statistics: Vol 3*. (London: Charles Griffin and Co.).

Kung, S. (1978), 'A New Low-Order Approximation Algorithm via Singular Value Decomposition', *Proc. Control and Decision Conference*, California.

Kydland, F. E. and Prescott, E. C. (1977), 'Rules Rather than Discretion: The Inconsistency of Optimal Plans', *Journal of Political Economy*, vol. 85, pp. 473–92.

Laursen, S. and Metzler, L. (1951), 'Flexible Exchange Rates and the Theory of Employment'. *Review of Economics and Statistics*, vol. 32. pp. 281–99.

Layard, P. R. G. and Nickell S. J. (1985), 'Unemployment, Real Wages and Aggregate Demand in Europe, Japan and the United States', *Carnegie-Rochester Series on Public Policy*, vol. 23, pp. 143–202.

Layard, P. R. G. and Nickell, S. J. (1986), 'Unemployment in Britain', *Economica*, supplement, vol. 53, pp. 121–70.

Levine, P. and Currie, D. (1985), 'Optimal Feedback Rules in an Open Economy Macromodel with Rational Expectation', *European Economic Review*, vol. 27, pp.141–163.

Levine, P. and Currie, D. (1987), 'The Design of Feedback Rules in Linear Stochastic Rational Expectations Models, *Journal of Economic Dynamics and Control*, vol. 11, pp. 1–28.

Levine, P. and Smith, P. (1987), 'The Gains from Optimal Control in a Small Econometric Model', 8th SEDC Conference, Boston.

Lipton, D., Potterha, J., Sachs, J. and Summers, L. (1982), 'Multiple Shooting in Rational Expectations Models', *Econometrica*, vol. 50, pp. 1329–1333.

Lucas, R. (1976), 'Econometric Policy Evaluations: A Critique', in K. Brunner, and A. Meltzer, (eds), *The Phillips Curve*, Carnegie-Rochester Conferences on Public Policy, vol. 1, (Amsterdam: North Holland), pp. 19–46.

Maciejowski, J. and MacFarlane, A. G. J. (1982), 'CLADP: The Cambridge Linear Analysis and Design Programs', *Control Systems Magazine*, vol. 2, pp. 3–8.

Maciejowski, J. and Vines, D. (1984), 'Decoupled Control of a Macroeconomic

Model using Frequency-Domain Methods', *Journal of Economic Dynamics and Control*, vol. 7, pp. 55–77.

MacFarlane, A. G. J. and Postlethwaite, I. (1977), 'The Generalised Nyquist Stability Criterion and Multivariate Rool Loci', *International Journal of Control*, pp. 1–27.

Matthews, R. C. O. (1968), 'Why has Britain had Full Employment since the War?', *Economic Journal*, vol. 78, no. 3, pp. 555–69.

McKay, A. D. (1987), 'Can Estimates of UK National Income be made more Timely?', presented to European Meeting of the Econometric Society, Lyngby.

McKinnon, R. I. (1984), 'An International Standard for Monetary Stabilisation', *Policy Analysis in International Economics, no. 8*, (Washington DC: Institute for International Economics).

McKinnon, R. I. (1986), 'Monetary and Exchange Rate Policies for International Financial Stability: a Proposal'. Economic Paper no. 53 (Brussels: Commission of the European Communities).

Meade, J. E. (1966a), 'Exchange Rate Flexibility', *Three Banks' Review*, no. 70, pp. 3–27.

Meade, J. E. (1966b), 'Life-Cycle Saving, Inheritance and Economic Growth', *Review of Economic Studies*, vol. 33, pp. 61–78.

Meade, J. E. (1978), 'The Meaning of Internal Balance', *Economic Journal*, vol. 88, pp. 423–35.

Meade, J. E. (1981), *Stagflation: Volume 1. Wage-Fixing* (London: Allen and Unwin).

Meade, J. E. (1982), 'Domestic Stabilisation and the Balance of Payments', *Lloyds' Bank Review*, no. 143, pp. 1–18.

Meade, J. E. (1985), 'Full Employment, Wage Restraint and the Distribution of Income, in D. Steel and R. Holme (eds), *Partners in One Nation* (London: The Bodley Head).

Meade, J. E. and Vines, D. A. (1988), 'Monetary Policy and Fiscal Policy: Impact Effects with a New Keynesian "Assignment" of Weapons to Targets', in S. Howson (ed.) *The Collected Works of James Meade*, Vol. 3 (London: Unwin Hyman).

Miller, M. and Salmon, M. (1985), 'Dynamic Games and the Time Inconsistency of the Optimal Policy in Open Economies', *Economic Journal*, supplement, vol. 95, pp. 124–37.

Miller, M. H. and Williamson, J. (1988), 'The International Monetary System', *European Economic Review*, vol. 32, pp. 1031–54.

Minford, P. and Peel, D. (1983), *Rational Expectations and the New Macro-economics*, (Oxford: Martin Robertson).

Moore, B. (1981), 'Principal Components Analysis in Linear Systems: Controllability, Observability and Model Reduction', *IEEE, Trans. AC*, vol. AC-26, no. 1, pp. 17–31.

Mundell, R. A. (1962), 'The Appropriate Use of Monetary and Fiscal Policy for Internal and External Stability', *IMF Staff Papers*, vol. 9, pp. 70–77.

NIESR (1984), National Institute Model 7. Mimeo.

Nurkse, R. (1945), 'Conditions of International Monetary Equilibrium' in *Essays in International Finance*, no. 4, International Finance Section, University of Princeton.

Obstfeld, M. (1980), 'Imperfect Asset Substitutability and Monetary Policy under Fixed Exchange Rates', *Journal of International Economics*, vol. 10, pp. 177–200.

Oulton, N. (1981), 'Aggregate Investment and Tobin's Q: the Evidence from Britain', *Oxford Economic Papers*, vol. 33, pp. 177–202.

Phillips, A. W. (1954), 'Stabilisation Policy in a Closed Economy', *Economic Journal*, vol. 64, pp. 290–323.

Phillips, A. W. (1957), 'Stabilisation Policy and the Time-form of Lagged Responses', *Economic Journal*, vol. 67, pp. 265–77.

Poole, W. (1970), 'Optimal Choice of Monetary Policy Instrument in a Simple Stochastic Macro Model', *Quarterly Journal of Economics*, vol. 84, pp. 197–216.

Posner, M. (ed.). (1978), *Demand Management* (London: Heinemann Educational Books).

Rustem, B., Westcott, J., Zarrop, M., Holly S. and Becker, R. (1979), 'Iterative Re-Specification of the Quadratic Objective Function', in S. Holly, B. Rustem, and M. Zarrop, (eds), *Optimal Control for Econometric Models* (London: Macmillan), pp. 106–33.

Sachs, J. and Wyplosz, C. (1984), 'Real Exchange Rate Effects of Fiscal Policy', Harvard University Discussion Paper no. 1050.

Sargent, T. and Wallace, N. (1975), 'Rational Expectations, the Optimal Monetary Instrument and the Optimal Money Supply Rule', *Journal of Political Economy*, vol. 38, pp. 241–55.

Schaefer, S. M. (1981), 'Measuring a Tax-Specific Structure of Interest Rates in the Market for British Government Securities', *Economic Journal*, vol. 91. pp. 415–38.

Shiller, R. J. (1979), 'The Volatility of Long-Term Interest Rates and Expectations Models of the Term Structure', *Journal of Political Economy*, vol. 87, pp. 1190–1219.

Spencer, P. D. (1984), 'The Effect of Oil Discoveries on the British Economy – Theoretical Ambiguities and the Consistent Expectations Simulation Approach', *Economic Journal*, vol. 94, pp. 624–32

Taylor, J. B. (1979), 'Staggered Wage Setting in a Macro Model', *American Economic Review*, vol. 69, pp. 108–13.

Tirelli, P. (1988), 'Target Zones and Wealth Effects: Current Account Implications of Alternative Policy Assignments'. University of Glasgow. Mimeo.

Tirole, J. J. (1983), 'On the Possibility of Speculation under Rational Expectations', *Econometrica*, vol. 50, no. 5, pp. 1163–82.

Tobin, J. (1969), ' A General Equilibrium Approach to Monetary Theory', *Journal of Money, Credit and Banking*, vol. 1. pp. 15–29.

Tobin, J. (1980), *Asset Accumulation and Economic Activity* (Oxford: Blackwell).

Tobin, J. and Buiter, W. H. (1976), 'Long-run Effects of Fiscal and Monetary Policy on Aggregate Demand', in J. Stein (ed.) *Monetarism – Studies in Monetary Economics* (Amsterdam: North-Holland).

Tobin, J. (1982), 'Money and Finance in the Macroeconomic Process', *Journal of Money, Credit and Banking*, vol. 14, pp. 171–204.

Turnovsky, S. J. (1977), *Macroeconomic Analysis and Stabilisation Policy* (Cambridge: Cambridge University Press).

Vines, D. A., Maciejowski, J. and Meade, J. E. (1983), *Stagflation: Volume II. Demand Management* (London: Allen and Unwin).

Vines, D. A. (1986), 'Macroeconomic Policy after Monetarism', *Royal Bank of Scotland Review*, no. 152, pp. 3–19.

Weale, M. R. (1986), 'The Structure of Personal Sector Short-term Asset Holdings', *Manchester School*, vol. 54, pp. 141–61.

Weale, M. R. (1987), 'Wealth Constraints and Consumer Behaviour', Department of Applied Economics. Mimeo.

Weale, M. R. (1988), 'Industrial Prices and Profits' in Barker and Peterson, op. cit.

Westaway, P. (1985), PhD. Dissertation submitted to the University of Cambridge.

Westaway, P. (1986), 'Some Experiments with Simple Feedback Rules on the Treasury Model', *Journal of Economic Dynamics and Control*, vol. 10, pp. 239–48.

Whittaker, R., Wren-Lewis, S., Blackburn, K. and Currie, D. (1986), 'Alternative Financial Policy Rules in an Open Economy Under Rational and Adaptive Expectations', *Economic Journal*, vol. 96, pp. 680–95.

Whiteman, C. H. (1986), 'Analytical Policy Design under Rational Expectations', *Econometrica*, vol. 54, pp. 1387–1406.

Williamson, J. (1985) *The Exchange Rate System* (Washington DC: Institute for International Economics).

Williamson, J. and Miller, M. H. (1987), *Targets and Indicators: A Blueprint for the International Co-ordination of Economic Policy* (Washington DC: Institute for International Economics).

Index

NB: Reference numbers of Figures in text are italicised and follow relevant page-numbers